Culture and Conflict in Seventeenth-Century France and Ireland

Culture and Conflict in Seventeenth-Century France and Ireland

EDITED BY

Sarah Alyn Stacey and Véronique Desnain

FOUR COURTS PRESS

Set in 11 on 13 point Bembo for
FOUR COURTS PRESS LTD
7 Malpas Street, Dublin 8, Ireland
e-mail: info@four-courts-press.ie
and in North America
FOUR COURTS PRESS
c/o ISBS, 920 N.E. 58th Avenue, Suite 300, Portland, OR 97213.

A catalogue record for this title
is available from the British Library.

ISBN 1–85182–717–X

Printed in Great Britain
by Antony Rowe Ltd, Chippenham, Wilts.

Contents

Acknowledgements   7

Introduction   9

I. WOMEN, MEN AND TEXTS IN CONFLICT

1   'Aux pieds de l'Eternel je viens m'humilier': Racine and the Bible   21
    Véronique Desnain

2   'By the sword divided': cultural and confessional conflict in the
    life and writings of Madame de St Balmont (1607–59)   30
    Kate Currey

3   From 'Ex ovo omnia' to ovism: the father function in
    seventeenth-century treatises on generation   41
    Rebecca Wilkin

4   Medicine and religion in seventeenth-century France:
    La Rochelle, 1676–83   52
    Jean-Paul Pittion

5   'Il n'y a plus de Mecenas': *Le Roman bourgeois* and the crisis
    of literary patronage   72
    Craig Moyes

6   'Ce miracle du monde': harmony and disharmony in
    Saint-Amant's representation of the cosmos   82
    Sarah Alyn Stacey

II. MORAL CONFLICTS

7   The problem of freedom in Arnauld's defence of Jansenius   103
    Michael Moriarty

8   Free will, determinism and providence: the ideological context
    of the *Histoires Tragiques* of Jean-Pierre Camus   117
    Mark Bannister

9   *Raillerie, honnêteté* and 'les grands sujets': cultured conflict in
    seventeenth-century France   128
    David Culpin

10 Mutations judiciaires dans la seconde moitié du XVIIe siècle   135
     Pascale Feuillée-Kendall

           III. THE THEATRE IN CONFLICT

11 On humour and wit in Molière's *Le Misanthrope* and Congreve's
     The Way of the World   151
     Andrew Calder

12 The stage controversy in France and England – a confessional
     convergence?   163
     Henry Phillips

13 Conflicting cultures as reflected in some seventeenth-century
     English translations of French plays   183
     Pat Short

14 'If Egypt now enslav'd or free A Kingdom or a Province be':
     translating Corneille in Restoration Dublin   194
     Deana Rankin

15 Rebel hearts: La Calprenède's transformation of political
     conflict into drama   210
     Guy Snaith

16 Conflicting signals: images of Louis XIV in Benserade's ballets   227
     Julia Prest

           IV. MILITARY CONFLICT

17 Franco-Irish military relations in the Nine Years War, 1689–97   245
     Harman Murtagh

18 Voltaire's slanted vision of the Fronde as *commedia buffa* in *Le
     Siècle de Louis XIV*   256
     Marc Serge Rivière

Bibliography   271

Index   283

Acknowledgements

This collection of articles was inspired by a conference of the same title held at Trinity College Dublin, 11–13 November 1999. I am most grateful to Trinity and to the French Embassy for its generous support of that conference. Special thanks must also be expressed to Mr Charles Benson, the Keeper of Early Printed Books at Trinity College, and to Professor Pauline Smith and Dr Gerald Morgan for the advice and encouragement they gave throughout the venture. My very great thanks must, of course, be expressed to the contributors both to the conference and to this volume for their invaluable participation and cooperation. My sincere gratitude, finally, to Dr Véronique Desnain for her assistance in the editorial process.

Sarah Alyn Stacey

I would like to thank the contributors for their help and patience and Sarah Alyn Stacey for giving me the opportunity to participate in this project.

Véronique Desnain

Introduction

PART I: SARAH ALYN STACEY

In 1999, Trinity College Dublin acquired a large proportion of Geoffrey Aspin's collection of seventeenth-century books, many of which are very rare theatrical works. To mark this acquisition, which will undoubtedly prove invaluable for scholars in the field both in and outside of Ireland, I organized a conference, 'Culture and Conflict in Seventeenth-Century France', which was held in Trinity on 11–13 November 1999. This collection of essays, based largely on the papers given at that conference, represents the second stage in the commemoration of this highly important acquisition.

If the contexts in which conflict may arise are infinite, intrinsic to any such context is a suppression and suspension of harmony. The conflict ends or is suspended when, or if, it cedes, for whatever reason, to harmony. Any conflict, then, is essentially a struggle between two states of being, disharmony and harmony. As the range of articles in this volume indicates, although contained within the poles of disharmony and harmony, each conflict has its own particular dynamic, whether it be military, religious, sexual, political, or textual, or a combination of these or other factors, and it is this dynamic which bestows upon a conflict its uniqueness. What is of particular interest, then, is the complexity and diversity characterizing conflict's expression, and it is with this that each of the articles in this volume is concerned.

The organization of the volume follows, with only slight modification, that of the original conference. The first section, 'Women, men and texts in conflict', comprises six articles. The first article, by Véronique Desnain, '"Aux pieds de l'Eternel je viens m'humilier": Racine and the Bible', examines Racine's use of biblical sources in his final two tragedies, *Esther* and *Athalie*. This article presents a threefold conflict – the conflict between the original text and its rewritings, a religious conflict between the disciples of a monotheist faith and those of a polytheist culture, and a conflict between the sexes in a bid for power. In this last-mentioned conflict, we see Racine engaging with a highly topical issue in the seventeenth century, and, as we find in his other dramatic texts, what emerges is that the very fact of being a woman is a disadvantage, so that the female is presented as being faced either with accepting subjugation or, if she resists, with accepting her ultimate destruction.

In sharp contrast to any such notion of women accepting subservience to men is the example of Barbe d'Ernecourt, the 'amazone chrestienne' who is the subject of the article by Kate Currey, '"By the sword divided": cultural and confessional conflicts in the life and writings of Madame de St Balmont (1607–59)'; this article reviews the life of Barbe d'Ernecourt and focuses in particular on her representation by her two early biographers, the Franciscan Jean-Marie Vernon and the Jesuit Des Billons. What emerges is the portrait of a woman who, as the self-appointed guardian of Neuville-en-Verdunois, embraces two diametrically opposed modes of behaviour, the one belligerent and traditionally associated with the masculine (she was captain of Neuville's army); the other spiritual and caring and traditionally associated with the feminine (she was a mother, directed her community's spiritual affairs, taught music, nursed plague sufferers, and finally ended her days in a convent). In Currey's view, underlying this behaviour is not a fundamental dissatisfaction on d'Ernecourt's part that she is a woman, but rather her moral and religious convictions which, to be fulfilled, required her to conflate the two genders. However, it is not only her conflation of male and female roles which makes d'Ernecourt an interesting icon of conflict. She was born in contested territory to which both France and Lorraine laid claim. Moreover, although officially French with a political allegiance therefore to Louis XIII, her husband fought for the enemy, Charles IV. A conflict also exists between the two biographers. Whereas in the seventeenth century Vernon emphasizes her combination of soldiership and piety, Des Billons, writing in the following century, seems instead more concerned with her as an 'historical curiosity', and tends to play down her military exploits. Moreover, whereas in the seventeenth century she is viewed as a heroin of France, in the eighteenth century she is transformed into a heroin first and foremost of Lorraine, a divergence highlighting how the writing of history is always subject to the cultural and political context and perspective of the historian/biographer. The final section of the article examines briefly d'Ernecourt's *Les Jumeaux martyrs*, a play constructed around the conflict between personal desire and duty, and in many respects a reflection of the conflictual issues in the author's own life.

Rebecca Wilkin, in her article '"Ex ovo omnia" to ovism: the father function in seventeenth-century treatises on generation', focuses more specifically on the question of conflict in the writing process. She takes as her starting point Michel Foucault's distinction between the author as a socio-historical entity and the author function, that is, the proper name which shapes the work, and his conclusion that when scientific authority shifts from a canon of proper names to an ensemble of universal truths, then the author function no longer obtains. Looking specifically at what she perceives as the rhetorical empiricism of a number of seventeenth-century texts on generation, Wilkin challenges Foucault's view, arguing that a specific author function does in fact obtain, at least until the 1670s. Central to this analysis is the trope of paternity to signify authorship. It is argued that the effectiveness of this traditional metaphor of aesthetic creation is undermined by new theories about ovism which emerged in the seventeenth century and which played down the importance of the father in the procreative process. Wilkin argues that these theories led some scientific authors to forego a visceral connection to their work, whilst others, for whom 'authorial dispossession' would have been tantamount to denying the father function, resisted the denial of the author function.

Jean-Paul Pittion's article, 'Medicine and religion in seventeenth-century France: La Rochelle, 1676–83', considers seventeenth-century medicine from an historical perspective. Drawing on a wealth of archival material, Pittion considers the practice of medicine in La Rochelle, 1676–83, and focuses particularly on the conflict which arose between Catholic and Protestant physicians following letter patents and statutes of 1680 which excluded the latter from practising. Up until then, however, Catholics and Protestants alike had practised harmoniously together, putting La Rochelle very much at the forefront of medicine in France. This article examines the cause of the professional exclusion, attributing it to widespread unresolved hostility between Catholics and Protestants, a hostility arising from political, economic and demographic imbalances between the two confessions, but also from intolerance of religious difference. In Pittion's view, it was this last factor, religious conflict, which played a determining role in shaping medical practice in La Rochelle, as elsewhere in seventeenth-century France.

'"Il n'y a plus de Mecenas": *Le Roman bourgeois* and the crisis of literary patronage' by Craig Moyes considers Antoine Furetière's *Roman bourgeois* (1666), arguing that in order to understand this curious, innovative, and frequently maligned work the context of its publication must be taken into account. Moyes highlights the importance in this respect of the fall from grace of Nicolas Fouquet, the patron of a considerable proportion of the period's artistic elite. His trial, conducted in 1661–5, signified, it is argued, the end of the Golden Age of patronage, and Furetière's *Roman* should be read as a direct and pessimistic response to this fundamental change in the nature of artistic exchange.

This first section concludes with my own article, '"Ce miracle du monde": harmony and disharmony in Saint-Amant's representation of the cosmos'. This article suggests that through his particular presentation of the cosmos, Saint-Amants' engages indirectly with the debates on authority and free-will which were so prominent in the seventeenth century. His poetry, both in *fond* and *forme*, that is, through its evocation of literal conflict and through the exploitation of certain stylistic techniques, points to a precarious coexistence between harmony and disharmony in a nonetheless strictly organized cosmic hierarchy. What is accentuated is the fundamental instability both of the cosmos and of Man's place within it.

The second section, 'Moral conflicts', comprises four articles. The first of these, 'The problem of freedom in Arnauld's defence of Jansenius' by Michael Moriarty, examines very thoroughly one of the most important grounds for conflict in the mid-seventeenth century, the question of human freedom. Moriarty examines the theological and philosophical issues relating to this question as they are expressed in Antoine Arnauld's *Seconde apologie pour Jansenius* (1645). The question is considered specifically in relation to necessity and constraint, indifference, love and action, passion and constraint, and what becomes clear from this discussion is the extent to which Arnauld in fact diverges from the views of Jansenius. Whilst writing what is perhaps the most systematic exposition in French of the theology of Jansenius, Arnauld, it seems, was not afraid to modify that theology, and this may be seen as a reflection of how he sought to build alliances with other schools of thought. The work may, therefore, be considered as distilling both a theological conflict and a textual conflict.

In 'Free will, determinism and providence: the ideological context of the *Histoires Tragiques* of Jean-Pierre Camus', Mark Bannister also considers the question of free will. The *histories tragiques* would seem to serve a deliberately didactic purpose, as they articulate the position of the Catholic Church on the passivity of Man to higher forces. However, as Bannister argues, the literary merits of these tales deserve appreciation and would suggest that the genre is more closely linked to the novel or *nouvelle* than is generally acknowledged.

David Culpin, in '*Raillerie, honnêteté* and "les grands sujets": cultured conflict in seventeenth-century France', considers the various often conflicting seventeenth-century views on whether an *honnête homme* may indulge in raillery to make a serious point. What becomes apparent is the precariousness of communication by such a form of humour: it is not sufficient to intend *raillerie* for it to be understood, but what is essential is that it should be correctly decoded.

In the final article in this section, 'Mutations judiciaires dans la seconde moitié du XVIIe siècle', Pascale Feuillée-Kendall examines the draconian legal reforms put in place by Colbert and Louis XIV in the second half of the seventeenth century to suppress rebellion. These reforms, notably the *ordonnance civile* of 1664 and the *ordonnance criminelle* of 1670, suggest a tyrannical regime which sought to suppress at any cost the voice of any dissenting individual.

PART II: VÉRONIQUE DESNAIN

The third section, 'The theatre in conflict', comprises six articles. Certainly, the importance of the theatre in the seventeenth century is clearly illustrated by the number of essays in this section which deal with it either as a social phenomenon (Philips) or by concentrating on specific authors (Calder) and their translators (Short, Rankin, Snaith).

Andrew Calder's analysis, in 'On humour and wit in Molière's *Le Misanthrope* and Congreve's *The Way of the World*', concentrates on perceptions of what constitutes acceptable forms of humour and the notion that those perceptions are nationally influenced. Looking at older sources (Erasmus, Cicero) through to Montaigne and seventeenth-century philosophers, Calder demonstrates the essential differences between the comedies of Molière and those of Congreve. Based on an examination of the difference between humour and wit, Calder's article shows that despite their common aim (to expose the folly and ridicule of human behaviour), the two play-wrights offer radically different visions of the world, with Congreve relying heavily on his characters' wit to elicit sympathy, admiration and, perhaps more surprisingly, pathos. Calder convincingly puts forward the argument that whilst Congreve's characters may appear even more flawed than Molière's, his use of witty dialogue makes the audience laugh with them, rather than at them and that we, the spectators, are therefore more inclined to identify with the characters and forgive them their shortcomings.

Attitudes to the theatre as a social phenomenon were often similar in France and England despite the differences in practice and styles exposed in other chapters. In 'The stage controversy in France and England – a confessional convergence?', Henry Philips offers an overview of the debates about the status of theatre taking place through the best part of the century in both countries, and hence provides a fascinating perspective on the strategies used by religious moralists to condemn or defend the theatre. If anything, this article demonstrates that a common goal can in itself be a source of conflict. Theatre was condemned by both Catholic and Protestant authorities and both sides often used the same sources to support their arguments, but for Ridpath and other English advocates against the theatre, it was equally important that their arguments should not be seen as falling in line with their 'popish' counterparts or that Protestants should not appear to be less stringent in their condemnation than Catholics. The more rigid stance adopted by the English side can perhaps be linked to the respective out-comes of the Fronde and the Civil War: French moralists, Protestants among them, were more inclined to dissociate the temporal and spiritual aspects of the king's personae (a rather delicate operation not dissimilar to the one which forms the basis of Prest's essay) and to argue that political preoccupations may justify behaviour by the king which would be unacceptable in his subjects. There is no such leniency on the part of the English moralists who staunchly denounce the theatre as the road to perdition.

When we examine the relationship between France and its anglophone neighbours, translation has much to tell us about both cultural differences and mutual perceptions. J.-P. Short's 'Conflicting cultures as reflected in some seventeenth-century English translations of French plays' examines the alterations made by translators to French plays by Corneille and reminds us of the different expectations of audiences in France and England. Short introduces some unexpected statements about the French and English temperaments before examining translations by Joseph Rutter, William Lower, Katherine Philips and Charles Cotton. Whilst these clearly show stylistic variations (English translations are more 'action-driven' and do not shy away from depictions of violence), they also bring to the fore the fact that culture and politics are closely related. On the most basic level this was because the Restoration of 1660 led to the re-opening of the theatres which had been closed during the Commonwealth, but it was also because political preoccupations, such as the stability of the crown and the threat against the ruler's life, which are emphasized in the English versions, can be linked to the anxieties generated by the Civil War.

Like Short, Deana Rankin, in her article, '"If Egypt now enslav'd or free A Kingdom or a Province be": translating Corneille in Restoration Dublin', presents the translations of original French texts and shows the thematic and stylistic choices made by translators to be strongly linked to the particular political circumstances of the country for which they are destined. With particular emphasis on the works of Katherine Philips and John Dancer, Rankin argues that the very plays they chose to translate, *La Mort de Pompée* and *Nicomède*, are representative of the effort by members of Dublin society to establish their own identity rather than simply consider themselves English exiles. More importantly perhaps, both plays deal with the need for mediation following a time of crisis and the transition from military conflict to political stability. As such *Pompée* would have had strong personal connotations for Philips who had been caught up in the upheaval of the 1650s. As for *Nicomède*, it highlights the tensions between the military temperament and the need for political compromise to ensure peace, although Rankin points out that the version by Dancer (himself a military man) favours the soldier-hero over the diplomat, something which is reflected in the language of the translation. Despite the additions or alterations made by the translators, Rankin argues that it is nonetheless clear that Corneille's plays fitted the preoccupations of a Dublin audience still coping with the aftermath of the Civil Wars, and that their translations played a role in the formation of a settled, cultured Protestant Anglo-Irish society.

The links between the arts and politics are a common theme throughout the chapters in this section and Guy Snaith's 'Rebel hearts: La Calprenède's transformation of political conflict into drama' concentrates on the processes, both conscious and unconscious, which lead to the sublimation of a specific political situation into dramatic tension. Here a phenomenon similar to the one exposed by translation in Rankin can be observed but in the opposite direction: La Calprenède occasionally draws on English history for his plays (*Jeanne, Reine d'Angleterre, Le Comte d'Essex*), as well as on more ancient subjects (*La Mort de Mithridate, La Mort des enfants d'Hérode*), but Snaith argues that La Calprenède's choice of subjects and composition are influenced by the political upheaval which marked the late 1630s and early 1640s in France, 'La Calprenède's protagonists behaving in a fashion not only worthy of tragedy but also of the real rebels of Louis XIII's reign'. Whilst this may not have been a conscious process on the part of the writer, Snaith successfully shows that in seeking to provide his audience with all the poetry, thrills and visual pleasure that tragedy could offer, La Calprenède also provides us with a dramatic record of the mood of France in the early seventeenth century.

That theatre was less violently attacked in France can probably be explained in part by Louis XIV's passion for the arts and the fact that he himself took part in performances, but an examination of Louis the actor exposes how conflict can occasionally be embodied in a single individual. Julia Prest's 'Conflicting signals: images of Louis XIV in Benserade's ballets' highlights the paradoxes that emerge from Louis' participation in ballets which put forward the 'natural' body whilst the state machinery attempts to construct the monarch as a political figure beyond the mere physicality of lesser mortals. Benserade's task in writing the 'livrets' for the ballets was an exercise in diplomacy, and the verse writer had the uneasy task of praising the king's superhuman qualities whilst the audience was faced with the physicality and humanity of the man on stage. Since ballet verse often referred to the actor's life as much as to the role, Benserade's fine balancing-act involved alluding to the king's human weaknesses (exemplified by reference to his mistress) and his official projection as a god-like figure overshadowing all aspects of his subjects' lives, without the disparity between the two becoming obvious. In a departure from previous writings on the subject of the 'dancing king', Prest concentrates on the tensions created by the superposition of the 'Body natural' and the 'Body political', and hints that the conflict could not be resolved despite Benserade's best efforts.

Certainly, the conflicts which this collection seeks to highlight could take a far bloodier turn as shown by the articles by Harman Murtagh and Marc Serge Rivière in the fourth and final section, 'Military conflict'. Towards the end of the century, Ireland, the refuge of ousted Jacobean power, became the object of a 'tug-of-war' between England and France, with religion once again at the root. Whilst Rankin's examination of translations highlights cultural divergence, Murtagh's 'Franco-Irish military relations in the Nine Years War, 1689–97' shows that France and Ireland were nonetheless natural allies when it came to resisting the threat posed by Protestant England. The overthrowing of James II by William of Orange turned England from a potential ally into a dangerous rival for Louis and left Catholic Ireland in a vulnerable position. The Jacobites turned to France for support against the new Protestant English powers that threatened Ireland. Although the French view of Ireland was not always flattering ('la nation du monde la plus brutale et qui a le moins d'humanité'), men, weapons and supplies were sent to support the Jacobite efforts. This was not an altruistic gesture. William of Orange was a real threat to France and forcing him to divert resources to Ireland was a strategic move. To a large extent, the Franco-Irish alliance benefited France more than Ireland: whilst the Jacobites were ultimately unable to resist the Protestant advances, the treaty of Limerick meant that thousands of Irish soldiers were incorporated into the French army at a time when Louis faced some serious military challenges.

The final article, which is by Rivière and entitled 'Voltaire's slanted vision of the Fronde as *commedia buffa* in *Le Siècle de Louis XIV*', offers an eighteenth-century perspective on the internal conflicts which marked the beginning of Louis XIV's reign. It concentrates on the difficulty Voltaire-the-historian experienced in maintaining a neutral stance when confronted with the beliefs of Voltaire-the-philosopher. As a defender of the 'thèse royale', Voltaire chooses to present La Fronde as a ridiculous rebellion, both in its origins and in the events that unfolded. Rivière shows that Voltaire's choice of sources (in particular Madame de Motteville) and the credence he gives them despite their links to the royal family, his vocabulary, the occasional lack of accuracy in his citations and his predilection for amusing anecdotes all conspire to present the Fronde not as a serious political conflict but as a ludicrous, farcical display of posturing which exposed the foolishness of those involved in the rebellion. Rivière clearly demonstrates the way in which Voltaire's presentation reduces the Fronde to an amalgam of comic characters and comic 'vignettes' which can be linked back to the *commedia* traditions. Rivière points out that Voltaire, who despised such vulgar entertainment, uses those elements to play down the significance of the events in order to highlight the need for strong, absolute monarchy and that Voltaire's bias can be identified in the tone of his writing as much as in his use of data. Despite good intentions, Voltaire found it almost impossible to remain objective but, as Rivière reminds us at the beginning of the article, Voltaire saw the historian as a man with a moral purpose – to prevent the repetition of past mistakes. His presentation of the Fronde as a despicable and ridiculous episode in the history of France seems, therefore, to make sense in the light of his own convictions.

I. WOMEN, MEN AND TEXTS IN CONFLICT

'Aux pieds de l'Eternel je viens m'humilier': Racine and the Bible

VÉRONIQUE DESNAIN

In this article I intend to examine the role of biblical sources in Racine's last two tragedies, *Esther* (1689) and *Athalie* (1691). I will attempt to show that although the Bible itself is strongly rooted in androcentric tradition, Racine's portrayals and the alterations he made to the original sources serve to reinforce the patriarchal message and emphasize the didactic qualities of the original stories. I will show that the biblical context and its necessarily androcentric nature emphasize that, for female characters, any attempt to challenge the patriarchal structure is seen as heretical, a notion hinted at in previous plays but which truly comes into its own in *Athalie*. In this play, the queen's conflict with Yahweh's followers closely parallels and sometimes conceals the battle between the genders. Thus the play revolves around not one but two conflicts – a religious one, which involves the establishment of a monotheist faith in a polytheist culture, and a social one which involves the subjection of women to male power. The first gives us a straightforward plot, the outcome of which, in the tragic tradition, is already known to the audience. The second, more covert and insidious, reflects some of the debates which were taking place in France in the seventeenth century and concerned the place of women in society, and more particularly their 'ability' to hold positions of power. Although this is most obvious in *Athalie*, since the heroine is already in such a position of power, concerns about this are also hinted at in *Esther*. Finally, this article will conclude with a look at the way in which women in the two tragedies are used to seal the alliance with the male god. I will suggest that Racine's biblical plays establish a double standard according to which women are inherently 'sinful' in that they are positioned outside the realm of the religious and can only redeem themselves by serving the interests of men who achieve secular power through their access to the spiritual.

We know that a didactic purpose was intended, at least for the original actors and audience members, since Racine tells us in the 'Préface' to *Esther* that Saint-Cyr was established to teach the Demoiselles 'tout ce qui pouvait contribuer à les rendre capables de servir Dieu dans les différents états où il lui plaira de les appeler'.[1] Readings, recitations and singing were used both

---

1 All quotations from Racine are taken from *Théâtre complet*, ed. J. Morel and A. Viala (Paris 1980).

to get rid of unacceptable provincial accents and to provide some basic moral grounding, but unfortunately 'la plupart des plus excellents vers de notre langue [furent] composés sur des matières fort profanes, et nos plus beaux airs [sont] sur des paroles extrêmement molles et efféminées, capables de faire des impressions dangereuses sur de jeunes esprits'. Racine's mission in providing new material is, therefore, clearly pedagogic as well as artistic and it could be argued that *Esther* and *Athalie* present us with two different strategies for a common purpose: to educate by positive example in the first case, and to provide a dire warning, through the fate of the 'anti-heroine', in the second.

It may be interesting to consider first the biblical episodes chosen by Racine to form the basis of his plays. Despite some alterations made by Racine, alterations which will be discussed in this article, the plot of *Esther* remains essentially the same as in the original: Assuérus (Ahasuerus/ Xerxes),[2] having banished his wife, Vashti, for disobeying him, chooses as his new wife Esther who has been sent to the palace by Mardochée (Mordecai) in the hope that her great beauty would secure the king's love. But Esther is a Jewess and the Jews have been persecuted by the king's adviser, Aman (Haman). When Mardochée hears of Aman's plot to exterminate the Jews, he urges Esther to reveal herself to the king and to speak in favour of her people, despite the fact that this might mean losing her own life. The king, however, is won over: he has Aman put to death and gives his estates to Mardochée, who becomes his new adviser and ensures the safety of the Jews.

It might seem ironic, however, that Racine should choose to convey his moral message through the Book of Esther, a work described by biblical scholars as 'a light book, a ribald and funny story featuring concubines and drunken parties'[3] in which 'Ahasuerus and his courtiers appear as hapless buffoons before the calm strength of Vashti and, by implication, of all their wives'.[4] It may seem odd, also, that Racine should have chosen a text so controversial, both in its mockery of authority and in the fact that God's name is never pronounced in it, so that it was, for a long time, not allowed to appear alongside the other biblical books. However, it should be remembered that his source was the Greek translation in which 'un pieux traducteur [grec] avait corrigé l'aspect trop païen de ce livre par de nombreuses additions que Saint Jérome met en appendice dans la *Vulgate* [. . .] [ce texte] devait lui être familier depuis longtemps sous cette forme puisque le théologien le plus révéré à Port-Royal, Saint Augustin, l'utilise à plusieurs reprises dans ce sens'.[5]

2 The biblical forms of the names appear in brackets.   3 S.R. Driver, *The Hebrew scriptures* (New York 1963), p. 127.   4 S.A. White, 'Esther' in C.A. Newsom and S.H. Ringe (ed.), *The women's Bible commentary* (London 1992), p. 127.   5 E. Zimmermann, *La Liberté et le destin dans le théâtre de Jean Racine* (Saratoga 1982), p. 120.

Whereas the original biblical text of the Book of Esther paints the picture of a much stronger woman than the Esther of Racine's play, some additions were made to the Greek translations, such as Esther's fainting, which totally change the tone of the text:

> The atmosphere of the book is made more romantic by the change in the character of Esther in Additions C and D [. . .] When she appears before Ahasuerus in Addition D, her beauty and her fear are emphasized. At the climactic moment, when the king sees her in court, she faints! Ahasuerus's response to her is motivated by pity for her weakness and fear; Esther becomes a negative stereotype of a weak, helpless woman.[6]

However, Racine does make one specific change of his own which alters the characters of both Esther and Mardochée. In Act I iv., Mardochée tells his niece that she represents 'tout l'espoir de [ses] malheureux frères' (185). Whilst this heightens dramatic tension, 'tout l'espoir' obviously contradicts Mordecai's warning in the Old Testament in which he says: 'For if you keep silent at such a time as this, relief and deliverance will rise for the Jews from another quarter, but you and your father's family will perish. And who knows but that you have come to royal position for such a time as this?' (Book of Esther 4:14). Several implications are apparent in this change. Firstly the biblical version throws doubt on Mardochée's supposed 'knowledge' in that it ends with a question and therefore the power he possesses in Racine as the 'voice of God' far exceeds the power he has in the original. Racine's version also removes the notion of a personal danger limited to Esther and those close to her should she fail to act and replaces it with more far-reaching consequences. The appeal made by Mardochée to Esther in Racine may appear less emotional as it does not play on direct family relationships, yet the choice of the word 'frères' suggests much wider implications for the outcome of Esther's decision (hence making this a religious tragedy where the future of Christianity depends on the heroine), and shifts the emphasis from real blood ties to ethnic ones (which makes for a universal tragedy rather than a personal one). Finally his appeal shifts the theme of the play from the profane to the sacred: Esther's failure to act would, in Racine's version, threaten the future of Christianity itself, something which cannot be inferred from the original story. As Th. Malachy observes, in the Bible Mordecai's allusion 'souligne précisément l'absence de rapport automatique entre Dieu et l'action de Mardochée. Car le destin de son peuple pris en charge par Dieu ne fait pas nécessairement un avec son destin personnel et celui de sa famille.'[7] But Racine suppresses any reference to

---

6 White, 'Esther', p. 127.   7 Th. Malachy, 'Esther: une tragédie de Racine et de l'Ancien

another source of help for the Jews, hence putting their future and survival entirely in the hands of Esther. By blurring the boundaries between Mardochée's political ambitions and God's will, he turns 'une chronique commençant par une révolte du harem et se dénouant, après une série de coups de théâtre, en une révolution de palais'[8] into a religious drama. In doing so, he also produces a social model in which men have a direct link to the divine, while ignorance and obedience are the preserve of women for Esther accepts her role but does not necessarily understand it. Whilst her compliance is crucial to Mardochée's plan, Esther's strength, if it can be described as such, resides solely in her influence on a powerful man, an influence exerted by her physical beauty – 'Le sceptre offert à la beauté' (42) – and her 'womanly' traits, such as crying and fainting at times of crisis. Her act of defiance is entirely dictated by Mardochée.

Furthermore, the religious figurehead of Racine's tragedy is only a distant relation of the original Mordecai. Malachy highlights some major discrepancies, pointing out that the biblical Mordecai, 'loin d'être l'homme de Dieu peint par Racine, est avant tout un fin politique qui voit dans la beauté de sa cousine Esther (elle n'est pas sa nièce) une occasion de s'introduire dans le palais royal . . .'[9] Indeed we must wonder at the biblical Mordecai's initial motivation for placing Esther among the many women rounded up to try to distract the king from the memory of the banished Vashti. We are given to understand that some divine foresight made him aware of the threat to come, which enhances his status as a religious visionary. Yet Malachy reminds us that in the Bible, at the point of crisis, 'il n'invoque point la mission sacramentelle dont l'investit Racine. C'est davantage l'impératif d'un réaliste qui, tout en jugeant la gravité de la situation, voit dans l'intervention d'Esther l'occasion de se distinguer.'[10] It is a plan which evidently works since the last verse of the Book of Esther is entitled, tellingly, 'The greatness of Mordecai'. Similarly, in Racine's play, although Esther's intervention leads to safety and social recognition for the Jews, her own position remains unchanged whereas Mardochée reaps the benefits, both material and social, of the risks she has taken on his orders:

> Viens briller près de moi dans le rang qui t'est dû.
> Je te donne d'Aman les biens et la puissance:
> Possède justement son injuste opulence.
> (Assuérus, III. vii. 1179–81)

Testament', *Lettres Romanes* (août 1989), 143–5 (p. 146).   **8** Ibid., 147.   **9** Ibid., 145.   **10** Ibid., 145–46.

Whilst the end result is the same as in the Bible, Racine's presentation of events shifts the emphasis away from Mordecai's use of Esther's body as a commodity which serves his own ends, be they political or religious. In the play, his accession to a high social position in the wake of Aman's death appears almost incidental whilst the consequences of the shift in power for the Jews (and therefore the advancement of the Christian faith) remain at the forefront.

A final point needs to be made about *Esther* which will bring us to the more overt presentation of the relationship between religion and secular power found in *Athalie*. As I mentioned in my introduction, the topic of women and power was widely discussed in seventeenth-century France. A few forward thinkers highlighted the inequalities between the sexes and advocated greater parity,[11] but the overall image left by most of the evidence is of a society (or at least its male thinkers) terrified by the possibility of being ruled by women, a fear which justifies the subservience of women in the private sphere on the grounds of various arguments about their physical and moral weakness. Once the patriarchal organization of the family has been established, it can be used as a basis for the exclusion of women from the political scene. The thrust of the argument, in a simplified form, would be that 'la loi de la nature, [. . .], ayant créé la femme imparfaite et débile, tant du corps que de l'esprit, l'a soumise à la puissance de l'homme',[12] and so a woman must submit to her father or husband. This naturally rules her out as a sovereign who must have absolute authority. The danger of putting a foreign power on the throne through marriage was also a salient preoccupation of the day which is strongly reflected in *Athalie* in which the eponymous character's gender and origins are emphasized, making her doubly 'other' and hence doubly threatening. In *Esther*, the 'necessity' of keeping women away from overt power is hinted at when Assuérus tells Esther:

> Venez, derrière un voile écoutant leurs discours,
> De vos propres clartés me prêter le secours.
>
> (II. vii. 707–8)

This concept of 'power behind the throne' suggests that the king does recognize and value his spouse's opinion, but it also serves to highlight the unacceptability of overt power for women and consolidates the idea that

11 See Le Père Le Moyne's *La Gallerie des femmes fortes* (Paris 1647); Poulain de la Barre's *De l'égalité des deux sexes* (Paris [1673] 1984); Gabrielle Suchon's *Traité de la morale et de la politique* ([Lyon 1693] Paris 1999). The first two in particular were undoubtedly successful, with five editions in the seventeenth century, although Pierre Ronzeaud suggests that this may have been a 'succès de curiosité': 'La femme au pouvoir ou le monde à l'envers', *Dix-septième Siècle*, 108 (1975), 9–33.
12 Cardin Le Bret, *De la souveraineté du roy* (Paris 1632), vol. 1, 4.

women should not appear to play any part in the decision-making process. Some might argue that this 'invisible power' is sometimes stronger than that bestowed by most overt positions but it is also dangerous and precarious. It is very likely that a monarch seen to rely heavily on his wife for advice would invite criticism and hence jeopardize his own position.[13] It is therefore in his own interest to keep any female intervention carefully hidden. The idea of being governed by a female monarch is anathema in seventeenth-century France, much as it was in the Old Testament:

> My people – children are their oppressors, and women rule over them. O my people, your leaders mislead you, and confuse the course of your paths. (Isaiah 3:12)

Moreover, if the female adviser recognized and attempted to use her power, it is more than likely that her sovereign would take offence, regardless of their relationship, and endeavour to get rid of her, as Agrippine's fate in *Britannicus* amply demonstrates.

In *Athalie* the issue is addressed in a much more direct way and the biblical setting should not distract from the fact that the subjugation of women is as central a theme as the establishment of the monotheist faith. In fact the two issues are intrinsically linked since the advent of the 'new' god can only be achieved through the destruction of the cult of Baal which is dominated by a strong mother figure. The recognition of Yahweh as the one and only god signals the exclusion of women from the realm of the spiritual since they cannot recognize themselves in, or hope to represent, the male god. Athalie therefore represents transgression in various forms – a foreigner at the head of the state, a woman without a man and a follower of a polytheist faith which allowed women priests (the reviled Jezebel, for example, had a religious as well as a political role). She has sinned by becoming the dominant member of her family as much as she has in seizing political power, the two aspects being inextricably linked.[14] Thus Athalie is the embodiment of

---

13 A fact exemplified by the biblical presentation of Ahab. A. Brenner notes that 'The prophetic narratives establish the opinion – which the editorial passages reinforce – that one of Ahab's greatest sins was his subordination to Jezebel's views and beliefs (1 Kings 16:31–34; 21:25)'. However she goes on to point out the political reasons behind Ahab's attitude: Jezebel was a priestess of Baal whilst Ahab's authority stemmed from Yahweh, therefore 'such a doubly strong legitimation of the monarchy suited Ahab's best interest [. . .] thus [. . .] he let his wife administer internal affairs on her own. Rational political considerations of this type seem much more in keeping with his thinking than the Samson-like motif of masculine weakness for corrupt feminine wiles' (*The Israelite woman: social role and literary type in biblical narrative* (Sheffield 1985), pp 23–5). However, Ahab is most often presented as a weak ruler, an impression which also emerges in Racine's *Athalie*, owing to the emphasis on Jézabel's role. **14** As Ronzeaud reminds us: 'L'argument décisif des théoriciens du XVIIe reste le fondement patriarcal du pouvoir, la correspondance entre l'Etat et la

the prevalent worries of seventeenth-century thinkers regarding the unsuitability of women for power. As Ronzeaud points out:

> [Sa] faiblesse [physique et mentale] s'accompagnant de dépendance, la femme ne sera pas libre, et cette soumission à autrui constitue le troisième argument par lequel on écarte du pouvoir celles qui seraient obligées de se reconnaître un maître en leur mari, et ce faisant, de livrer l'autorité étatique à une domination étrangère.[15]

Athalie, although there is nothing to suggest that she was a less than obedient wife, is 'usurpatrice' both by virtue of her gender and her 'foreignness', although it seems clear that her enemies find the former far more distasteful than the latter. She has come to power through her husband but refuses to surrender it when her son is killed. She assumes her status through marriage in the same way that a man might claim it through his wife. Furthermore 'c'est généralement dans l'organisation patriarcale de la famille que les théoriciens politiques vont chercher la justification de l'exclusion féminine du gouvernement',[16] but Athalie is also a widow, a woman without a husband. She has no interest in relinquishing her power to a man and is therefore doubly a threat to patriarchal power – on the private level, since the absence of a husband means that she has no 'master' and therefore only recognizes her own authority, and on the public level since she is the highest political authority in the land. If it is accepted that 'on doit obéir au Prince plus qu'à son père,'[17] then 'permettre alors à une femme de régner reviendrait donc à établir et à accepter le plus impensable des matriarcats absolus et tout puissants'.[18]

In this light it could perhaps be argued that the numerous references to Athalie as 'mère' are symptomatic of this fear of matriarchy: Athalie has become a metaphoric mother, a symbol of female power which threatens the very existence of the phallocentric monotheist supremacy. The religious setting of the play compounds this since, as Marie-Florine Bruneau argues,

> Ce sentiment de l'horreur et de la peur ressenti par les juifs à l'égard d'Athalie et de Jézabel fait écho à la notion collective de l'abject et de l'abomination que Kristeva tente de délimiter dans son essai sur l'abjection [. . .] 'Celles-ci [les femmes] placées apparemment dans une position d'objets passifs, n'en sont pas moins ressenties comme des puissances rusées. Comme si deux pouvoirs essayaient de se partager la

---

famille, tous deux soumis à l'autorité masculine' ('La Femme au pouvoir', 14).   **15** Ibid., 13. **16** Ibid., 11.   **17** Barthélémy de Chasseneux, quoted in Ronzeaud, art. cit., 14.   **18** Ronzeaud, art. cit., 14.

société. L'un masculin, en apparence vainqueur, avoue dans son acharnement même contre l'autre, le féminin, qu'il est menacé par une puissance asymétrique, irrationnelle, rusé, incontrôlable. Cet autre sexe, le
féminin, devient synonyme d'un mal radical à supprimer' (Kristeva).[19]

In this context, what is at stake is far more than the struggle of Christianity
against polytheism. It is the establishment through a monotheist faith of a
social structure which will ensure the subjugation of women to male
authority. When Bernard Chedozeau states that 'la tragédie raconte la
destruction d'un des obstacles dressés sur la route du salut des hommes –
l'obstacle que représente Athalie',[20] it must not be overlooked that this 'salvation' is inseparable, in the Judæo-Christian perspective, from a strict hier-
archization of the sexes. In most of Racine's tragedies womanhood becomes
a negative attribute when linked to certain acts or behaviours. In *Athalie*,
being a woman can, in itself, be a violation of the law. Zacharie's reaction to
Athalie's arrival in the temple is fairly symptomatic of this:

> Une femme . . . Peut-on la nommer sans blasphème?
> Une femme. C'était Athalie elle-même.
>
> (II. ii. 395–6)

His description of events stresses both her gender and her apparent pride:

> Dans un des parvis, aux hommes réservés
> Cette femme superbe entre, le front levé,
> Et se préparait encore à passer les limites
> De l'enceinte sacrée ouverte aux seuls lévites.
>
> (II. ii. 397–400)

It is obvious that in his mouth 'superbe' and 'front levé', which would normally suggest admiration, are unforgivable flaws in a woman's character. He
continues by quoting Joad's reprimand to the queen:

> Reine, sors, a-t-il dit, de ce lieu redoutable,
> D'où te bannit *ton sexe* et ton impiété.
>
> (II. ii. 404–5; my italics)

By implying that both attributes are equally blasphemous, the priest makes
it clear that even a pious woman is irredeemably tainted by her gender. The
very word 'femme' becomes negative when uttered among the faithful, as

19 Marie-Florine Bruneau, *Racine, le Jansénisme et la modernité* (Paris 1986), pp 135–6.   20 Bernard
Chedozeau, 'Le Tragique d'Athalie', *Revue d'Histoire Littéraire de la France* (juillet-septembre 1967),
494–501 (p. 499).

demonstrated by the fact that it is never used in its generic sense to describe 'the good woman' of the play, Josabet.

Ultimately women, sinful by virtue of their gender, are denied access to a spirituality which mirrors their selves and they can only hope to access the divine by reinforcing the position of the men to whom they are attached by family links. To do this they may have to sacrifice themselves, like Esther, or their children, like Josabet, but most importantly they must accept their subordinate position or else become the enemy and, like Athalie, face destruction.

'By the sword divided': cultural and confessional conflict in the life and writings of Madame de St Balmont (1607–59)

KATE CURREY

During the mid-seventeenth century, a period when Europe was riven by warfare, a remarkable woman, Barbe d'Ernecourt, Madame de Saint Balmont (1607–59), defended her husband's estates in the duchy of Lorraine, in present-day north eastern France.[1] It should be noted that Barbe d'Ernecourt was not alone in her activities. Another noblewoman who marshalled her retainers against the duke of Savoy during the Nine Years' War was Philis de la Tour du Pin de La Charce.[2] Louis XIV rewarded her for her loyalty with a colonel's pension, unlike Barbe d'Ernecourt who, as John Lynn points out, 'never actually bore a commission from either the king of France or the duke of Lorraine'.[3] However, Barbe d'Ernecourt was recognized by her contemporaries for the nature of her martial activities, which Lynn acknowledges as 'impressive'.[4] To them she was known by the nickname 'l'Amazone chrestienne'. Certainly, Barbe d'Ernecourt's life presents us with a fascinating paradox. Under the guise of 'amazon' it was possible for her, even as an early modern woman, to live a life which challenged the accepted codes within which her sex was supposed to operate. But, unlike Jeanne d'Arc, another of Lorraine's 'Amazons' with whom her career invites at least a partial degree of comparison, Barbe d'Ernecourt did not fall from public acclaim into opprobrium.

The first part of this article will provide a brief survey of Barbe d'Ernecourt's life. The second part will examine how she was portrayed by her two biographers, Jean-Marie Vernon and Le Père Des Billons, in the seventeenth and eighteenth centuries respectively. The third and final part will present an analysis of her drama, the *Jumeaux martyrs* (1650).

---

1 Lorraine, a territory in the present-day north eastern corner of France, suffered considerably from the depradations of the Thirty Years War, depicted graphically in Jacques Callot's engravings, *Misères de la Guerre*', the 'Miseries of War'. On the duchy's experience of war, see S. Gaber, *La Lorraine meurtrie* (Nancy 1979). 2 I am grateful to Dr Guy Rowlands of Exeter College, Oxford, for drawing my attention to the existence of Philis de la Tour du Pin de La Charce, whose adventures are recounted in the *Histoire de Madamoiselle de la Charce de la maison de la Tour du Pin, ou Mémoires de ce qui s'est passé sous le règne de Louis Quatorze* (Paris 1731). 3 John A. Lynn, *Giant of the Grand Siècle: the French Army, 1610–1715* (Cambridge 1997), p. 343. 4 Ibid.

THE LIFE OF BARBE D'ERNECOURT

Barbe d'Ernecourt's life is relatively well documented. Micheline Cuénin's study of Barbe d'Ernecourt makes extensive use of primary sources in the Bibliothèque Nationale, and (among others) the Archives départementales de la Marne and the Archives départementales de la Meuse.[5] Much of this evidence formed the basis of the earlier biographical studies of Barbe d'Ernecourt by the Franciscan Jean-Marie Vernon and the Jesuit Des Billons.[6]

There is also a remarkable equestrian portrait by the Lorraine court artist, Claude Deruet. This shows Barbe d'Ernecourt seated on horseback, amidst the backdrop of her husband's estates at Neuville-en-Verdunois. Clad in male attire, the Barbe d'Ernecourt of this picture possesses an innate theatricality which reflects Deruet's involvement in producing the decorative ephemera required by festivals held at the court of Nancy.[7] Some of Deruet's other paintings, especially the series commonly called the 'Four Elements' or 'Seasons', depict court entertainments, where female courtiers are dressed in the fantastic guise of Amazons. Doubtless conceived as just this kind of 'general scheme of decoration', Deruet's picture belies the serious implications of Barbe d'Ernecourt's outlook and activities.[8] Moreover, despite the glamourizing effect of his portrait, she was, in reality, short and stocky and her complexion was pitted with smallpox scars.[9]

Barbe d'Ernecourt was born in May 1607 at Neuville-en-Verdunois, between Bar-le-Duc and Verdun. Her birthplace, like Jeanne d'Arc's Domrémy, was an area of contested territory over which France and Lorraine jockeyed for control. Her father, Simon d'Ernecourt, belonged to

---

5 Micheline Cuénin, *La Dernière des Amazones: Madame de Saint-Baslemont* (Nancy 1992). This is the most detailed biography to date. For a useful, briefer survey, see the preface to C. Abbott and H. Fournier's edition of *Les Jumeaux martyrs* (Genève 1995). **6** See Jean-Marie Vernon, *L'Amazone chrestienne ou les avantures de Madame de Saint Balmon, qui a joint une admirable dévotion et la pratique de toutes les vertus avec l'exercice des armes et de la guerre* (Paris 1678). A new edition of this work was brought out in 1873, prefaced by René Muffat and published in Paris by E. de Soye. See also Le Père Des Billons, *Histoire de la vie chrétienne et des exploits militaires d'Alberte-Barbe d'Ernecourt connue sous le nom de madame de Saint-Balmon* (Liège 1773). **7** For example, the 1627 *Combat à la barrière* staged by Duke Charles IV of Lorraine for the duchesse de Chevreuse's visit to the court of Nancy, a project which witnessed the collaboration of Claude Deruet and Jacques Callot. **8** Christopher Wright, *The French painters of the seventeenth century* (London 1985), p. 40. On depictions of Barbe d'Ernecourt, see also F.G. Pariset, 'Claude Deruet', *Gazette des Beaux Arts*, I (1952), 153–72; idem, 'Les Amazones de Claude Deruet', *Le Pays Lorrain* (1956), 97–114. For a more recent perspective, see Carmeta Abbott, 'The portrait as text: two depictions of Madame de Saint-Balmon 1607–1660', *Atlantis: Revue d'Études sur les Femmes, numéro spécial sur la femme sous l'Ancien Régime* (1993), 122–33. **9** Cuénin, *La Dernière des Amazones*, p. 61.

the Lorraine nobility and held the position of gentleman of the chamber to duke Henri II.[10] Barbe's mother, Marguerite, also belonged to the Lorraine nobility. It is interesting to speculate, therefore, on where their daughter's strong allegiance to the French cause originated, especially given that her parents had such close ties to the ducal court. As a young girl, Barbe d'Ernecourt was educated by her aunt, Madame d'Estrepis, at Vitry-le-François. Whilst she mastered such feminine accomplishments as playing the lute, she was also highly literate. She read philosophy and history and wrote religious poetry. Certainly, her later foray into the genre of religious drama would seem to reflect these interests.

In 1625, Barbe d'Ernecourt married a young nobleman, Jacques d'Haraucourt, the seigneur de Saint Balmont. His family estate was based just south of Toul and the ducal capital of Nancy. Jacques d'Haraucourt enjoyed life at the court of Nancy to which he repaired in 1625. Under the flamboyant rule of duke Charles IV, who inherited the duchy in 1624, the Nanceian court experienced a constant round of lavish entertainments such as the controversial 1627 'Combat à la barrière'.[11] However, the newly-wed Madame de Saint Balmont did not join her husband at court, although her noble background made her eminently suitable to do so. She chose instead to remain on her husband's estates. Throughout their marriage, in fact, the couple spent little time together owing to the political upheaval in the duchy. This could have served as a uniting rather than a divisive factor given that, like many individuals contracted into a family alliance, Madame de St Balmont and her husband seem to have had very little in common. This said, it would appear that the couple did share a mutual enjoyment of hunting, a pursuit popular amongst the nobility, the court of Nancy being no exception.[12] It is possible that Madame de Saint Balmont's involvement in martial pursuits originated from her experience of hunting and the time that she spent with her husband riding around his lands.

Madame de Saint Balmont's marriage to Jacques d'Haraucourt produced two sons and a daughter. Her sons were not long-lived: one died at two days old and the other died in 1644 aged fourteen. However, her daughter, Marie Claude, seemed to have had more of her mother's resilience. She married in 1646 and went on to have a son who was to inherit his grandmother's possessions.

---

10 Henri II (1563–1608) was the eldest son of duke Charles III and ruled Lorraine between 1608 and 1624. 11 The published account of this festival is Henry Humbert's *Combat à la barrière* (Nancy 1627). 12 On court entertainments during this period, see Henri Roy, 'La vie à la cour de Lorraine sous le duc Henri II', *Mémoires de la Société d'Archéologie Lorraine et de Musée Historique Lorrain*, 63 (1913), 53–206. The ducal palace's so-called 'Galérie des cerfs' was decorated with painted scenes of stag-hunting.

In 1629 an imperial army overran Lorraine. Duke Charles IV raised an army to defend his territories. Madame de Saint Balmont's husband went to join Charles' forces, but was captured and taken prisoner. His wife, who stayed at Neuville, sold off family possessions to pay for his ransom. Her own immediate concern was to defend Neuville from ravaging troops.[13] Indeed, Neuville was to become a refuge for surrounding villagers as a number of artisans were given board and lodging in return for work. Neuville was, in effect, a self-sufficient community. It even had its own cavalry and infantry companies of which Madame de Saint Balmont was captain.

Madame de Saint Balmont also assumed the role of the community's spiritual director and encouraged her residents to attend mass, while she herself rose at 4.30 a.m. to pray. She was the self-appointed guardian of the local shrine of Benoîte-Vaux, where a statue of the Virgin was venerated by the locals and also by Madame de Saint-Balmont. When it was attacked in July 1643, although she was seriously ill, she left her sick-bed to defend it. As well as teaching music to her residents so that they could sing the daily office, Madame de Saint Balmont took her charitable obligations seriously, distributing bread to 200 paupers every week.

It is interesting to observe that, in her capacity as self-appointed guardian of Neuville, Madame de Saint Balmont assumed the 'masculine' duty of defending the community. Her overseeing of the spiritual lives of her charges fits more neatly into the duties commonly performed by noblewomen during the period. Certainly, between 1636 and 1643, Madame de Saint Balmont's military career flourished and she took part in over twenty-five expeditions and skirmishes.

Indeed, her activities read like something in a Dumas novel. In 1637 she was granted a permit by the French which allowed her to move freely within their occupied territory. At this point it is necessary to ask why these concessions were granted. It is possible that we shall have to accept the interpretation that Madame de Saint Balmont's pro-French loyalties assured her safety. She actually intervened on behalf of the French when the governor of Bar-le-Duc was taken prisoner by Charles' forces. He was rescued by her own soldiers, but a reprisal action was mounted and Charles IV's troops attacked Neuville, killing five women and taking prisoners. However, the French subsequently rescued the hostages, such was their respect for Madame de Saint Balmont. The conflicts of the situation were, then, even reflected in Madame de Saint Balmont's marriage, where husband and wife not only supported opposing sides, but witnessed these opposing sides in active opposition.

---

13 See Gaber, *La Lorraine meurtrie.*

It is beyond the scope of this article to examine the many other military exploits of Madame de Saint Balmont, exploits which are recounted in considerable detail by Vernon and with somewhat less enthusiasm by Des Billons.[14] One incident will suffice to give a flavour of Madame de Saint Balmont's exploits during this period. One of her enemies, having been captured in a skirmish, was due to be executed. He remarked with chagrin that it was not his capture which he found humiliating so much as the fact that it had been effected by a woman!

These were, indeed, testing times, even for someone of Madame de Saint Balmont's energy and determination. Inevitably, the ongoing conflict brought other difficulties to Lorraine besides marauding troops. One of these was the plague. Madame de Saint Balmont added the care of plague sufferers to her roll-call of duties. In this she was assisted by her aunt, the abbess of a nearby nunnery. Her own health would suffer as a result of her exertions.

During the last portion of her life, Madame de Saint Balmont, despite ill health, chose to pursue her strong sense of religious vocation and entered the convent of Sainte-Claire at Bar-le-Duc. Her strict adherence there to the convent regime caused her health to deteriorate to the extent that the abbess forced her to leave. In 1659 she had made her will, leaving all her goods to her grandson, and she then returned to Neuville where she died in May 1660 aged 52. Her biographers paint an edifying picture of her virtuously conducted illness, and, in her words, death brought release from fear of 'le joug tyrannique de la mort'.[15] She was buried next to her husband in the church at Neuville. An inscription placed there in the eighteenth century praises her 'charité inépuisable/par ses exploits guerriers/pour la défense du pays'.[16] Here, as Cuénin notes, an interesting shift of attitude had occurred by the eighteenth century. In place of the pro-French propaganda of the seventeenth century, the 'pays' which Madame de Saint Balmont's epitaph praised her for defending was Lorraine and not France.

When considering Barbe d'Ernecourt's life, it is necessary to avoid the understandable temptation to treat her as a swashbuckling heroine in the Dumas mould, a 'véritable héroine de cape et d'épée'.[17] Instead, a more profitable line of enquiry is to attempt to understand how her contemporaries were able to place such a positive gloss upon her activities. Here the key point seems to be that, in the first instance, her early biographers were both

---

14 Des Billons describes Vernon's account as a 'discours fort ennuyeux' (*Histoire de la vie*, p. 33). **15** Cuénin, *La Dernière des Amazones*, p. 168, citing Vernon. **16** Ibid., p. 169, note 8. **17** Claude Gével, 'Une héroine du dix-septième siècle: Madame de Saint-Balmont', *Revue de Paris* (octobre 1930), 168–80 (p. 168).

Catholic clerics. Such individuals would be familiar with the typology of Catholic militancy, a common topos used by early modern rulers. The dukes of Lorraine, especially Charles III (who reigned between 1559 and 1608), were no exception in their pursuit of pro-Catholic policies.[18] These were realized through such actions as the brokering of dynastic marriages with another Catholic dynasty, the Bavarian Wittelsbach, or by the founding of a Jesuit university at nearby Pont-à-Mousson in 1574.[19] Thus Barbe d'Ernecourt can be seen as a virtuous exponent of just this kind of Catholic militancy.

As Marina Warner has established, by the late sixteenth century, Jeanne d'Arc was rehabilitated and becoming well integrated into the extant symbolic repertoire of heroines from both biblical and classical sources.[20] It is also quite possible that this presentation of Barbe d'Ernecourt as a virtuous heroine owes something to the presence of Jeanne d'Arc in the duchy of Lorraine's repository of local symbols. For example, in 1581, a Jesuit father at the University of Pont-à-Mousson wrote a play about Jeanne d'Arc entitled *L'Histoire tragique de la pucelle de Dom-Remy, aultrement d'Orléans*.[21] In this play, Jeanne's virtue lies in her essential obedience to divine will, as perceived in the terms of duty. Barbe d'Ernecourt's actions and, indeed, the theme of her religious drama may be interpreted in the same way. However, it should also be borne in mind that Barbe d'Ernecourt, although identified closely with the duchy by virtue of her marriage, remained French by both her birth and her loyalty to Louis XIII.

Like Jeanne d'Arc, it is possible that Barbe d'Ernecourt may be appropriated to serve the needs of a wider audience. But, in the final analysis, what interests us should be how she located herself in relation to the many conflicts which she faced in her life. These included her desire to pursue her religious convictions and her divided personal loyalty, whether to her husband or the king of France, or to Lorraine as her marital home and France as her country of birth. In addition, Barbe d'Ernecourt was expected to enact the roles of wife and mother. On the other hand, she seems to have felt the

---

18 For example, Philip Soergel has established how the Bavarian Wittelsbach dynasty deployed Corpus Christi processions to convey their anti-Protestant stance. See Philip Soergel, *Wondrous in his saints: Counter-Reformation propaganda in Bavaria* (Berkeley and Los Angeles 1993), p. 89. **19** Charles III's sister, Renée, married Wilhelm of Bavaria in 1568, while his daughter Elisabeth married her first cousin, Maxmilian of Bavaria, in 1595. On the founding of the university of Pont-à-Mousson, see Eugène Martin, *L'Université de Pont-à-Mousson et les problèmes de son temps* (Nancy 1972). **20** See Marina Warner, *Joan of Arc: the image of female heroism* (London 1981), pp 189–200. **21** Le Père Fronton du Duc, *L'Histoire tragique de la pucelle de Dom-Remy, aultrement d'Orléans* (Nancy 1581).

compulsion to embrace a masculine role as shown by her adoption of male clothing and her defence of her husband's estates.

BIOGRAPHICAL ACCOUNTS

By what process did Madame de Saint Balmont become the subject of several biographies? Of these biographies, the best-known are, firstly, *L'Amazone chrestienne* (1678) by the Franciscan Jean-Marie de Vernon, and, secondly, the *Histoire de la vie chrétienne et des exploits militaires d'Alberte-Barbe d'Ernecourt'* (1773) by the Jesuit author Des Billons. The motivations governing the production of each book are interesting, in that both works reveal a shift in attitudes towards Madame de Saint Balmont experienced between the late seventeenth and late eighteenth centuries respectively.[22]

Madame de Saint Balmont's first biographer, Jean-Marie de Vernon, was attached to the household of Louis XIV's chancellor, Pierre Seguier. In the late 1660s, he was entrusted by his superiors in the Franciscan order with the task of collating a list of personal professions of faith made by those who were lay members. One signature appeared twice, that of Madame de Saint Balmont. It was written in ink and also in blood. This demonstration of faith impressed Vernon who resolved to discover more about the owner of the signature.

Vernon decided that such a pious individual deserved to be the subject of a book. It is interesting to note that he was not put off by Madame de Saint Balmont's masculine behaviour, but rather regarded her as someone of superior spiritual stature. He pursued research in the region of Lorraine where she had lived and spoke to many people who had known her, including family servants, her priest, and surviving members of her family, of whom the most important was her daughter who had preserved her mother's letters. Amongst those he interviewed, Vernon found that Madame de Saint Balmont was not without her critics.[23] Nonetheless, what seems to be significant here was that Vernon's high opinion of his subject's spiritual sincerity caused him to become her self-appointed defender. Indeed, he defends her thus: 'Je n'appelle point le discours présenter une apologie pour justifier nostre Amazone Chrestienne, ny pour la deffendre contre ceux qui la voudroit accuser: l'integrité des moeurs, et les avantages qu'elle a parcourt à la Religion [. . .] la rendent assez recommendable.'[24]

Dedicated to the Virgin Mary, in recognition of Madame de Saint

---

22 For a brief account of this process, see Cuénin, *La Dernière des Amazones*, pp 7–9.   23 Ibid., p. 8.   24 Vernon, *L'Amazone chréstienne*, p. 139.

Balmont's martial virtue, Vernon's book devotes sixty-eight chapters to the exploits of his heroine. Twenty-seven of these focus upon her virtues, deploying a traditional range of female role-models, such as Judith, Deborah and Jeanne d'Arc, all of whom shared the appropriate qualities of courage and virtuous conduct.[25] In addition, Judith 'symbolized heroic courage in rescuing a besieged and starving city on the verge of surrender'.[26] However, as if to acknowledge Madame de Saint Balmont's adoption of a masculine role, Vernon also offers several comparisons with relevant male role-models such as Caesar and Alexander.[27] Vernon also comments that Madame de Saint Balmont carried a man's heart in a woman's body.[28]

This dual combination of gender roles recurs throughout Vernon's depiction of Madame de Saint Balmont and reflects the dichotomy of her activities. On one hand, she is presented as a virtuous, godly woman, on the other, she is a spirited warrior and man of affairs.[29] Nonetheless, it is always her virtue which provides the justification for her conduct or her feminine guile which serves to offset her masculine behaviour. In a quotation typical of the work, Vernon argues that 'son humeur guerrière estait accompagnée ou plustost reglée par une conduite delicate et honneste'.[30]

Both Vernon and Des Billons get round the issue of her adoption of male attire by arguing that her husband encouraged her to dress as a man because his estates were isolated and dangerous.[31] Thus, unlike Jeanne d'Arc, Madame de Saint Balmont did not have to persuade a sceptical contemporary audience that God had told her to dress as a man, but rather that she was simply obeying her husband. Taken into consideration with her pious conduct, this explanation seemed sufficient to exonerate Madame de Saint Balmont from any potential charge of unnatural conduct. It is worthy of mention, however, that contemporary accounts confirm that she seemed uncomfortable in women's clothes. As Antoine Arnauld, the governor of Verdun, observed: 'C'était une chose assez plaisante de voir combien elle était embarrassée en habit de femme.'[32]

It is interesting to compare Vernon's motivation for writing the life of Madame de Saint Balmont with that of the Jesuit Des Billons. Des Billons

---

25 Ibid., pp 135–6.   **26** See Ulinka Rublack, 'Wench and maiden: women, war and the pictorial function of the feminine in German cities of the early modern period', *History Workshop Journal* (Autumn 1997), 1–21 (p. 5).   **27** Vernon, *L'Amazone chrestienne*, p. 203.   **28** Ibid., p. 238.   **29** Ibid., p. 225.   **30** Ibid., p. 184.   **31** According to Vernon, 'Alberte d'Ernecourt, montant tous les jours plusieurs fois à cheval en présence de son mari, devint [. . .] une illustre cavalière' (*L' Amazone chréstienne*, p. 20). Des Billons makes a similar comment: 'Il faut remarquer icy ce que la coustume de se travester luy vint du commandement de son mary' (*Histoire*, p. 21).   **32** Cited by Cuénin, *La Dernère des Amazones*, p. 61. Arnauld makes this observation in his *Mémoires* which were written between 1677 and 1678, more or less at the same time as Vernon's work was published.

came across Vernon's book by chance, as only a few copies had been published. Unlike his predecessor, he was less concerned with his subject's piety and more with her status as a historical curiosity. However, like Vernon before him, Des Billons categorizes Madame de Saint Balmont as a heroine cast in the mould of Deborah, Judith and Jeanne d'Arc.[33] As previously mentioned, he plays down her military exploits, but still refers to her as 'l'humble et dévoute Guerriere'.[34] Des Billons sums up Madame de Saint Balmont thus: 'une héroine, qui faisait honneur à la Lorraine, à la France et à son siècle'.[35] Interestingly, he places Lorraine before France in this list, a shift noted (as mentioned above) by Cuénin with reference to Madame de Saint Balmont's epitaph.

'LES JUMEAUX MARTYRS'

Turning to the play written by Madame de Saint Balmont, the *Jumeaux martyrs*, this religious drama is the only surviving published example of her work, although she produced several others and also wrote religious verse.[36] Her writings were evidently a vehicle for her spiritual and personal preoccupations, given that they deal with conflicts between personal desire and duty. The *Jumeaux martyrs* is important as it evidences the fact that Barbe d'Ernecourt was not just literate but also highly educated. It is also possible to analyze this drama for the light it sheds upon Barbe d'Ernecourt's strong religious convictions which seem to have impelled most of her actions and her outlook.

Research on the theatrical traditions in Lorraine identifies religious dramas such as those written at the Jesuit University of Pont-à-Mousson as having evolved in the French classical style.[37] Certainly, the *Jumeaux martyrs* also owes much to drama of the time. Indeed, in the choice of its theme and subject matter, the *Jumeaux martyrs* resembles in particular a religious play, *Maurice* (1606), written by Nicolas Romain, a court secretary at Nancy.[38] *Maurice* explores the dilemma faced by its eponymous Roman emperor whose army revolts when he refuses to pay the ransom for some of his soldiers who are being held hostage by a heathen overlord. Similarly, the plot

---

33 Des Billons, *Histoire*, p. 33. **34** Ibid. **35** Ibid., p. 100. **36** Their subjects were the death of Julius Caesar and the life of St Godelave. On this, see Abbott and Fournier's preface to their edition of *Les Jumeaux martyrs*, p. 25. **37** For more on this, see H. Lépage, 'Étude sur le théâtre en Lorraine', *Mémoires de l'Académie de Stanislas'*, 14 (1886), 265–303. **38** Nicolas Romain, *Maurice. Tragoedie* (Pont-à-Mousson 1606); for a discussion of this play and a brief account of Romain's career, see Alain Cullière, 'La vie culturelle en Lorraine dans la seconde moitié du XVIe siècle', Université de Nancy II, Ph.D. thesis (Nancy 1978), pp 403–17.

of the *Jumeaux martyrs* turns on the theme of refusal. Set during the reign of Diocletian, it concerns the martyrdom of two Roman Christian converts, Marc and Marcellin, who were followers of St Sebastian. Despite constant threats of execution, the two refuse to abjure their faith. Their wives, families and friends are all equally determined to save them. Everyone, apart from Marc and Marcellin, is distressed and exasperated at their desire to martyr themselves. Nonetheless, the two men get their own way in the end and die bravely.

Themes of conflict and duality run through this drama. The use of the twin motif is interesting because it allows the author to reinforce the sense of duty shared by Marc and Marcellin. Other pairs of characters, such as the twins' parents and their wives, unite themselves in opposition against them. For example, their wives, Camille and Silenie, complain: 'Nous avons deux jumeaux, et nos maux sont les mesmes.'[39] Madame de Saint Balmont accepts the conflicting desires which divide the twins and their families. For example, instead of arguing that the wives of Marc and Marcellin should uncomplainingly accept their fate, she acknowledges their need to express their grief. So it is that one wife, Camille, asks, 'Pour avoir mon espoux, qu'est-il que je ne fasse?'[40]

Madame de Saint Balmont is especially sympathetic to the desperate and exasperated parents, wives, and friends of the future martyrs. She shows how they try to understand what has led the pair to act in this way. For example, Cephas says 'leur crime est commun, plus il est pardonable, et leur jeunesse le doit rendre excusable'.[41] But neither the strongly united front presented by friends and family, nor the great risks which they are prepared to take on their behalf (even resorting to bribing the judge who is to try them), can overcome the twins' determination to die for their faith. As the play progresses, it becomes increasingly obvious that the chosen destiny of the twins is ineluctable. Whilst the other characters rail against the implacability of fate, it is as if the twins are resigned to their fate.

Undoubtedly Madame de Saint Balmont had herself faced such conflicts between duty and desire, especially in her support of the French cause, while her husband retained his loyalty to the exiled duke of Lorraine, Charles IV. Where her life differed from that of her characters was that her actions had empowered her well beyond most women of her time. In her drama she is exploring the conflicts faced by individuals who are literally helpless in the face of destiny. Yet she is able to demonstrate that those who are the most vulnerable, Marc and Marcellin, are also the strongest. It is their religious

---

39 Madame de Saint Balmont, *Les Jumeaux martyrs*, ed. C. Abbott and H. Fournier, p. 48. All quotations in this article are taken from this edition. **40** Ibid., p. 48. **41** Ibid., p. 53.

faith that is the source of their strength. As Marc comments: 'L'âme d'un vray Chrestien ne doit estre offensé.'[42] This seems to reflect the fundamental outlook of Madame de Saint Balmont herself. Another character, the mother of Marc and Marcellin, expresses an opinion which could also have come from Madame de Saint Balmont: 'Le vray moyen d'avoir un peu d'humilité, est de se voir tombée en quelque adversité.'[43] In other words, she recognizes suffering as part of the human condition, especially as a mother facing the death of her two sons. Madame de Saint Balmont had also lost two sons, a fact which adds yet another personal dimension to this drama.

In the final analysis, this is a very human drama. The threats faced are real and immediate, and the characters are fearful and resentful but also brave and determined. Whilst one should not make too many conscious connections between Madame de Saint Balmont's life and her play, it is undeniable that, through her own experiences, she played out conflicts of the kind faced by her characters. In her view, adversity breeds strength and religious faith breeds both hope and the courage to face death. Freedom of conscience and action were both very necessary to Madame de Saint Balmont, and she allows her twin heroes to face their death knowing they have been true to their convictions. Indeed, her own attitude to life may be summed up by the following line from the play spoken by Sébastien: 'Ce grand dieu nous créant en pleine liberté fait dépendre le choix de nostre volonté.'[44]

Even if Madame de Saint Balmont's life was not quite what she would have chosen – it is tempting to think that she would perhaps have preferred to have been a man – unlike most women of her time, she lived it in a way that reflected both her moral outlook and her desire for action. Maybe this was as a consequence of the social dislocations experienced by her homeland during the Thirty Years War, or as a result of the indulgence of her husband, but it is certainly a testimony to her own personal bravery. She was a woman upon whom many conflicts centred, notably those of gender, territorial allegiance, peace and war, motherhood and religious duty. However, despite these personal conflicts, Madame de Saint Balmont's identity achieved coherence through her religious conviction and her assumption of a masculine role. Ultimately, despite her atypical and unfeminine actions, Madame de Saint Balmont, at least according to the terms of early modern social stereotyping, was still identifiable as fitting the mould of a contemporary noblewoman. Unlike Jeanne d'Arc, Madame de Saint Balmont's sense of personal duty and strong religious conviction took precedence over her desire to do the job of a man.

---

42 Ibid., p. 75.   **43** Ibid., p. 82.   **44** Ibid., p. 109.

From 'Ex ovo omnia' to ovism: the father function in seventeenth-century treatises on generation

REBECCA WILKIN

In his famous essay, 'Qu'est-ce qu'un auteur?', Michel Foucault distinguishes between the author as a socio-historical entity, and the 'author function', or the proper name that gives shape to a work and whose own contours are defined by that work. In order to underscore the emergence of a literary author function during the seventeenth century, Foucault contrasts the trajectories of literary and scientific discourses. Before the seventeenth century, he argues, scientific works were only valid if they invoked a proper name (such as Aristotle or Galen), whereas literary works 'were accepted, put into circulation, and valorized without any question about the identity of their author'.[1] Basing his timeline on the works of historians of science such as Alexandre Koyré and Thomas Kuhn, Foucault argues that at the very moment when literary works acquired authors, scientific authority shifted from a canon of proper names to an ensemble of universal truths.[2] Consequently, Foucault suggests, there was no 'author function' for scientific discourse; unlike the proper name gracing the title page of a literary work, that appearing on a scientific treatise was not seen to belong in any organic way to the ideas contained within it.

Foucault uses scientific discourse as a foil against which to dramatize the rise of the literary author function. It is perhaps for this reason that he takes at face value the claims to scientificity articulated in the texts that he classifies as scientific. He does not question, for instance, the extent to which empiricism was a theory as much as a practice. One proponent of the idea that one should base one's knowledge of nature on interactions with nature was Pierre Bayle (1647–1706), the prodigious author of the monthly

---

1 M. Foucault, 'Qu'est-ce qu'un auteur', *Bulletin de la Société française de Philosophie*, 44 (1969), 73–104 (p. 149). 2 Authors of *Du monde clos à l'univers infini* (Paris 1957) and *The structure of scientific revolutions* (Chicago 1962), respectively. Koyré's idea that '[le remplacement de la conception aristotélicienne de l'espace [. . .] par celle de la géométrie euclidienne] impliqua le rejet par la pensée scientifique de toutes considérations basées sur les notions de valeur, de perfection, d'harmonie, de sens ou de fin, et finalement, la dévalorisation complète de l'Etre, le divorce total entre le monde des valeurs et le monde des faits' bears particular affinity with Foucault's portrayal of seventeenth-century scientific authorship.

Nouvelles de la république des lettres. In his review of a newly published treatise about the fœtus, Bayle champions empiricism when he condemns the use of metaphor in medicine:

> cela est ordinaire partout où les sentimens sont fort partagez [que] l'on s'amuse à des comparaisons, à des allusions, & à des Métaphores mystérieuses. Ces ornemens bons pour les harangues, ne valent rien du tout ailleurs. Cependant les Medecins qui devraient uniquement nous rapporter en simples historiens ce qui se passe dans la Nature, & comment se fait chaque chose, ne sont pas toujours exempts de ce faux goût qui donne dans des Analogies imaginaires.[3]

Bayle's argument that the frivolous ornamentation of rhetoric has no place in the objective discourse of medicine appears to confirm Foucault's claim that, during the seventeenth century, the discourses of science and literature, together with the notions of scientific and literary authorship, definitively went their separate ways. Bayle characterizes doctors as simple historians of a Nature that functions according to its own laws. Analogously, Foucault treats empiricism as an idea that stands alone, disembodied from the texts in which it appears. Yet through his allusion to the rhetoric engendered by controversy, Bayle suggests that the mere act of representing nature clouds its self-evidence. And examining the idea of empiricism in the context of medical discourse leads us to question the idea that seventeenth-century science consisted of a faceless revelation of Nature's truths.

Certainly, although physicians characterized the body – as opposed to books – as a source of pure and unmediated knowledge, the very notion of an entity free of artifice emanated irresistible rhetorical appeal. Doctors called on the body to witness the transparency of their representations and theories about it; they supplemented empirical knowledge with a rhetorical claim to empiricism. Thus, although in principle doctors agreed with Bayle that rhetoric was none of their business, in practice their works were 'harangues' and they employed the tricks and tropes of classical rhetoric to persuade their readers. The consideration of empiricism as an ideal as well as a practice, as a rhetorical device as well as a technique, begs the question of the author's purpose. With what aim in mind does a doctor insist on the imitative perfection of his work? In seventeenth-century medicine, as in classical rhetoric, imitation went hand in hand with invention, for one asserted

---

3 P. Bayle, *L'Histoire du fœtus humain, recoeüillie des extraits de Monsieur Bayle; & publiée par Monsieur du Rondel* (Leyden 1688), p. 25. The works on generation that Bayle reviews are all by Charles Drelincourt (1633–97), who, like Bayle, was the son of a Protestant minister and an exile who taught medicine and then anatomy at Leyden. This one is on the membranes of the fœtus.

one's difference from others through one's accurate imitation of nature.[4] Doctors and anatomists characterized their books as faithful representations of a body that lay in wait of discovery, but nonetheless re-vindicated their intellectual property rights, as it were, to those representations. Like their literary counterparts, therefore, physicians emphasized their organic filiation to their works. Moreover, they expressed possession through one of the oldest metaphors of aesthetic creation: they characterized authorship as paternity.

It is this metaphor which is the focus of this article. By analyzing both the rhetoric of empiricism and what I call the 'father function' in seventeenth-century medical discourse, I shall argue, contrary to Foucault, that there was in fact a scientific author function. However, I shall also show that the new theory of ovism called into question the importance of the father in generation, and, as a result, diminished the potency of the trope of paternity as an expression of authorship.

In 1685, when Bayle makes his critique of metaphor in science, few medical topics inspired more harangues, and consequently more metaphors, than that of the generation of Man. 'Jamais on n'a tant foüillé dans le corps de l'homme que depuis un siécle, pour en découvrir la structure surprenante,' writes Bayle, '[mais] de toutes les parties qu'on a examinées avec une incroyable curiosité, il n'y en a point qu'on ait le plus exactement épluchées que celles qui servent à la génération.'[5] The most recent theory of generation, developed in fits and starts in Italy, England, Holland, and France, was that of ovism. Colluding his systematic dissections of Charles II's does in all stages of pregnancy and parturition with the anatomies of chickens which he and Hieronymus Fabricius d'Aquapendente had studied, William Harvey, in his *Anatomical exercitations, concerning the generation of living creatures* (1653), postulated that an egg resulted from the fertilization of the womb by male semen.[6] Although Harvey's theory remained Aristotelian to the extent that

---

4 Despite the different aims of art and science, William Harvey recognizes their similar need for representations which resemble as closely as possible the real thing: 'For as art is a habit whose object is something to be done; so science is a habit, whose object is something to be known: and as the former proceedeth from the imitation of Exemplars; so this latter from the knowledge of things naturall. The Sourse of both is from sense and experience; since it is impossible that Art should rightly be purchased by the one, or Science by the other, without a direction from Ideas. Yet in both Art & Science too, that thing which in sensible objects wee perceive, differs from the perception itself, which is kept in the memory, or imagination. That, is the exemplar, the Idea, the forme informing : this, the Representation, the Idos, the abstracted Species. That, is a natural thing, a real entity; this, a resemblance, or similitude' (*Anatomical exercitations, concerning the generation of living creatures* (London 1653), preface). **5** Bayle, *Nouvelles de la république des lettres* (juillet–1684), I: 536. **6** Harvey, *Anatomical exercitations*, p. 139. Harvey studied under Fabricius (1533–1619) at Padua where he was Professor Supraordinarius of anatomy. Fabricius wrote *De formatio foetu* (1604) and *De formatione ovi et pulli* (1621). It is from Fabricius that Harvey gets the idea that the semen is

he claimed that the egg came into being thanks to male semen, the inscription of the frontispiece of his book 'ex ovo omnia' (all comes from the egg) took on a new resonance with the publication of Reinier de Graaf's *De mulierum organis generationi inservientibus* (1672). Extrapolating to women from his experiments on rabbits, De Graaf argued that eggs pre-existed male fertilization. De Graaf and his rival, Jan Swammerdam,[7] inspired in turn Nicolas Malebranche's theory of 'emboitement.' In *De la recherche de la vérité* (1674), Malebranche speculated that Eve's egg had contained all the future eggs of humanity.

Ovists made a great deal of the fact that they were viewing the human body and its functions objectively, not through words borrowed from others, but through their own interactions with it. Harvey writes in his preface to his treatise on generation that '[t]he Reader, instructed by his own eyes, shal discover [. . .] how unsafe, and degenerate a thing it is, to be tutored by other mens commentaries, without making tryal of the things themselves: especially, since Natures Book is so open, and legible.' Similarly, Bayle compares a physician's role to that of a portraitist. He says in his review of a publicitary pamphlet announcing a forthcoming *Système du fœtus humain* that the author, Charles Drelincourt, 'fait espérer au lecteur que [l'opinion] qu'il lui prépare est un vrai Original tiré au vif, & sur la nature, & non pas sur les fausses vûës d'autrui'.[8] In order to avoid being 'tutored by other mens commentaries' or misled by 'les fausses vûës d'autrui,' both Harvey and Bayle maintain that one should consult the 'Original book' of Nature.

Nevertheless, although they privileged the original over the derivative, and the natural over the artificial, doctors' representations of the original and the natural were necessarily derivative and artificial. To mask this fact and to impart the illusion of perfect equivalency between their representations of

the efficient cause of generation. For a very good account of Fabricius' 'Aristotle project,' see Andrew Cunningham, 'Fabricius and the "Aristotle project" at Padua', in A. Wear, R.K. French and I.M. Lonie (ed.), *The medical renaissance of the sixteenth century* (Cambridge 1985), pp 195–222. **7** In *Biblia mundi* (published posthumously in 1680), Swammerdam claims to have discovered the human ovum before De Graaf. On Swammerdam's microscopic work on insects and his influence on Malebranche, see Clara Pinto-Correia, *The ovary of Eve: egg and sperm and preformation* (Chicago 1997), pp 25–32. **8** Bayle, *Nouvelles de la république des lettres* (mai 1685), III: 553. It is significant that the *Remarques sur la conception* in which Drelincourt claims to detain the most resemblant theory of generation is a publicitary preview for his soon-to-be-published *Système du fœtus humain*. His portrait of generation is, in fact, nowhere to be found in the *Remarques*. Rather, in a 'conduite très-bien entenduë,' to quote Bayle, Drelincourt prepares his reader to receive his system as the 'Original' by discounting all extant theories. As Bayle remarks, 'Personne n'ignore que des esprits desabusez de leurs vieilles opinions, & pleins d'espérance qu'on va leur en proposer de meilleures, sont dans les plus favorables dispositions, & dans toute la docilité qu'on puisse raisonnablement souhaiter': *Nouvelles de la république des lettres*, (mai 1685), III: 553.

the body and the actual body, doctors tautologically called upon the body to symbolize lack of mediation, thereby revealing the rhetorical basis of their empirical assumption that nature exists outside of and independently of Man's artifice. Indeed, as Jacques Derrida argues, since an anti-rhetorical stance is inherently rhetorical, a thing's rhetorical value increases the less it appears constructed and artificial.[9] As a result, the empirical claim for an unmediated body made metaphors involving that body all the more persuasive, and thus all the more appealing, for those whose rhetorical strategy it was to insist upon the resemblance of their portrait to the original.[10]

So it is, for instance, that the ovist physician from Marseille, Louis Barles, paradoxically mobilizes the body in order to emphasize his lack of recourse to rhetoric. He prefaces his 1672 French translation of De Graaf's book, *Les Nouvelles Decouvertes sur les organes des femmes, servans à la generation*, by blindly asserting that the modern theory of generation is free of figures: 'Ce ne sont pas icy [. . .] des figures de Rhetorique, ny des Paradoxes: Ce sont des veritez toutes nues. C'est une Doctrine receüe aujourd'hui de tous les Sçavans, & dont nous sommes convaincus par nos propres experiences faites a l'Hotel Dieu, sur des Cadavres de Femmes.'[11] Through his highly rhetorical equation of nude female cadavers with the truth laid bare, Barles implies that, for the first time, the process of generation has been represented transparently, unmediated by ambiguous language. Barles paradoxically deploys metaphor here to argue for the absence of rhetoric; he argues for the objectivity of his 'doctrine' by highlighting its resemblance to, as much as its origin in, the body.

---

9 Jacques Derrida, 'La Mythologie blanche', in *Les Marges de la philosophie* (Paris 1972).
10 Certainly, the stance against metaphor was not unanimous in medicine. At the same time as theologians and rhetoricians such as Nicole, Bossuet, Boileau, Malebranche, Arnauld, François Lamy and Goibaud du Bois were debating the place of metaphor (and the imagination to which it appealed) in predication, doctors debated metaphor's role in medicine. Some doctors were conscious that avoiding metaphor was impossible. Harvey, for example, apologetically acknowledges the inevitability of analogy in the practice of anatomy, and faced with a choice between expressing 'new inventions by old words' and 'mint[ing] up new and fictitious terms,' he chooses the former, that is, metaphors, as the lesser of two evils, although he is fearful lest they obfuscate rather than illustrate what they are meant to represent. Similarly, the ovist physician Guillaume de Houppeville responds thus to his anti-ovist opponent's attack on his use of metaphor: 'il est necessaire quelquefois de [se] servir [des fables et des figures], pour faire concevoir un objet rare & particulier; c'est ce qui a donné lieu à Licetus, Paré, & plusieurs autres de donner tant de figures dans les traitez qu'ils ont fait des Monstres, afin de faire comprendre des objets, qui parce qu'ils sont nouveaux & inconnus, se representent mieux par les traits du burin, qui peut bien les imiter, que par ceux de la plume, qui n'a pas toûjours des paroles pour les expliquer' (*La Génération de l'homme par le moyen des œufs* (Rouen 1676), p. 18). In Cartesian fashion, Houppeville attributes to images the same illustrative function as metaphors.   11 L. Barles, *Les Nouvelles Decouvertes sur les organes des femmes, servans à la generation* (Lyon 1674), p. 3.

Just as they supplemented their claims to accurate imitation of the body by alluding rhetorically to its nudity, physicians bolstered their claims to invention through the ancient trope of authorship as paternity. The source of this trope would seem to be Plato's *Symposium* in which it is argued that authoring a work is like engendering a child only better, because a work serves as an eternal monument to its author, while a child is made of flesh and blood and is therefore mortal.[12] Marsilio Ficino, the son of a Florentine physician, translated this trope in his commentary on the *Symposium*, the *De amore* (1469), a neo-Platonic work widely disseminated during the sixteenth century in European courts.[13] However, the trope of authorship as paternity did not wane with the decline of Neoplatonism; in 1575, the Spanish physician, Juan Huarte, refutes the neo-Platonic notion of knowledge acquisition, but nonetheless retains the Platonic analogy between engendering children and producing knowledge.[14]

Certainly, it was common during the Renaissance for an author to personify his book as his natural progeny in prefaces. For example, in a poem entitled 'L'Autheur à son livre,' Agrippa D'Aubigné apostrophes the *Tragiques* as his son, saying,

> Va Livre, tu n'es que trop beau
> Pour estre né dans le tombeau
> Du quel mon exil te delivre:
> Seul pour nous deux je veux périr:
> Commence mon enfant à vivre
> Quand ton père s'en va mourir.[15]

D'Aubigné here contrasts his own imminent extinction with the book's immortality, and although the child's life begins where the father's ends, the

---

12 See Diotima's speech on pregnancy in 'The Symposium' in *Dialogues on love and friendship*, translated by Benjamin Jowett (New York, 1968), p. 100.　**13** Ficino, *De amore*, translated by Sears Reynolds Jayne (Columbia 1944), ch. XIV, p. 207: 'Whence Comes Love for Men, and Whence That for Women, according to Plato, the soul is as pregnant as the body, and they are both aroused to procreation by the stimuli of love. But some men, either on account of their nature or their training, are better equipped for offspring of the soul than for those of the body. Others, and certainly the majority of them, are the opposite.'　**14** Huarte's point is that 'Nature fait habile'; in other words, each boy (Huarte did not consider girls capable of any sort of knowledge) has inherent strengths that must be diagnosed through humoral analysis in order for him to embark upon a course of study and thus a career. Huarte says that just as Socrates' mother, a midwife, could not make a woman give birth if she were not pregnant, '[de même] Socrate, faisant le mesme office de sa mere, ne pouvoit, par maniere de dire, faire enfanter la science à ses disciples, devant qu'ils fussent enceins d'icelle' (*Anacrise, ou Parfait jugement et examen des esprits propres & naiz aux sciences*, translated by Gabriel Chappuis (Lyon 1580), p. 4).　**15** A. d'Aubigné, *Les Tragiques*, ed. A. Garnier and J. Plattard (Paris 1990), p. 27.

implication is that the author will live on through his literary lineage. This convention was not specific to poetry, for Ambroise Paré, Henry IV's appointed surgeon, offers a similar send-off to his complete works of 1598:

> Or sus donc maintenant, va t'en mon fils trescher,
> Que depuis quarante ans n'ay cessé de lecher
> [. . .] eternellement
> On verra [. . .] ce mien ouvrage vivre.[16]

A work is superior to a child not only because it is immortal, but also because it satisfies the fantasy of engendering without woman. Indeed, although both D'Aubigné and Paré identify themselves as fathers, and although their expectation to live on through their works derives from the assumption of patrilinearity, they also adopt a maternal role: the father in D'Aubigné's poem dies when the child is born, recalling his own mother's death in childbirth, and Paré licks his son clean of the final debris of delivery. That an author is both father and mother of a work makes his possession of it all the more total. In this respect it is interesting to recall that Michel de Montaigne, in his essay, 'De l'affection des peres aux enfans', explains that products of the intellect are 'plus nostres' – more ours – than children, because authors are both father and mother in intellectual production:

> ce que nous engendrons par l'ame, les enfantemens de nostre esprit, de nostre courage et suffisance, sont produicts par une plus noble partie que la corporelle, et sont plus nostres; nous sommes pere et mere ensemble en cette génération; ceux cy nous coustent bien plus cher, et nous apportent plus d'honneur, s'ils ont quelquechose de bon. Car la valeur de nos autres enfans est beaucoup plus leur que nostre; la part que nous y avons est bien legiere; mais de ceux cy toute la beauté, toute la grace et pris est nostre. Par ainsin, ils nous representent et nous rapportent bien plus vivement que les autres.[17]

Montaigne here characterizes intellectual production as a profitable investment; the energy that 'we' put into a work yields returns that are all 'ours'. When 'nous sommes pères et mères ensemble', the resulting brainchild yields a mirror, as it were, of its sole genitor. By contrast, one cannot take full credit for natural progeny, for as composites created by man and woman together, children are not really 'autres nous-mêmes'. Thus in the preface to his complete works, Paré counters accusations of plagiarism by asserting that he is his book's father and mother:

---

16 A. Paré in preface to *Œuvres complètes* (Paris 1598).   17 M. de Montaigne, 'De l'affection des peres aux enfans' in *Essais*, ed. Alexandre Micha (Paris 1979), book 2, p. 71.

à fin [que quelques trop severes censeurs] n'ayent occasion de se plain-
dre de mon entreprise, comme homme qui ait moissonné aux champs
des autres, [. . .] je dy donc, que tout cest œuvre est à moy, & n'en [peut]
estre fraudé, comme attentant nouvelleté, puis que j'ay basti en mon
propre fond, & que l'edifice & les materiaux m'appartiennent.[18]

To harvest in the fields of others is not only to steal another man's ideas, but
also, according to Aristotle's metaphor of generation as planting, to abscond
with another man's offspring. And to this accusation Paré retorts that he has
contributed both the form and the matter, 'l'edifice & les materiaux' – in
sum, that he is both the father and mother of the work at hand.

However, asserting authorial possession through the trope of parent
begetting child proved problematic in the case of ovism, since ovism called
into question the father's primacy in generation, a tenet that Aristotle and
Galen had taken for granted.[19] In effect, although not all ovists believed that
the egg altered the distribution of labour between men and women in generation,[20] others, and especially the opponents of ovism, feared that it did. In

---

18 Paré, 'Au lecteur' in *Œuvres complètes*, ed. cit. For an account of Paré's detractors, see Paul
Dumaître, 'Autour d'Ambroise Paré: ses adversaires, ses ennemis', *Histoire des Sciences médicales*, 32
(1998), 2, 203–10.   19 In suggesting that women might contribute more to generation than men,
ovism rekindled one of the core themes of the *querelle des femmes*. Beginning with the occult
philosopher Heinrich Cornelius Agrippa in *De nobilitate et praecellentia foeminei sexus* in 1529, it was
a standard feature in the pro-woman side of the *querelle* to argue that women contribute more to
their offspring than men, sometimes to the point of being able to engender alone. The
phenomenon of parental singularity also had currency as a sort of theoretical *cas-limite* in medical
discussions of abnormal generation. The medical philosopher Jourdain Guibelet affirms in his *Traité
de la génération de l'homme* (Evreux 1603): 'Je dis que si quelques femelles sans l'ayde du masle
peuvent engendrer leur semblable [. . .] la femme qui est beaucoup plus parfaite, à tort sera privée
de ce principe' (138). Whilst the pro-women interlocuters of the *querelle* relied on exceptional and
erudite examples, ovists claimed to base their arguments on empirical evidence. More radically than
those who had argued for the superior merit of women in the textual tradition of the *monde à
l'envers*, therefore, ovists threatened to minimize the relevance of paternity in general. Moreover,
they threatened to destroy syllogisms such as that put forth by Nicolas de Cholières in his
misogynist mise-en-scène of the *querelle* in *La guerre des males et des femelles* (Paris 1588). He
challenges his pro-woman opponent who argues that women play a greater role in generation than
men, asking 'Avez-vous le jugement si morfondu que ne sçachiez bien que le grain qu'on seme en
une terre ne porte point le nom de la terre; [mais] de froment ou d'orge, ou de feves ou autre
graine? Pourquoy donc voudriez-vous que la famille print le nom de la femme, puisque la semence
est virile en non feminine?' This particularly tautological formulation of Aristotle's theory of
generation – barley is called barley rather than clay, therefore children are called by their father's
name rather than by their mother's – reveals the extent to which metaphors mask man's
construction of nature and, by the same token, naturalize patriarchy.   20 For example, Charles
Drelincourt, despite being an ovist, maintains that 'Il y a cette différence entre un grain qui germe
dans la terre & un œuf qui germe dans la matrice, que celui-ci n'a pas au dedans de soi comme
l'autre le principe de la génération, car avant que d'avoir été imprégné des atomes acides & salins

a public lecture at the Jardin du Roi in 1690, the royal demonstrator of anatomy, Pierre de Dionis, emphasizes the diminished role that the modern theory of generation accords to men: 'de manière que c'est la femme, selon ces Modernes, qui fournit la semence dont l'enfant est fait, le lieu où il est formé, & le sang dont il est nourri; & que l'homme ne contribuë à la generation que de quelques esprits qui vivifient la semence de la femme & la rendent feconde'.[21] As Dionis puts it, ovism 'prive l'homme [de son avantage] pour le donner tout entier à la femme'.[22]

If ovists continued to express their filiation to their work in terms of the 'father function', the anxiety of paternal dispossession eventually infiltrated their claims to intellectual possession. This shift towards anxiety can be seen by comparing the prefatory paratext to Harvey's *On the generation of living creatures* of 1653, in which ovism is still conceived of in Aristotelian terms that equate father with form and mother with matter, with that of Louis Barles, who, twenty years later, translates De Graaf's discovery that the egg pre-exists sexual intercourse. Because Harvey was reluctant to publish his research before he came to clearer conclusions, his friend and fellow member of the College of Physicians, Sir George Ent (1604–89), had to convince him to relinquish his manuscript. Ent purports to 'have performed no more then the meer office of a Midwife' in publishing Harvey's *Anatomical exercitations*, but he nonetheless takes it upon himself to supplement the lacking 'author-to-his-book' poem. In the 'Epistle Dedicatory', Ent sends Harvey's book out into the world with these lines:

> Live Modern Wonder, and be read alone,
> Thy Brain hath Issue, though thy Loins have none.
> Let fraile Succession be the vulgar care;
> Great Generation's selfe is now thy Heire.

True to the Platonic metaphor, Ent contrasts the frailty of natural succession with the eternal heir that is Harvey's theory of generation. Yet Ent's emphasis on Harvey's childlessness is ambivalent. On the one hand, it can be taken to mean that while others (presumably women) concern themselves with the 'vulgar care' of child-rearing, Harvey has nurtured the 'Issue' of his brain. On the other hand, it can be interpreted thus: Harvey can rest assured that

de la semence virile l'œuf des femmes n'a aucun germe, ce n'est qu'une cristalline enveloppée de deux tuniques sans coque qui sont fort poreuses, & qui peuvent prêter [. . .] le principe actif & matériel de l'embryon vient de l'homme, & [. . .] la femme ne fait autre chose que fournir un sujet passif & nutritif': Bayle, *Nouvelles de la république des lettres* (octobre 1685), IV: 1130–31. **21** Pierre Dionis, *L'Anatomie de l'homme suivant la circulation du sang, & les dernières découvertes, démontrées au Jardin Royal* (Paris 1690), pp 279–81. **22** Ibid., p. 282.

his progeny is of his own making, while natural fathers have the 'vulgar care' of worrying about the legitimacy of their children.

A mere twenty years later, however, the 'vulgar care' of legitimacy was overshadowed by that of the mother's predominance in generation. In his introductory summary of the process of generation, Barles makes no mention of a father:

> Ce n'est que de nos jours, [. . .] que l'on a découvert que les femmes fournissent toute la matiere de la Generation; que leurs testicules sont des ovaires, que par occasion il s'en détache des œufs descendant dans la Matrice par des canaux aussi agréables que necessaires, pour s'y échauffer & s'y couver, pendant quelques mois, qu'enfin apres un certain temps destiné de la Nature leur coquille se casse, leurs membranes se déchirent, & nous avons le plaisir de voir sortir un homme de dedans un œuf.[23]

Although Barles quite conventionally compares women to chickens through his analogies of gestation to incubation and birth to hatching, the process of generation that he relates is actually gleaned from De Graaf's dissections of rabbits. In rabbits, copulation triggers ovulation, and De Graaf thought that in women too the egg migrated to the uterus as a direct result of sexual intercourse.[24] Thus when Barles says that 'par occasion, il s'en détache des œufs descendant dans la Matrice,' he is alluding to woman's brief interlude with man. Once the former of female matter or the purveyor of the stronger seed, the father has been reduced to the *occasion* or chance that initiates an otherwise all-female affair.

If the impossibility of ascertaining paternity was already a source of great anxiety to the husbands of pregnant women in the early modern period, the increasingly evident implications of ovism and 'emboitement' – that the identity of the father of the imminent child might not matter very much anyway – could only have undermined the father function.[25] And true enough, by contrast with Ent's confident bravado, Barles does not purport

23 Barles, *Les Nouvelles Decouvertes sur les organes des femmes, servans à la generation*, p. 3.   **24** On this see Jacques Roger, *Les Sciences de la vie dans la pensée française du 18e siècle* (Paris 1971), p. 284. **25** I have not yet had a chance to explore the potential repercussions of ovism on the father function in literary discourse. Nevertheless, I do not think it a coincidence that Molière mocks this convention. In *Les Femmes savantes*, first performed in 1672, the same year that De Graaf and Swammerdam published their findings on the human ovum, Trissotin says to Philaminte of an epigram he composed, 'Hélas! c'est un enfant tout nouveau-né, madame. Son sort assurément a lieu de vous toucher, et c'est dans votre cour que j'en viens d'accoucher' (III.i.720–22). Terry Castle argues that, as a result of new aesthetic exigencies, in seventeenth- and eighteenth-century England, English authors abandoned the paternity-authorship trope, or else associated it specifically with bad authorship: 'Lab'ring Bards: Birth topoi and English Poetics, 1660–1820', *Journal of English and Germanic Philology*, 78 (1979), 193–208. While this may be true, I suspect that the perspective of

to have served as midwife to 'great Generation's selfe' in translating De Graaf's work. In the dedicatory epistle, Barles asks protection for 'la nouvelle doctrine' as if he were seeking a surrogate father for a bastard. 'Les livres sont comme des Enfans exposez,' he writes, 'qui cour[ent] mille hazards de périr,' and this is why authors 'mett[ent] à la teste des Livres, le nom de quelque personne considerable par sa Naissance ou par sa meule'. Barles does not claim any relation to the book he presents to his dedicacee, and, further-more, by speaking of books in the plural he casts authorial dispossession as a general phenomenon. The rupture between author and work results from the suspicion that fatherhood no longer assures a visceral connection to progeny. To compensate for the weakness of their filiation to their works, authors supplement their own name with that of someone considerable; they look for an adoptive father to care for a child over which they have no authority. Patrilinearity still determines legitimacy, but arbitrarily so. Indeed, although Barles defines a person's status in terms of his 'Naissance', that per-son, the dedicacee – in this case, the governor of Marseille – can choose either to accept or reject the foundling 'doctrine' of ovism. So it is that the father and the name of the father are no longer one and the same, and a book may boast a name, but no father.

Barles' picture of a world in which names and books circulate and, once in a while, collide, bestows a glimmer of confirmation on Foucault's claim that the practitioners of the 'New Science' of the seventeenth century aban-doned the authority of the proper name in favour of universal truths that could be uncovered but not authored. Nevertheless, this disinvestment from authorship did not result from a new, empirical ideal of science in which doctors, to return to Bayle, 'devraient uniquement nous rapporter en simples historiens ce qui se passe dans la Nature'. On the contrary, the age-old 'analogie imaginaire' by which both scientific and literary authors expressed authorial possession, that is, what I have been calling the 'father function', continued to have currency at least until the 1670s. Only when empirical evidence revealed the father's near superfluity in generation did the scien-tific man forego the claim to a visceral connection to his work. Even then, individual authors, however scientific their pretensions, resisted the author-ial dispossession that resulted from the revocation of the father's prerogatives in generation. In Barles' epistle, the death of the author function produced a profoundly human sense of loss. An author deprived of his status as the sin-gular possessor of a textual creation and lacking the authority to protect his 'enfans exposez' could only be compared to a father bereft of his child.

female predominance in generation also contributed to the reconceptualization in England of generation as mere reproduction.

Medicine and religion in seventeenth-century France: La Rochelle, 1676–83

JEAN-PAUL PITTION

Until the last decades of the seventeenth century, in La Rochelle, as in many other towns or cities in France, the practice of medicine was 'free': to practise, physicians needed only to obtain a licence from the municipal authorities. La Rochelle physicians, once licensed, became members of a municipal body which had its own statutes dating back to before the siege of 1628. This corporation elected its own doyen. In a similar way, apothecaries were formed into a loosely organized *compagnie* whose statutes also dated back from before the siege. Physicians and apothecaries together provided a form of municipal health service.

In the early 1670s, the physicians' corporation was composed of seven members. Three of them, J. Dumont, P. George and I. Gille, were Catholics, whilst four of them, É. Bouhéreau, P. Colomiés, P. Hamelot and É. Richard, were members of the French Reformed Church. During the following decade, the religious make-up of the town medical corporation changed. Hamelot died and Colomiés appears to have left La Rochelle. They were replaced by Jean Seignette, most probably a son of the apothecary Élie Seignette, the inventor of a proprietary medicine, the *sal polychrestum*, which remained listed in pharmacopoeias for over two centuries, and by Nicolas Venette, whose treatise, *De la génération de l'homme ou Tableau de l'amour conjugal* (1696), was to become a standard work of reference for over a century. Seignette belonged to the Reformed churches; Venette was a Catholic. Dumont, also a Catholic as already mentioned, was elected doyen. In 1680, the four Catholic doctors petitioned the king's council and obtained letter-patents, incorporating the town physicians into a new 'Corps et Collège de Médecine'. As 'Collège royal', the new body had the right to confer degrees and to award licences. The first public defence took place 'in publico Rupellae Fano' in 1681.[1] New statutes were immediately drafted and written into the record of the *Présidial* at La Rochelle. The letter-patents and the new statutes included a clause according to which 'aucuns médecins ne pourront estre aggrégez [. . .] s'ils ne sont catholiques'. The three *réformé*

---

1 A copy of the theses defended on that occasion is among Elie Bouhéreau's papers in Marsh's Library, Dublin.

physicians, Bouhéreau, Richard and Seignette, appealed the clause to the king's council. They argued that at La Rochelle medicine remained a free profession and that no royal edict or order had ever excluded *réformés* from it. In 1683, the three lost their appeal and were debarred from their practice. A public polemic then followed between Venette and Richard on the issue of the right of patients to choose their doctor, but the debate was short-lived. Within two years, the edict of Nantes was revoked, sealing the fate of all *réformés* in the kingdom.[2]

Until these events, religion does not appear to have been a source of conflict or an issue between the La Rochelle physicians. On the contrary, all available evidence suggests that, for many years, in the medical community *réformés* and Catholics were united by a sense of service to their fellow citizens and by a strong *esprit de corps*. These attitudes were encouraged by the particular conditions that the physicians faced in their practice and by the common tradition of care to which they were heirs.

The population of La Rochelle, like any other during the period, suffered from common fevers, flu, food poisoning and parasite infestation, whilst women were particularly at risk during pregnancy and labour. But La Rochelle had its own particular health profile, reflecting both its geographic situation and its economic activity. La Rochelle is situated on a promontory, between the Breton and Poitou marshlands. Close by, Colbert developed the naval base of Rochefort on such marshy flatland. Around the town, the coast of Saintonge, low and with many estuaries, was, at the time, partially covered twice daily by the rising tide. The climate is mild and damp in winter, dry and sunny in summer. Since the sixteenth century, the marshes had produced vast quantities of salt for export to England, Holland and the Hanseatic ports. After a period of stagnation in the decades that followed the siege of 1628, trade from La Rochelle had undergone a remarkable recovery. Trade with the East and the West Indies played a major part in this recovery and merchant tonnage trebled between 1664 and 1686.[3] When John Locke visited La Rochelle in 1677, he noted that fevers and 'dropsy', undoubtedly due to the proximity of marshes, were common.[4] Long-term

---

2 On the history of France under the edict of Nantes, see Elisabeth Labrousse, *'Une foi, une loi, un roi?' La Révocation de l'Édit de Nantes* (Genève 1985). **3** On this, see John C. Clark, *La Rochelle and the Atlantic economy during the eighteenth century* (Baltimore and London 1981). **4** J. Locke, *Journal*, entry for 7 September 1677, Bodleian Library, MS Locke f.3, p. 282–3 (new pagination). The term 'dropsy' was generally applied to swellings affecting the connective tissues of the body, characteristically the inflammation of joints and the presence of fluid in them. Locke could refer to rheumatoid arthritis or to tuberculosis of the joints. But his interest in *sal polychrestum* (see below, note 9) suggests that he also had in mind abdominal dropsies, ascites, which can also be the result of infection by the Koch bacillus.

residents were affected by the 'Poitou colic', an endemic form of lead poisoning caused by the pipes through which drinking water was brought to the town.[5] Seamen returned from their voyages ill from scurvy, and there also appears to have been a high incidence of venereal diseases among them.[6] In dealing with these conditions, local physicians could draw on the lessons learnt by their predecessors and by long-established town apothecaries. During the second siege of La Rochelle (1627–8), physicians and apothecaries had struggled to save lives ravaged by malnutrition, starvation and epidemics. One of the physicians, Mathias Goyer, had identified as a form of scurvy 'un certain mal de bouche' which affected children during the siege, and he successfully treated it by decoctions of wild herbs growing on the sand dunes.[7] The experience was not forgotten and Goyer's successors were proud of his achievements and paid homage to him.[8]

In caring for the town inhabitants, the medical corporation of La Rochelle was in a very favourable situation compared to physicians in other town and cities. There was a wide variety of *materia medica* available. Rare drugs from the Levant and newly discovered ones, notably cinchona from the West Indies, were in ready supply thanks to the sea-trade, and for the preparation of their prescriptions the town physicians could rely on highly-skilled apothecaries.[9] Hamelot, for example, had assembled a *cabinet de curiosités*, and by 1683 Élie Bouhéreau's library contained some 3,000 volumes, including many up-to-date treatises on medicine or natural philosophy, while the apothecary Isaac Baulot was a true virtuoso who designed experiments to test the theory of the transmutation of metals. In 1677, he published his *Mutus liber*, which presented in sets of engravings the procedures, protocols and results of his experimentation.[10] La Rochelle apothecaries were familiar with the processes of fractional distillation, perhaps owing to the fact that the Charentes region was emerging as a producer of brandies. Grey salt from local salt marshes had many impurities and offered rewarding challenges to experimentation. The apothecaries were familiar

---

5 See Jacques Boucher de Beauval, *Traité de la populaire colique bilieuse du Poitou* (La Rochelle 1673). It seems that the disease peaked in 1632–6 and 1640–6. 6 These conclusions are drawn from a survey of surviving prescriptions. On these, see below, note 33. 7 The herbs in question were 'berle' (perhaps *sium latifolium*) and 'herbe de moutarde' (probably a species of the *Linnean sinapis*). 8 The episode is described by Pierre Mervault in *Journal des choses plus mémorables que ce sont passées au dernier siège de La Rochelle* (no place, no date [1641]), p. 184. Venette pays tribute to him in his own *Traité du scorbut* (La Rochelle 1673), p. 114. 9 Locke was certainly impressed by them. During his stay in La Rochelle, he met Bouhéreau, Baulot and Seignette and took notes on both the composition and the therapeutic properties of *sal polychrestum* and on the use of *aqua regis* to dissolve gold. 10 The *Mutus liber* has generally been interpreted as a working of esoteric and spiritual alchemy. In a forthcoming article, I argue that the *Mutus liber* is also and above all a handbook of experimentation, giving protocols and identifying results.

with the actions of sulphuric and hydrochloric acids. From the deposit of wine (cream of tartar, that is, bi-tartrate of potash), they made tartaric acid, of use in the preparation of soda powders. By treating cream of tartar and sulphates of antimony with sulphuric acid, they obtained antimony oxide and potassium antimonate. Two metallic preparations were particularly in favour. One of these, chloride of mercury, was obtained by boiling together mercury and sulphuric acid, triturating the resulting persulfate of mercurate with mercury and further treating the mixture with sodium chloride. A sugar of lead, that is, acetate of lead, based on litharge, that is, lead oxide, resulted from the separation of silver from lead with refined vinegar. It is apparent, then, that the prescriptions which the apothecaries made up were sophisticated and required precision in dosages and in mixing.

A taste for learning, a sense of duty and of professionalism encouraged co-operation amongst physicians and apothecaries. So it was that Venette and Dumont, as well as Bouhéreau and Richard, used Baulot as their apothecary. Among prescriptions written by La Rochelle physicians which have survived and which cover the period 1676–8, two at least result from joint consultations. On one occasion, Catholic and *réformé* physicians attended 'une dame de la religion' who was dying in labour. When the apothecary Boucher de Beauval published his *Traité de la populaire colique bilieuse du Poitou* (La Rochelle 1673), he dedicated the work to the 'Docteurs en Médecine de la Ville', and the book includes a testimonial signed by all of them. The physicians praised Boucher de Beauval for 'la guérison [. . .] qu'il spécifie sur un grand nombre de malades qu'il a traité conjointement avec nous'. Venette's *Traité du scorbut* (La Rochelle 1671), dedicated to the *Intendant de Marine*, Colbert du Perron, was published with a solemn 'approbation' by the whole medical corporation.

However, by 1683 this collective ethos had disappeared and the *réformé* physicians were debarred from practice by their Catholic colleagues. There are other examples of measures aimed at excluding *réformé* physicians from practice during the period,[11] but in the case of La Rochelle, given the strong sense of corporate identity which existed in the town's medical milieu, how are we to explain the expulsions of 1683? Were they caused by a general

---

11 As early as May 1670, *lettres-patentes* were issued which forbade 'aux médecins du Collège de Rouen en cas de vacance d'y admettre aucun d'entre eux qui fit profession de la R[eligion] P[rétendue] R[éformée]'. In 1683, The *réformé* physician Jean Rangeard was expelled from the *médecins jurés* of Bordeaux. These and other cases are illustrated in 'Memoires et pieces pour servir a l'histoire generale de la persecution faitte en France contre ceux de la religion Reformée depuis l'année, 1656, jusqu'a la Revocation de l'Edit de Nantes, faitte par celuy donné a Fontainebleau au Moys d'Octobre, 1685', a collection of legal documents gathered by a contemporary, Abraham Tessereau (Bouhéreau MS, Marsh's Library, Dublin).

deterioration of the religious situation in the town which eventually affected the medical profession? Or, as the polemic between Richard and Venette which followed the exclusion of 1683 suggests, did the public manifestations of professional *esprit de corps* conceal real differences in the medical outlook of *réformé* and Catholic doctors, differences which local factors brought out into the open? What can we discover about the role of confessional allegiances from the way La Rochelle physicians understood and practised medicine, and, more generally what can the case of La Rochelle tell us about the interplay of medicine and religion in late seventeenth-century France?

France experienced a period of relative religious peace during the minority of Louis XIV, but daily coexistence between members of the two rival confessions did not eradicate feelings of suspicion. In a town with such a militant past as La Rochelle, good neighbourly relations concealed a great deal of reciprocal misunderstanding.[12] In the 1670s, the religious frontier, which still divided the population, re-asserted itself with new vigour. Local pressures exacerbated conflicts between members of the two confessions, leading to a general increase in tensions in the town. The political and economic as well as the demographic imbalance between the two confessions could not but fuel resentment on both sides of the religious divide. Protestant La Rochelle had never recovered from the siege of 1628 during which an estimated 15,000 died. By the 1670s, the town population had reached its pre-siege numbers of nearly 23,000, but it included only 5,000 *réformés*.[13] *Réformés* still formed a significant percentage of the population, but as a shrinking minority they felt threatened by a continuing influx of new Catholic inhabitants. Moreover, since the abolition of the municipal authority by royal edict after the siege, royal officers, all of them Catholics, administered the town. Resentful of having lost the right to govern their city, the great patrician *réformé* families nevertheless continued to dominate the economic life of the city and were in control of much of the sea trade. This in turn created feelings of resentment among newly-settled Catholics envious of those who still considered themselves their betters and who remained proud of their glorious Protestant past.

A major cause of the deterioration of community relations was the militant activity of members of the local Compagnie du Saint-Sacrement, present in La Rochelle from 1644 onwards. The Compagnie was a lay sodality

12 These attitudes are discussed by L. Pérouas in *Le Diocèse de La Rochelle: sociologie et pastorale* (Paris 1964).   13 See D. Parker, *La Rochelle and the French monarchy: conflict and order in seventeenth-century France* (London 1980).

which was first formed in the 1640s and which attracted the most militant amongst the Catholic notabilities in the town. Its aim was to encourage new forms of piety amongst the laity and to make frequent and regular Communion the foundation of religious practice. The Compagnie was one of the numerous manifestations of the new devotional culture which spread through Counter-Reformation France. For its members, the reformation of the religious life of the laity also required the extirpation of heresy. Against what they saw as the dangerous obstinacy of heretics, members of the Compagnie would use all forms of pressure to bring about their conversion.

Most royal office holders belonged to the Compagnie. In 1660, one of these royal officers, Pierre Bomier, on the occasion of a fiscal disturbance, succeeded in having some 300 *réformé* families expelled from the town, claiming they had settled in the town after 1628 in contravention of the Edict. It was only after five years and numerous legal suits that some of those expelled recovered their right to residency.[14]

The new bishop of La Rochelle, Henri de Laval, encouraged his clergy to be actively involved in campaigns of conversion.[15] In 1674, André Lortie, one of La Rochelle's pasteurs, reacted by publishing a treatise against the Catholic doctrine of the Eucharist. Later the same year, another pasteur, Pierre Hespérien, preached a sermon on another point of Catholic doctrine, the worshipping of saints.[16] By reaffirming Protestant doctrine, and by asserting that Catholic worship, and particularly the liturgy of the Eucharist, was the manifestation of the superstitious beliefs of the Roman Church, the two pasteurs were warning their flock against what they saw as a strategy designed to entrap them, for Catholic controversialists had tended to play down doctrinal differences between the two churches since the first attempts at a reconciliation of the two confessions earlier in the century.[17] The two pasteurs realized, however, that doctrinal concession and equivocation could open the way to entrapment: a member of the Compagnie might inveigle a *réformé* to attend mass and attempt to lead him to the Communion table. If the latter refused Communion, he might be accused of sacrilegious conduct; if he accepted, he would be deemed to have expressed a wish to convert. To

---

14 The Compagnie was dissolved by Louis XIV in 1666, but its members remained active in La Rochelle. The activities of local *convertisseurs* are detailed by Daniel Henri Delaizement, one of the rochellais pasteurs, later exiled in Holland, in his *Histoire des réformés de La Rochelle depuis l'année 1660 jusqu'à l'année 1685* (Amsterdam 1689). 15 On the religious situation prevailing at La Rochelle, see the important study by Pérouas, *Le Diocèse de La Rochelle*. 16 See André Lortie, *Traité de la sainte cène* (La Rochelle 1674); Pierre Hespérien, *Sermon sur St Jean iv 22* (La Rochelle 1674); et André Lortie, *Défense du sermon de Mr Hespérien sur S. Jean ch.iv v.22* (Saumur 1675). 17 It is significant, for example, that a draft plan for the uniting of the two Churches, in the archives of the Reformed church of La Rochelle, stresses the need for major changes in the form of worship, but plays down doctrinal differences.

retract would provoke the accusation of being relapsed which would bring the risk of heavy penalties. This applied also to the pasteur who dared to receive a relapsed person back into his church.

The pasteurs were also issuing a direct challenge to Catholic controversialists. As expected, the publication of Hespérien's sermon drew an immediate reply from Michel de Bordaille, chaplain to the chapter and vicar general of La Rochelle. Over the next two years there appeared several works dealing with the two issues, including two substantial treatises by Bordaille.[18] By the mid-seventies, the conversion of local *réformés* had become a public issue in La Rochelle. They appeared to be on the defensive, whilst Catholics were increasingly militant.

The first sign that heightened confessional tensions were having an impact on the medical milieu of the town was a confrontation between the *réformé* apothecary, Élie Seignette, and some of his Catholic fellow tradesmen. Seignette's *sel polychreste* was reputed to give excellent results in remedying a number of complaints.[19] The proprietary medicine brought fame and commercial success to its inventor. Some of his colleagues tried to imitate it. In 1673, to protect his trade, Seignette was granted by Colbert du Perron 'une concession qui revient quasiment à des lettres-patentes'.[20] Four or five of the town apothecaries who lost the right to manufacture the medicine tried to put Seignette out of business. In 1676, they succeeded in obtaining from the *lieutenant général* of La Rochelle new statutes for their corporation. The trade of apothecary was to cease to be 'free' and to come under the control of a newly-formed professional body. To be admitted to it and to be allowed to open shop, one needed to produce new *lettres de maîtrise*. As Élie Seignette had inherited his trade from his father, without being formally admitted as master apothecary (as the old statutes did not require him to do so), he would now be out of business.

Greed and jealousy were the main motives of Seignette's rivals, but they made his religion an issue in the conflict.[21] They quoted an *arrêt du Conseil* of July 1669, according to which 'les habitants de la Rochelle faisant profession de la Religion Prétendue Réformée ne pourront estre admis à l'advenir

---

18 Michel de Bordaille, *Éclaircissement de la doctrine de l'Église touchant le culte des saints, pour servir de réponse à un sermon* . . . (La Rochelle 1675) and *Défense de la foi de l'Église touchant l'Eucharistie, contre le livre de Mr de Lortie de la sainte cène* (La Rochelle 1676). See also his *Défense de la doctrine de l'Église touchant le culte des saints, contre le livre de Mr de Lortie* (La Rochelle 1677). **19** *Sal polychrestum*, or 'Rochelle salt', is prepared by boiling tartrate of potassium in a solution of carbonate of sodium, and crystallizing it. It was used as a general purgative, particularly as a treatment for abdominal dropsy. **20** See *Apologie pour le sel polychreste de Monsieur Seignette, maistre apoticaire de la Rochelle* (no place [La Rochelle], no date [1674]). **21** In his *Apologie*, Seignette attacked the quackery of his colleagues, denouncing the 'effets pernicieux' of counterfeit preparations based on salpetre, but playing down the religious antagonism of his adversaries.

aux arts et métiers'.[22] They wrote into the new draft statutes a clause that excluded from the award of *maîtrise* those who did not profess the Catholic religion, and used it against Seignette.[23] A legal case battle followed the publication of the new statutes.[24] No doubt thanks to the patronage of the *intendant*, Seignette won his case: we know that he was still trading well after the Revocation of 1685.[25] However, for the physicians of the town, the Seignette affair became a test of confessional solidarity. In a published *Apologie*, Seignette claimed that he had received support from '*certains* médecins de la ville' (my italics). Though he does not name them, one suspects that only his co-religionists among them showed public support.

What is certain is that the affair created a mood of suspicion amongst the town's *réformé* physicians. In the *factum* which they issued in 1683, they claimed that their exclusion was the result of a conspiracy hatched by their Catholic colleagues with the help of the local magistracy. In their opinion, the reason for the erection of the new *collège* had nothing to do with professional qualifications, but was simply an excuse to exclude them 's'ils ne se font pas catholiques'.[26] Whether or not such a plot was actually hatched during the Seignette affair, professional attitudes could not thereafter be kept insulated from confessional allegiances. In this new climate, while the affair was at its height, Élie Richard, one of the three later to be excluded, intervened in the controversy between Lortie and Bordaille by publishing a short treatise entitled *Réflexions physiques sur la transsubstantiation et sur ce que Mr Rohault en a écrit* (Saumur 1676). Élie Richard's intervention broke with the conventions of the genre, as theological controversy was understood to be the preserve of clerical specialists. On the question of transubstantiation, both Lortie and Bordaille borrowed their theological and historical arguments from a previous lengthy controversy between the Jansenists Antoine Arnauld and Pierre Nicole, and the leading *réformé* pasteur from Charenton, Jean Claude. Richard shifted the ground of the controversy from the theological to the scientific. He wrote from the standpoint of a learned

---

22 The *arrêt* in question is listed in Abraham Tessereau's *Mémoires* (Bouhéreau MS, Marsh's Library, Dublin). 23 Without a *maîtrise*, no apothecary would be allowed to keep open shop 'sous quelque prétexte que ce soit'. 24 See *Factum pour Élie Seignette apoticaire et exerçant l'art de la pharmacie à La Rochelle, intimé. Contre la communauté des maistres apoticaires de la mesme ville appellans* ([La Rochelle] [1676]). Seignette argued that subsequent to the *arrêt*, the more important *Déclaration royale* of 1669 had reaffirmed the rights of *réformés* already practising 'arts et métiers' at La Rochelle to continue to do so. 25 Seignette was briefly banished to Besançon in 1691, which suggests that he had resisted further attempts to convert him, but there is no doubt that he retained at least the right to produce and sell his preparation. His sons built up one of the most powerful merchant houses of La Rochelle during the eighteenth century. See John C. Clark, *La Rochelle and the Atlantic economy*, pp 10–11. 26 *Factum pour Élie Richard, Élie Bouhéreau et Jean Seignette contre Jacques du Mont . . .* ([La Rochelle] [1683]).

physician. Taking as his starting point Jacques Rohault's recent attempt to reconcile scholastic species and Cartesian substance, Richard argued that the new mechanistic philosophy made nonsense of the dogma of transubstanti-ation.[27] Élie Richard's intervention amounted to a public declaration that physicians had a duty to speak out and to put their expert learning at the service of their religious convictions.

In publishing his tract, Richard was deliberately polemical as he knew that Catholic theologians continued to raise strong objections to Cartesian doctrine. Nevertheless, the tract shows that he took the new Cartesian sci-ence of nature seriously. As a contribution to the contemporary debate con-cerning Descartes' philosophy, his tract is not particularly remarkable, but what makes it interesting is what it tells us about Richard as a *réformé* physi-cian. The tract makes it plain that Richard supported the new mechanistic philosophy of nature. For a physician of the time, this meant being on the side of the Moderns in medicine. Though Élie Richard did not publish any medical treatises, the letters which he wrote to his cousin, Élie Bouhéreau, while studying at Groningen and Leyden, have survived.[28] They show that his studies there gave him a knowledge of mechanistic physiology and of iatrochemical pathology. In this he differed from his colleague and soon-to-be adversary, Nicolas Venette. We get a good idea of Nicolas Venette's med-ical doctrine from his *Traité du scorbut.* The work contains much speculation about the nature of the disease, but Venette seems unaware of the more recent medical literature on the subject. In the preface to the treatise, he alludes to current debates on the circulation of the blood, but the signifi-cance of the discovery in terms of rival physiological models escapes him.[29] His theory of sanguinification relies on the Galenic concept of coction. His account of the various disorders which he groups under scurvy is based on the traditional pathology of humoural disorder, though the treatise also shows some influence of Jean Fernel's *Universa medicina* in mentioning fer-mentation as a possible cause. However, Venette's main authorities remain Galen and the sixteenth-century Spanish physician, Francisco Valles.

By training, Richard and Venette were heirs to two different doctrinal

27 Jacques Rohault's *Entretiens sur la philosophie* were published in Paris in 1671. The first *Entretien* discusses transsubstantiation, the second the animal-machine. On Rohault's interpretation of Cartesian physics, see Paul Mouy, *Le Développement de la physique cartésienne, 1646–1712* (Paris 1934), pp 113–37. **28** The letters, which begin in 1664, are among the Bouhéreau manuscripts in Marsh's Library, Dublin (MS Z. 2. .2.14). **29** 'Le sang a du mouvement de soi-même, ou plutot c'est le cœur qui en est le principe . . .' (*Traité du scorbut*, preface, sig. 2Bv). Venette appears to be aware of the difference between Harvey and Descartes on the cause of the motion of the blood, but does not see that the circulation of the blood entails a new physiological model whereby the heart replaces the liver as the central organ of the system.

traditions. In Paris, where Venette studied more than two decades after Jean Riolan The Younger's death, the Faculty was moving towards accepting the circulation of the blood, but doctrinally it remained firmly committed to the humoural model in physiology.[30] In Protestant lands, at Groningen and Leyden, or even at Orange where Bouhéreau took his degree, the teaching of medical doctrine was not so concerned with orthodoxy; it was more open and flexible. Fundamental humoural physiology remained a reference, but it was treated as capable of accommodating iatrochemical pathology and the iatrophyical model of body functions.[31] In the late seventeenth century, the difference between the two traditions remained, although it had become essentially one of style and of emphasis. Nevertheless, from this point of view, Richard's medical culture may be termed Protestant, and Venette's Catholic.

However, analysis of a sample of forty prescriptions written by the two physicians during the same years shows that this difference of style in their training and in their doctrine did not significantly influence the way they approached treatment.[32] Allowing for the bias inherent in the sample, the *materia medica* used by our two physicians reveal remarkable similarities in the way they approached therapy. Though the apothecary they used, Isaac Baulot, was particularly expert in chimiatry, both Richard and Venette often relied on 'general' remedies, that is, panaceas inherited from the Ancients. It is worth noting that, in the sample, Richard is the one who prescribes theriac, the grandest and most universal of these panaceas. Secondly, considered in relation to their alleged therapeutic effects, the remedies used by both physicians reflect the commonly-accepted classification of remedies into, on the one hand, specific remedies, that is, purgatives (defined as vomitives, purges, diuretics and diaphoretics), and, on the other hand, cordials. This means that both Richard and Venette considered treatment to be about the flushing out of the root cause of malignant humours by progressively more drastic purgation, followed by the restoring of humoural balance with

---

30 As L. Brockliss and C. Jones write, in French faculties, particularly in Paris during this period, conversion to Harvey's ideas had 'surprisingly little impact' on doctrine, and acceptance of the heart's machinery did not diminish opposition to Descartes' mechanistic model of the body. Cf. L. Brockliss and C. Jones, *The medical world of modern France* (Oxford 1997), I, 2, pp 138–50. **31** Cf. Mirko D. Grmek, 'Le concept de maladie' in M. M. Grmek & B. Fantini (ed.), *Histoire de la pensée médicale en Occident* (Paris 1997), pp 163–7. **32** Some two hundred prescriptions written by at least four of the La Rochelle physicians during the years 1676–8 have survived and are found among Bouhéreau's papers, in Marsh's Library, Dublin. Those by Richard and Venette make up aproximately half of the total number. We have examined all the prescriptions and have selected the first forty which divide equally between Richard and Venette. The prescriptions were all filled by Isaac Baulot who, in most cases, added the name or the occupation of the patient.

cordials. Both, in fact, acted according to the received therapeutic wisdom of the time.

Furthermore, the two showed the same rational approach to prescribing, particularly when complex and potent substances were involved. As regards iatro-chemical remedies, the prescriptions show a common concern for accuracy in dosage and for purity. Both Venette and Richard favoured distillations for herbal remedies and both knew the role of specifics in the treatment of particular conditions, for instance venereal diseases. Surprisingly, only Venette is shown using cinchona, a recent and important addition to the treatment of recurrent fevers, but this may just be due to the bias in the sample. If Venette appears to have prescribed a wider range of drugs, Richard seems to have been more cautious or more restrictive in his approach to cure. Both, though, made extensive use of palliatives.

The armamentarium of both Élie Richard and Nicolas Venette was self-consciously scientific. It reflected what might be called the normal professional expertise of a trained physician of the period. Both were careful physicians, clearly concerned to use their learning for the good of their patients. Yet it is on the question of how important a doctor's professional expertise really is for patients that they were most at odds. This is made obvious by the pamphlets which they published in 1683, soon after the exclusions were confirmed. Richard's pamphlet is entitled *Lettre à Mademoiselle D. B. sur le choix d'un médecin*. It was answered by Venette in *Response à une lettre écrite à Mademoiselle D. B. sur le choix d'un médecin*. Despite the immediate context in which they were published, the pamphlets are relatively free of personal polemics. The *Lettre à Mademoiselle D. B.* makes no direct references to the recent events or to the persons involved. Only in his brief rejoinder to the *Response* do we find Richard (or perhaps Bouhéreau) indulging in some sarcastic comments on the style of his adversary. As for Venette, except for one slip into argument *ad hominem*, his reply is expressed in a language that is restrained.[33]

According to Richard, what prompted him to write his piece was a question put to him by one of his patients: how does one choose one's physician? In answer, Richard sketched the portrait of the ideal physician as he saw it. Venette responded with criticisms, stating his own view of the qualities to look for in a physician. For Richard, a doctor should be judged by the way in which he conducts himself 'dans ce qui ne regarde pas sa pro-

---

33 Richard's tract was published anonymously, but its typography and mode of composition leave little doubt that it was printed by Desbordes in Saumur. Venette's reply was printed in La Rochelle by Toussains de Gouy. Copies of these rare pamphlets are among Bouhéreau's books in Marsh's Library, Dublin (pressmark R. 3. 8. 27).

fession'. 'Bon sens' and 'esprit droit' in the doctor's conduct as a person are the only criteria on which patients can base their choice for laymen are not familiar with 'les termes de l'art' and cannot judge how good the expert knowledge which the physician claims to possess really is. Expertise is not a question of learning, but of experience. Richard warns against 'ces [médecins] grands parleurs qui disent beaucoup de paroles et [font] fort peu de choses'. Patients should be wary of a doctor 'qui parle et agisse légèrement', particularly 's'il est sans expérience et qu'il faille essayer tous ses coups d'essay'.

Venette agrees that patients must expect that their physician will be experienced in his art. He also agrees that a cautious use of his specialized knowledge is what makes a good doctor. But he lays great stress on the risk attached to experimental treatment: 'Les expériences sont dangereuses et l'on ne doit user d'un remède nouveau qu'après quarante bon succès [*sic*].' The point of this becomes clear later when Venette makes a reference to the controversy which had opposed Galenists and Iatrochemists on the use of *vinum emeticum* in the treatment of some conditions. The controversy was already more than two decades old, and Venette was not interested in debating the pros and cons of the remedy as such.[34] Venette used *vinum emeticum* as an argument in support of the need for an official body whose authority was sanctioned by the law and whose function was to approve qualification and treatment.[35] Venette was reacting to a provocative piece of advice on which Richard had ended his tract: if no doctor is available whom a patient can trust, the patient may dispense with the service of a trained physician. According to Richard, in such circumstances it was better to seek advice from an apothecary, or even from friends or relatives suffering from similar complaints. And a sufferer could also make use of such handbooks of medical self-help as were at his disposal. It was this advice which led Venette to focus on the question of control and to stress that treatment must remain the preserve of qualified professionals.

Beyond the immediate circumstances which occasioned it, the polemic between the two and the arguments they used in support of self-help, or in defence of professional expertise, reveal different presuppositions about the

---

34 Tartar emetic was obtained by dissolving 2 grains of *antimonium tartaratum* in one fluid ounce of strong wine. *Antimonium tartaratum* was prepared by boiling in water, evaporating and crystallising a paste of oxide of antimony and acid tartrate of potassium. Cf R.I. McCallum, *Antimony in medical history: an account of the medical uses of Antimony and its compounds since early times to the present day* (Edinburgh 1999). 35 'Ça été [*sic*] le sentiment du premier Parlement de France qui par un arrêt condamne à 500 li. d'amande ceux qui ont la hardiesse de donner des remèdes violents et principalement du vin émétique sans l'avis et l'ordonnance du médecin' (*Response*, p. 19).

nature of the art and the role of the practitioner. For Venette, the nature of medical knowledge makes it accessible only to specialists; for Richard, the hermetic form of medical knowledge can be used to restrict access to it. This means that for Venette, the physician is at the centre of the healing relation, whilst for Richard, it is the patient. To say this may appear anachronistic until one recalls the central positions of the two confessions on the question of access to the Scriptures as a way to salvation. For the Reformed faith, all true believers under the guidance of their learned pastors can have access to the revealed text. For the Catholic Church, the Church and tradition provide, through the priest, the essential mediation between the faithful and revealed Truth. This, in the final analysis, is where religion coloured the conceptions that Richard and Venette had formed of the role of the physician as an expert who controls knowledge. Venette took a more clerical and Richard a more pastoral view of the role of the professional.

What conclusions may we draw from this analysis on the interplay of religion and medicine in France during the period? One conclusion concerns the role played by religion in the popularization of medicine during the second half of the seventeenth century.[36] The evidence that we have discussed supports the view that in France, as in Protestant England, religion and an emphasis on experience made *réformé* physicians more open to the idea of breaking down the barriers between learned and popular medicine.[37] On the other hand, it was from his experience as a professional that Richard wrote when he advocated self-help. And two decades later, the staunch defender of professional expertise, Nicolas Venette, published one of the period's most successful books of popular advice on sexual matters.[38] This also fits in with what is known about the factors which led to the popularization of medical literature in France during the period.[39] Manuals of self-help for laymen and handbooks for charitable persons were produced in increasing numbers during the second half of the seventeenth century. But in France, at least, the impetus for the dissemination of medical knowledge largely came from within the ranks of professional practitioners. Undoubtedly religion played a part in this, if by religion we understand

36 Cf. Roy Porter, 'Introduction', in Roy Porter (ed.), *The popularization of medicine, 1650–1850* (London & New York 1992).　37 Cf. Andrew Wear, 'The popularization of medicine in early-modern England', in Roy Porter (ed.), *The popularization of medicine, 1650–1850*, pp 17–41 (see in particular pp 27–9).　38 Nicolas Venette, *De la génération de l'homme, ou tableau de l'amour conjugale. Septième edition, reueuë, corrigée, augmentée & enrichie de figures* (Cologne [i.e. Paris] 1696).　39 See in particular Matthew Ramsey, 'The popularization of medicine in France, 1650–1900', in Roy Porter (ed.), *The popularization of medicine*, pp 97–133.

Christian charity. But charity was a value shared by both the Catholic and the Reformed Churches. In physicians, charity found its expression in a professional concern for improving the way that people managed their health. The multiplication of specialized treatises which France witnessed during the same period also shows that physicians were becoming conscious of their duty, as professionals, to keep themselves informed of new developments in medicine.[40] In so doing, the physicians were answering the expectations of an increasing number of patients who wanted to use their services. But the expectations of patients during that time were not solely or even primarily about how learned their doctor should be. Then, even more than now, trust depended on other factors, and we should not underestimate the part played by the patients' religious convictions in determining who their doctor should be and how he should behave. In the France of the edict of Nantes in particular, belonging to one or the other of the two confessions was an important facet of a person's received public identity. In the case of the French *réformés*, being a member of the minority faith could foster a sense of exclusiveness, of belonging to the 'bourgeoisie du ciel', to quote a term often used in *réformé* sermons. Without the painstaking identification of the religion of the patients named in the prescriptions, it is difficult to judge if confessional links were a determining factor in the formation of the physicians' clientèles. But there is little doubt that Richard's eagerness to promote self-help was a reaction to the distress felt by many of his co-religionists at being deprived of the services of a professional they could call their own.

Finally, the cases studied illustrate the role of corporate as well as political and ideological factors in the history of the medical profession, as indeed in that of related occupations during the period. These cases and other similar ones occurred in the context of a determined policy on the part of the crown to achieve religious conformity in the kingdom. They were also the consequence of exacerbated tensions between the rival confessions at local level. But in La Rochelle, as elsewhere in France, the moves to debar *réformés* from trades and professions, though supported *a posteriori* by the crown, originated from within the corporations. These moves took the form of the redrafting of old statutes and the imposition of new criteria for qualification to membership and, therefore, to practice.[41] This suggests that there were pressures at work within these trades and professions to reinforce the control that corporate bodies exercized over the occupations which they organized.

---

40 Whilst comprehensive treatises by long-established authorities continued to be used for reference, the new works in the vernacular works focused on single issues in physiology, pathology and therapeutics. Their style was often polemical, and their contents claimed to be innovative.
41 Cf. A. Th. van Deursen, *Professions et métiers interdits; un aspect de l'histoire de la révocation de l'édit de Nantes* (Groningen 1960).

Long before religious conformity became one of the criteria, the academic medical establishment had been asserting its right to decide who was entitled to practise not only medicine but also the other trades.[42] As the profession gained in status and social prestige, access to it became increasingly competitive. Increased competition within the profession and with the other trades accelerated the trend towards the imposition of stricter qualifications and of well-defined professional boundaries. The drive towards establishing faculty monopoly on qualification and practice continued long after the edict of Nantes was revoked in 1685. It culminated in an edict issued in 1707 that conferred the sole right of licensing physicians on the joint authorities of faculty and crown.[43] Considered in this perpective, the debarring of *réformé* physicians was one stage in a process which had more to do with protectionism than with ideological purity. Nevertheless, for a brief period, during the last decades of the edict of Nantes, corporate politics mingled with religious prejudice to make the imposition of religious conformity a means of restricting access to practice. This occurred at a time when, largely as a result of increased professionalization, most physicians were practising what can be termed 'normal medicine'. La Rochelle physicians shared the same know-how common to the majority of professional practitioners, that is, a seasoned knowledge made up of recognized procedures and of reliance on well-tried remedies. But the events of 1683 show that in the history of medicine, as in that of other fields of learning, the politics of knowledge cannot be separated from the politics of religion in France under the edict of Nantes.

---

42 On the intervention of the Faculty in the lengthy struggle for formal recognition and control of their own trades by apothecaries and surgeons in Paris, see R. Lespinasse (ed.), *Les Métiers et corporations de la ville de Paris XIVe–XVIIIe*, 3 vols (Paris 1886–97), vols 1 and 3. As regards midwives, in Paris, by 1600 statutes brought them under the strict control of physicians and surgeons. The regulation of midwifery by the medical profession took longer to achieve in the provinces. On this and related matters, see Susan M. Broomhall, 'Connaissances et pratiques de santé chez les femmes françaises de la Renaissance', ch. 8, pp 178–86 (unpublished *mémoire de DEA* supervised by J.-P. Pittion and submitted to the Centre d'Études Supérieures de la Renaissance, Tours 2000).
43 The stated objective of the edict was to 'ranimer l'attention et la vigileance des Facultés établies dans ce Royaume'.

APPENDIX

Materia medica as used in a sample of forty preparations by Richard and Venette	Richard	Venette	Descriptions
Traditional Galenic confections and electuaries			
Electuarium catholicum	2	1	Purgative and diuretic	Extract of coloquinth, agaria, helleborus and diarrhodon abbatis
Electuarium diacarthum	2		Cathartic and carminative, used in chronic conditions, also to treat scurvy	A preparation of cardamom, gum tragacanth and scammony)
Hyacynth	2		Astringent, against fluxes	A Galenic confection
Rheum Electuarium	2	5	Purgative	A preparation of rhubarb and liquorice roots
Theriac	1		A narcotic preparation, used to treat diarrhea	As aqua theriaci
Prepared vegetable substances for confections and compounds, macerated, in decoctions or syrups			
Althea (marsh mallow)	3		Demulcent lenitive	In syrup
Amomum (fragrant balsam)	1		For contusions	As liniment
Amygdala (almonds kernels)	1		For liver complaints and against constipation	In decoction
Anisum pimpinella (anise seeds)	2	1	Carminative	As powder for dissolution

Materia medica as used in a sample of forty preparations by Richard and Venette	Richard	Venette	Descriptions	
Artemisia	2	2	Emmenagogue	In syrup
Assa foetida (garlic)		1	Enema	In a nodule
Camphor		1	For coughs, carminative and antispasmodic	In a bole
Capillaris herba (capillaire de Montpellier), the maidenhead fern	1		Lenitive, for catarrhs	In syrup
Cassia (daphe)		3	As a mild narcotic	In decoction
Chicory		2	Fiuretic, also used in inflammatory rhumatism	In syrup
China (bark)		1	Febrifuge	In decoction
China (root)		2	Diaphoretic for lues veneriae	In decoction
Cinnamon	2	1	Carminative and stimulant	
Cornua corvinis (hart's tongue)		1	Astringent	In decoction
Croccus orientalis (safran)	1		Anodyne against palpitations and convulsions	In powder
Cydonia		1	Astringent	
Diacrydium (gum resin of scammony)		1	Stimulant of liver or stomach	Dissolved in white wine
Fava (husks of broad beans)		1		In powder

Folia orientalia (Indum malabathrum)	4	Carminative and restorative	
Gentian (root of)	1	For pituitous affections	In mixture or tincture
Glycyrrhyza (liquorice root)	3	Emollient for bronchii	Macerated
Guaiacum (bark)	1	Diaphoretic, anti-inflammatory, for VD	In decoction
Lemon	1	Tonic, for scurvy	Syrup
Macis (nutmeg oil)	1	To relieve swelling	
Manna (sap of manna–ash)		Purgative	Dissolved
Myrobalan	2	Astringent	
Myrthum	1	Astringent	In syrup
Oleum	1	Demulcent	
Omphacium (olive oil)	1	As laxative or vermifuge	
Oxalis (sorrel)	1	Stomachic	In decoction
Pimpinella (poterium sanguisorba)	1	Used post partum or against candida	In decoction
Plantago (plantin)	2	Against hemorages	In decoction
Populus (leaf of poplar)	1	Used in ear or eye ointments	
Rosa (as mellis ros. or sacc. ros.)	1	As adjunct	
Rosa (as oxyrrodium)		As ointment	
Rosa, syrup of	4	Mild laxative	As syrup

Materia medica as used in a sample of forty preparations by Richard and Venette

	Richard	Venette	Descriptions	
Sagapenum		1	Emmenagogue and antispasmodic	Gum of
Santalum citrinum (bark of yellow sandalwood)		1	Febrifuge, against palpitations	In decoction
Terebinthina (turpentine)		3	Diaphoretic and diuretic	
Spagyrics (essences, tinctures, distillations)				
Aqua artemisiae	2	2	Emmenagogue	
Aqua imperialis	2	1	Stimulant	Distillation of cinnamon, nuts and aromatic herbs
Aqua betonica	1			Obtained ffrom betony
Aqua borraginea	1	1	Roborant	Obtained from borage
Aqua cardui benedicti	1		Febrifuge	Distillation of holy thistle
Aqua floris cassiae		3	Purgative	Distillation of daphne
Aqua hyssopi	2		Roborant	Distillation of hyssop
Aqua melissae	2		Purgative	Essence of melissa
Aqua papaveri	2			Laudanum tincture
Aqua parietariae		2	Astringent, anti-inflammatory	Distillation of pellitory of the wall
Centinodia			Roborant	Rye alcool

Sal absinthii	4	Anthelmentic, tonic	Essence of wormwood
Iatro-chemical materia, metal compounds			
Crocus metallorum	1	Emetic	Compoud of iron salts
Crystallum minerale	2	Astringent, for external use	Alum
Diasema rullandi (vinum emeticum)	1	Emetic	Protosulphide of antimony, disolved in wine
Kermes minerale	1	Diaphoretic, emetic in high doses	In powder sulfide of antimony + carbonate of sodium
Mercurium dulce	4	In pill, against luis venereae	Chloride of mercury
Sal polychrestum (Seignette salt)	2	Purgative	Sodium potassium tartrate
Sals prunella	2	Roborant	Potassium sulphate and nitrate
Sal saturnii	1	Against ulcerations	Lead acetate
Tartarus emeticus	1	Emetic	Antimonium diaphoretum (mixed antimony oxide and potassium antimonate)
Others			
A pigeon recently killed	1		To be applied on head wound (as haemostatic)
Veal meat (in broth)	1		Diet

'Il n'y a plus de Mecenas': *Le Roman bourgeois* and the crisis of literary patronage

CRAIG MOYES

Antoine Furetière's *Roman bourgeois* (1666) generally falls rather uneasily between two critical stools, depending on whether one approaches it as a seventeenth-century specialist or as a theorist of literary genres. For *dix-sep-tièmistes*, it has traditionally been seen as a particularly egregious example of what one should *not* be writing in 1666. With its disarticulated narrative, its lack of central character, its enumerations in the forms of tables and lists, its seemingly gratuitous nastiness towards Charles Sorel, the *Roman bourgeois* seems a far cry from the nascent canons of French classicism which were elsewhere being established. Antoine Adam, in his magisterial *Histoire de la littérature française au XVIIᵉ siècle*, went so far as to say:

> Si Furetière n'avait pas été l'ami de Racine et de Boileau, s'il ne s'était rendu fameux par son *Dictionnaire* et par son conflit avec l'Académie française, il n'est pas certain que l'on parlât encore du *Roman bourgeois*. L'œuvre ne s'impose pas par sa valeur. Elle n'a même pas le mérite d'être le témoin d'une époque et d'un moment dans l'histoire de notre littérature. Mais parce qu'elle continue d'être rééditée, lue et citée, il n'est pas possible de la passer sous silence.[1]

The equanimity grudgingly shown by Adam's sense of scholarly duty does little to attenuate the attack which follows, however, and Furetière fares badly, to say the least, in comparison with the major writers of his day.

For historians of the novel, on the other hand, the judgment is not nearly so damning. Since the 'rediscovery' of the *Roman bourgeois* by Charles Asslineau in 1854, Furetière has been read as a precursor, albeit a clumsy one, of the great novelists of the nineteenth century. Thus recuperated as a realist novel *avant la lettre* (le 'premier roman d'observation qu'ait produit la littérature française,' writes Asslineau),[2] the *Roman bourgeois* could fit neatly into the standard development of the genre. This is still its place in most textbook histories of French literature.

What both these camps hold in common, however, is an approach which

---

1 Antoine Adam, *Histoire de la littérature française au XVIIᵉ siècle* (Paris 1962), vol. 4, p. 194.   2 *Le Roman bourgeois* (Paris 1854), p. 16.

willy-nilly abstracts the novel from the immediate context of its publication. For a literary historian like Antoine Adam, this decontextualization is, in the first instance, Furetière's own fault. By choosing to write a poor burlesque of an outdated genre when other writers were at the same time busy producing the masterpieces of French classicism, Furetière shows himself to be inevitably out of step with his age. 'Quinze ans plus tôt,' writes Adam, 'la littérature burlesque avait fait la parodie des épopées. Le livre de Furetière veut être la parodie des romans héroïques. On ne peut s'expliquer autrement ce langage volontairement bas et ignoble, ces plaisanteries fades d'un vulgaire goguenard.'[3] But of course one can explain these things otherwise, providing one is armed with a different methodology. By looking forward instead of backward, by seeing Furetière as a precursor of narrative realism rather than as an outdated burlesque parodist, the *Roman bourgeois* can be understood as confusedly blazing a trail towards a genre whose time had not yet come. What is important to note here, however, is that the effect of decontextualization is essentially the same, and it matters little whether one is working on behalf of an intemporal humanism or a generic teleology. Indeed, as fine a reader as Henri Coulet shows that these two positions are in no way incompatible. For Coulet, Furetière is both a 'pédant mal embouché et retardataire' and an innovator ahead of his time: 'Quand le public et les écrivains seront sensibles au pittoresque de la réalité vulgaire, sa cruauté et sa sèche crudité seront comprises; tout un courant du roman qui passe par Diderot et Restif au XVIIIe siècle, par Champfleury et Zola au XIXe, pourra se rattacher à lui.'[4] Recent re-readings which, seizing on the same 'unreadability' and 'incoherence' that so repelled Antoine Adam, see the *Roman bourgeois* as an early literary experiment akin to the *nouveau roman*, have done little to overcome this critical impasse.[5]

This article will not attempt to offer a reception history of the *Roman bourgeois* (although that would be a fascinating study in itself),[6] but will simply argue for an approach to the novel which would take into account the

---

3 Adam, *Histoire de la littérature française au XVIIe siècle*, vol. 4, p. 196.   **4** Henri Coulet, *Le Roman jusqu'à la Révolution* (Paris 1967), pp 277–88.   **5** Witness two of the titles presented at a 1986 conference devoted to Furetière: Jean Alter, 'Vers des re-lectures du *Roman bourgeois*: du lisible, du scriptible, de l'illisible et du relisible' and Michèle Vialet, 'L'écriture de l'incohérence', in Michel Bareau, Jacques Barchilon, Donna Stanton and Jean Alter (ed.), *North American Society for Seventeenth-Century French Literature, Actes de Banff* (Paris, Seattle, and Tübingen 1987), pp 237–48 and 373–88. Jean Serroy calls the *Roman bourgeois* a 'prodigieux raccourci' which, in a single work, marks both the beginning and the end of the realist novel. See his *Roman et réalité. Les Histoires comiques au XVIIe siècle* (Paris 1981), p. 656.   **6** Readers are referred to Ulrich Döring's recent study *Antoine Furetière: Rezeption und Werk* (Frankfurt am Main 1995); partial results of this research have appeared in French: *idem*, 'La réception critique du *Roman bourgeois* au dix-neuvième siècle', *Œuvres & Critiques*, 2, no. 2 (hiver 1977–8), 99–115.

oft-forgotten context of its publication. When Adam writes that one cannot even say in its favour that it bears witness to a moment in French literary history, he is, I think, quite wrong: on the contrary, it is precisely because the *Roman bourgeois* appears when it does that it merits renewed study. For whatever else it is − burlesque, satire, novel, or anti-novel − it is also a response to the massive shift in literary economics that occurred in the first decade of Louis XIV's personal reign, a shift that was both publicly emblematized and practically consolidated with the arrest and conviction of one of the most important literary patrons of the preceding decade, Nicolas Fouquet, and the concommittant establishment of Colbert's list of pensionable writers. From a period during the first half of the century in which artistic patronage flourished, when the epistle dedicatory became an art form in its own right, under Louis XIV France moved squarely towards a system of centralized state support for writers which is still to this day known as *mécénat d'état*.

Now why should this change be important? After all, what matter who pays so long as writers are supported? There is much to be said, and indeed much that has been said, on the extraordinarily rich figure of Mecenas who was so important to seventeenth-century letters. For Guez de Balzac, writing in the 1640s, Mecenas was much more than simply a source of financial support for writers of the Roman empire; rather, his role was fundamentally political. 'Ce fut Mecenas,' Balzac writes, 'qui dora un siècle de fer; qui rendit supportable la Monarchie à des Ames passionnées pour la Liberté; qui respandit son bonheur de tous cotez; qui mit l'amitié d'Auguste en commun; qui ne demanda que pour donner.'[7] The role of Mecenas is, then, both political and economic, at least in the general sense of the term, as it is he who is responsible for the equal exchange and circulation of value in an unequal polity. Under a political regime of absolutism, Mecenas alone ensures distributive justice in the imaginary sphere, taking only in order to give, as Balzac puts it, that is, taking the essentially incommensurable love of the autocrat and allowing it to flourish within a new imaginary republic, the Republic of Letters.[8] This may have been true in the 1640s, but compare now Furetière's terse example written some thirty or forty years later in his dictionary (published posthumously in 1690) under the heading 'Mecenas': 'Il n'y a plus de Mecenas, aussi n'y a-t-il plus d'Horaces ne de Virgiles.'

---

7 J.-L. Guez de Balzac, 'Entretien XXI', *Les Entretiens* [1657], ed. B. Beugnot (Paris 1972), vol. 1, pp 317–18. **8** For two excellent discussions of the role of Mecenas in the seventeenth century, see Bernard Beugnot, 'La figure de Mecenas', in Roland Mousnier and Jean Mesnard (ed.), *L'Âge d'or du mécénat (1598–1661)* (Paris 1985), pp 285–93; see also Christian Jouhaud and Hélène Merlin, 'Mécènes, patrons et clients. Les médiations textuelles comme pratiques clientélaires au XVIIe siècle', *Terrain*, 21 (octobre 1993), pp 47–62. The politico-economic role of Mecenas is brilliantly pointed up by Merlin and Jouhaud's discussion of Richelieu.

To be sure, such isolated examples prove nothing in themselves; nevertheless, they can be read as indicative of a major shift in the understanding of the place in society at the time of both the patron and the poet. The year 1661 is often invoked in this context. It is, of course, the year in which Mazarin died and the year in which Louis XIV seized personal power. The year therefore marked the beginning of a regime whose constant desire for personal and national glory would indelibly mark the entire century, a century shortly to be known as 'le siècle de Louis XIV'. It also marks the end of what has been termed 'l'âge d'or du mécénat'. It is worth observing, however, that the end of this golden age is not so abrupt as the mythic date of 1661 would have us believe. It stretches out, I would argue, over the long judicial erasure of Nicolas Fouquet.

From 1661 to 1665, all of Paris, if not all of France, was transfixed by the most famous trial of the century. Indeed, d'Ormesson, the public prosecutor, called it 'le procès le plus célèbre qu'on ait vu depuis plusieurs siècles'.[9] The superintendant of finances, the patron of Corneille, Scarron, Madeleine de Scudéry, Pellisson, Molière, La Fontaine, Le Brun and Le Nôtre — in short, the patron of most of the artistic elite of the period — found himself suddenly on trial for his life, having been accused of diverse State crimes and set, it seemed, to fall. The outcome is well known: before a stacked jury, Fouquet defended himself well enough to save his life, but in doing so he lost everything else. For the first and only time in French history the king exercised his privilege of regal grace not to lighten the sentence, but to overrule it. Fouquet's banishment was commuted to life in prison and all his possessions, as well as his protégés, were to be seized and put directly into the royal service. Colbert was left, on behalf of the king, the sole artistic paymaster of the realm.

It would, of course, be untrue to affirm that artistic patronage, or mécénat, disappeared in one fell swoop with the imprisonment of Fouquet. Writers continued to be supported by various grandees, though none, perhaps, with the éclat of the former superintendant.[10] The important change, however, is, as always, symbolic. Again it is instructive to compare the figuration of artistic patronage under Louis XIV with that described and applauded by Balzac twenty years before. The essential mediating function

9 Quoted in Jules Lair, *Nicolas Foucquet, procureur général, surintendant des finances, ministre d'état de Louis XIV* (Paris 1890), vol. 2, p. 389. At the end of the trial, d'Ormesson would write: 'Ainsy voilà ce grand procès fini, qui a esté l'entretien de toute la France du jour qu'il a commencé jusques au jour qu'il a esté terminé', *Journal d'Olivier Lefèvre d'Ormesson*, ed. M. Chéruel (Paris 1860), vol. 2, p. 288. 10 It is a mark of that *éclat* that, under the heading 'Mescene' in the key to Somaize's *Grand dictionnaire historique des prétieuses* (Paris 1661), we find the following reference: 'Monsieur le Sur-Intendant des Finances' (vol. 3, p. 21).

of Mecenas pointed up by Balzac, and linking the absolute monarch to the author on the one hand and to the aggregate of individual readers or subjects on the other, fades away behind a putatively immediate relation in which the Sun King can, as it were, shine undiminished as the only star in the cultural firmament.[11] In the 1660s, Chapelain, Pellison and Boileau all reiterate, in one form or another, the new imperative of royal patronage. As Pellisson, who had only recently returned to royal favour, wrote in 1670: 'Il faut louer le roi partout, mais pour ainsi dire sans louange.'[12] 'Louer sans louange', a phrase which can only mean that the epideictic mechanisms of laudation – those very same mechanisms which were personnified and put into action by the figure of Mecenas a generation before – must henceforth disappear behind the unique glory of a unique object of praise.

But is it possible to conceive of a direct, that is, unmediated exchange between the king, the author and the literary public? By effacing Mecenas is not the writer also somehow diminished or effaced? Boileau, rallying to the new literary policies of Colbert, thought that this was not the case, but it is not by chance that Virgil and Augustus take pride of place in his *Art poétique* of 1674, and Mecenas, still invoked in his 'Satire I' of 1666, is now nowhere to be seen.[13] There is only the stark choice between ignoble sale and royal glory:

> Travaillez pour la gloire et qu'un sordide gain
> Ne soit jamais l'objet d'un illustre Ecrivain.
> Je sçai qu'un noble esprit sans honte et sans crime,
> Tirer de son travail un tribut legitime:
> Mais je ne puis souffrir ces Auteurs renommez,
> Qui dégoûtez de gloire et d'argent affamez,
> Mettent leur Apollon aux gages d'un Libraire,
> Et font d'un Art divin un métier mercenaire.

---

11 Jouhaud and Merlin note the parallelism between the nascent figure of the author, who was, in the following century, to go on to establish an unmediated relation with his public, and the absolutist monarch, who was meant to rule singlehandedly over his subjects: 'Dans le seconde moitié du siècle, le modèle du Mécène s'estompera : ce qu'on nomme le mécénat d'État sera surtout un clientélisme centralisé, libéré des ambiguïtés politiques et esthétiques propres aux années 1590–1660. C'est ainsi que naîtra l'imaginaire d'un rapport direct entre l'auteur et son public, et que s'établira le face à face du Prince et du public des particuliers' ('Mécènes, patrons et clients', p. 61).   **12** *Œuvres diverses de Monsieur Pellisson de l'Académie françoise* (Paris 1735), vol. 2, p. 326; for a sustained discussion of this letter, see Louis Marin, *Le portrait du roi* (Paris 1981), pp 49–107. **13** 'On doit tout esperer d'un monarque si juste. / Mais sans un Mecenas à quoy sert un Auguste?'. This satire was begun in 1657, published first in 1666, and reworked for the definitive edition of 1701. The lines quoted, however, are the same in both editions. See note by A. Adam in his edition of Boileau, *Œuvres complètes* (Paris 1966), p. 866.

Now if this dilemma between honest tribute and vile gain is also Furetière's, he is definitely less sanguine about the prospects than is Boileau. Let me quote him again: 'Il n'y a plus de Mecenas, aussi n'y a-t-il plus d'Horaces ne de Virgiles.' Without Mecenas, there can be no poetry, or at least no great poetry. Indeed, if glory and money can be exchanged without recourse to this imaginary and essential mediation, has not the exchange become tantamount to a sale, and therefore somehow fundamentally anti-thetical to the theoretically disinterested aristocratic generosity which underwrote the aesthetic of *mécénat*?

When the *Roman bourgeois* was granted its privilege in March 1666, Fouquet had been in prison for just over a year but he was far from forgotten. Colbert was filling the void left by the arrest of the superintendant on two fronts at once, pursuing the kingdom's financiers through the Chambre de Justice established in 1661, and continuing his new artistic policy through the *liste de pensions* which he had initially set up in 1662. The first of these lasted until 1669,[14] and the second, though running out of steam somewhat before the end of the decade, remained in place for thirty years. It is clear, in any case, that the 1660s were a period of fiscal and artistic consolidation for Colbert, and that Fouquet was, as it were, *l'homme à abattre* on both fronts. For all its generic incoherence, and indeed for all its lack of direct reference to the trial, the *Roman bourgeois* can be read, in part at least, as a response to this fundamental change in the nature of artistic exchange.[15]

---

14 A French judicial record; see Daniel Dessert, 'Finances et société au XVIIᵉ siècle : à propos de la Chambre de Justice de 1661', *Annales E.S.C.*, 29, no. 4 (juillet-août 1974), pp 847–81.
15 Although the textual evidence is slim, two possible references to Fouquet are nevertheless worth mentioning. The first, evoked by Charosselles in a general conversation on the exchange value of different types of literature, harks back to 1654, to the Salon of Mme Du Plessis-Bellière and the famous decease of her parrot – famous because it spawned a small poetic movement to which, by the way, Fouquet himself contributed (Urbain-Victor Chatelain, *Le Surintendant Nicolas Foucquet, protecteur des lettres, des arts et des sciences* (1905; Genève 1971)). According to Charosselles, it is not the gravity or intrinsic value of the rhymes themselves which count in this poetic economy, but the speed of their circulation, a speed which depends ultimately on fashion. The second reference is more telling. Inserted into the 'Historiette de l'Amour égaré', it also refers to an event that took place before Fouquet's fall from grace. The story recounts the seduction of one of the 'Néréides', or filles d'honneur of Thétis, the 'Reine-mère', by the 'Intendant des Coquilles de Néptune', and the subsequent denunciation of the affair by a 'Triton jaloux'. As the editor of the Folio edition glosses, the Intendant is, of course, Fouquet and the 'Triton Jaloux' is the conte de Brion. But to this clear event of the 1650s a more contemporary reference is added. Following the discovery of the seduction, Thétis 'condamna la pauvre Néréiade à être enfermée le reste de ses jours dans une prison de glace au fond de la mer Baltique, et le séducteur fut emprisonné dans une coquille de limaçon, où toujours depuis il se tint caché, et n'osa montrer ses cornes, sinon quelquefois à la fin d'un orage.' Now this last phrase, which Prévot does not pick up, refers not only to the imprisonment of Fouquet at Pignerol, but also – and this would not have escaped the readers of 1666 – to the thunderbolt that struck the prison in June of 1665 and destroyed the very

To my mind, one of the least compelling interpretations of Furetière is that of a realist writer awaiting his public. The *Roman bourgeois* is *not* the bourgeois novel. As the narrator warns us, it is important not to be misled by the title. When once again the *auteur/libraire* appears in the second half to apologize for the 'irregularity' of the novel, he says, 'Que si vous y vouliez rechercher cette grande régularité que vous n'y trouverez pas, sachez seule-ment que la faute ne serait pas dans l'ouvrage, mais dans le titre: ne l'appellez plus roman, et il ne vous choquera point.'[16] True enough, it is clearly not a romance in either the heroic or even the comic mode, but we might also add that we should not assume, as many critics do, that it is 'bourgeois' or even a 'novel', at least not in the post nineteenth-century sense of these terms. The first and only English translator of the *Roman bourgeois* got it right first time in 1671, translating the title not as *The bourgeois novel*, but as *The city romance*.[17] For indeed the city is not only the place where one finds a collection of vaguely ridiculous characters, like so many variations on the theme of the *bourgeois gentilhomme*, but it is also, more fundamentally, the *polis*, the space of exchange.

If exchange in general is evoked and satirized in the first half of the novel through the burlesque courtship of Nicodème and Javotte, and inverted in the second with the legalistic squabbling of Charoselles and Collantine, it takes an explicitly literary, and, indeed, quite contemporary turn with the introduction of the court bailiff, Volaterran, who arrives carrying the papers of the recently deceased poet, Mythophilacte. Amongst these is the 'Somme dédicatoire' – literally, a *Summa Dedicatoria* indicating to poets the ways and means of flattering prospective patrons – the table of contents of which is

room where Fouquet was kept. Fouquet miraculously escaped unharmed, a fact which was considered, by his allies at least, as a clear sign from God of the injustice of his imprisonment. The story quickly spread through Paris and it was used as a pretext to try to intercede once again on behalf of the superintendant. Despite being borne by respected members of the literary community, the intercession failed miserably. Ménage, who imprudently penned an occasional poem addressed to the clemency of the monarch, found himself struck off the list of pensions: Daniel Dessert, *Fouquet* (Paris 1987), pp 268–9. Despite the unreliablilty of the narrative voice that prefaces the *Roman bourgeois*, can we not credit the declaration of the *auteur/libraire* that what he is giving us is a 'livre qu'il s'est diverti à composer en sa plus grande jeunesse'? To be sure, that voice is undermined by its context, aliminary epistle from the bookseller to the reader where it is suggested that the bookseller is in fact the author and that the preface, like the rest of the book, has been 'accomodé pour le mettre à la mode'. Although it is a hypothesis impossible to prove, an 'accomodement' in 1665 of a text from the 1640s or 50s would at least help to explain the abrupt transition from the first book to the second, and indeed might also go some way towards explaining the later reception of Furetière which sees him as both an outmoded satirist and a novelistic precursor. **16** *Roman bourgeois*, ed. Jacques Prévot (Paris 1981), p. 168. **17** However, the anonymous English translator misattributed the *Roman bourgeois* to Scarron, giving it the title of *Scarron's city romance, made English* (London 1671).

read by Volaterran to the assembled company. Whatever Furetière's own position was regarding Fouquet – his early satire, *Le Voyage de Mercure*, roundly attacked the excesses of financiers and his later split with La Fontaine was probably at least partially a result of the latter's support for the disgraced superintendant – it is hard not to read the 'Somme dédicatoire' as anything but a response to the public change in the status of literary patronage brought about by the trial. This is no to say that Furetière's attitude is in any way nostalgic; his critique is too keen and his humour too dark. But he does recognize that if the figure of Mecenas is no longer able to underwrite literary production as it did when Guez de Balzac was writing, neither is the figure of the author yet in a position to become the sole origin of 'literature', as it would in later centuries. Mythophilacte, who spent his life suffering and died penniless, caught between 'ses pretendus Mecenas' and 'ces méchans libraires', is surely a figure of this transitional economy.

In a novel where a contemporary writer, Charles Sorel, is so shamelessly mocked under the transparent key of Charroselles, we might be tempted to ask whether Mythophilacte too refers with a wink to a particular writer known to the readership of 1666. Perhaps he does, and critics have suggested several possibilities. But to search for a 'key' here as elsewhere in the novel is to ignore the narrator's warning that 'les serrures sont mêlées', the locks have been tampered with. As a lexicographer, Furetière was keenly aware of the possibilities of the signifier, of the power and significance of names. Even if Mythophilacte does have an extra-textual reference, his name, like Volaterran's (which, moreover, is explicitly glossed by the narrator), means something quite precise: 'guardian – or protector – of the tale'. It is no accident that when the protector of the tale is no more, little remains by way of story in the *Roman bourgeois* itself. The text of the exchange between Charoselles and Collantine, already a jumble of legalistic jargon, gives way to the paratext of a deceased writer's life: catalogues, titles, scraps of paper, and plans for impossible dedicatory epistles. Indeed, with the reading of the 'Somme dédicatoire', the titles and headings themselves take over the entire printed space of the page. And at every head or title in the lexical sense the question of title in the judicial or commercial sense is also posed. More often than not the question is reduced to this: what is the actual value of *mécénat* or patronage if it is henceforth to be conceived in terms of an unmediated exchange between praise and money? And as the distance between *mécénat* and commercial exchange is reduced to zero, the writer, like his text, is effectively squeezed out. 'Il n'y plus de mécènas, aussi n'y a-t-il plus d'Horaces ne de Virgiles.'

It is a mark of Furetière's pessimism on these matters that the last thing Mythophilacte leaves is a dedicatory epistle to the hangman. More than simply a joke, it is the only exchange left in this degraded literary economy that might still be in some way disinterested: in return for smoke ('de l'encens') the hangman gives 'de belles accolades', where accolade is to be understood etymologically as an embrace about the neck. 'Il est vrai,' Mythophilacte writes, 'que vous leur donniez incontinent après un tour de vostre metier; mais combien y a-t-il de courtisans qui vous imitent, et en mesme temps qu'ils baisent un homme et qu'ils l'embrassent, le trahissent et le précipitent' (p. 248). The hangman is the only one who can *donner incontinent*, that is, immediately, according to the seventeenth-century use of the word, but there is here a play on the well-known effect that such 'accolades' have on hanged men. Compared to courtiers and lawyers, or to crooked booksellers and false patrons, that is, those who give only to take, only the hangman, who takes (life) in order to give (justice and salvation), can be seen as properly disinterested. Unfortunately, the result in all cases is the same: no longer the production of artistic gold, as in the time of Augustus and Mecenas, but the production of the classical figure of anti-value – *la merde*.

Finally, and without putting too fine a point on it, can we not read Collantine and Charoselles along the lines of the same axiological reversal? Taking as its root the old word *cole*, which Furetière defines as bile,[18] and *tine*, which he defines as a small vessel, Collantine thus becomes *Cole en tine*, just as Charoselles would become '*char aux selles*', so that both act not so much as characters in a romance than as vehicles for the transport of bilious and excremental evacuations. In this particular literary economy, where the noble generosity of *mécénat* is supplanted by the involuntary scatology of the *palais*,[19] it should come as no surprise that at the end of the *Roman bourgeois* there is no place for any exchange – or for that matter, any tale – save that of the cynical and empty gainsaying of judicial debate. And so the final lines: 'La resolution de cette difficulté est qu'ils courent encore. Il en est de même des procès de Collantine et de Charoselles: ils ont toujours plaidé et plaident encore, et plaideront tant qu'il plaira à Dieu de les laisser vivre.'

---

18 Cf. the following entry: 'COLERA MORBUS, s.m., Desgorgement de bile fort subit, qui donne un grand dévoyement par haut & par bas, qui est si dangereux qu'on l'appelle autrement un *trousse-galand*. Il procede d'une continuelle indigestion des viandes. Cette maladie est ainsi appellée, à cause qu'elle fait sortir la bile fort violemment par haut & par bas, selon Galien & Celse; ou parce que la matiere est incessamment jetée hors des intestins, qu'on appeloit autrefois *cholades*.' **19** The 'involuntary scatology' which here characterizes the literary representation of the legal profession in the *Roman bourgeois* would ironically be reversed in the 'legal' representation of the Académie française against Furetière himself twenty years later. When Furetière's project of a rival French dictionary became known to his colleagues at the Académie, they immediately snapped into action, appealing to the chancellor for the suspension of his privilege as well as voting his immediate expulsion from their ranks. Charpentier, one of Furetière's most implacable enemies, went so far as

Ordure, smoke and empty words — we are a long way from the solid mediation incarnated by Mecenas a generation before. The glory that was so confidently assured by Balzac's Mecenas, drawing from Augustus in order to give to the poet, is here reduced at every turning to an impossible and/or spurious transaction. Patrons are counterfeit, booksellers are thieves, the guardian of the tale is dead. Between the recent passing of aristocratic patronage and the as yet undeveloped commercial relation between an author and his public, Furetière leaves us with a pessimistic account of literary exchange. But for all its negativity and bile, it does, *pace* Antoine Adam, bear witness to a crucial moment in French literary history.

---

to design an emblem showing a turd with the motto 'Ab expulso corporis sanitas' ('Through expulsion the health of the body'). Furetière lost no time in responding in kind:

> Infame Autheur, quand vostre bile boust
> Vous faites voirs [*sic*] des traits de votre ame grossière,
> En vous jouant d'une sale matiere;
> Qu'on di estre de vostre goust.
> On ne peut pas changer la nature,
> Votre brutalité jointe à votre embonpoint,
> Fait que vous pouvez bien vous veautrer dans l'ordure,
> Car on tient qu'aux Cochons la merde ne peut [pue] point.

Cited in Alain Rey, 'Antoine Furetière, imagier de la culture classique', introduction to *Le Dictionnaire universel d'Antoine Furetière* (Paris 1978), pp 65–6.

'Ce miracle du monde': harmony and disharmony in Saint-Amant's representation of the cosmos

SARAH ALYN STACEY

In one of Saint-Amant's most quoted poems, 'Le Cantal', the poet explains why this, not Brie, is now his favourite cheese:

> Que vous avez d'appas! Que vostre odeur me plaist!
> Et que de vostre goust, tout horrible qu'il est,
> Je fay plus d'estat que d'une confiture
> Où le fruit déguisé brave la pourriture![1]

This paradoxical attraction to the cheese in question provides a humorous example of a frequent duality in Saint-Amant's representation of the world about him: harmony and disharmony are frequently shown to coexist, as here in a paradoxical attraction to the unattractive. This emphasis on what may be defined as the poles of all conflict manifests itself in the text in a variety of ways, notably through the representation of literal conflict in the universe, and this is frequently conjoined with and mirrored by stylistic and textual conflict.[2] Central to this conflict would seem to be a preoccupation with stability, both the stability of Man's place in the cosmos, and the stability of the cosmos itself. This article will examine both the way in which this conflict shapes Saint-Amant's text and his poetized cosmos, and how this conflict engages with fundamental existential concerns.

I. COSMIC POLITICS: HIERARCHIES, CONTRADICTIONS, AND MORAL PRINCIPALS

In his 'Epistre à l'hyver', written to commemorate the departure for Poland of his protectress, Marie de Gonzague, in December 1645, Saint-Amant

---

[1] 'Le Cantal' in *Œuvres*, ed. Jean Lagny and Jacques Bailbé, 5 vols (Paris 1967–79), vol. 2, p. 150, ll. 5–8. All quotations in this article from Saint-Amant's works are taken from this edition. On Marc-Antoine Girard, sieur de Saint-Amant (1594–1661), see in particular the following: P. Durand-Lapie, *Un académicien du XVIIe siècle: Saint-Amant, son temps, sa vie, ses poésies* (Paris 1898); Raoul Audibert and René Bouvier, *Saint-Amant: Capitaine du Parnasse* (Paris 1946); J. Lagny, *Le Poète Saint-Amant (1594–1661): essai sur sa vie et ses œuvres* (Paris 1964). [2] Notably devices which exploit contradiction, for example, oxymoron, paradox, antithesis, contradiction.

evokes a strictly hierarchized Nature in which each of the seasons, although unique in character, is dependent upon one another. Winter's participation in this harmonious cycle is highlighted as paradoxical, when, for example, the poet addresses the season as a

> . . . Demon qui fais que la Nature
> Lasse d'agir, est comme en sepulture
> Dans un Lict froid, où sa fecondité
> S'eschauffe et dort sous la sterilité
> Qui l'enlaidit pour la rendre plus belle,
> Qui sa vigueur irrite et renouvelle,
> Et qui luy sert à reproduire au jour
> Le gay Printemps, les Graces, et l'Amour.
>   [. . .] et sur qui nos raisons
> Fondent l'espoir des trois autres Saisons.[3]

The allusions here to Nature's apparent death at the hands of winter, and to the process whereby Nature, through a temporary disfigurement by the season, in fact becomes yet more beautiful and vigorous, points both to a discrepancy between appearance and reality and to the paradox of an advantage bestowed through violence. Both the discrepancy and the paradox, examples of conflict as they juxtapose opposing ideas, also recall and subvert the stereotype of winter as a negative season associated with death.[4]

The importance of winter's place in Nature's hierarchy is conveyed by the personification of the season as a mighty king. This personification occupies most of the poem from line 17 onwards and embeds in the poem a political discourse on kingship, a highly topical subject at the time when there was a great preoccupation with establishing and preserving social harmony through efficient government, and the relationship between monarch and subject was hotly debated.[5] This personification of winter therefore participates indirectly in this debate by articulating a particular view of kingship, one which, as we shall see, goes counter to the absolutism so favoured by Richelieu and his followers.

'Tu ranges tout sous ton Sceptre fatal' (l. 20), observes the poet, assuming the role of winter's humble subject, as he addresses to the season a petition to show clemency towards the princess on her long journey. The power

3 'Epistre à l'hyver', ed. Lagny and Bailbé, vol. 3, pp 171ff., ll. 1–8, 11–12. 4 Cf. also 'L'Hiver des Alpes', ed. cit., vol. 2, pp 124, where the poet again extols the virtues of the harsh season. Incidentally, the conflict between appearance and reality is found here also, but in contrast the appearance is presented as preferable to the reality. See ll. 10–11: 'Sa Robbe d'innocence, et de pure splendeur,/Couvre en quelque façon les crimes de la Terre.' 5 On this preoccupation, see in particular the article in this volume by Pascale Feuillée-Kendall.

of winter would seem to be supreme, as denoted by 'tout' which indicates the all-encompassing geographical breadth of its dominion, and also by 'fatal' which highlights the nature of this power, namely that it is ineluctable. Nonetheless, the poet tries to persuade it, for the benefit of the princess, to 'suspendre un peu l'aspre et dure vertu/Dont aujourd'huy ton bras est revestu' (ll. 23–4). This request is tantamount to asking winter to act contrary to its harsh character, from which it follows that the harmonious interaction of the seasons, which, it has been emphasized earlier in the poem, depends upon such harshness (see ll. 1–12), may be threatened. However, there is an implicit justification of such an aberration on both the poet's part and winter's part, for the princess (as well as her forthcoming marriage) is presented as an harmonious and highly-revered element in the cosmos, so that, it is implied, any adjustment on her behalf to Nature's normal patterns will maintain cosmic harmony: she is 'Un rare Objet, que le Ciel mesme adore,/ Une Deesse, un Miracle charmant' (ll. 26–7), for whom Nature, recognizing her merit, and, it is implied, her superiority, willingly modifies itself:

> Des-ja l'eclat d'un si sublime honneur
> A disposé, par sa fameuse course,
> Le Pole mesme à donner à son Ourse
> Une autre forme, un plus benin aspect;
> Et la Nature approuve son respect.
>
> (ll. 36–40)

The poet reminds the season that, although it is a mighty ruler, it is accountable to a higher force, the Heavens ('Ciel', l. 43), and must therefore obey orders from this higher force even if this means modifying and acting contrary to its usual character:

> Donc, ô Demon, qui regnes sur la Glace,
> Puis qu'un devoir porte à changer de face
> Les feux du Ciel, dont tu reçois la Loy,
> On n'en peut pas attendre moins de toy.
>
> (ll. 41–4)

What appeared initially to be a plea for clemency therefore evolves into a reminder to winter of its obligation, its subordination to a higher force, a reminder which implies that the season cannot and should not disobey if harmony in the cosmos is to be preserved. The reward for such obedience will be a recognition and celebration by the poet and Nature of winter as a benevolent, purifying, regenerative and, above all, unique force essential to Nature's cycle:

Je me prepare à te bastir un Temple
Si magnifique, et si noble en Autels
Qu'il ravira tous les coeurs des Mortels [. . .]
Et sous tes pieds, mainte feuille, et mainte herbe,
Que le froid garde, afin de te parer,
Diront aux yeux qu'on te doit reverer,
Comme le seul, qui couve et fortifie
Les Biens qu'aux Champs le Laboureur confie;
Comme le seul, qui donne ame à Ceres,
Qui rend l'Air sain, qui purge les guerets,
Et qui fabrique en un moment sur l'Onde
Des chemins secs, les plus riches du monde.

(ll. 46–8, 54–62)

If winter's aberration from the norm is, in these particular circumstances, presented as non-conflictual but as positive and in accordance with the will of the cosmos, divergences within Nature are not always characterized by such harmony. The poet reminds winter that autumn revolted against the natural succession of the seasons 'de despit de ce que tu destruits/Sa pompe verte, et son regne, et ses fruits' (ll. 95–6), and, together with the unfaithful sea (l. 91), caused the shipwreck of the princess' ambassador (ll. 89–92). However, 'l'affection triompha de la haine' (l. 110), and autumn resumed its correct place in the cycle so that harmony was restored. The passage, through its representation of a season in revolt against the rest of Nature and dangerous to Man, highlights the precariousness of order and harmony in the cosmos, and also the precariousness of Man's fate at the hands of unpredictable natural elements,[6] an awareness of which essentially motivates the poem.

To persuade winter to comply with his request, the poet tells the season that if it shows clemency towards the princess it will be celebrated in verse: Ronsard's 'Hymne de l'Hyver' (1563) and perhaps Saint-Amant's own composition, 'L'Hiver des Alpes', will be read (ll. 64–8). There is a parallel implicit here between the regenerative roles of both winter and poetry: just as winter is a key element in Nature's continuity (see ll. 11–12), so too is poetry a means of perpetuating someone's name even beyond death, in this case the names of Ronsard, Saint-Amant, winter, and, at the end of the poem it is emphasized, the name of the princess (ll. 193–200). Moreover, the allusion here to two earlier compositions embeds these texts into the poem, that is, it regenerates them just as winter regenerates Nature's elements, and also

---

6 For further evocations of Nature's hostility to man, cf. 'L'Esté de Rome', ed. cit., vol. 2, pp 122ff (great heat); 'La Seine extravagante', ed. cit., vol. 4, pp 264ff (flood).

points to their participation (and also this poem's participation) in a tradition or cycle of poems celebrating winter. The threat implicit in this condition is, of course, that if winter does not comply with the poet's request, then the poet will not celebrate the season, his earlier poem and the one by Ronsard will not be read, and so the poetic tradition of celebrating the season will be broken. The perpetuation of the season's reputation is clearly at stake.

The urgency of the poet's request for winter to be clement towards the princess reaches a climax in the closing sections of the poem when he tells the season:

> Apprens, au reste, et soit dit sans menace,
> Que si bien-tost on ne voit la bonace;
> Si pour deux Mois tu ne laisses en paix
> L'Air agité de tourbillons espais,
> Ce beau soleil pour qui ton Roy souspire,
> D'un seul rayon destruira ton Empire;
> Te montrera combine tu luy desplus;
> Et de l'Hyver on ne parlera plus.
>
> (ll. 177–84)

Despite the poet's affirmation to the contrary in line 177, this is very obviously a threat of annihilation, and this explicit contradiction, implying as it does despair and panic, serves to highlight his urgency. Moreover, this threat signals a transformation of the relationship between the king/winter and the humble petitioner/poet, with the latter revolting, at least verbally, against his subordinate position. However, the revolt is ineffectual, and the threat of annihilation shown to be empty for the poem concludes with an acceptance by the poet that he and the rest of the cosmos are, in fact, powerless over winter and unable to restrain it: 'Or en tout cas, *si* ta fureur ne cesse. . .'(l. 189; my italics). One arm remains which has been alluded to already and that is poetry. The poet will use it to preserve the integrity of the princess' reputation even though her physical safety cannot be assured by the potentially hostile winter (ll. 193–200). Moreover, he uses it to issue a combined warning and final plea to winter:

> Ne pense pas venir au devant d'elle,
> En Vassal mesme et discret, et fidelle;
> Mais fay luy voir, avec tranquillité,
> La Courtoisie en l'Incivilité.
>
> (ll. 201–4)

   This demotion of winter from the status of a king so that he is not worthy (it is implied) to stand before the princess even as a vassal reflects the hostility the poet feels towards the potentially unyielding season, and the esteem in which he holds his protectress, who, it is indicated, is superior to the season in the cosmic hierarchy. The oxymoron in the final line defines winter as fixed in its barbarity ('en l'incivilité'), with 'courtoisie', a characteristic of civilization, the opposite of barbarity, a hypothetical trait that the poet can only hope the season will display: it is not intrinsic to it. Certainly, the negative tone of these closing lines contrasts sharply with the opening sections of the poem where praise of the benefit derived from winter's harshness prevails.

   Complementing and reinforcing this representation of conflict and harmony within Nature and between Man and Nature is the evocation of the conflicting emotions felt by the French as they prepare for the departure of their princess for Poland (ll. 113–36). Happy for her marriage, yet sad to see her leave,

> [. . .] tout Paris en revient esploré
> [. . .] Et la plaignant, mesme à peine sa veuë
> De son aspect se trouve despourveuë,
> Qu'il en gemit, comme si le tombeau
> Avoit enclos tout ce qu'il eut de beau.
>
> (ll. 152, 157–60)

   This image of the tomb recalls the evocation of Nature at the beginning of the poem as 'comme en sepulture' (l. 2), and suggests an equivalence between the apparent effects of winter's arrival and the princess's departure. Just as winter's arrival is, contrary to appearances, positive, as it regenerates Nature, so too is the princess' departure positive, even though the French do not want to lose her, as it brings honour to both her and to France (ll. 123–8).

   In 'Le Contemplateur' (ed. cit., vol. 1, p. 49), as in 'L'Epistre à l'hyver', a cosmic hierarchy is also clearly defined, although here God is presented very explicitly as being at the head of Nature which is used by Him as an instrument both for divine retribution and for forgiveness.[7] Drawing upon Genesis, Saint-Amant evokes how God sent the great Flood as a punishment to Man for his sins (ll. 61–70), and how He chose a dove bearing an

---

7 For further examples of Nature as an instrument of divine justice, cf. among others 'La Pluye', ed. cit., vol. 1, pp 137ff, where the drought is evoked as a punishment to man for his sins (ll. 21–2); in 'L'Arion', ed. cit., vol. 1, pp 108ff, the dolphin who saves Arion functions as an instrument of divine justice (ll. 237–40).

olive-branch as a messenger to Noah 'Pour luy-mesme annoncer la paix' (l. 80), the dove being an indication that dry land was near. Noah's blessed state is suggested by the evocation of how his tears, instead of increasing the flood waters, paradoxically made them dry up (ll.68–70), the implication being that they moved God to pity for him.

Man's perception of his place in this cosmic hierarchy is shown to be problematic. The poet expresses great confidence that he understands Nature:

> Nature n'a point de secret
> Que d'un soin libre, mais discret,
> Ma curiosité ne sonde,
> Ses cabinets me sont ouvers,
> Et dans ma recherché profonde
> Je loge en moy tout l'Univers.
>
> (ll. 85–90)

This image of Nature being physically contained within the poet implies the poet's intellectual superiority within the cosmic hierarchy. However, the poet then contradicts this view, drawing attention to an internal dichotomy, namely the desire and aspiration to understand Nature, but the awareness that Nature eludes Man's comprehension, and is therefore beyond his intellectual abilities. This contradiction, together with the articulation of this dichotomy through a series of antithetical images which contrast Man and Nature – the rhythmical ebb and flow of the tides (a very topical conundrum at the time the poem was written), the contrasting lack of clear direction felt by the poet, his intellectual 'paralysis' which contrasts with the movements of the sea – highlights the fundamental conflict here between Man's limited intellect and Nature's unfathomable mysteries:

> Là, songeant au flus et reflus,
> Je m'abisme dans cette idée;
> Son mouvement me rend perclus,
> Et mon Ame en est obsedée [. . .]
> Mais quand je veux bien l'esplucher,
> J'entends qu'on n'y peut rien entendre,
> Et qu'on se pert à le chercher.
>
> (ll. 91–4, 98–100)

It is the sea which particularly fascinates the poet and it is presented as a contradictory force, being both destructive and nurturing. The poet observes, for example, how

Tantost comme un petit batteau,
Dans la bonace non suspecte,
J'appercoy voguer sur cette eau
Le nid que l'orage respecte:
Pour luy le flot amer est doux . . .

(ll. 141–5)

A conflict is here presented between Nature and Man, a conflict which contrasts with the harmony between Nature and the birds. 'Le flot amer' indicates that for the poet, that is, Man, the waves are hostile; moreover, the syntagma 'la bonace non suspecte' may be read as an allusion to the saying 'la bonace trompe souvent le Pilote', and this therefore embeds in the text the idea that Nature can deceive Man, and introduces, incidentally, another conflict, that between appearance and reality. In contrast, the sea does not deceive the birds (it is 'non suspecte') but is protective of the eggs in the nest, as is indicated by the adjective 'doux'; moreover, the north wind becomes calm (l. 146), and Saturn 'a l'influence heureuse' (l. 147), although the allusion recalls the generally accepted view that the planet is the cause of all the ills on earth, that is, it is hostile to Man's happiness. Finally, the sun warms the eggs and helps them to hatch (ll. 148–50).

Nature's hostility towards man is reciprocated, however, and by similar means: the sea's deception is matched by Man's deception of Nature. The poet sets traps for the unsuspecting animals, and his detailed evocation of the artful process indicates no remorse, rather pleasure at the death of his prey:

Je tens aux Lapins quelque piege:
Tantost je tire aux Cormorans,
Qui bas dans les flots murmurans
Tombet percez du plomb qui tuë:
Ils se debattent sur ce bort,
Et leur vie en vain s'esvertuë
D'eschapper des mains de la mort.

(ll. 194–200)

Consider also the poet's evocation of how he traps the sea bream, a passage which highlights his paradoxical attitude towards Nature: he appreciates its beauty (he refers to 'ce beau Poisson'), but has no desire to preserve it:

Nous laissons après nous traisner
Quelque ligne pour la Dorade;
Ce beau Poisson qui l'appeçoit
Pipé de l'espoir qu'il conçoit
Aussi tost nous suit à la trace;

Son cours est leger et bruyant,
Et la chose mesme qu'il chasse
En fin l'attrape en le fuyant.

(ll. 203–10)

This paradox of Man killing something he admires is compounded by
the poet's pantheistic view that Nature's magnificence, which he attacks,
reflects the greatness of God (ll. 221–4, 301–10).

Fused with these reflections which highlight the conflictual character of
Nature and Man's relationship with it, are references to the difficult political context in which Saint-Amant wrote this poem while at Belle-Ile in
1628.[8] The poet evokes a conversation with the duke of Retz:

Nous celebrons du Grand LOUYS
L'heur, la prudence, et le courage,
Et disons que le Cardinal
Est à la France dans l'orage
Ce qu'au navire est le fanal.

(ll. 266–70)

The comparisons here between a storm and the political troubles of
early seventeenth-century France, and between a navigation lamp and
cardinal Richelieu battling in the metaphorical storm, complement, and are
in turn themselves complemented by, the idea of the literal conflict between
Nature and Man evoked in the earlier sections of the poem. Given the
explicitly articulated political allegiances of the poet (l. 264), an equivalence
is clearly implied between the storm and the Ligue, with the stereotypical
associations attached to the storm at sea - namely destruction, loss of human
life, loss of direction – being transferred to the activities of the Ligue to sig-
nal how destructive it is. In contrast, the comparison between the cardinal
and the navigation lamp implies Richelieu's perspicacity in dealing with the
political strife caused by the Ligue, a perspicacity which will, against the
huge odds suggested by the comparison between mighty Nature and the
troublesome Ligueurs, prevent France from metaphorically 'running
aground' and will restore social and political order.

The poem concludes with a final section evoking the poet's vision of the
Day of Judgment, with the emphasis placed, largely through adynaton and
enumeration, on a Nature in chaos, its laws overturned, as God destroys his
creation:[9]

---

8 Saint-Amant had accompanied the duke of Retz to Belle-Ile during the siege of La Rochelle.
9 Cf. Agrippa d'Aubigné's evocation of the Day of Judgment in *Les Tragiques*, Jugement, ll. 697ff.

> Les Estoilles tombent des Cieux,
> Les flames devorent la terre,
> Le Mongibel est en tous lieux,
> Et par tout gronde le tonnerre:
> La Salemandre est sans vertu;
> L'abeste passe pour festu,
> La Mer brusle comme eau-de-vie
>
> (ll. 410–17)

If, as we are told explicitly, 'la Nature est exterminée/[. . .] Tout est destruit
. . . (ll. 432, 439), Man, in contrast, has the opportunity to resolve his conflict
with God. He has the chance of salvation (ll. 445–50) and also of immortality through his artistic creation (ll. 455–60), but on one condition, the text
implies – that he accept his loyalty and subordination in the cosmic hierarchy to God alone:

> O Dieu! qui me fais concevoir
> Toutes ces futures merveilles,
> *Toy seul à qui pour mon devoir*
> *J'offriray les fruits de mes veilles,*
> [. . .] fay qu'en ce terrible Jour
> Je ne brusle point d'autre flame
> Que de celle de ton amour.
>
> (ll. 441–4; 448–50, my italics)

Some inconsistencies occur within Saint-Amant's cosmic hierarchy. If, as
we have seen, Saint-Amant highlights the uniqueness of each season, implying thereby that this uniqueness is an essential characteristic of the cosmic
hierarchy,[10] this order is contradicted in the sonnet 'L'Autonne des Canaries'
(ed. cit., vol. 3, p. 149). Here, the poet presents an earthly paradise where this
uniqueness of the seasons has been effaced. Throughout the whole year,
Nature yields its fruits, so that 'durant tous les Mois on peut voir en ces
Lieux/Le Printemps et l'Esté confondus en l'Autonne' (ll. 13–14). The omission of a reference to winter implies that here it does not exist. Moreover,
the conflation of the three other seasons effectively cancels the differences
between them and therefore their individuality. Here, there is only one season of constant fruitfulness, and the names of the four seasons are relevant
only as markers of time, and not as markers of time *and* of climatic change
as is usual. There is then a discrepancy between what these names usually
signify and what they signify in the Canaries.

See also Saint-Amant's 'Le Bel Œil malade', ed. cit., vol. 1, pp 160ff, ll. 4–5.   **10** See for example
'L'Epistre à l'hyver', ed. cit., vol. 1, pp 171ff, ll. 1–12.

If, as in 'L'Epistre à l'hyver' and more explicitly in 'Le Contemplateur', Nature is presented as part of a Christian order, elsewhere, in contrast, Saint-Amant focuses on specific sections of the cosmic hierarchy with no reference to God. For example, in his poem 'Le Soleil levant' (ed. cit., vol. 2, p. 5), it is the sun that is celebrated as a source of order in the universe:

> C'est le Dieu sensible aux Humains,
> C'est l'oeil de la Nature;
> Sans luy les oeuvres de ses mains
> Naistroient à l'advanture,
> Ou plustost on verroit perir
> Tout ce qu'on voit croistre et fleurir.
>
> (ll. 55–60)

In 'La Metamorphose de Lyrian et de Sylvie' (ed. cit., vol. 1, pp 96ff), Nature is presented as an instrument of divine pagan, not Christian, justice. Apollo and Pan, sympathizing with the broken-hearted Lyrian, transform his intransigent beloved into an elm, while he is transformed, at his request, into an ivy which covers the tree. As it is divinely motivated, this metamorphosis from the human state to the vegetative state is presented as a justified violence against the proud Sylvie, whilst in contrast Lorian's metamorphosis is a divine reward for his perseverance, a happy end to the amatory conflict, as it allows him the physical gratification he was denied while he and Sylvie were in human form. So it is that the ivy

> Cherche en sa passion qu'il tasche d'apaiser,
> La place où fut la bouche afin de la baiser [. . .]
> Et tout se pert en luy horsmis les sentimens:
> Car on diroit à voir ses branches enlacées
> Que se ressouvenant de ses peines passées
> Et voulant conserver son bien present aussi,
> De peur qu'il ne s'échappe il l'environne ainsi.
>
> (ll. 291–2, 296–300)

II. NATURE'S CYCLE: LIFE VERSUS DEATH?

Nature is often shown to be engaged in a paradoxical cycle of constant renewal and self-destruction. In 'Le Printemps des environs de Paris' (ed. cit., vol. 3, p. 147), various elements of Nature are personified as pairs of lovers engaged harmoniously with each other, the sight of which engenders a sense of well-being in the poet and a desire to participate in this harmony:

> Qui ne seroit ravy d'entendre sous l'Aurore
> Les Miracles volans qu'au Bois je viens d'ouyr?
> J'en sens avec les fleurs mon Coeur s'espanouyr,
> Et mon luth negligee leur veut respondre encore.
>
> (ll. 5–8)

However, the sonnet concludes: 'Tout ayme, tout s'embraze, et je croy que le Monde/Ne renaist au Printemps que pour mourir d'amour' (ll. 13–14). There is, then, a duality to this harmony which cyclically permeates the natural world in spring, for it is also a cause of disharmony, which is denoted by the allusion to suffering and death through love sickness.

Similarly, in 'Élégie à damon' (ed. cit., vol. 1, p. 154), the beloved, through her beauty, charms the cosmos, and exercises over it a certain power, albeit involuntarily, in a way which negatively reverses Nature's laws. For example, in her presence the rose becomes pale (l. 81), the lily reddens and droops (ll. 85, 89), but this destruction is presented as positive: it is a sign of Nature's willing and proper homage to her beauty (ll. 82–4, 86–92). Her paradoxical status as a force of positive destruction is clarified further when the poet tells us: 'jamais la Nature/N'employa tant de soin à l'humaine structure' (ll. 69–70). As she is both a part of Nature (and this is emphasized also by the comparisons between her attributes and those of the natural world), yet destructive of Nature, she reflects how Nature can be self-destructive, a duality frequently encountered, as we have seen, in Saint-Amant's representation of the cosmos.[11]

III. MAN AND NATURE: THE PRECARIOUS ALLIANCE

The relationship between Man and Nature is frequently shown to alternate between harmony and disharmony, suggesting that the relationship between them is essentially precarious and unstable. For example, in his 'Sonnet à feu Monsieur Des-Yveteaux' (ed. cit., vol. 3, p. 180), Saint Amant evokes his friend's garden as a harmonious combination of the cultivated (signified by the word 'jardin', l. 1) and the uncultivated, which induces a sense of well-being in the appreciative beholder:

> Que les tresors fueillus de ces rameaux divers,
> Formant un beau desordre en leurs ombrages vers,
> Me charment les esprits et me comblent de joye!
>
> (ll. 9–11)

---

11 See for example, the role of winter in 'L'Epistre à l'hyver', ed. cit., vol. 1, p. 171; see also 'Le Printemps des environs de Paris', ed. cit., vol. 3, p. 147, ll. 13–14;

If such an appreciation signals a harmony between Man and Nature, this harmony is contradicted in the final tercet, the complementarity of *fond* and *forme* highlighting the shift from harmony to disharmony. The poet here comments on a regrettable disharmony between the two. Although Nature allows trees to age slowly and without debilitation, unfortunately, in the poet's view, it does not bestow this privilege upon Man, and so, for this implied injustice, he denies Nature his unlimited praise:

> Et combien la Nature on me verroit benir
> Si par un heureux Sort, qu'aux Arbres elle octroye,
> En vieillissant comme eux tu pouvois rajeunir!
>
> (ll. 12–14)

In 'Sonnet sur la moisson' (ed. cit., vol. 3, p. 182), Saint-Amant again presents a landscape which reflects a 'meslange gracieux' (l. 2), a harmonious conflation of the cultivated and the uncultivated, the man-made and the natural. The cultivated is denoted by the reference both to fields and fallow ground (l. 2), images which denote a formal organization of the ground, and to the wheat sown on the plane (ll. 5–8), whilst the uncultivated is indicated by the 'rustique Amphitheatre', formed naturally by the trees which graduate in height down the slopes (ll. 3–4). The harmonious topography is transformed in the tercets, however, where the cutting of the wheat is evoked in terms of violence suggesting a conflict between Man and Nature:

> L'or tombe sous le fer; des-ja les Moissonneurs
> Despouillant les sillons de leurs jaunes honneurs,
> La Desolation rendent et gaye et belle.
>
> (ll. 9–11)

The paradoxical notion articulated in line 11 that this stripping away is positive is clarified in the final tercet:

> L'utile Cruauté travaille au bien de tous;
> Et nostre oeil satisfait semble dire à Cybelle,
> Plus le ravage est grand, plus je le trouve dous.
>
> (ll. 12–14)

There is, then, an approval here of Man's violence against the earth on the grounds that it brings benefits for 'tous', which implies the cosmos as a whole, and, therefore, paradoxically also the earth to whom the violence has been done. As the earlier reference to fields lying fallow (l. 2) denotes that Man nurtures Nature in return for what it yields, the text suggests that the relationship is one of mutual and equal benefaction which alternates paradoxically between violence and nurture.

IV. THE POET IN NATURE: NURTURE AND CONFLICT

In a liminary poem for the 1621 edition of Théophile de Viau's *Œuvres* (ed. cit., vol. 1, p. 3), Nature is presented – appropriately enough given Théophile's preoccupation with it – as a nurturing environment for poetical inspiration and creativity:

> Vous qui dedans la solitude
> D'un bois, d'un antre, ou d'un estude
> Imaginez voz beaux escrits,
> Lors que la saincte Poësie
> Vous anime. . .
>
> (ll. 25–9)

The poet tells us that he has put his finest poems in this book 'Comme en un coffre de Ciprés/Pour le garder de pourriture' (ll. 53–4), but then rejects the analogy as he recognizes the incompatibility between the symbol, a plant associated with death as it is commonly found in cemeteries, and the book, commonly associated with immortality:

> Mais vrayment c'est bien sans raison,
> Que j'en fais la comparaison
> Puis qu'en ces choses l'on remarque
> Une contraire qualité:
> Car l'un se dedie à la Parque
> Et l'autre à l'immortalité.
>
> (ll. 55–60)

The passage highlights then the potential conflict which characterizes the writing process: what the poet aspires to, as Saint-Amant clearly indicates here, is a harmony between his thoughts and his mode of expression, and to achieve this he must engage in a careful examination of a word's associations before he selects it. Moreover, the rejection of the image because of its particular associations highlights the poet's belief that poetry immortalizes and is itself immortal, that is, it defies Nature's law governing death.

The difficulties of the writing process are also alluded to in Saint-Amant's poem 'Les Visions, à damon' (ed. cit., vol. 1, pp 125ff). Here, what is fore-grounded is the subjectivity of the poet's perception/presentation of Nature, as we are told how, grieving for his friend, François de Molière, certain sights activate certain negative associations for him and colour his representation:

Si j'y rencontre un Cerf, ma triste fantaisie
De la mort d'Acteon est tout soudain saisie;
Les Cygnes qu'on y voit dans un paisible Estang,
Me semblent des Corbeaux qui nagent dans du sang . . .

(ll. 145–8)

What is implied is that the way in which the poet presents the world around him will depend upon his personal associations and mood, which signals a conflict between objective observation and subjective observation, that is, in this particular context, between Nature as an absolute construct and Nature as a poeticized construct. However, if objectivity is undermined, there is a correspondence between Nature, as constructed by the poet, and his mood, the former reflecting the latter, so that poetic creation and author are psychologically in perfect harmony.

In one of his best known poems, 'La Solitude' (ed. cit., vol. 1, pp 33ff), which again focuses closely on the link between poetic inspiration and Nature, Saint-Amant evokes a natural world inhabited by mythical and supernatural creatures, such as naiads, nymphs, ghosts, witches and goblins, where the interaction of all the elements is harmonious in part because of predatory Man's exclusion from it. So it is that

Là, cent mille Oyseaux aquatiques
Vivent, sans craindre en leur repos,
Le Giboyeur fin, et dispos
Avec ses mortelles practiques; [. . .]
Jamais l'Esté, ny la froidure
N'ont veu passer dessus cette eau
Nulle charette, ny bateau
Depuis que l'un et l'autre dure.
Jamais Voyageur alteré
N'y fit servir sa main de tasse;
Jamais Chevreüil desesperé
N'y finit sa vie à la chasse;
Et jamais le traistre hameçon
N'en fit sortir aucun poisson.

(ll. 51–4, 61–70)

Indeed, all reference to the human world suggests that it is anxiety-ridden and to be fled, in contrast to the peaceful and harmonious natural world which offers Man healing solace. The poet, for example, reveals how the solitude afforded by 'ces lieux sacrez à la Nuit' (l. 2) 'plaisent à mon inquietude' (l. 4); it is not in the human world but in the natural world that he finds inspiration for poetic creativity (ll. 191–4); it is Nature which offers respite to those who desire suicide, perhaps because of unrequited love (ll. 85–90), although the text is ambivalent as to whether Nature provides a means for them to accomplish their suicide or, on the contrary, dissuades them from it:

> Que je prens de plaisir à voir
> Ces Monts pendans en precipices,
> Qui pour les coups du desespoir
> Sont aux malheureux si propices,
> Quand la cruauté de leur sort
> Les force à rechercher la mort!
>
> (ll. 25–30)

Such textual ambivalence highlights Nature's duality as a force capable of both extreme gentleness and extreme violence, as a force which both bestows life and takes it away, that is, as a force of opposites, of contradictions. This duality is further emphasized in the poet's highly graphic reflection on the sea's variability between extremes:

> Tantost, l'onde broüillant l'arene,
> Murmure et fremit de courroux,
> Se roullant dessus les cailloux
> Qu'elle apporte, et qu'elle r'entraine.
> Tantost, elle estale en ses bors,
> Que l'ire de Neptune outrage,
> Des gens noyez, des Monstres mors,
> Des vaisseaux brisez du naufrage, [. . .]
> Tantost, la plus Claire du monde,
> Elle semble un miroir flottant . . .
>
> (ll. 151–8, 161–2)

If the poet admires this duality ('Que je trouve doux le ravage/De ces fiers Torrens vagabonds', ll. 31–2), and appreciates Nature for the poetic inspiration it affords him (ll. 175–8, 191–4), there is, as he tells Alcidon (Charles II Maignart de Bernières) to whom the poem is addressed, an internal conflict between his appreciation, on the one hand, of the sociability offered by the human world, and his appreciation, on the other, of the creative solitude offered by the natural world, and the poem concludes with this dichotomy unresolved:

> O que j'ayme la Solitude!
> C'est l'Element des bons Esprits,
> C'est par elle que j'ay compris

> L'Art d'Apollon sans nulle estude:
> Je l'ayme pour l'amour de toy,
> Connoissant que ton humeur l'ayme,
> Mais quand je pense bien à moy,
> Je la hay pour la raison mesme;
> Car elle pourroit me ravir
> L'heur de te voir, et te servir.
>
> (ll. 191–200)

In 'La Jouyssance' (ed. cit., vol. 1, p. 63), in contrast, the poet combines an enjoyment of Nature with an enjoyment of company, that of his mistress. Here, the poet contrasts his two conflicting lifestyles, that of the court, 'ce pompeux Edifice' (l. 1), and that of his country house. The characteristics of the first, summed up as pomposity (l. 1), 'contrainte' and 'artifice' (l. 4), connote a conflict between the appropriate and the inappropriate, between freedom and constraint, between truth and deceit. In contrast, in the country, the poet is, quite simply, 'libre' (l. 5), leads 'la plus douce vie' (l. 9), and enjoys a correspondence between his desires and his senses:

> Mes sens en bonne diligence
> S'entendoient avec mes desirs,
> Me recherchans mille plaisirs
> D'une soigneuse diligence.
>
> (ll. 11–14).

Nature and Man coexist here harmoniously, the beautiful landscape forming a complementary backdrop to the poet's reciprocated love, and the poet embellishing Nature with his luth-playing (ll. 155–80). As the poet states that he enjoys all this when he is far from the court (ll. 1–4), embedded in the text is the implication that this earthly paradise is the opposite in every respect of his life at court, the negative portrait of which is, therefore, present implicitly throughout the text.

This championing of the country over the court is contradicted, however, in 'Les Cabarets' (ed. cit., vol. 1, pp 208ff), where the poet extols the virtues of urban life over those of the country, as he exhorts his friend, Nicolas Faret, to leave the countryside of Fontainebleau to return to Paris, 'ce petit Monde,/Où tout contentement abonde' (ll. 97–8). Highlighting through an allusion to 'La Solitude' the contradiction here of his usual attitude, he recommends that the countryside should only be experienced vicariously through the text, while the urban world, better suited to both their temperaments, should be experienced directly:

> Ne cherche point la solitude
> Si ce n'est par-fois dans ces Vers
> Que j'ay donnez à l'Univers
> [. . .] La campagne n'a point d'appas
> Qui puissant attirer tes pas,
> Et de l'air dont tu te gouvernes,
> Les moindres Escots des taverns
> Te plaisent plus cent mille fois
> Que ne font les Echos des bois.
> ET A MOY AUSSI.
>
> (ll. 106–8, 115–21)

However, the prevailing view articulated in Saint-Amant's works is that the poet enjoys a privileged status in Nature. This is emphasized particularly in 'L'Arion' (ed. cit., vol. 1, p. 109). Drawing on Ovid's version of the Orpheus story, Saint-Amant presents Arion as capable of taking control of Nature (and, indeed, of the human world) through the charming qualities of his voice and luth playing: he

> Ostoit l'ame aux humains pour la donner aux marbres,
> Domtoit les animaux, faisoit marcher les arbres,
> Arrestoit le Soleil, precipitoit son cours,
> Prolongeait à son choix ou les nuits, ou les jours,
> Réveilloit la Clemence, endormoit la tonnerre.
>
> (ll. 25–9) [12]

Although Arion disturbs the natural order, there is no suggestion that he causes chaos. He is presented, rather, as an harmonious element in the natural world. So it is that when his crew try to kill him and he is forced to jump into the sea, Nature saves him by sending a dolphin to take him to land (ll. 190–2), night is turned into day (ll. 217–20), and the stars shine brightly so that he may see where he is going (ll. 221–3). Arion is, therefore, a paradox in the cosmos, as the threat he presents to the normal patterns of the natural world is presented as acceptable to the cosmos. [13]

---

12 See also ll. 145–62. **13** Cf. 'La Jouyssance', ed. cit., vol. 1, pp 163ff, ll. 155–80, where the poet evokes how his luth playing charms Nature and even prompts an oak tree to speak. Cf. also L'Epistre à L'hyver', ed. cit., vol. 1, pp 171ff., ll. 35–40, where Marie de Gonzague provokes a change in natural patterns, but this is not through any power she wields but because Nature respects her.

To conclude, it may be said that Saint-Amant's representation of the cosmos engages indirectly with the controversial eternal debates on authority and free will which were particularly to the fore during the seventeenth century. He presents a strictly organized cosmos in which the harmony between its various elements is preserved only when all are in strict obedience to the supreme cosmic force, which is at times defined as a god, whether Christian or pagan, or, more generically, as Nature. Despite this strict hierarchy, there is a flexibility within it which allows for harmonious aberrations from expected and usual patterns of behaviour, but only if these aberrations are endorsed by the head of the hierarchy. Otherwise, such divergences are shown to have destructive consequences. If the poet enjoys a privileged status in Nature, Man is, on the whole, at the mercy of Nature's laws, and it is this precariousness which defines the relationship as essentially conflictual. Man is presented as being both a friend and a foe to a Nature which equally both nurtures and harms him, but there is one constant: despite his aspirations, he always remains fundamentally subordinate to Nature in the cosmic scheme, and it is this with which he must come to terms.

II. MORAL CONFLICTS

The problem of freedom in Arnauld's defence of Jansenius

MICHAEL MORIARTY

The Jansenist controversy displays the re-emergence, in the new context of post-Tridentine Catholicism, of issues that had been crucial to the early phases of the Reformation. Whereas in Spain and Italy the Catholic Church had managed to contain theological controversy to the extent of, largely, confining it within the ecclesiastical sphere, the French experience was very different: it was when the political threat arising from the existence of a strong Protestant movement had been defused that bitter divisions broke out within the Catholic Church, and new engagements took place on some of the battlegrounds of the Reformation controversies. These new conflicts were, of course, affected by the outcome of the earlier ones. It is the problem of human freedom which emerges as one of the most important grounds of conflict in the mid-seventeenth century, as it had been a hundred years earlier. In what follows I shall discuss some of the attendant theological and philosophical issues, in particular as they appear in Antoine Arnauld's *Seconde apologie pour Jansenius* (1645), which is perhaps the most powerful systematic exposition in French of Jansenius' theology, Pascal's brilliant *Écrits sur la grâce* being incomplete, but I shall not attempt to integrate these issues into a general political and social treatment of the 'Jansenist' phenomenon. True, Arnauld's intervention is essentially tactical: he is writing a defence of Jansenius, not providing, as Jansenius attempts to do, a fully worked-out theory of freedom. Indeed, he later denied that he had any interest in the philosophical problem of freedom at all.[1] But for that very reason we can learn something from his selection and development of material for theological and polemical purposes.

The first *Apologie* (1644) had been a reply to a series of sermons against Jansenius by Isaac Habert in 1642–3. Habert replied in the *Défense de la foi de l'Église* (late 1644), and the *Seconde apologie* was Arnauld's counterblast.[2] A certain part of the material is *ad hominem*, and Arnauld sometimes digresses

---

1 See the editorial preface to Antoine Arnauld, *Œuvres*, ed. Gabriel Du Pac de Bellegarde and Jean Hautefage, 42 vols (Paris 1775–81), vol. 10, pp xxix–xxxi (p. xxx). **2** On Habert's role in the Jansenist controversy, see Antoine Adam, *Du Mysticisme à la révolte: les Jansénistes du XVIIe siècle* (Paris 1968), pp 151–2, 163–4, 197.

from his theological argumentation to analyze the networks of personal and institutional relationships that have filtered the theological issues.[3] He remarks, for example, that Habert's scandalized reaction to Jansenius' assertion that liberty and necessity are compatible sits oddly with the praise he earlier bestowed on a work by the Oratorian Gibieuf, which upheld a similar position to that of Jansenius.[4]

Behind the specific criticisms which Arnauld aims to refute lies a more general accusation: new Jansenist is but old Protestant writ large, or, as Habert puts it, Jansenism is but a 'Calvinisme de longue robe'.[5] And it is easy to see why the opponents of Jansenius latched on to the question of freedom. One of Luther's most prominent works is entitled *De servo arbitrio*.[6] Book Two of *L'Institution chrétienne*, in which Calvin begins to develop the distinctive positions that separate him from the Roman Catholicism of his day, affirms with equal vigour the bondage of the will to sin.[7] If the position of Jansenius could be equated with that of Luther and Calvin, then a very effective controversial blow would have been struck against his followers.

Now although Luther and Calvin expressed their views on freedom with particular trenchancy, the views themselves were not totally new. Broadly speaking, Luther and Calvin belong, as did many Catholic theologians, to an intellectual tradition derived from St Augustine and, beyond him, from the St Paul of the Epistle to the Romans, in which the preoccupation is not so much with free will or choice as with freedom. What characterizes freedom is first of all the absence of constraint: we are free insofar as we act voluntarily. In this sense, the sinner can be said to be free, but, for Luther and for Calvin at least, he has no choice between sinning and not sinning.

The approach of St Thomas Aquinas, on the other hand, reflects an Aristotelian concern with the problem of choice. Not all voluntary action is free, for children and even animals may be said to act voluntarily, but they do not act on the basis of a rational judgment selecting one out of a number of possible courses of action. The presence of alternatives is essential to Aquinas' conception of free will or free choice.[8] It was this aspect of his

3 Pascal does the same, in comic mode, in the first two *Provinciales*. 4 On the relationship between the conceptions of liberty of Gibieuf and Descartes, see Étienne Gilson, *La Liberté chez Descartes et la théologie* (Paris 1913), pp 198–206, 216–23, 309–12. 5 Quoted by Arnauld in his *Second apologie pour M. Jansenius, Évêque d'Ypres* [1644; text of 1645], in *Œuvres*, ed. cit., vol. 17 (1778), pp 1–637 (p. 13 and cf. p. 48). 6 Martin Luther, *De servo arbitrio* in *Luthers Werke in Auswahl*, ed. Otto Clemen, 4 vols (Berlin 1966–7), vol. 3, pp 94–293. See in particular p. 125 for Luther's views on freedom and necessity. 7 Jean Calvin, *Institution de la religion chrétienne*, ed. Jean-Daniel Benoît, 5 vols (Paris 1957–63), vol. 2, II.ii. 7, p. 30. 8 'Potest enim homo velle et non velle, agere et non agere: potest etiam velle hoc aut illud, et agere hoc et illud' (Saint Thomas Aquinas, *Summa theologiae*, I-II, q. 13, a. 6; cf. I-II, q. 10, a. 2).

thought that was emphasized by many Roman Catholic theologians in reaction to the Lutheran and Calvinist stress on man's helpless bondage to sin.

Jesuit theologians like Luis de Molina and Francisco Suárez (who was also a major philosopher) insisted that freedom requires 'indifference'. That agent, says Molina, is said to be free who, given all that is required in order to act, may act and not act, or may perform one action in such a way that he could also perform the contrary, and who acts in virtue of a prior judgment of the reason.[9] He speaks elsewhere of freedom as involving the possibility to choose 'indifferently' between alternatives, and Suárez offers a broadly similar definition.[10]

When the Flemish theologian Jansenius took it upon himself to expound the true doctrine of St Augustine with regard to grace, he devoted several chapters of his massive work *Augustinus*, published posthumously in 1640, to the problem of freedom.[11] And the issue was in turn highlighted by his critics and censors. Of the famous Five Propositions (originally seven) condemned by Innocent X in the bull *Cum occasione* of 1653, no fewer than four relate to aspects of the problem: whether the just have the power always to fulfil the commandments (I); whether interior grace is resistible (II, IV); whether in order to merit or demerit the agent must be free from necessity or merely free from compulsion (III).[12] Arnauld's *Seconde apologie* dates from 1644, nine years before the papal pronouncement, and five before the first

---

9 'Illud agens liberum dicitur, quod positis omnibus requisitis ad agendum, potest agere & non agere, aut ita agere vnum, vt contrarium etiam agere possit. Atque ab hac libertate facultas, qua tale agens potest ita operari, dicitur libera. Quoniam verò non ita operatur nisi præuio arbitrio, iudicioq; rationis, inde est, quòd quatenus ita præexigit iudicium rationis, liberum appelletur arbitrium' (Luis de Molina, *Liberi arbitrii concordia cum gratiae donis, divina praescientia, providentia, praedestinatione et reprobatione*, 3rd edn (Antwerp 1609), p. 8). **10** Ibid., p. 335. According to Suárez, the definition of a free faculty must meet two conditions: 'Unum est quod illa sit potentia activa, ex se et ex sua interna facultate habens vim ad exercendam et suspendendam actionem suam. Aliud est quod illa facultas, dum exercet actum, ita sit disposita et proxime (ut ita dicam) præparata ad opus ut, positis omnibus requisitis ad agendum, possit agere et non agere' (Francisco Suárez, *Disputationes metaphysicae*, XIX.iv.8, in *Disputaciones metafísicas*, edited and translated by Sergio Rábade Romeo, Salvador Caballero Sánchez and Antonio Puigcerver Zanón, 7 vols, Biblioteca hispánica de filosofía (Madrid 1960), vol. 3, p. 362. **11** For a good succinct account of Jansenius's conception of freedom, see Elmar J. Kremer, 'Grace and free will in Arnauld' in Elmar J. Kremer (ed.), *The great Arnauld and some of his philosophical correspondents* (Toronto 1994), pp 219–39 (pp 219–23). The bulk of Kremer's article is a careful and illuminating scrutiny of Arnauld's later positions, rather than those of the *Seconde apologie*. See also his article 'L'Accord de la grâce avec la liberté selon Arnauld', in *Antoine Arnauld (1612–1694): philosophe, écrivain, théologien,* Chroniques de Port-Royal, 44 (1995), 145–61. **12** The Five Propositions may be found in *Enchiridion symbolorum, definitionum et declarationum de rebus fidei et morum,* ed. Heinrich Denzinger, revised by Adolf Schönmetzer, 35th edn (Barcelona/Freiburg im Breisgau/Rome/New York 1973), nos 1092–96 (old numbering)/2001–5 (new numbering). They are also listed in many works on Jansenism; see, for example, Louis Cognet, *Le Jansénisme*, Que sais-je?, 6th edn (Paris 1991), pp 50–1.

appearance of the five propositions in a list drawn up by Nicolas Cornet for condemnation by the Sorbonne. But liberty had already emerged as a vital battleground: it is involved in several of the points of discrepancy alleged by Habert to exist between the respective doctrines of Augustine and Jansenius. Thus, the fifth of Habert's 'articles' deals with the irresistibility and efficacy of grace. Habert accuses Jansenius of holding that grace is irresistible because it imposes necessity on the will. In the sixth article, Jansenius is accused of denying co-operation between grace and the will. These two charges are serious because the council of Trent had anathematized the view that the will does not co-operate with grace, and cannot dissent from it, being completely passive.[13] The seventh article deals with the possibility of the commandments, another issue addressed by Trent;[14] the ninth with the compatibility of liberty and necessity. These subjects coincide with those of the second, first, and third of the Five Propositions respectively. The twelfth article concerns the actions of infidels, which Jansenius holds are necessarily sinful. This thesis was included in Cornet's original list of seven propositions. It may not at first sight appear to have anything to do with freedom, but the structure of the *Augustinus* makes the connexion clear: the inauthenticity of the virtue to which infidels might lay claim reinforces the thesis that they have no freedom to act virtuously, or even to avoid sin. And, in fact, Arnauld's most extensive discussion of the nature of voluntary action is used to support the denial of virtue to infidels.

Although it would be more faithful to the structure of Arnauld's text to summarize his argument in relation to the specific articles of the controversy between himself and Habert, the interest of the argument goes so far beyond that particular quarrel that it will be more useful, for the purposes of this article, to reconstitute it around a more general series of issues. There is a risk posed, however, by an excessively systematic approach. Jansenius is systematic: he methodically surveys the historical and doctrinal issues, and patiently expounds his theory (or rather his master's theory), while refuting those errors opposed to it. He is happy to accumulate other writers in support of his view, but their role is ancillary. Arnauld is writing apologetically, and his goal is to demolish the fake image of Jansenius, the crypto-Protestant, constructed by his adversaries. So he is more willing to use *ad hominem* arguments, tending to show that even if one disagrees with Jansenius on certain issues, one may find that the implications of his theory do not run counter to those of one's own. The issue of indifference is precisely a case in point. It is essential to Arnauld's tactical defence of Jansenius. But since it is theo-

13 Council of Trent, session VI, *Canones de iustificatione*, can. 4, in Denzinger/Schönmetzer, op. cit., no. 1554/814.   14 Ibid., can. 18, no. 1568/828.

retically peripheral to the conception of freedom held by both Arnauld and Jansenius, it is better to begin elsewhere.

NECESSITY AND CONSTRAINT

Jansenius is accused by Habert of holding that:

(i)   freedom is compatible with an inevitable necessity to act;
(ii) freedom is compatible with an inevitable necessity to sin;
(iii) freedom is utterly destroyed in the will of sinners.

The obvious aim is to tar Jansenius with a Lutheran and Calvinist brush. However, Arnauld accepts that Jansenius holds (i) and (ii), but denies that he holds (iii).[15]

First of all, Arnauld endeavours to show in what sense freedom is compatible with necessity. Augustine distinguishes between a necessity 'de contrainte & de violence' and a necessity that is 'simple & volontaire'.[16] Death is a necessity of the first kind: we shall die whether we like it or not. But the will is not under this kind of necessity: it makes no sense to say 'I must will x whether I like it or not', since if I do not like it, I am not willing it. The other kind of necessity is 'celle par laquelle il est nécessaire que quelque chose se fasse, la volonté n'y répugnant point, mais au contraire le voulant immuablement', and this is sometimes referred to as necessity of immutability.[17] By such a necessity God loves himself and the blessed love God, but there is no constraint here. In heaven, we shall be unable to sin, yet we shall be freer than now.[18]

Arnauld cites a long line of authors who define liberty first and foremost as the absence of necessity of constraint, for example, not only Aquinas but also St Bonaventure, Alexander of Hales, Peter Lombard, Richard of St Victor and Hugh of St Victor.[19] This army of authorities is tactically highly important, since it shows that Jansenius is neither an eccentric nor a mere echo of Luther and Calvin who also identify liberty with absence of constraint.

---

15 Arnaud, *Seconde apologie*, ed. cit., p. 238; cf. p. 263.   **16** Ibid., p. 238. Arnauld's ultimate source here is Augustine's *De civitate Dei*, V.10, but more immediately he is drawing on Jansenius, *Augustinus*, 3 vols (Rouen 1643 [first published 1640]), vol. 3, *De gratia Christi salvatoris*, book VI, ch. 6, pp 264–7.   **17** Arnaud, *Seconde apologie*, ed. cit., p. 238.   **18** Ibid., p. 239. This is an Augustinian position. See for example *De civitate Dei*, XXII.30.   **19** Arnaud, *Seconde apologie*, ed. cit., pp 239–41, 244–6. I allude here only to passages that specifically define liberty as opposed to constraint. The Aquinas passages are from *Contra gentiles*, III, c. 138 and *De potentia*, q. 10, a. 2, ad 5. However, Arnauld later realizes that these are not an adequate statement of Aquinas' mature view (see below, and n. 8 above).

Augustine's distinction between the two types of necessity can be assimilated to Aquinas' distinction between necessity of constraint and necessity of inner inclination: the former diminishes the praise of virtuous actions because they have not been performed voluntarily, the latter does not (Arnauld, *Seconde apologie*, p. 240). This necessity of inner inclination leaves freedom intact, and Arnauld propounds the following case to show why this is so:

> Seroit-ce diminuer la louange que mériteroit un sujet, pour n'avoir pas consenti aux sollicitations violentes qu'on lui auroit faites, de trahir son Prince, que de dire, que son action, ayant été comme nécessaire, et faite presque sans aucune liberté, ne mérite pas de louange; parce que sa générosité & sa fidélité le rendoient incapable de commettre cette trahison, qu'il auroit peut-être commise, s'il avoit esté moins fidelle & moins généreux? (*Seconde apologie*, p. 257)[20]

The argument presupposes another traditional argument for freedom, namely that it is postulated by such speech acts as praise or blame.[21] In this sense, then, Arnauld argues, we can hold that a sinner is necessitated to sin by inner inclination, without conceding that he has forfeited his freedom. But Arnauld follows Jansenius in denying that all human action in this life is subject to an immutable necessity of inner inclination. Had both men not denied this, then they could certainly have been accused of Lutheranism.

INDIFFERENCE

Arnauld argues, however, that Man here on earth is capable of both good and evil, action and non-action or, in scholastic parlance, he enjoys indifference of contrariety and of contradiction. Where there is indifference, there is plainly liberty. Indifference is not essential to liberty, else God and the blessed, who cannot sin, would not be free, but it is an aspect of human liberty in this life (*Seconde apologie*, pp 241–3). Those scholastics who hold that indifference is essential to human freedom mean only indifference of contradiction, that is, not the freedom to do good or evil, but the freedom to act or not to act (*Seconde apologie*, p. 260). So they need not take offence at Jansenius' view that sinners are subject to a necessity to sin, for this is a general necessity:

---

20 The characterization of the action as 'faite presque sans liberté' must be that of Arnauld's hypothetical opponent, and not his own.   **21** On this, see Cicero, *De fato*, XVII.40; discussed by Augustine, *De civitate Dei*, V.9, V.10; cf. also Aquinas, *Summa theologiae*, I, q.83, a.1.

parce que ce n'est point une nécessité particulière de commettre chaque péché, en sorte que celui qui fait un péché ne se puisse abstenir de le faire; mais seulement une nécessité générale de pécher, qui vient, de ce que le libre arbitre est tellement environné de ténèbres, & esclave de l'amour des créatures, avant qu'il ait reçu la lumière de la foi, & quelques étincelles de l'amour de Dieu, que, de quelque côté qu'il se tourne, il est impossible qu'il ne pèche (*Seconde apologie*, p. 259).

We can always escape one sin by embracing another. The point here is tactical: even if you disagree with Jansenius on the essence of human liberty, you need not take issue with his view of the necessity to sin. In other words, Jansenius can be absolved of the accusation that he suppresses human freedom.

The compatibility of Jansenius' account of freedom with indifference arises over another issue, that of grace. Jansenius' critics contend that he makes grace irresistible, a thesis condemned by Trent.[22] This seems plausible because Jansenius does not think that we are free to co-operate or not with grace (that is, efficacious grace, the grace of Jesus Christ), as Arnauld himself emphasizes (*Seconde apologie*, p. 184). Grace, however, acts in conjunction with the will: 'La grâce n'agit pas seulement avec le libre arbitre des hommes déchus, mais [. . .] de telle sorte, que c'est elle qui le fait faire, qui le fait vouloir, & qui le determine à l'action par une force invincible' (*Seconde apologie*, p. 174). Elsewhere he remarks that the power of grace over the will is 'aussi douce qu'elle est invincible' (*Seconde apologie*, p. 199). Grace is not violent: it makes us want to act in the appropriate way.

Even under the influence of grace, we enjoy indifference both of contradiction and of contrariety, properly understood. We cannot sin while under the influence of grace but while under the influence of grace we retain the capacity to sin. We could sin if we would, but we do not want to. To say that 'while under the influence of grace, we have the *capacity* to sin' is true in one sense, and not in another: that is, in scholastic terminology, it is true in the 'divided' sense, but false in the 'composite' sense.[23] In the composite sense, it would mean 'We have the capacity to sin while under the

---

22 See note 13 above.   **23** Arnauld seems to state that it is true in the composite but false in the divided sense, but Jansenius' text quite clearly implies the reverse (*Augustinus*, vol. 3, *De gratia Christi salvatoris*, VIII.20, p. 307). If the Tridentine proposition is understood in the composite sense, it would mean 'it is possible that a free will moved by grace can dissent from it', which Jansenius would deny. In the divided sense it means 'a free will moved by grace has the power to dissent, if it will', which he concedes, simply asserting that that power would never be exercised, since if influenced by grace one would not want to refuse consent. See also Kremer, 'Grace and free will', pp 222–3.

influence of grace.'[24] According to Jansenius and Arnauld that is false, but they would agree that while under the influence of grace, we have the capacity to sin, for although contrary acts (doing God's will or sinning) cannot exist simultaneously in the same will, contrary powers or possibilities can. In this sense, the free will, moved by God, can refuse consent if it wills (as Trent stipulates), and in this sense we possess indifference of contrariety and contradiction.[25] To put the matter in traditional terms, Arnauld and Jansenius are insisting that the effectual nature of grace does not destroy nature, or, in more anachronistic terms, that it does not so reprogramme the human being as to change his or her personality radically. One might suggest the following analogy: X has given up his excessive drinking, apparently for good, because he is in love with Y; but supposing Y's influence were removed from X's life, he might well revert to his former habit. If, then, one wants to maintain that indifference is an essential aspect of human freedom, Arnauld argues that, provided we understand indifference correctly, it is not jeopardized by Jansenius' doctrine of grace or by his account of sin.

So far, in his analysis of the relationship between freedom and indifference, Arnauld has been walking in the tracks of Jansenius. But, beyond a certain point, he ceases to follow his guide. For, having explained that the view of sinners as necessitated does not clash with the scholastic conception of indifference, Jansenius abandons this apparently eirenic approach in order to insist on the difference between Augustine's conception of freedom and that of the scholastics.[26] For obvious tactical reasons, Arnauld is disposed, on the contrary, to soft-pedal the contrast between them. I shall presently mention a significant point of divergence.

LOVE AND ACTION

We have seen that a necessity of inner inclination is not incompatible with freedom. This is partly because, as in the example of the faithful subject, it can be construed as a form of love: 'Qu'y a-t-il de plus libre que l'amour, & que fait-on plus librement que ce qu'on fait par amour?' (*Seconde apologie*, p. 255). The ultimate inspiration here is doubtless Augustine: 'Recta igitur voluntas est bonus amor et voluntas perversa malus amor.'[27] But there is also a closer verbal parallel to Aquinas' 'nihil magis est voluntarium quam amor'.[28]

---

24 This seems to be implied by the quotation from Suàrez given in n. 10 above.   **25** Arnauld, *Seconde apologie*, ed. cit., pp 181–3; cf. p. 187.   **26** Jansenius, *Augustinus*, vol. 2, *De statu naturae lapsae*, IV.20–21, pp 260–1.   **27** Augustine, *De civitate Dei*, XIV.7. On the relation between love and will in Augustine, see Étienne Gilson, *Introduction à l'étude de saint Augustin* (Paris 1929), pp 165–6.   **28** St

This notion of love as the fundamental motivation is developed by Arnauld in relation to the problem of pagan virtue, an issue foregrounded in La Mothe le Vayer's *De la vertu des payens* of 1642, and covered, as we saw, in Nicolas Cornet's first list of seven condemnable Jansenist propositions. Arnauld's demonstration that all actions by infidels are sinful is an elaborate compound syllogism of the type sometimes termed 'epicheirema', in which the premisses are themselves furnished with proof.[29] The major premiss is: 'toute action volontaire, qui ne procède point de quelque mouvement d'amour de Dieu, est nécessairement péché'. The minor premiss is: 'on ne peut pas dire, qu'il y ait aucune action dans les Infideles, qui procède de quelque mouvement d'amour de Dieu' (*Seconde apologie*, p. 305). The conclusion follows that all actions by infidels are sins (*Seconde apologie*, p. 333).

The major premiss is proved in three steps: 'toute action volontaire procède de quelque amour'; 'tout amour est nécessairement ou amour de Dieu, ou amour de la créature'; 'tout ce qui procède de l'amour de la créature est vicieux' (*Seconde apologie*, p. 306). Arnauld argues as follows:

> Personne n'agit volontairement qu'il n'agisse pour quelque fin, & la volonté ne sauroit se porter à une fin, que comme à un bien, parce qu'il est impossible que l'homme désire le mal comme mal. Or l'amour n'est autre chose que la pente & l'inclination de la volonté vers le bien: & par conséquent, il ne peut jamais y avoir d'action volontaire qui ne procède de quelque amour. (p. 307)

The words 'pente' and 'inclination' echo Augustine's analysis of love. Augustine refers to love as a 'pondus', which here means not exactly weight but the tendency of a given type of body to seek its place upwards like fire, or downwards like a stone.[30] But this way of thinking is taken up by Aquinas. Thus his theory of the will starts with the most basic form of appetite, the inclination that goes with a certain form, his example being the tendency of fire to rise and to reproduce itself.[31] Up to a point, then, it seems fair to equate his 'inclinatio' with Augustine's 'pondus', or at least there is a corridor here from Augustine's theory to that of Aquinas. Again, in linking will and love, Arnauld is certainly following Augustine, but here too Aquinas is

---

Thomas Aquinas, *Summa theologiae*, I, q. 41, a. 2, 3. This statement forms part of an objection to Aquinas' own view, but it is not itself rejected in his reply (ibid., ad 3). Strictly speaking, there is a distinction, since Aquinas would not necessarily equate 'voluntary' and 'free': animals can act voluntarily in a sense (ibid., I–II, q. 6, a. 2), but we would not say that they act freely. Arnauld, however, does not seem to acknowledge the distinction at this point.　**29** On epicheirema, see Antoine Arnauld and Pierre Nicole, *La Logique ou l'art de penser*, ed. Pierre Clair and François Girbal, Bibliothèque des Textes Philosophiques, 2nd edn (Paris 1993), pp 228–9.　**30** Cf. Augustine, *Confessions*, XIII.9; *De civitate Dei*, XI.28.　**31** Aquinas, *Summa theologiae*, I, q.80, a.1.

an Augustinian: love, he holds, is the first motion of the will, and the root of all motions of the appetite.[32] Indeed, the very notion advanced by Arnauld that love is the source of all actions is an echo of Aquinas' claim that any agent performing any action does so out of love of some kind.[33] The reason that Aquinas held this view is that all agents act for an end, and the end is always some good that is loved and desired. But Arnauld too, in the passage just quoted, registers this link between acting out of love and acting for an end. Again, his assertion that the will can aim only at what is good, or what we perceive to be good, is thoroughly Thomist.[34] For Jansenius, the influence of Aristotle on conceptions of freedom had been absolutely disastrous, so it is striking that his disciple, via St Thomas, should be building bridges with the Aristotelian tradition, with its distinctive stress on the purposive dimension of action.[35]

This theory of love as the ultimate motivation is extremely suggestive, especially when combined with the notion of voluntary action as fulfilling some purpose of the agent. By showing that sin is voluntary, because inspired by love, it makes it easier to exempt God from blame for human wrongdoing. At first sight this view seems to ignore the problem of acrasia (weakness of will), the experience of being unable to avoid some action we want to avoid or to perform one we want to perform. But in fact it throws light on the problem: sinners persists in sin because there is something they want from their sinful behaviour, some need to which it corresponds, some goal it fulfills. At some level they do not want what they think they want, and vice versa. The theory thus leaves room for a theory of unconscious motivation, and, indeed, Arnauld speaks of the desire in human beings for independence as 'caché dans les replis les plus secrets de la volonté' (*Seconde apologie*, p. 326).[36]

Arnauld's theory, then, may be summarized as follows. All voluntary action is action for an end. The end is a perceived good. The inclination towards good is synonymous with love. Thus all voluntary action is inspired by love of some kind, whether of God or of the creature. But love itself is free, since it is an inclination of the will, the distinction between the free and the voluntary being discounted. What we do for the sake of love, we do

---

32 Aquinas, ibid., I, q.20, a.1; see also Brian Davies, *The thought of Thomas Aquinas* (Oxford 1992), p. 150. 33 See Aquinas, ibid., I–II, q.28, a.6: 'omne agens, quodcumque sit, agit quamcumque actionem ex aliquo amore'. 34 Cf. Aquinas, ibid., I–II, q.8, a.1. 35 See Jansenius, *Augustinus*, ed. cit., vol. 3, *De gratia Christi salvatoris*, book VI, preface, p. 255. 36 Paradoxically, Arnauld challenged the notion of 'pensées imperceptibles' developed by Nicole, while admitting that there are thoughts of which we are not fully conscious at any given time. See Geneviève Lewis, *Le Problème de l'inconscient et le cartésianisme* (Paris 1950), pp 200–18, and E.D. James, *Pierre Nicole, Jansenist and humanist: a study of his thought* (The Hague 1972), pp 38–42.

freely. It follows that the sinner and the saint alike are free in what they do, since in the end they are doing what they want, even if both are subject to a certain form of necessity. Again, in this life, we enjoy indifference with respect to particular actions, and this is a sure sign of liberty. Now it is not quite clear that Jansenius would altogether agree with this solution.

PASSION AND CONSTRAINT

Jansenius makes plain that his definition of will does not cover indeliberate impulses of rage, fear, concupiscence, and the like. In his view, the will is that element in us, that apex of the mind, that consents to or withholds consent from an impulse.[37] Thus sin consists in consent to concupiscence, and not in concupiscence itself.[38] Concupiscence is an habitual force: 'pondus quoddam habituale, quo anima inclinatur ad fruendum creaturis' (*De statu naturae lapsae*, II.7, p. 129). In this sense, it is clearly not voluntary, since it is an inescapable part of the condition of fallen man.

The will is free to the extent that it is in our power.[39] An act is in our power when, if we want it to take place, it will, and conversely if we do not want it to take place it will not.[40] Jansenius takes over the scholastic distinction between immediate acts of will ('elicited' acts) and acts commanded by the will but requiring the mediation of another power.[41] These latter are not wholly within our power: if I choose to walk, I may be impeded by an injured leg. The act of will in general is completely within our power, since if I will x, then the act of willing x necessarily takes place. But particular volitions may not be at a given time: I may want to love God, and yet be unable to.[42] Freedom, then, is a matter of gradations. But although it can coexist with certain kinds of necessity, for instance the necessity of an immutable will, it is intrinsically incompatible with necessity of coercion.[43]

Now Arnauld seemed to be saying very much the same thing. But Jansenius gives a fuller account of what he means by coercion. For he argues that when Augustine defines the act of will in opposition to coercion, he does not just mean physical coercion. He also means to exclude moral or psychological coercion.[44] Thus a motion originating in fear ('terrente metu

---

37 Jansenius, *Augustinus*, ed. cit., vol. 3, *De gratia Christi salvatoris*, VI.5, p. 264. **38** Jansenius, *Augustinus*, ed. cit., vol. 2, *De statu naturae lapsae*, II.24, pp 167–71. **39** Jansenius, *Augustinus*, ed. cit., vol. 3, *De gratia Christi salvatoris*, VI.3, p. 260. **40** Jansenius' source is Augustine, *De spiritu et littera*, XXXI.53 (PL 44, 235). **41** See Aquinas, *Summa theologiae*, I-II, q.6, introduction. **42** Jansenius, *Augustinus*, ed. cit., vol. 3, *De gratia Christi salvatoris*, VI.4–5, p. 261. **43** See Jansenius, *Augustinus*, ed. cit., vol. 3, *De gratia Christi salvatoris*, VI.6, p. 266 and VI.38, p. 306. **44** This conception has a later history. Leibniz speaks of the passions as exerting a 'violence [. . .] douce',

mali') or concupiscence ('concupiscentiâ stimulante') is not voluntary but coerced or necessary, and the fear or concupiscence is itself a form of necessity. And this is so whether or not an alternative volition is possible (fear driving out fear, or one concupiscence another). In this sense, the indifference that Jansenius concedes does sometimes obtain when we act is not a sufficient condition of voluntary action in Augustine's sense, that is, action exempt from any form of constraint. In general, what we do unwillingly or reluctantly we do under compulsion, and, therefore, involuntarily.[45] The line of thought is clear enough: the more concupiscence is in operation, the less I am master of my actions, and the greater the tension between what I wish and what I do. If I yield to concupiscence, part of me may want not to have done so, but even if I refrain from it, another part of me may wish I had not. To this extent, there is an element of unwillingness, and hence necessity, in whatever action I pursue. Whether this view of volition is compatible with Jansenius' definition of will as the part of the personality that resists or consents to indeliberate motions is another question.

Certainly, this view held by Jansenius clashes altogether with that of Aquinas. Following Aristotle, St Thomas argues that actions caused by fear, such as jettisoning a cargo to save the ship in a storm, are involuntary in that one would not want to perform them in general, yet voluntary in the particular case – we want to save the ship and ourselves at the expense of the cargo if necessary – while concupiscentia increases the voluntary element, since its nature is, precisely, to incline the will towards an object.[46] Moreover, Arnauld is dissenting from Jansenius' view when he asserts that all voluntary actions are inspired by love, for then an action inspired by concupiscence can be voluntary, and again when he asserts that where there is indifference there is freedom, even though freedom does not require indifference.

One could say that this doctrine held by Jansenius does not imply that sinful man's freedom is entirely destroyed, since, in the divided sense, he retains the capacity to do good even when under psychological compulsion.[47] But this does not seem to satisfy his account of Augustine's conception of liberty. And Jansenius does state that necessity of coercion 'secundum quid atque moralis' (in a relative psychological sense) does destroy freedom in a relative psychological sense ('secundum quid etiam & moralem destruit

although he asserts that, under their influence we are still acting freely (*Essais de théodicée*, ed. J. Brunschwig (Paris 1969), §289 (p. 290)). Kant defines freedom as the 'independence of the will of coercion by sensuous impulses': *Critique of pure reason*, translated by J.M.D. Meiklejohn, with an introduction by A.D. Lindsay, Everyman's Library (London and New York 1934), p. 317. **45** Jansenius, *Augustinus*, ed. cit., vol. 2, *De statu naturæ lapsæ*, IV.21, p. 261. Cf. vol. 3, *De gratia Christi salvatoris*, VII.4, p. 313.   **46** Aquinas, *Summa theologiae*, I-II, q.6, a.6–7. See also Davies, *The thought of Thomas Aquinas*, pp 224–5.   **47** See Kremer, 'Grace and free will', pp 222–3.

libertatem').[48] Since Arnauld wished to rebut Habert's charge that Jansenius holds that freedom is destroyed in sinners, it is not surprising that he did not defend the view of psychological coercion that seems to lead to that conclusion.

It is beyond the scope of this article to examine Jansenius' conception of freedom in further detail, especially the problem of reconciling the view of psychological forces as coercive with the concept of double delectation, whereby the effect of grace is to provide a delectation that overmasters the delectation of sin. But enough has been said to suggest that Arnauld's presentation of the issue, which stresses the voluntary nature of sin, diverges somewhat from Jansenius' conception of freedom and the voluntary. And this corresponds to Arnauld's polemical design: to emphasize the compatibility of Jansenius' way of thinking with other traditions, especially that of Aquinas. Perhaps for this reason he does not lay particular stress here on the concept of double delectation: he is more concerned to show that although the Thomists do not speak of grace as delectation, they agree with Jansenius in rejecting the Molinist idea that its efficacity depends on human consent (*Seconde apologie*, p. 184). It is as if, despite the title of his work, Arnauld's concern is to defend not so much the author Jansenius as a current of thought that he represents.

If it is fair to say that in the *Seconde apologie* Arnauld seems to tone down the anti-scholasticism of his master in a quest for common ground with Thomism, it is striking to observe how his position develops over time.[49] For he came to realize that St Thomas' position, to which he had tried in the *Seconde apologie* to assimilate Jansenius', had evolved by the time he wrote the *Summa theologiæ*. Aquinas there upholds a conception of freedom as essentially involving alternatives: it is a 'potestas ad opposita'. Surprisingly, Arnauld found that he positively preferred this later position. 'Potestas ad opposita' seemed a better expression than 'indifference', because the latter term implies a psychological state of equilibrium, the former does not, and is compatible with the notion of an infallible determination to act in a particular way. As he explains to Bossuet:

> On offre des présens à un bon juge pour le corrompre; quoiqu'il se trouve absolument déterminé à ne les point accepter, il est certain néanmoins que c'est librement qu'il les refuse. On demeure d'accord de la chose; il ne s'agit que de l'expression. Ne semble-t-il pas, Monseigneur,

---

48 Jansenius, *Augustinus*, ed. cit., vol. 3, *De gratia Christi salvatoris*, VII.4, p. 313.   49 For this change of heart, see the editorial preface to volume 10 of the *Œuvres*, ed. cit., and also Letter DCCCCLXV to Bossuet, July 1693, in *Œuvres*, vol. 3, pp 661–4, as well as Kremer, 'Grace and free will', pp 223–39.

que ce seroit faire tort à la vertu de ce juge incorruptible, si pour marquer qu'il a fait cela librement, on disoit qu'il a été dans l'indifférence
d'accepter ou de refuser ces présens? Car cela pourroit marquer la disposition d'un homme médiocrement vertueux, qui auroit hésité s'il les
accepteroit ou s'il les refuseroit; mais on ne donne pas cette idée, quand
on dit seulement qu'il a eu le pouvoir d'accepter ou de refuser ces
présens; puisque l'on conçoit facilement, que, de deux choses opposées
qui dépendent de notre libre arbitre, quelque déterminé que l'on soit de
faire l'une, ou pourroit bien faire l'autre, si on le vouloit.[50]

There is a plain analogy with the example of the loyal subject: both show
how Arnauld's imagination still moves within the robe milieu from which
he came, with its ideal of service of the ruler by the disinterested application
of the law. In the earlier case, however, the stress was on the force of the inner
inclination: the subject's moral qualities made him incapable of treachery.
Here, although the judge is still 'absolument déterminé' to refuse the bribe,
the evaluation of his action requires us to acknowledge that he could accept
it if he wanted to. It is true that this perspective is not incompatible with
Arnauld and Jansenius' solution to the particular problem of the resistibility
of grace discussed above. What is significant is the decision to adopt Aquinas'
general model of freedom. How Arnauld does so, in the late treatise on liberty he refers to in this letter to Bossuet, there is no space to discuss here.[51]
What one can say is that the choice of model is essentially pragmatic, thus
where Aquinas and Augustine differ in terminology, though their views are
substantially at one, we can ask 'qui sont ceux qui en parlent mieux, & d'une
manière plus conforme aux idées que les hommes en ont communément'
(*Seconde apologie*, p. 619). In this case, Aquinas is preferred. Arnauld has come
a long way from Jansenius' uncompromising commitment to Augustine's
formulations. His eighteenth-century editors point out that he was criticized
for abandoning the views of Augustine, but they themselves hold that 'il
changeoit tout au plus de langage'.[52] What does emerge, I think, from his
various treatments of the issue of freedom is that, even when he set himself
to defend Jansenius, Arnauld was more concerned to uphold the general
truths that Jansenius sought to defend, and to build alliances with other
schools, than to vindicate Jansenius' system as a whole.

---

50 Arnauld, Letter DCCCCLXV to Bossuet, July 1693, in *Œuvres*, ed. cit.,vol. 3, pp 661–4.
51 Arnauld, *De la liberté de l'homme* in *Œuvres*, ed. cit., vol. 10, pp 614–24.   52 Preface to Arnauld's
Œuvres, ed. cit., vol. 10, p. xxxi.

Free will, determinism and providence: the ideological context of the *Histoires Tragiques* of Jean-Pierre Camus

MARK BANNISTER

The *histoires tragiques*, which reached the peak of their popularity with the output of François de Rosset and Jean-Pierre Camus between 1610 and 1630, have been the object of considerable study in recent years. Their lineage has been traced back to the French translations of Bandello by Boaistuau and Belleforest in the sixteenth century; the influence of the *canards*, popular pamphlets reporting on amazing or bloodcurdling incidents, has been measured; critical editions of *histoires tragiques*, unpublished since the late sixteenth or early seventeenth centuries, have been appearing. Their anomalous position between realist fiction and the reporting of actuality at a time when the pastoral and sentimental novels were taking fiction away from realism has led to their being viewed as a sub-genre in their own right. That in its turn has inevitably led to attempts to make the sub-genre as substantial and significant as possible by including in it large numbers of sometimes disparate works. S. Poli, for example, has listed no fewer than forty-five collections of tales published over more than a century between 1559 and 1666 which he describes as *histoires tragiques*.[1]

A further effect of the assumption that the *histoire tragique* is a sub-genre in its own right is the general desire to demonstrate that all the works bearing that label emerge from a uniform ideological base and share a common aim. Anne de Vaucher Gravili argues that all the *histoires* published by Rosset, Camus, Malingre and Parival between 1614 and 1656 rigorously illustrate the principle that any transgression of the moral law leads ineluctably to exemplary punishment.[2] Poli contends that one of the most important aims of the *histoire tragique* is to 'rétablir la cohérence d'un monde bouleversé, une cohérence selon laquelle toute infraction est punie, et toute punition reconstitue l'ordre troublé'. The aim of Camus in particular, he claims, is to reassure the reader by demonstrating the profound rationality of the reality that surrounds him.[3]

1 S. Poli, *Storia di storie: considerazioni sull'evoluzione della storia tragica in Francia dalla fine delle guerre civili alla morte di Luigi XIII* (Abano Terme 1985). 2 A. de Vaucher Gravili, *Loi et transgression: les histoires tragiques au XVIIe siècle* (Lecce 1982), pp 22–4. 3 S. Poli, *Histoire(s) tragique(s):*

There is much that is valuable and convincing in the analyses carried out by these scholars, especially when they show the concern of the authors to establish their own version of *vérité* as opposed to *vraisemblance*, thus positioning them in relation to one of the crucial debates of the seventeenth century. However, in literature, labels can obscure as many aspects of a topic as they illuminate, and the desire to produce an all-embracing definition of the *histoire tragique*, covering the output of a range of authors over a long period, has inevitably tended to distort a number of important features of the works in question. The tales written in the 1580s, such as those of Poissenot, which are concerned almost entirely with illustrating the effects of fortune on human affairs,[4] cannot be identified with those written forty years later when the major preoccupation was with questions of guilt, retribution and the cosmic order. The ideological contexts of each of the two periods differ radically from each other, and it is necessary to consider the factors at work in the 1620s when the literary form of the *histoire tragique* (as opposed to the *canard*) was at the height of its popularity.

Jean-Pierre Camus, bishop of Belley, had learned from his mentor, François de Sales, the importance of making Catholic doctrine accessible to the greatest number of the faithful, and undertook the writing of *histoires tragiques* as a means of achieving a wider dissemination of that doctrine than the pulpit alone could allow, having been impressed by the success of Rosset's *Histoires tragiques* (1614 and 1619). It goes without saying that he had a strong belief in a divinely ordained moral order, and he constructed the great majority of his tales in such a way as to stress that belief as fact, but it nonetheless becomes apparent in many of the stories he selected for inclusion in his collections that he was not absolutely sure what the terms of that order were or how it operated in the human sphere. A few of his tales recount the sort of sad accident, usually found in a *canard*, to which there is no moral dimension, for instance, the account of an incident in which a boat carrying a family is accidentally overturned by a passing barge, causing most of the family to be drowned.[5] In some of his tales he works hard to formulate a moral message which emerges only tortuously from the situation he

---

anthologie/typologie d'un genre littéraire (Fasano and Paris 1991), p. 30. Poli in fact categorizes the *histoire tragique* as an *histoire de loi* ('Autour de Rosset et de Camus', *Romanciers du XVIIe siècle, Littératures Classiques*, 15 (octobre 1991), 29–39 (p. 33); cf. D. Rieger, '"Histoire de loi" – "Histoire tragique": authenticité et structure de genre chez F. de Rosset', *XVIIe Siècle*, 184 (juillet-septembre 1994), 461–77.   **4** See B. Poissenot, *Nouvelles Histoires tragiques*, ed. J.-C. Arnould and R. A. Carr (Genève 1996), Prologue.   **5** J.-P. Camus, *Les Spectacles d'horreur* (Paris 1630), II, 22. All the examples I give are taken from the two books which comprise this text of which there is a modern reprint (Genève 1973). Equally valid examples can be found in two other works by Camus, *L'Amphitheatre sanglant* (Paris 1630) and *Les Rencontres funestes* (Paris 1644).

depicts. The chain of events, mostly fortuitous, that results when a peasant throws a stone at his son with whom he is angry, inadvertently killing him, and which leads to the deaths of the entire family, elicits no more of a moral than that, since the devil is constantly looking for opportunities to do mischief, we should treat children with moderation (*Les Spectacles d'horreur*, I, 2). The case of two boys who, having watched their father cutting a calf's throat, try the same thing with their baby brother, then, horrified by the blood, hide in the stove and are unwittingly burned to death by their mother, calls forth only the warning that we should be careful what we do in front of children because they have the capacity to bring evil out of what appear to be the most indifferent things (*Les Spectacles d'horreur*, I, 18).

Camus may well recognize a moral imperative which, in a sermon, would be presented as an absolute, but, in his *histoires tragiques*, he is prepared to accept gradations in his condemnation of those who transgress such a moral. Suicide, although a mortal sin and often assumed to be caused by demonic possession, is judged variously according to the motivation that provokes it. A girl who burns herself to death rather than give in to the lust of a soldier is presented as a case of heroic virtue, all the more praiseworthy for being found in someone of humble origin (*Les Spectacles d'horreur*, I, 19); a man who prefers to die fighting against impossible odds rather than take his chances on survival is certainly 'blasmable' but, because his despair is motivated by 'la ialousie de l'honneur', it may be called 'honorable', even though he has rejected the approved course of trusting in providence (*Les Spectacles d'horreur*, II, 4); however, a wife who starves herself to death because her husband has been killed must be condemned because virtue lies in avoiding excess, and she has died following 'la rage d'vn aueugle desespoir' rather than 'vne iuste affection raisonnable' (*Les Spectacles d'horreur*, I, 17).

Some of Camus' stories are, in effect, no more than historical *exempla* of the kind used in educational manuals, citing cases, for example, of kings being magnanimous and of captains dealing with treachery either with clemency or ruthlessness.[6] He also enjoys collecting striking incidents for their own sake. One of his tales consists entirely of two incidents showing the power of the imagination. During an intensely bad winter, a traveller rides across what he takes to be a large plain but, when he is told he has just crossed a deep lake, he falls into a fever and dies. A man riding on a donkey falls asleep and is carried across a ravine on a narrow plank. When shown where he has been, he collapses (*Les Spectacles d'horreur*, II, 5). These stories are not used, as they would have been by Pascal, to demonstrate the power

---

6 See, for example, *Les Spectacles d'horreur*, ed. cit., I, 4, 12; II, 17, 20.

of the *puissances trompeuses*: they are simply curiosities from the notebooks of Camus.

It is difficult to accept, therefore, that the *histoire tragique* necessarily presents a coherent vision of a moral order in which transgressions are clearly identifiable and every transgression receives its just punishment. Camus was not, of course, primarily concerned with writing moral treatises, despite the claims he makes.[7] Whether or not the *histoire tragique* counts as fiction, he treats his material in the same way as writers of fiction would. He gives his characters the kind of name found in novels, for example, Métrodore, Crisèle and Amphiloque. Unlike most writers of *canards*, he manipulates the events he is recounting to produce a rounded, more satisfying structure. In some places, he is clearly more interested in the pathos and tragedy of the situation than in the moral message. One story, for instance, recounts the tragedy of a young woman who, prevented by her father from marrying the man she loves, is drawn into a clandestine marriage with her brothers' tutor, and this leads to poverty, despair and suicide (*Les Spectacles d'horreur*, I, 23). It is evident that Camus is primarily concerned with the suffering endured by the characters but, in order to fulfil his moral mission, he is reduced to attaching to his tale various *passe-partout* truisms to which he frequently has recourse when there is no obviously clear conclusion to be drawn. For example, parents should not force their will upon their children; disordered passions will take control if allowed to do so; the devil is constantly looking for opportunities to do evil; and, of course, the moral that 'on ne cognoist bien les deffauts que quand ils sont commis, & les hommes ne voyent dans l'aduenir que des obscuritez & des incertitudes'.

If Camus, committed to affirming a divinely created moral order, does not in fact demonstrate a straightforward progression from transgression to punishment, it is necessary to look more closely at the terms of his depiction of the moral universe. The clue lies in the constant references to providence. The seventeenth century had inherited from the sixteenth century a confusing range of positions on the perennial uncertainty about the forces of free will and determinism in the human condition. It was not only that the Calvinists denied free will. The Paduan school of philosophy, following the direction set by Pomponazzi, had argued in favour of determinism in the natural world, with the fideistic escape-clause that the argument was valid in

---

7 Camus claimed on numerous occasions that he had been encouraged by François de Sales to write Catholic novels and histories in order to counter the corrupting influence of the romances of the day, and he continually stressed the moral purpose of his writing. See notably 'Dessert au lecteur' in *La Pieuse Jullie* (Paris 1623); 'Dilude' in *Petronille* (Lyon 1626); preface to *Les Euenemens singuliers* (Lyon 1628).

the philosophical sphere but not necessarily in the theological sphere. The council of Trent was curiously restrained about this key area. It issued a general anathema against those who denied the existence of free will in human affairs but it avoided involving itself in the more complex aspects of what was an essential prerequisite for any understanding of the question of grace. As a result, the dispute about the nature of grace which broke out in 1582 between the Dominicans and the Jesuits revealed a major fault in the foundations of the Counter-Reformation. Molina's treatise, *Concordia liberi arbitrii cum gratiae donis* (1589), in which he expounded the reconciliation of grace and free will, provided a target against which the Dominicans used all their weaponry. The dispute focused increasingly on the definition of physical predetermination or predisposition which the Dominicans claimed was the equivalent in the natural order of efficacious grace in the supernatural order, while the Jesuits argued that efficacious grace was necessarily united to the consent of the will. The Jesuits were accused of Pelagianism, the Dominicans of Lutheranism. After more than twenty years of acrimony, as much politically as theologically motivated, the debate was left unresolved when Pope Clement VIII died in 1605.

Of those who had made a major contribution to the debate in the 1580s, the Flemish Jesuit Lessius in particular continued to publish treatises in support of Molina's case, but it is noticeable that he turns increasingly to the concept of a providence which enfolds predestination and thereby guarantees its inclusiveness. Predestination is a part of providence, which furnishes the means by which human beings, through the exercise of their will, can achieve salvation: it corresponds to the call of grace and is consummated by man when he responds to that call.[8] Lessius developed this line of argument further in his treatise *De providentia* (1613), examining there the crucial questions of free will, determinism and grace in terms of the broader concept of providence, for the existence of which he adduces fifteen arguments. They include the classic arguments that it derives from cosmic order, from first causes and so on, but, in particular, providence is expressed as the daily experience of God's justice and concern for ordinary people. Nothing is otiose in the world: everything fulfils its own purpose. Humans have different talents, aptitudes and attitudes, but they are all complementary and enable society to function effectively. If God did not exist, there would be no providence and therefore no need to be moral: the highest wisdom would be to extinguish virtue.[9]

8 L. Lessius, *De praedestinatione et reprobatione angelorum et hominum disputatio* (Antwerp 1610), pp 245–8. **9** L. Lessius, *De providentia numinis et animi immortalitate libri duo adversus atheos et politicos* (Antwerp 1613), septima/duodecima ratio.

It is not surprising that such an approach engaged the interest of François de Sales, dedicated as he was to making the spiritual life accessible to those whose business did not allow them to withdraw from the world. In 1613 he wrote to Lessius, enthusiastically endorsing his views, and in his *Traité de l'amour de Dieu* (1616) included several chapters on the subject of providence. He expounds the classic optimistic doctrine, traceable back to Boethius, that the complexity of individual events visible to humans conceals the providential pattern behind them which will bring about ultimate good:

> Il y a des cas fortuits & des accidens inopinez: mais ils ne sont ny fortuits, ny inopinez qu'à nous, & sont sans doute tres-certains à la prouidence celeste, qui les preuoit & les destine au bien public de l'vniuers. Or ces cas fortuits se font par la concurrence de plusieurs causes, lesquelles n'ayant point de naturelle alliance les vnes aux autres produisent vne chacune son effet particulier en telle sorte neantmoins que de leur rencontre reüssit vn autre effect, d'autre nature, auquel, sans qu'on l'ait peu preuoir, toutes ces causes differentes ont contribué.[10]

This easily comprehensible doctrine corresponded to that set out in the various handbooks written to advise parish priests and confessors on the most effective ways of presenting the faith to their flock. One such book, for example, the *Hortus pastorum,* addressed the need to combat the passivity that such a doctrine might engender by stressing the role of free will working in conjunction with providence.[11] The spiritual adviser should ensure that the faithful veer neither to the right with the Protestants, who deny free will, nor to the left with the Pelagians, who credit the will with superhuman power: 'Nos vero viam regiam ingrediamur, & primariam quidem operationem Deo eiusque gratiae tribuamus, sed cooperationem & quidem liberam, voluntati adscribamus' (We however tread the royal road, attributing the primary operation of grace to God, but ascribing to our will its free cooperation with grace).[12]

The need to argue in favour of a specifically Catholic concept of providence was reinforced during what has been called the 'crisis of 1619–25' when, according to the self-appointed guardians of orthodoxy, a tide of *libertinisme* threatened to engulf France. Neo-Epicurean freethinkers argued that the only way in which providence could be said to operate was through

---

10 François de Sales, *Traicté de l'amour de Dieu* (Rouen 1626), p. 82. 11 J. Marchant, *Hortus pastorum et concionatorum sacrae doctrinae floribus Polymitus* (Paris 1638); see pp 37–40. 12 J. Marchant, *Candelabrum mysticum septem lucernis adornatum, sacramentorum ecclesiae doctrinam pastoribus, concionatoribus, sacerdotibus pernecessariam illustrans* (Mons 1630), pp 590–1.

the workings of nature. Others rejected free will on the grounds that an omniscient and omnipotent deity must know the ultimate fate, whether salvation or damnation, of each individual, thus rendering free will redundant. One of the key premises on which Vanini based his philosophical exploration of the universe was that God's providence consisted solely in having created necessary and unchanging laws in nature, thereby leaving no scope for divine intervention in human affairs. Everything depended on providence, certainly, but there was no question of miracles or of prayer persuading God to interfere with the inevitability of events dictated by natural laws.[13] The furious denunciations hurled by Garasse at the 'atheists' contained more indignation than argument, but his case ultimately had to rest on the need to accept the will of God in all things. Instead of blaming fortune or destiny,

> nous pouuons nous seruir auec toute humilité du nom de Dieu: disant, si nous auons quelque bon succez en nos affaires, que c'est par la grace de Dieu: Si nous n'auons pas l'issuë que nous desirons, que c'est par la permission de Dieu, qui a mille ressorts dans sa prouidence, qui peut auoir destourné le cours de nos affaires, pour exercer nostre patience, pour chastier nos offenses, pour se faire recognoistre maistre & souuerain de ses creatures, &c.[14]

It can be seen, then, that Camus began writing his *histoires tragiques* at a time when the Catholic Church needed to re-assert both the specificity of its doctrines (and especially that of the concept of providence), and also that acceptance of God's will to bring ultimate good out of the moral morass produced by human actions was the response required of the mass of the faithful. Camus had, in fact, made his own contribution to the debate in treatises on a number of occasions, though he was aware of the difficulties involved in reconciling free will and providence:

> Que Dieu cognoisse les choses futures d'vne preuoyance & d'vne Prescience certaine, il est indubitable. [. . .] sçachant les causes necessaires des choses futures, il en sçait par consequent les effets par vne voye indubitable. Mais la question est grande, de sçauoir comment se peuuent accorder ces deux choses, qui semblent de prime abord contraires: la Prescience infaillible de Dieu & le libre arbitre de l'homme. [. . .] le poinct decisif est, que ceste Prescience diuine est si libre qu'elle n'impose aucune necessité à l'euenement des choses futures. Ce qui se peut

---

13 G.-C. Vanini, *Amphitheatrum aeternae providentiae divino-magicum, christiano-physicum, nec non astrologo-catholicum* (Lyon 1615), pp 287–9. 14 F. Garasse, *La Doctrine curieuse des beaux esprits de ce temps, ou pretendus tels* (Paris 1623), p. 461.

assez clairement manifester par cet exemple; pour sçauoir qu'vn homme en va tuer vn autre, ou faire quelque meschant acte, il ne s'ensuit pas que sçachans son dessein, nous le contraignions pour cela de faire mal, il est de mesme en la prescience de Dieu, pour sçauoir que les peruers se damneront par leurs meschantes œuures, il ne laisse pas de les laisser en leur franc arbitre, & libre volonté.[15]

His non-theological writings always contained a strong moral and didactic element, though that element arguably did not necessarily overrule the desire to develop the more 'literary' aspects of the work. It is clear, however, that a great many of his *histoires tragiques* are framed in such a way that the events recounted and their outcome match the arguments commonly advanced to prove the existence of providence. In some cases that is easy enough. One of the standard proofs was the exemplary punishment visited in the Bible on those guilty of serious crimes such as blasphemy, sacrilege or perjury (the examples of Belshazzar and Nebuchadnezzar were commonly cited). Camus was keen to show through many examples that, in the modern world, Heaven was as active as ever, both in singling out those who blaspheme, indulge in witchcraft, or defile sacred places, and in visiting usually supernatural retribution on them.[16] Direct and spectacular divine intervention can equally well support the *ex miraculis* argument in favour of providence, as Camus shows in his story 'Les trois testes' in which the three calves' heads carried in a net by a murderer are seen by those around as the heads of his victims. The ways of God are incomprehensible but striking: 'Par combien de manieres & douces & fortes sçauez-vous atteindre à vostre but, & faire connoistre aux hommes qu'il n'y a point de prudence qui puisse parer aux decrets de vostre prouidence' (*Les Spectacles d'horreur*, I, 24; see also II, 16).

One of the central arguments in favour of providence was the fact that human beings have different faces and voices. If it were not so, according to Lessius, society would not be able to function and the world would be even more full of adultery, incest, fraud and other crimes than it is, since husbands would not be able to recognize their wives, parents their children, nor creditors their debtors and so on (*De providentia*, 109). Mersenne quotes the case of Martin Guerre as an example of the confusion and sin that arise when individuals cannot be clearly distinguished.[17] When Camus comes across a

15 J.-P. Camus, *Les Diuersitez* (Paris 1613), fols. 307 v°, 308 v°, 309 r°-v°. **16** See for example *Les Spectacles d'horreur*, ed. cit., I, 8, 11; II, 24. **17** M. Mersenne, *Quaestiones celeberrimae in Genesim* (Paris 1623), cols. 123–4.

story illustrating the importance of distinctive voices, he is keen to emphasize that providence is at work behind the structure of events. A case in point is 'Le Tesmoin aveugle' (*Les Spectacles d'horreur*, I, 6). This story relates how an Italian merchant is attacked and murdered by a servant, but during the assault a blind man who is passing by enquires about the cause of the cries and is told by the servant that the merchant is ill. We are told that the blind man is passing near the scene of the crime 'par permission de Dieu'; later on, 'par prouidence de Dieu', he happens to be in the inn where enquiries are being made; it is 'par inspiration divine' that the magistrate investigating the murder has a hunch that the servant is the assassin; finally, the servant, whose voice is recognized by the blind man and therefore incriminates him, dies a Christian death, demonstrating that 'l'œil de la iustice diuine est tousiours ouuert sur les crimes'.

The attempt to extract the same message from another tale, *La Funeste Ressemblance* (*Les Spectacles d'horreur*, I, 7), involving facial similarity this time, reveals how difficult it is to relate the theory of providence to the 'reality' depicted. In this story, Procle, a student at Leipzig, lives a riotous life, kills Sindulphe in a brawl and flees, not daring to return home to Grafenthal. He finds his way to Ulm from where Artème has eloped with Irèce. Her brothers see Procle in the street, think he is Artème, kill him and flee. Artème's parents get the law to condemn the brothers to death *in absentia*. Meanwhile, Artème and Irèce, short of money, are near Grafenthal and meet Procle's cousin, Maurice, who takes Artème for Procle. Realising the potential of the mistake, Artème pretends to be Procle and explains that he has not been home because he has married without permission. Maurice intercedes with Procle's parents who receive their supposed son and his bride with joy. Sindulphe's family, however, have been watching for Procle's return and Artème finds out his double has been killed in Ulm. When one of Irèce's brothers, Hans, turns up in Grafenthal, Artème offers not to denounce him as the killer of the real Procle in return for being forgiven for eloping with Irèce, and he suggests they all return to Ulm. Artème tells Procle's father he is going to visit Irèce's family. When Artème's parents see him again, they drop their case against Irèce's brothers and the murder is treated as that of an unknown stranger.

The story is explained as a triumph for providence both in sorting out the messy situation created when fortune gives two men the same face, physique and voice and in ensuring that justice ultimately prevails. The relationship between fortune and providence is complex. While in Grafenthal, Artème enjoys the 'visage riant de la fortune' for a time, but fortune grows tired of favouring him and 'luy excita vne tempeste dont se seruit la Prouidence pour le remettre au port heureux qu'il n'eut osé esperer', that is, he hears about his own 'murder' in Ulm and meets one of the murderers. The implication is that providence can deflect potentially disastrous situations away from those it protects, though in this case it must have done so by inspiring in Artème the stratagem he puts to Hans which saves him from human justice. The reader is left puzzled as to the nature of divine justice. By the end of the story, the murderer Procle has been killed but for the wrong reason, as the victim of another murder. Procle's parents are happy that their son is, as they think, still alive, but they are deceived. Artème, who has deceived them, is allowed to enjoy his married life with Irèce, and the brothers, who have committed murder, are not held to account for their crime. Clearly, if that is providence at work, it moves in mysterious ways. Camus can only conclude: 'Contentons-nous de contempler en la funeste Ressemblance de Procle à Artème vn traict de la main de la diuine Iustice.'

La Funeste Ressemblance demonstrates the fundamental problem experienced by Camus in trying to relate the events recounted in such a wide and diverse selection of stories to the concept of an all-embracing providential justice. He himself has to admit in many instances that he cannot see how divine justice is working through the tangled plot. He can only assure the reader that it is unfailingly active in all circumstances: 'qui est-ce qui cognoist le sens de Dieu, & qui peut penetrer les secrets de sa prouidence? [. . .] Qui n'admirera les ressorts de la diuine conduitte, & les moyens dont elle se sert pour rendre à vn chacun selon son œuure?' (*Les Spectacles d'horreur*, II, 8). However, in order to be convinced of this on the evidence presented by his tales, the reader would have to be prepared to accept a wide range of assumptions. Firstly, that divine justice may allow an innocent person to be wrongly accused and put to death because he or she was guilty of some undiscovered crime known only to God. Secondly, that the punishment for a crime may be visited upon the guilty person's descendants. Thirdly, that providence may use the violent and inhuman actions of one person in the grip of unbridled passions, actions which would certainly merit damnation, as the vehicle for retribution against another person led into sin by passion, that is, a case of sinful passion punishing sinful passion. Fourthly, that a man wrongly executed for a crime he did not commit may be receiving the punishment for a number of acts unacceptable to God but not considered unduly heinous by human law, such as wife-beating. Fifthly, that divine justice may be selective, punishing some but not all of the criminals or sinners involved in an incident. We are shown that providence sometimes intervenes at the very moment of a crime to bring instant retribution but that, alternatively, it may allow the course of events to become more and more convoluted, with the innocent suffering and possibly being put to death under human law, until finally it turns the situation back on itself to bring a kind of justice out of the mess.

We can conclude that Camus certainly predicated his collections of *histoires tragiques* on the existence of a divine providence and that, whenever possible, he was happy to use individual stories to illustrate the all-embracing security provided by the certainty of divine justice. However, he freely admitted that the workings of divine justice were inscrutable and, given the fallibility of human justice, especially as a result of the ease with which confessions could be extracted from innocent men under torture, he found it impossible to use his tales as a demonstration of the providential structure within the world. It is more accurate to say that his *histoires tragiques* are an investigation into the workings of the moral order carried out *a posteriori* through a consideration of the complexities of human behaviour. That investigation puts the *histoire tragique* firmly into the same camp as imaginative literature, and shows that it is more closely related to other forms of the novel or the *nouvelle* than is often claimed. Those for whom Camus was writing were the same readers who devoured *L'Astrée* for its investigation of the affective side of human nature and the chivalric romances for their depiction of the heroic potential in humankind.[18] In addition to the shock of horrific events peddled by the *canards*, they found in the *histoires tragiques* the same kinds of situation brought about by strong emotions, social constraints and fortune as those imagined by novelists or *nouvellistes*, albeit with a more theologically oriented approach. If Camus had been writing sermons or treatises, he would have selected his exemplary material carefully to illustrate the moral point he was making. As it is, his interest in the human and literary aspects of the stories he composes arguably equals and perhaps exceeds his commitment to the didactic effect.

18 François de Rosset, author of the most successful collection of *histoires tragiques*, was well aware of the tastes of contemporary readers and responded by both translating romances of chivalry and by compiling a collection of *lettres amoureuses et morales*.

Raillerie, honnêteté and 'les grands sujets': cultured conflict in seventeenth-century France

DAVID CULPIN

In 'Des ouvrages de l'esprit', La Bruyère wrote: 'un homme né chrétien et français est contraint dans la satire; les grands sujets lui sont défendus'.[1] His remark, if true, suggests that the *honnête homme* in his conversations and the *moraliste* in his writings must confine themselves to the relatively anodine domain of 'le cœur humain' and that they cannot engage with potentially controversial topics including religion and politics. Such a view reinforces the impression of intellectual conformity too often associated with the 'siè-cle de Louis le Grand'. La Bruyère's remark should not, however, be accepted uncritically, if only because his chosen form of discourse, like the *Maximes* of La Rochefoucauld, depends for its impact on an occasionally reductive over-simplification. Moreover, contemporary evidence also suggests a crucial link between *honnêteté* and *raillerie*, and extends to mockery a discreet but potentially conflictual role in the discussion of even 'les grands sujets'.

According to the first edition of the *Dictionnaire de l'Académie Française* (1694), the verbs describing mockery – *railler*, *moquer* and *plaisanter* – occupy overlapping semantic fields. Each deploys a variety of techniques to achieve its polemical goal, techniques which may include 'bons mots' and particu-larly satire. The seventeenth century, from Régnier to Boileau, is the century of satire, though the legitimacy of satire is more or less accepted depending on the sphere in which it is employed. What Molière, in the preface to *Les Précieuses ridicules* (1659), termed 'la satire honnête et permise' is relatively uncontentious when used by him or by Boileau for poking fun at literary rivals or contemporary social mores; but Pascal, in the eleventh of the *Lettres provinciales* (1656–7) feels called upon to defend its use in a serious, theolog-ical context. Racine is aware of the same constraint, and in the *Lettre aux deux apologistes de l'auteur des 'Hérésies imaginaires'* (1666) justifies the use of mockery by arguing that 'la raillerie est permise, que les Pères ont ri, que Dieu même a raillé'. However, if the literary use of satire is a familiar feature of seventeenth-century literature, little attention has been given to the close relationship which existed during that period between *raillerie* and *honnêteté*.[2]

---

1 J. de La Bruyère, 'Des ouvrages de l'esprit' 65, in *Les Caractères* (Paris 1st edition 1688; final edition 1694). 2 On the 'honnête homme', see the following: Emmanuel Bury, *Littérature et politesse:*

A number of seventeenth-century theoreticians of *honnêteté* consider the question of whether an *honnête homme*, whose behaviour is governed by good taste and *bienséance*, may permit himself to indulge in *raillerie*. Morvan de Bellegarde's *Réflexions sur ce qui peut plaire ou déplaire dans le commerce du monde* (1689) include a chapter entitled 'Les plaisanteries', which begins with the question: 'Un honnête homme, peut-il faire quelquefois le rôle de plaisant?' He concludes that 'La belle raillerie peut être permise à un honnête homme', and adds: 'C'est cette belle raillerie qu'un de nos bons auteurs appelle la fleur du bel esprit, et il n'est point d'honnête homme qui n'en puisse faire à ce prix-là, sans craindre de se déshonorer'.[3] François de Callières poses a similar question in *Des Bons Mots et des bons contes, de leur usage, de la raillerie des Anciens, de la raillerie et des railleurs de notre temps* (1692). He begins by asking whether Pascal, in the *Pensées*, was suggesting that 'bons mots' should be outlawed from civilized society when he said 'diseur de bons mots mauvais caractère'. Callières concludes by re-affirming his initial contention that 'les bons mots' are 'le sel de la conversation des honnêtes gens'. Later he adds an illustration which takes up the terminology of Bellegarde: Sarrasin, the poet, he says, excelled in 'cette fine raillerie que quelques modernes ont appelé "la fleur de l'esprit"'.[4]

But what exactly is 'la belle raillerie'? Méré recognized both the need for piquancy in polite conversation and also the need for constraints to be placed upon the astringency of an individual's remarks. As he put it in his *discours* 'De la conversation': 'La conversation veut être pure, libre, honnête, et le plus souvent enjouée, quand l'occasion et la bienséance la peuvent souffrir.'[5] If *raillerie* is not to transgress against 'l'occasion et la bienséance' there are three principal dangers about which the theoreticians of *honnêteté* are broadly in agreement. The first restriction concerns the tone of the remark: *raillerie* should not be hurtful to the person against whom it is directed. Callières' approval of mockery is limited to 'ces railleries ingénieuses qui ne

l'invention de l'honnête homme, 1580–1750 (Paris 1996); Louis van Delft *Le Moraliste classique: essai de définition et de typologie* (Genève 1982); Jean-Pierre Dens *L'Honnête homme et la critique du goût: esthétique et société au XVIIe siècle*, French Forum Monographs, 28 (Lexington, Kentucky *c*.1981); Maurice Magendie, *La Politesse mondaine et les théories de l'honnêteté en France au XVIIe siècle* (Genève 1970); Oscar Roth 'L'Honnête-Homme chez La Rochefoucauld', in Alain Montandon (ed.), *L'Honnête-homme et le dandy* (Tübingen 1993), pp 59–76; and Domna C. Stanton, *The aristocrat as art: a study of the 'honnête homme' and the dandy in seventeenth- and nineteenth-century French literature* (New York and Guildford 1980).   **3** J.B. Morvan de Bellegarde, *Réflexions sur ce qui peut plaire ou déplaire dans le commerce du monde* (Paris 1689), p. 227.   **4** François de Callières, *Des bons mots et des bons contes, de leur usage, de la raillerie des Anciens, de la raillerie et des railleurs de notre temps* (Amsterdam 1692), pp 5, 3, 261. The reference is to Pascal's *Pensées*, fragment 549 in Sellier's edition (Paris, Bordas 1991).   **5** Antoine de Gombaud, chevalier de Méré, 'De la conversation' in *Œuvres complètes*, ed. Charles-H. Boudhors, 3 vols (Paris 1930), vol. 2, p. 103.

laissent après elles aucun venin';[6] or, as Méré says of 'la vraie honnêteté', 'si elle raille quelquefois, sa gaieté ne tend qu'à donner de la joie à ceux même qu'elle met en jeu'.[7] The second restriction concerns the topic to be dealt with. Religion is not a suitable subject for *raillerie*. In the 'Avertissement' to his work, Callières says of 'bons mots': 'Il faut surtout qu'ils soient exempts de toute sorte d'impiété.' Bellegarde concurs, for he writes: 'Il faut bien se donner de garde de railler sur des choses saintes.'[8] More generally, any *licence* or remark of a morally dubious nature is to be avoided. And third, as with all jokes, timing is important: *raillerie* must be used with discretion since listeners quickly tire of 'bons mots' which are forced, misplaced or used with too great a frequency. As Méré put it: 'Il faut avoir l'esprit bien juste et le goût bien confirmé, pour en dire souvent qui fasse de bons effets.'[9] La Rochefoucauld was aware of the same danger, and he notes: 'Il est malaisé d'avoir un esprit de raillerie sans affecter d'être plaisant, ou sans aimer à se moquer; il faut une grande justesse pour railler longtemps sans tomber dans l'une ou l'autre de ces extrémites.'[10]

When *raillerie* conforms to these conditions it not only can but should go together with *honnêteté*. In his *Réflexions diverses*, La Rochefoucauld writes:

> La moquerie est une des plus agréables et des plus dangereuses qualités de l'esprit: elle plaît toujours, quand elle est délicate; mais on craint toujours aussi ceux qui s'en servent trop souvent. La moquerie peut néanmoins être permise, quand elle n'est mêlée d'aucune malignité et quand on y fait entrer les personnes mêmes dont on parle.[11]

Descartes is even more emphatic. He writes in his *Traité des passions de l'âme* (1649):

> Pour ce qui est de la raillerie modeste, qui reprend utilement les vices en les faisant paraître ridicules, sans toutefois qu'on en rie soi-même, ni qu'on témoigne aucune haine contre les personnes, elle n'est pas une passion, mais une qualité d'honnête homme, laquelle fait paraître la gaieté de son humeur, et la tranquillité de son âme, qui sont des marques de vertu; et souvent aussi l'adresse de son esprit, en ce qui sait donner une apparence agréable aux choses dont il se moque.[12]

---

6 Callières, *Des bons mots et des bons contes*, ed. cit., p. 7.   **7** Méré, *Œuvres complètes*, ed. cit., vol. 1, p. 76.   **8** Morvan de Bellegarde, *Réflexions sur ce qui peut plaire ou déplaire dans le commerce du monde*, p. 220.   **9** Méré, *Œuvres complètes*, ed. cit., vol. 2, p. 41.   **10** La Rochefoucauld, *Réflexions diverses*, XVI. 'De la différence des esprits', in *Maximes et Réflexions diverses*, ed. Jean Lafond (Paris 1976), p. 194.   **11** Ibid.   **12** Descartes, *Les Passions de l'âme*, Art. CLXXX. 'De l'usage de la raillerie', ed. Geneviève Rodis-Lewis (Paris 1970), p. 196.

Concrete examples of the relationship between *honnêteté* and *raillerie* can be found in Charles Perrault's *Les Hommes illustres qui ont paru en France pendant ce siècle*, which provides pen-portraits or *éloges* of one hundred famous Frenchmen who had lived and died during the century.[13] For the most part Perrault's biographies confine themselves to external matters: books published, battles won, honours received. On a number of occasions, however, Perrault defines individuals as 'honnêtes gens' in relation to the notion of *raillerie*. The maréchal de Gramont was, for example, 'un seigneur d'un mérite extraordinaire, honnête, généreux, bon ami, bien fait de sa personne autant qu'on le peut être, parlant agréablement, raillant de bonne grâce, et pourvu de toutes les qualités qui forment un véritable grand seigneur'.[14] Similarly, according to Perrault, 'il entrait dans les écrits de Voiture, soit en prose soit en vers une certaine naïveté et une sorte de plaisanterie d'honnête homme, qui n'avaient pas d'exemple [. . .] jamais le grave et le sérieux n'ont été tempérés par une raillerie plus délicate et plus ingénieuse'.[15]

These examples illustrate the function of *raillerie* in its spoken form, as used by 'honnêtes gens', a function summed up in the phrase 'plaire et instruire'. Mockery is, in the first place, intended to bring pleasure. Méré says with respect to 'la conversation enjouée' that 'celui qui parle, s'il veut faire en sorte qu'on l'aime, et qu'on le trouve de bonne compagnie, ne doit guère songer, du moins autant que cela dépend de lui, qu'à rendre heureux ceux qui l'écoutent'. This is why *raillerie* is potentially so dangerous, because 'on ne saurait plaire de bon air quand on choque des personnes qui ne l'ont pas mérité'.[16] Mockery may, however, also have a more instructive purpose. Callières says: 'Il y a d'autres espèce [*sic*] de bons mots qui consistent en des reproches piquants et plaisants contre ceux qui ne font pas leur devoir.' This gives to *raillerie* a dimension that goes beyond the realm of 'le cœur humain' to the social or political, for these *bons mots* 'servent en diverses occasions importantes à redresser les malhonnêtes gens et les ridicules, et à corriger l'injustice et l'orgueil des hommes puissants qui abusent de leur pouvoir'.[17]

But if such mockery is to achieve its ends there must also be a readiness on the part of those who are the subject of mockery to *entendre raillerie*. According to the first edition of the *Dictionnaire de l'Académie française* (1694), 'On dit, qu'un homme entend la raillerie, pour dire, qu'il a la facilité, l'art, le talent de bien railler; et, qu'il entend raillerie, pour dire, qu'il ne

---

13 Charles Perrault, *Les Hommes illustres qui ont paru en France pendant ce siècle*, 2 vols (Paris 1696–1700). A critical edition of this work by D.J. Culpin is forthcoming (Gunter Narr/Biblio 17, Tübingen, 2002). Perrault also knew Callières, and in 1698 dedicated to him a poem entitled 'A M. de Callières sur la négociation de la paix'. **14** Ibid., vol. 2, pp 29–30. **15** Ibid., vol. 1, p. 73. **16** Méré, *Œuvres complètes*, ed. cit., vol. 2, pp 103, 114. **17** Callières, *Des bons mots et des bons contes*, ed. cit., p. 8.

s'offense point de ce qu'on lui dit en raillant.'[18] The second half of this observation is as important as the first; it is underscored by La Rochefoucauld
who also points out the need to *entendre raillerie*:

> Il y a une sorte de politesse qui est nécessaire dans le commerce des hon-
> nêtes gens; elle leur fait entendre raillerie, et elle les empêche d'être
> choqués et de choquer les autres par de certaines façons de parler trop
> sèches et trop dures, qui échappent souvent sans y penser, quand on sou-
> tient son opinion avec chaleur.[19]

Morvan de Bellegarde expands on this point in his *Réflexions sur le ridicule et
sur les moyens de l'éviter* (1696) when he observes that 'Les personnes d'esprit,
et qui entendent raillerie, se mettent du côté des rieurs, et donnent quelque
chose à l'intention de celui qui parle'. He argues that this accommodating
attitude is essential because

> Il y a de certaines rencontres, où il faut avoir de la complaisance, et
> entendre raillerie, à moins que de passer pour bizarre et pour ridicule.
> Ce n'est pas savoir vivre, ni même entendre ses intérêts, que de se fâcher
> pour des choses que l'on dit légèrement, et sans intention d'offenser per-
> sonne.[20]

Callières makes a similar remark in respect of 'ces railleries ingénieuses [. . .]
qui chatouillent pour ainsi dire plutôt qu'elles ne blessent ceux sur qui elles
sont exercées, et dont ils peuvent et doivent se réjouir les premiers, lorsqu'ils
savent vivre, et qu'ils savent ce qu'on appelle entendre raillerie'.[21]

But what if the individual who is the subject of mockery is unable to
entendre raillerie? The *Menagiana* (1693) provides one illustration of the consequences of such an instance: 'M. le Fèvre', we read, 'n'entendait point raillerie sur ses opinions, et il eut une aigre dispute avec M. Gallois en 1666'.[22]
One explanation of the difficulty encountered in making successful use of
mockery is put forward by Callières. He explains that 'bons mots' flourished
in republican Greece of antiquity in a way that is impossible under a monarchy 'où les divers degrés qu'on y a établis entre les hommes empêchent souvent les inférieurs de dire ce qu'ils pensent de plaisant sur ce qu'il y a de
ridicule en ceux qui se trouvent au-dessus d'eux'.[23] In particular we cannot
be sure that 'les grands' will take a benign view of *raillerie* at their expense.

---

18 *Dictionnaire de l'Académie française* (1694), Art: *Raillerie*.   **19** La Rochefoucauld, *Réflexions
diverses*, II. 'De la société', in *Maximes et réflexions diverses*, ed. cit., p. 165.   **20** J.B. Morvan de
Bellegarde, *Réflexions sur le ridicule et sur les moyens de l'éviter* (La Haye 1729), pp 70, 206.   **21** Callières,
Des bons mots et des bons contes, ed. cit., pp 7–8.   **22** Gilles Ménage, *Menagiana, ou bons mots,
rencontres agréables, pensées judicieuses, et observations curieuses* (Amsterdam 1693), p. 194.   **23** Callières,
Des bons mots et des bons contes, ed. cit., pp 112–13.

The Spanish moralist, Gracián, makes this point in his *Oráculo manual*, translated by Amelot de la Houssaie under the title l'*Art de la prudence* and published in 1684. We read: 'Quand le lion est mort, les lièvres ne craignent pas de l'insulter. Les braves gens n'entendent pas raillerie.'[24] Perrault himself notes the importance of seizing the right moment if the message of the *railleur* is to be well received. This is illustrated in his *Mémoires de ma vie*, which contain an anecdote about Louis XIV. The King, he says, 'jouait à la paulme à Versailles, et, après avoir fini sa partie, se faisait frotter au milieu de ses officiers et de ses courtisans, lorsque M. Rose [. . .] le vit en bonne humeur et disposé à entendre raillerie'. Monsieur Rose wished to rectify an anomaly which allowed magistrates to harangue the king on the occasion of his military victories, but did not extend this privilege (as it appropriately might) to members of the Académie française. The petitioner therefore expounds a witty paradox:

> Sire, on ne peut disconvenir que Votre Majesté ne soit un très grand prince, très bon, très puissant et très sage, et que toutes choses ne soient très bien réglées dans tout son royaume; cependant j'y vois régner un désordre horrible, dont je ne puis m'empêcher d'avertir Votre Majesté.[25]

The ploy succeeds, and the king accedes to Monsieur Rose's petition, a petition that has been cleverly introduced by this *raillerie*.

La Bruyère's view that 'les grands sujets [. . .] sont défendus' has become the conventional wisdom in respect of the years that fall under the personal rule of Louis XIV. But it is a view that was challenged in La Bruyère's own lifetime by Pierre Bayle in his *Dictionnaire historique et critique* of 1697. In the article devoted to the historian David Blondel we read:

> Une infinité de gens s'imaginent que personne n'ose dire en France ce qu'il pense: cependant, on le dit et on l'écrit fort librement. D'où est-ce que nos nouvellistes apprendraient tout ce qu'ils débitent concernant la France, si on n'écrivait ses pensées avec la dernière franchise?[26]

And he concludes: 'On s'entretient encore plus franchement de ces choses, qu'on ne les écrit.' It is the very nature of *honnêteté* that ensured the intellectual freedom of the *entretiens* to which Bayle alludes. *Railler* and *entendre raillerie* are indispensable elements of the discourse on *honnêteté* practised 'viva voce' in the salons; and although *raillerie* is widely held to be incompatible with religious topics, theoreticians of *honnêteté* leave open the

---

24 Baltasar Gracián, *L'Art de la prudence*, translated by Amelot de la Houssaie (Paris 1994), par. 54.
25 Charles Perrault, *Mémoires de ma vie*, ed. Paul Bonnefon (Paris 1909); reprinted with an essay by Antoine Picon (Paris 1993), p. 198.   26 Pierre Bayle, *Dictionnaire historique et critique* (1697).

possibility that by means of mockery some change may be effected in political and social issues. All those who are 'honnêtes gens' (including 'les grands' and the sovereign himself) should, at least on a good day, be able to *entendre raillerie* and not censure those who call them to account.

Mutations judiciaires dans la seconde moitié du XVIIe siècle

PASCALE FEUILLÉE-KENDALL

Le siècle de Louis XIV fut incontestablement pour la France un siècle de grandeur, et jamais la nation française n'avait sans doute bénéficié d'un tel prestige. Jamais l'œuvre politique n'avait été plus étendue et la civilisation française si admirée. Pourtant il demeure des contradictions en particulier dans la seconde moitié du siècle, période de pénurie monétaire, entre un contexte économique devenu difficile et la magnificence du 'grand siècle', entre une période de goût, de raffinement et une permanence de la révolte et du crime qu'accompagne une répression organisée et impitoyable. Cette époque se caractérise en effet par le musellement, l'émasculation des parlements au lendemain des Frondes, puis par une volonté réformatrice de la monarchie qui procède à un énorme travail de codification sous le contrôle de Colbert. Le jurisconsulte Loyseau évoque, en effet, s'agissant du système judiciaire, un 'grand fleuve' qui 'de chute en chute traîne les plaideurs dans un gouffre où peu ont le bonheur de ne pas être engloutis'.[1] Naît de ce dessein de 'travailler à la justice du royaume' une série d'ordonnances, véritables codes aux qualités 'formelles' indéniables, mais à l'efficacité discutable sur le fond et destinées à vaincre un désordre fonctionnel qui régnera jusqu'à la Révolution. On retiendra surtout que l'ordonnance criminelle de 1670 constitue un modèle de cruauté et de longévité, et ne mérite pas l'indulgence qu'ont suggéré souvent les historiens prêts à la 'réhabiliter'. La torture continuera en effet à se pratiquer jusqu'à son abolition en 1788, et très certainement au-delà jusqu'à la première moitié du XIXe siècle. La violence qui, certes, habite et menace la société ne saurait justifier que la réponse judiciaire fut non pas simplement sévère, mais tyrannique : la pratique pénale contemporaine continue à s'inspirer de ces méthodes d'Ancien Régime, ce qui place par certains aspects la France à la remorque de ses voisins européens.

---

[1] Cité par J.-P. Royer, *Histoire de la justice en France* (Paris 1995), p. 25.

LES ANNÉES DE TROUBLES

Mazarin meurt le 8 mars 1661, 'dignement' et en bon chrétien, dit-on, en prononçant le mot de Jésus, et Louis XIV se trouve dans une position de 'rompre le cordon' avec un mentor efficace quand il l'a fallu, mais certes devenu pesant et incontournable. Homme de confiance de Richelieu, il avait achevé son œuvre. Pendant la Fronde, il eut à affronter à la fois le Parlement de Paris, la population parisienne, les Grands se sentant à l'écart des décisions du gouvernement et les armées rentrant d'Allemagne où venait de cesser la guerre de Trente ans.[2] Il y parvint et régna en maître incontesté après les quatre années de désordre. Ces insurrections, démarrées en 1648 lors d'un conflit insignifiant transformé en crise institutionnelle – une brimade de Mazarin contre le grand conseil de la Chambre de comptes et de la Chambre des aides au sujet de la vénalité des charges – visaient l'autorité du gouvernement, et le roi s'était réfugié à Rueil avec son entourage.[3] Le parlement règne alors en maître devant une population réjouie: c'est la Fronde de 1649. Cependant, rapidement débordés, les parlementaires chercheront appui auprès des princes de sang et de la haute noblesse, ces derniers 'alliés' n'ayant guère à l'esprit l'idée du bien commun. Utilisant habilement les rivalités entre les Grands pour les opposer les uns aux autres face à une bourgeoisie lassée du désordre et un peuple versatile, Mazarin contribue à discréditer ce qui peut encore limiter l'autorité royale, et ainsi le peuple met en elle tous ses espoirs. Ces années de trouble, engendrant la misère à Paris et en province, montrent l'inaptitude à gouverner de la haute noblesse et des parlementaires, parmi lesquels certains s'avèrent 'bornés', d'autres intrigants, ou intéressés avant tout par l'argent.[4]

N'allons pas croire cependant que se sont achevés avec Mazarin les 'troubles' ou rébellions populaires, et l'historien B. Porchnev montre que des révoltes ne cessent de se succéder au cours du XVIIe siècle.[5] Certes, on constate une absence de conscience de classe dans les milieux pauvres de l'époque, mais en revanche on peut souligner une réalité inhérente au grand siècle: les soulèvements populaires appartiennent à une longue tradition du désespoir, la spontanéité faisant de ces révoltes le témoin de la misère ambiante.[6] Aux révoltes endémiques de 1663–5, à la grande insurrection bretonne de 1673–5, suivis des mouvements de 1690, s'opposera une maxime, enseigne du siècle, celle de l'Ordre, car 'le désordre règne partout'. Ces

---

2 Voir P. Gaxotte, *Histoire des Français* (Paris 1951), pp 135–49.   **3** Voir Royer, *Histoire de la justice en France*, p. 29.   **4** Voir *Histoire des élites en France*, ed. Guy Caussinant-Nogaret (Paris 1991), pp 163–8.   **5** B. Porchnev, *Les Soulèvements populaires en France de 1623 à 1648* (Paris 1963), pp 473–92.   **6** Royer, *Histoire de la justice en France*, pp 31–3.

désordres, survenant à tous les échelons de la société, que ce fût chez la bourgeoisie ou la noblesse, ou bien au sein de ce 'quatrième état' que constitue le peuple, expliquent sans doute le travail de 'remise en ordre' et l'organisation de la répression.

LA MISE AUX PAS DES PARLEMENTAIRES

Ces assemblées, les parlements, disposent d'un pouvoir judiciaire ou policier mais aussi administratif et législatif. Ils constituent d'un côté une juridiction d'appel des juridictions inférieures royales, ecclésiastiques ou féodales, avec un recours en cassation devant le roi (lequel renvoie à une juridiction et ne juge pas sur le fond, comme c'est le cas aujourd'hui). D'autre part, les parlements rendent des arrêts qui s'imposent à tous, sauf opposition du roi. Enfin, ces assemblées enregistrent les décisions royales sur lesquelles le roi prend d'éventuelles ordonnances, c'est-à-dire nos actuels amendements. Dès 1661, cette 'année exemplaire', comme le souligne Jean-Pierre Royer,[7] le roi compte lui-même dans ses mémoires dix-sept mesures d'autorité, mesures concernant des gens de justice: les magistrats de la Cour des aides, pour certains inoccupés et insoumis, sont exilés, décision constituant le début d'une véritable entreprise royale destinée à briser la résistance au pouvoir. Deux ans plus tard, en effet, Colbert rédige une instruction pour les maîtres de requêtes, commissaires répartis dans les provinces, texte aux conséquences importantes s'agissant du passage de la monarchie judiciaire à une monarchie administrative.[8] Le texte de 1663 aboutit à la rencontre 'sur le terrain' entre une nouvelle génération de 'parvenus' ou de gens sur le point de l'être, ambitieux et sans fortune, constituant une fonction publique toute neuve, et la génération des magistrats installés, conscients de leurs privilèges. Selon les termes de cette 'déconcentration' avant la lettre, les nouveaux arrivés, intendants ou commissaires, dont la fortune dépend de la bonne volonté du roi, sont envoyés en mission pour l'exécution d'ordres, et non pour fronder contre le pouvoir.[9] Ils ont vocation à devenir le lien indispensable entre autorité et peuple.

En 1665, Louis XIV poursuit son œuvre autoritaire en instituant le lit de justice roi non présent, mesure vexatoire pour les gens de robe.[10] Royer

---

7 Ibid. **8** Sur la mutation de l'État de justice en un État de finances voir B. Kriegel, *Les Chemins de l'État* (Paris 1986). **9** Définition contemporaine de la déconcentration en droit public: elle consiste à donner compétence pour prendre certaines décisions à des organes qui exercent leurs fonctions dans une circonscription déterminée et qui demeurent soumis à l'autorité hiérarchique des autorités centrales. Source: G. Dupuis et M.-J. Guédon, *Institutions administratives* (Paris 1988), p. 158. **10** Voir Royer, *Histoire de la justice en France*, pp 31–2.

rapporte qu'en 1668, lors d'une représentation des plaideurs de Racine, la cour s'étonne des éclats de rires ostensibles du monarque. Cette satire impitoyable envers les gens de justice est sans doute appréciée par un roi désireux de réduire à néant les prétentions des juges à partager l'exercice du pouvoir.[11] Puis, en s'attaquant à leurs traditionnelles prérogatives, il achève de les assujettir. En 1673, en effet, les remontrances préalables à l'enregistrement sont supprimées. Les cours ne pourront qu'après enregistrement rédiger des remontrances, ce qui rend ces dernières inefficaces. Louis XIV, le 'monocrate', est allé ici jusqu'à la limite du point de rupture.[12]

Né en 1638, roi en 1643 et devenu majeur en 1651, le roi Louis est un personnage auquel bien des historiens se sont intéressés. Des constantes ressortent des portraits qu'on lui consacre, qu'il s'agisse de Saint-Simon, Gaxotte ou Leroy-Ladurie. Il reçoit une éducation plus pratique et politique que livresque et intellectuelle, rudimentaire, mais non négligée. On lui attribue un certain sens de la dissimulation. Son appétit de vivre et de jouir (plaisirs, intrigues, ballets et chasses) est légendaire, et on le dit emprunt d'une tenace rancune, car il n'oublie ni défaillances ni trahisons. On note une certaine indifférence dans sa sérénité impassible d'homme vieillissant, accompagnée d'une certaine robustesse. Tout à la fois 'honnête homme' et chef d'état, opiniâtre au travail, il possède incontestablement le sens du bien commun, celui de l'ordre et de la justice qu'accompagne une connaissance de la nature humaine et le respect des talents. Au moment où il établit son mécénat royal, permettant aux lettres de s'épanouir,[13] et que se jouent *Les Précieuses ridicules*, le *Don Juan* ou le *Tartuffe*, s'est mise au travail une commission d'experts qui a entrepris une vaste réformation de la justice.

L'ŒUVRE DE CODIFICATION

L''entrée' du roi se fait en 1661, année de la mort de Mazarin. Le lendemain, Louis réunit son conseil, et il y est question de 'progrès' consistant en une simplification des lois. Colbert aurait voulu remplacer les anciennes ordonnances par un corps entier et parfait;[14] il forma donc une commission que le roi présida de nombreuses fois. Louis soumit les projets de codification au premier président du Parlement de Paris, Lamoignon, qui les présenta à un comité de magistrats. Chacun reconnut que le projet était téméraire et sérieux, mais à la réalisation difficile. En 1665, Louis XIV prend la décision,

11 Ibid. **12** H. Metivier, *L'Ancien Régime en France* (Paris 1981), pp 16–18. **13** Voir Gaxotte, *Histoire des Français*, p. 146. **14** Voir M. Boulanger, 'Justice et absolutisme: la grande ordonnance de 1670', *Revue d'Histoire Moderne et Contemporaine*, 47, no. 1 (2000), 8–11.

sans consulter ni les Etats généraux tombés quasiment en disgrâce, ni les parlementaires, de réunir les meilleurs auteurs de mémoires sous le contrôle de Pussort et Lamoignon. Le critère qui domine semble être celui de la polyvalence de ces juristes qui devront être très 'recommandables', qualités nécessaires communes à la magistrature.[15] Conseillers d'État ou maîtres des requêtes, avocats sélectionnés *ad hoc*, ceux-ci se lancent ainsi dans une grande œuvre de codification. Bonaparte n'agira pas autrement pour la rédaction du code civil (le comité de travail émanant de la souveraineté du prince, qui ne sera plus indivisible, productrice du Législatif ainsi que de l'Exécutif et du Judiciaire). Lamoignon, célébré par tous pour ses qualités en tous genres, tentera d'apporter modifications et observations au travail de Pussort. Ce dernier, oncle de Colbert, a un ascendant sur Lamoignon tel qu'il dédaignera, par exemple, les tentatives d'humanisation des ordonnances.

Le premier mémoire constitue l'ordonnance civile de 1667. Bien composée, elle apparaît très claire et simplifie la procédure civile. Les historiens, historiens du droit ou philosophes, sont à peu près du même avis s'agissant de la codification elle-même : Royer semble dire que l'ordonnance civile édicte les règles servant de base à notre code civil, le code Portalis, soulignant une plus grande célérité des procédures.[16] Blandine Kriegel, notant comme Royer les succès très inégaux ce ces codifications, évoque aussi l'incontestable succès des réformations en procédure civile. Selon Kriegel, si le désir de destruction manifesté par la monarchie à l'égard des traditions susceptibles de l'assujettir a pu être assouvi, une volonté d'innovation juridique doit être soulignée. Le travail à cette unité juridique et de réformation a consisté dans un premier temps à rédiger – on constate le passage de l'écrit à l'oral – puis à codifier, et de ce point de vue on ne peut que se féliciter du travail effectué.[17]

La codification des ordonnances est ainsi désignée car ces dernières possèdent un ensemble de réglementations complètes et détaillées de telle ou telle branche du droit. En 1669, l'ordonnance portant règlement sur les eaux et forêts, inspirant plus tard la loi de 1827, est à l'origine de la politique administrative forestière et contemporaine. Puis en 1673 est édictée une ordonnance de commerce ou code Savary; elle servira au code de commerce de 1807. Vient également l'ordonnance de marine de 1681, complétée par l'ordonnance des armées navales et du code noir, véritable législation de la marine, à l'origine du code de 1807. Kriegel souligne que cette codification aurait la particularité de constituer une première tentative réussie de

---

15 Ce critère de 'respectabilité' semble l'emporter parfois sur celui de 'compétence,' et Boulanger souligne dans son article sur l'ordonnance de 1670 l'inégalité profonde des aptitudes des juristes. **16** Royer, *Histoire de la justice en France*, pp 33–4.   **17** Kriegel, *Les Chemins de l'État*, pp 116–18.

rédaction de 'codes à la française', un code consistant en une compilation de lois, un recueil de droit.[18] Si au plan de la forme on ne peut que s'incliner devant une telle œuvre, sur le fond et dans les principes il en va autrement. L'ordonnance pénale (criminelle), rattachée théoriquement à l'ordonnance civile de 1667, posera des problèmes aux rédacteurs, puis sera vigoureusement dénoncée par les auteurs des Lumières, en particulier Beccaria et Voltaire.

LA 'GRANDE' ORDONNANCE CRIMINELLE DE 1670

A la fois dans son *Journal* et ses *Mémoires*, Louis XIV s'attribue la gloire et l'idée première de l'ordonnance de 1670. Dès 1661, Pussort travaillait déjà à l'élaboration du projet et le communiqua au roi en 1664, lui faisant croire habilement, comme c'était l'usage, que l'idée venait du monarque. Royer considère que ce texte constitue certes une tentative de classement organisé de règles, mais qui n'ont pas laissé d'embarrasser les juges et les praticiens.[19] Par ailleurs, l'ordonnance sera sévèrement condamnée comme étant un véritable modèle de cruauté et de longévité. Ses vingt-huit titres, subdivisés en articles, en font un code méthodique et complet d'instruction criminelle. Ses règles rigoureuses révèlent le souci de punir immanquablement plutôt que de craindre de frapper un innocent. Consistant en l'ensemble des règles qui gouvernent la recherche, la poursuite et le jugement des délinquants, elle se présente comme la riposte aux difficultés économiques et sociales, au désordre permanent auquel Louis XIV semble vouloir apporter une réponse radicale. Et nouveau 'Justinien',[20] il souhaite une grande ordonnance à la hauteur de ses vœux. Les historiens du droit auraient aujourd'hui tendance à adopter une certaine 'modération' à l'égard de l'ordonnance de 1670 qui a même bénéficié d'une tentative de réhabilitation par des auteurs du XIXe.[21] Cette pondération se justifie difficilement aujourd'hui lorsque l'on observe que la période contemporaine subit encore les conséquences de la grande ordonnance: tous les caractères de notre système actuel y sont réunis en effet. Comme aujourd'hui, la procédure se faisait contre l'inculpé, et non pas à la suite de débats au cours desquels aucune décision 'coercitive' ou privative à l'excès de liberté ne serait prise sans qu'il y ait assez de preuves pour rendre une opinion.[22] La question est en permanence d'actualité en France, dans

---

18 Signalons que le terme de codification proprement-dit n'apparaît qu'au XIXe siècle.   19 Voir Royer, *Histoire de la justice en France*, pp 35–7.   20 Expression empruntée à Boulanger, 'Justice et absolutisme', 7.   21 Voir par exemple Adhémar Esmein, *Histoire de la procédure criminelle* (Amsterdam 1882).   22 Voir Casamayor, nom de plume pour Serges Fuster, *Les Juges* (Paris 1957),

l'histoire récente de la Vème République en particulier, au cours de laquelle, de façon récurrente, les réformes dans ce domaine échouent les unes après les autres, le poids de l'histoire semblant paralyser les réformateurs.[23] Autrement-dit, cette grande ordonnance, qui certes avait comme vocation de lutter contre la violence face à l'expansion impressionnante de la criminalité et de la rébellion qu'a stigmatisé la Fronde, porte en elle-même la responsabilité d'un système se posant délibérément contre l'accusé ou l'inculpé. Comme le dit Casamayor, la balance judiciaire n'a jamais tenu son fléau à l'horizontal.[24] Tout est si incliné depuis le départ de la procédure, (que l'on appelle aujourd'hui la phase préliminaire du procès), que pour tenter de rétablir l'équilibre on désigne un juge, le lieutenant criminel, qui interroge, réinterroge, confronte l'accusé. Ce juge, à l'origine, est en même temps procureur, ne l'oublions-pas. Il est aussi l'ancêtre du juge d'instruction, magistrat devenu aujourd'hui conscient de ses pouvoirs destructeurs depuis la véritable révolution culturelle des juges à partir de 1968. Ce personnage si controversé, si redouté et en même temps adulé, s'attaque désormais avec acharnement aux 'forts', lui qui s'en est longtemps pris aux 'faibles'. Pour agir comme le 'gardien des promesses',[25] il porte une triple 'casquette', semblable à son ancêtre: celle d'officier de police judiciaire, menant l'enquête et ordonnant des perquisitions; celle de procureur, lors de la mise en examen, (longtemps nommée l'inculpation), c'est-à-dire celui qui détermine l'existence d'indices graves et concordants de culpabilité; celle de juge, qui ordonne la détention ou prononce un non-lieu. Ce dernier devient à chacune de ses interventions à la fois juge et partie, les droits de la défense étant de ce fait inégalement garantis. Son rôle en somme est tel que l'on n'imagine plus pouvoir se passer de lui: 'Ce sont donc des réticences, des appréhensions, la peur du vide qui nous rendent un peu hostiles à l'idée de la suppression du juge d'instruction.'[26] Le défenseur, l'avocat, éprouve à juste titre le sentiment que lors de son intervention au stade de l'instruction, l'affaire est déjà 'ficelée' par la police dans le cadre de la garde à vue, et qu'au moment du jugement tout est déjà joué.

Par ailleurs le système inquisitoire est maintenu dans l'ordonnance de 1670 tel qu'il existait, conformément au texte de 1498. Ensuite, l'ordonnance de Villers-Cotterêt en 1539 est demeurée la référence majeure jusqu'à celle de 1670 qui entérine, renforce l'état du droit criminel précédent. Il était en

p. 11. **23** Voir mon article, 'La Réforme de la justice: velléité, ou réalité?', *French Politics and Society*, 16, no. 3 (1998), 30–7. A mon avis, l'histoire pèse incontestablement sur la procédure pénale: peur du vide ou peur de la perte des acquis constituent une leitmotiv 'justifiant' l'échec d'une réforme sans cesse repoussée. **24** Casamayor, *Les Juges*, p. 11. **25** Expression empruntée au titre de l'ouvrage d'Antoine Garapon, *Le Gardien des promesses* (Paris 1996). **26** Propos d'un juge rapporté dans *Procè pénal et droits de l'homme*, ed. Mireille Delmas-Marty (Paris 1992), p. 182.

effet impossible à l'accusé d'avoir accès aux pièces de la procédure, de connaître l'identité des dénonciateurs, de savoir le sens des dépositions avant de récuser les témoins, ou de faire valoir des faits justificatifs. A l'inverse, le magistrat avait des droits exorbitants, comme celui de recevoir des dénonciations anonymes, cacher à l'accusé la nature de la cause, ou l'interroger de façon captieuse en utilisant des insinuations, le 'prêcher le faux pour savoir le vrai', principes policiers d'aujourd'hui. Il incarnait à lui seul cet énorme pouvoir consistant à investir l'accusé. Une 'vérité' était ainsi reçue ensuite par les juges à la phase de procès, sous formes de pièces et rapports écrits. Ils ne rencontraient l'accusé qu'une fois. La situation a-t-elle tellement changé? S'agissant des relations entre magistrats et avocats, Rémi Lenoir, professeur a Paris I, enquête au Barreau de Paris : 'Ce qui est mis en avant par tous, c'est leur position inférieure face aux juges, la nécessité de s'en remettre à leur bon vouloir, de demander des faveurs pour obtenir ce qui leur permettrait d'assurer leur travail [. . .]. Au stade de l'instruction, le sentiment général est celui de l'impuissance alors que le pouvoir des juges d'instruction leur paraît exorbitant.'[27]

Cette procédure avait pour origine, pense-t-on, la peur du désordre, de la violence et des impétuosités contre les parties et les juges. Pourtant, déjà des voix s'étaient élevées par des contemporains contre l'ordonnance de 1539, préjudiciable à l'innocent tels les grands légistes Jean Constantin, Charles Dumoulin ou Pierre Ayrault.[28] Constantin s'élevait contre l'exclusion des avocats et indiquait de quels faibles moyens disposait la défense. Les observations de Dumoulin ont traversé les siècles, et Ayrault enfin démontra l'évidence des dangers de la procédure criminelle en France : 'On ne fait de la justice, comme des saints et sacrés mystères, qui ne se communiquent qu'au prêtre [. . .] Il est facile à huis-clos, d'ajouter ou de diminuer, de faire brigues ou impressions. L'audience est au contraire la bride des passions, c'est le fléau des mauvais juges.'[29] Ayrault a dépeint avec âpreté le juge d'instruction et la faiblesse de la défense, discours qui nous est au XXIe siècle terriblement familier. Et il faudra tout de même attendre 1897 pour que soit introduit un avocat pendant la phase d'instruction. *Pendant* mais pas *dès* le début de l'instruction, car en l'an 2003, on dénie toujours la véritable présence de l'avocat pendant la garde à vue au pays des droits de l'homme. Elisabeth Guigou, l'actuelle garde des sceaux, n'a réussi à imposer le défenseur que comme un 'assistant social' auprès du gardé à vue, sans possibilité d'accès au dossier, le ministère de l'Intérieur, les syndicats de police et de magistrats ayant usé d'énormes pressions sur elle. Les avocats ont eux-mêmes une part de responsabilité dans ce processus qui marginalise la

---

27 Ibid.   28 Voir Esmein, *Histoire de la procédure criminelle*, p. 160.   29 Ibid.

France, étant peu préparés à intervenir dans l'urgence, à la façon des médecins, comme c'est plus souvent le cas dans les pays anglo-américains.

Ces habitudes ancestrales, ce poids de l'histoire depuis Louis XIV, comme le souligne le praticien Daniel Soulez-Larivière (il est avocat à la Cour d'appel de Paris et auteur de nombreux ouvrages sur la justice), expliqueraient cette si grande difficulté à toucher à des pratiques qui se fondent dans la nuit des temps, régissant les rapports des hommes à l'univers de la faute, du crime et de la peine.

LE MAINTIEN DE L'USAGE DE LA TORTURE

Un des défauts majeurs de l'ordonnance de 1670 – peut-être le principal d'entre eux d'ailleurs – demeure indiscutablement le maintien de l'usage de la 'question', mot employé pour torture, ou encore 'tourments', alors que l'occasion était offerte au Législateur de l'époque (qu'incarnent Pussort, Lamoignon et leur 'comité de rédaction') de s'en débarrasser. Le supplice, quant à lui, a une fonction juridico-politique, comme un cérémonial pour reconstituer une souveraineté blessée.[30] Rendant indissociables l'exécution elle-même et ce qui la précède, on torture avant et après le prononcé de la sentence. 'Le cycle est bouclé: de la question à l'exécution, le corps a produit et reproduit la vérité du crime.'[31] Jusqu'au XVIIIe siècle, le supplice ne joue encore pas le rôle de réparation morale, mais a plutôt le sens d'une cérémonie politique, le délit étant un défi au souverain. Ce supplice public qui dure avait le but de reconstruire cette souveraineté. Dans le but initial d'arracher l'aveu, on soumettait donc le patient à la question. On distingue entre 'question préparatoire' et 'question préalable', la deuxième étant réservée aux condamnés à mort, pour obtenir la révélation de leurs complices. Puis il existe la 'question ordinaire' et la 'question extraordinaire', la dernière consistant en une aggravation et une augmentation de la durée du tourment. Les magistrats ne sont pas tendres, et le XVIIIe siècle semble encore plus cruel que le siècle précédent : dans certaines grandes villes, il est de coutume que l'on chausse les pieds du patient d'escarpins ou de brodequins, sans doute en cuir et soufrés, que l'on approche du feu. L'on procède trois fois à cette opération strictement réglementée. Or au XVIIIe siècle, on brûle cinq puis neuf fois le patient. Puis le condamné a droit à une mort chrétienne, assisté par des prêtres.[32] L'ordonnance de 1670 retardait l'exécution de quelques heures, puis, corde au cou, pieds nus et parfois sur une claie, le condamné

---

30 Voir M. Foucault, *Surveiller et punir* (Paris 1975), p. 45.   **31** Ibid., p. 59.   **32** Signalons qu'au siècle des Lumières, on ne note quasiment plus la présence des religieux du côté du supplicié.

était conduit sur le lieu d'exécution. Parfois, il faisait amende honorable, et une torche de cire ardente en mains, il se repentait s'il le voulait devant la porte d'une église. Lorsqu'il s'agissait d'un gentilhomme, ce qui était rare, on lui tranchait la tête avec une épée à deux mains; quant aux roturiers, ils étaient pendus jusqu'à l'étranglement. Ou bien on brisait bras, jambes, cuisses et avant la mise sur une roue. Puis le corps était jeté dans le feu et réduit en cendres jetées au vent. Ou encore, on pouvait être brûlé vif, comme ce fut le cas pour La Voisin.

Tous les peuples de l'Antiquité ont connu la torture à l'exception des Juifs.[33] La cité grecque a admis et pratiqué la torture politique et Pierre Ayrault observe que la question se donnait en public. Le mot grec pour torture, $\beta\alpha\sigma\alpha\nu\sigma\varsigma$, qu'il convient de rapprocher de $\beta\alpha\sigma\alpha\nu\iota\zeta\epsilon\iota\nu$ (torturer) signifie à l'origine, d'après les données de la philologie, 'examiner à fond, vérifier, éprouver.' Repose ici clairement l'idée selon laquelle la torture est au fond une épreuve de véracité, et que cette épreuve devant aboutir à l'aveu est une pratique se perdant ainsi dans la nuit des temps. L'Église fut à l'origine de la procédure pénale française, depuis qu'en 1229 Grégoire IX créa l'Inquisition pour lutter contre l'hérésie cathare.[34] La procédure d'instruction était directement inspirée de la procédure romaine réservée aux esclaves. Incluant la torture en 1252, l'Inquisition prévoyait ce tête-à-tête entre le moine et son patient, devenu le lieutenant criminel avec son suspect. On dit que l'empereur Auguste prétendait déjà que les tourments constituaient des moyens efficaces à rechercher la vérité. Cicéron ajoute que des paroles de ceux qu'on tourmente par le fer, le feu ou par toutes fortes douleurs, semble sortir la vérité même.[35]

Il est généralement admis qu'au XVIIe siècle la torture est approuvée par tous. Certes, les parlementaires, transformés en conservatoire rétrograde, soutiennent et appliquent de façon barbare et dans leur majorité le texte. Mais la réalité est plus mitigée dans une société ayant au plus haut degré le sens du goût, et la torture est en réalité depuis longtemps objet de critique. Un contemporain de Louis XIV, Nicolas, bien que se disant respectueux des lois, n'admet pas un système qui ne se fonde que sur des aveux obtenus dans la souffrance intense du supplice qu'on inflige au suspect. 'Ce n'est pas la douleur du corps humain qui pousse un criminel à la confession de son crime, mais la contrition et les douleurs de l'âme. [. . .] Tout y est contraint: tout est sujet à l'exception de la crainte, ennemi juré de la liberté, de l'ingénuité, de la vérité.'[36] Son étude consiste en une lettre qu'il adresse à Louis XIV. Dans sa préface, il invite le monarque de France à 'extirper de

---

33 Voir A. Mellor, *La Torture* (Paris 1949).   34 Voir D. Soulez Larivière, *Les Juges dans la balance* (Paris 1987), pp 44–5.   35 Ibid.   36 A. Nicolas, *La Torture* (Amsterdam 1681), p. 101.

son royaume par son pouvoir absolu et d'inviter par un exemple aussi noble que le sien les autres princes chrétiens à corriger dans leurs états tant d'injustes moyens de venir à la connaissance et au châtiment des crimes.'[37]

Dans les lettres de Madame de Sevigné, lorsqu'il est question du passage à la question de la Brinvilliers ou de l'exécution de La Voisin dans l'affaire des poisons, l'auteur ne semble pas particulièrement favorable aux méthodes de son époque. Elle est certes choquée par les blasphèmes ou l'absence de repentir de La Voisin, mais rapporte, amère, les propos d'un magistrat présent au procès vantant la douceur 'd'une peine infligée à cette femme condamnée au bûcher qui a bénéficié des faveurs du bourreau.'[38] Ce dernier lui arrachera généreusement la tête avec des crocs de fer, tandis que ses propres enfants, à son service, jetteront des bûches sur la suppliciée. 'Comment vous portez-vous de ce petit conte? Il m'a fait grincer des dents,' écrit la marquise à sa chère fille, Madame de Grignan.[39] Chez les philosophes, Beccaria et Voltaire sont les plus virulents : 'Qui ne frissonne d'horreur en voyant dans l'histoire tant de tourments affreux et inutiles?'[40] S'agissant de Lamoignon et Pussort, il ressort de différentes études qu'ils furent sur le point de procéder à l'abolition de la torture. Mais en désaccord sur biens des aspects de l'ordonnance, ils opérèrent lâchement en choisissant la sévérité. Une phrase de Pussort confirme ce 'conservatisme juridique' : 'Il n'y a rien de si contraire à l'ordonnance que l'indulgence.'[41]

L'ENFERMEMENT OU LE 'RENFERMEMENT'

A la torture physique s'ajoute un nouveau type de tourment utilisé au XXIe siècle en France à la fois comme peine mais aussi comme moyen de pression au stade de l'enquête préliminaire: il s'agit de la prison. Alors qu'au moyen-âge n'existait que le passage du cachot à la potence ou à la liberté, on commence à emprisonner au XVIIe siècle. Michel Foucault, dont la lecture a éclairé une nouvelle génération de magistrats depuis le début des années soixante, et induit chez eux de nouvelles attitudes, relève que l'enfermement coïncide avec la naissance du capitalisme. Selon ses chiffres, 6000 personnes sont détenues en permanence à Paris sur 300,000 habitants. C'est le début de l'enfermement de masse; s'entassent ainsi les vagabonds, les gens sans travail et sans domicile fixe. Selon Foucault, il s'agit donc d'accepter un emploi,

---

37 Ibid.   **38** Madame de Sévigné, *Lettres*, ed. B. Raffalli (Paris 1976), p. 261.   **39** Ibid.   **40** Cesare Beccaria, marchese di, 1738–94. *Dei delitti e delle pene. Traité des délits et des peines* / Traduit de l'italien. Neuchatel: [s.n.], 1797. HV8661.B28 1797.   **41** Cité par Boulanger, 'Justice et absolutisme', 29–30.

même mal payé, pour échapper au cachot. Ainsi, les salariés les plus modestes sont 'matés', stabilisés par la menace de l'enfermement, et les agitateurs ainsi éliminables, et cela grâce à une police aux pouvoirs quasi-judiciaires : 'Le procureur, qui naît autour du XIIe siècle en Europe, devient le représentant du souverain lésé par tort.'[42]

Un nouveau type de contrôle des individus par leur marginalisation, consistant en cet enfermement, devient une méthode qui se généralise. Dans *L'Histoire de la folie*, Foucault mentionne la création de l'Hôpital Général à Paris en 1656, qui n'est pas un établissement médical mais une structure juridico-administrative, une instance 'alternative' en somme qui décide, juge et exécute indépendamment des juges.[43] Les directeurs se voient donc octroyer des carcans, prisons et basse-fosses. En 1676, un édit du roi prescrit qu'il y aura un hôpital par ville de son royaume et l'Église prend une part active au projet. En 1662, 6000 personnes y sont déjà enfermées dont la masse indistincte comprend la population sans ressources, sans attaches sociales, la population délaissée. Et en 1657, Vincent de Paul approuve cette décision de 'ramasser tous les pauvres en des lieux propres pour les instruire, les entretenir et les occuper'.[44]

S'il faut attendre le milieu du XIXe siècle pour que s'efface la punition physique, en excluant du châtiment 'la mise en scène' de la souffrance, cela ne veut pas dire que des punitions 'plus discrètes dans l'art de faire souffrir, jeu de douleurs plus subtiles, plus feutrées et dépouillées de leur faste visible' n'aient pas immédiatement pris le relais.[45] L'enfermement par la méthode de la prison préventive au moment où, en France, on dénonce tous azimuts la condition des prisonniers, est une façon de punir le suspect en amont sous des prétextes divers parmi lesquels la nécessité de l'aveu. Ce dernier n'a du reste guère le droit à la parole que celle de s'expliquer pour prouver son innocence et d'apporter des éléments susceptibles d'entraîner sa propre condamnation (le droit 'de se taire' n'existant pas *stricto sensu*). La France tient de surcroît le triste monopole de la durée de la détention provisoire en Europe, sanctionnée régulièrement par la Cour européenne des droits de l'homme. Or pour saisir la Cour, il faut que toutes les voies de recours internes soient épuisées. Si un homme subit un traitement inhumain en détention, il devra attendre au moins cinq ans avant que l'État français ne soit sanctionné. La dernière condamnation marquante de la France remonte à 1999, et il s'agit d'une condamnation précisément pour torture, terrible humiliation depuis la période de la guerre d'Algérie. Que la France soit

---

42 M. Foucault, *Dits et écrits* (Paris 1994), p. 398. **43** M. Foucault, *Histoire de la folie* (Paris 1961), p. 47. **44** Saint Vincent de Paul, *Correspondance*, ed. Pierre Costa, 7 vols (Paris 1920–2), vol. 6, p. 245. **45** Foucault, *Surveiller et punir*, p. 21.

condamnée par la Cour européenne de Strasbourg n'est pas nouveau: depuis 1981, elle l'a été dans une soixantaine d'occasions. Mais s'agissant de la qualification de la torture, c'est la première fois, et elle devient le seul état (avec la Turquie) parmi les pays qui composent le Conseil de l'Europe à avoir subi une condamnation aussi infamante.[46]

CONCLUSION

Pour conclure, il existe de remarquables constantes et une certaine continuité dans l'histoire de la justice française. S'agissant de procédure 'consensuelle', civile ou commerciale, on observe aujourd'hui, tout comme hier, peu de difficultés insurmontables. En revanche, les principes régissant toute mesure légale privative de liberté doivent s'apprécier avec une attention très particulière, et la procédure pénale est ainsi devenue la bête noire pour les uns et une arme fatale pour autres. Les juges, en effet, ont retrouvé désormais une dignité perdue, et ne veulent en aucun cas céder les prérogatives que leur offrent leurs codes traditionnels. De plus, la justice française est envahie par des corporations hostiles, porteuses de haines ancestrales, et où personne ne veut céder. La France reste à cet égard l'un des seuls pays démocratiques à être affecté par le poids d'une histoire qui rend difficilement comprehensible la distinction entre les fonctions de juges et procureurs. De plus, la montée en puissance des magistrats a eu pour conséquence de médiatiser à l'extrême les acteurs judiciaires, devenus peut-être les seuls derniers vrais révolutionnaires.

---

46 Le 29 juillet 1999, la France est condamnée à l'unanimité pour torture par la Cour européenne des droits de l'homme. Ahmed Selmouni avait porté plainte fin 1992 contre cinq policiers pour de graves sévices subis lors de sa garde à vue en novembre 1991. La cour française avait condamné les fonctionnaires à des peines avec sursis. La France doit aujourd'hui verser 500 000 francs pour dommages matériels et moraux au requérant, qui purge actuellement une peine de treize ans de prison pour traffic de drogue à Montmédy (Meuse). Certes, Ahmed Selmouni n'a pas été soumis à la question; en revanche, on lui a, semble-t-il, enfoncé une petite matraque dans l'anus. L'homme a été frappé, les policiers lui ont uriné dessus, puis menacé avec un chalumeau, pensant qu'ils venaient (ce fut leurs termes) de procéder à un 'interrogatoire musclé.'

III. THE THEATRE IN CONFLICT

On humour and wit in Molière's *Le Misanthrope* and Congreve's *The Way of the World*

ANDREW CALDER

Both Molière's *Le Misanthrope* and Congreve's *The Way of the World* are variations on the Greek Golden Age and Roman genre of New Comedy.[1] Both, too, have a strong, if fairly broad, satirical thrust: they are evocations of worlds overtaken by folly and vice in the satirical and humanist tradition of Sebastian Brant, Erasmus, Rabelais and Ben Jonson. The two plays focus particularly on the *beau monde* and its hypocrisies. There are many parallels to be drawn between them. Célimène, in *Le Misanthrope*, presides over a salon which feasts on gossip, while, in *The Way of the World*, Congreve's Lady Wishfort and friends take it in turns three times a week to hold 'cabal nights', 'where they come together like the coroner's inquest, to sit upon the murdered reputations of the week'.[2] Mirabell's eulogy of the irresistible Millamant could apply equally well to Molière's Célimène: 'Her faults are so natural, or so artful, that they become her; and those affectations which in another woman would be odious serve but to make her more agreeable.'[3] Mirabell has more than a touch of Alceste's melancholic and jealous misanthropy: the latter is in a constant rage because he cannot have the company of Célimène to himself, while Mirabell begins the play in a black mood because, the evening before, Millamant had sent him away from a gathering at which the fools Witwoud and Petulant were invited to stay. In both plays, Arsinoé and Lady Wishfort, ageing and vengeful coquettes, full of dishonest schemes, play key roles. The comic pairing of Witwoud and Petulant echoes Molière's pair of *marquis*, Acaste and Clitandre, empty-headed fops always on hand to flatter and fawn. And yet the two plays are strikingly different.

Part of the difference lies in the two playwrights' uses of humour and wit. Both of these terms and concepts were very much more current in the English tradition than in the French. In his essay 'Of poetry' (1690), Sir William Temple wrote that the English stage surpassed all others, ancient and modern, in its portrayal of humour,

1 Molière's *Le Misanthrope* was first performed in Paris in 1666, while *The Way of the World*, Congreve's last play, was first staged in 1700. Line references to *Le Misanthrope* can be followed in any good edition; page references to *The Way of the World* are to *The comedies of William Congreve*, ed. Eric S. Rump (London 1985). 2 *The Way of the World*, p. 325. 3 Ibid., p. 328.

a word peculiar to our language too, and hard to be expressed in any other; nor is it, that I know of, found in any foreign writers, unless it be Molière, and yet his itself has too much of the farce to pass for the same with ours.[4]

The term 'humour', in the English sense of looking upon quirky or 'humorous' behaviour through a perspective of smiling irony or laughter, did not appear in France until the eighteenth century, where it arrived as an anglicism and has continued to have associations with *l'humour anglais* ever since. Even in England, however, humour had taken on this meaning only gradually over the 150 years or so before Congreve. In contrast, wit and the French equivalent *esprit* had both been long in common usage; in both languages, however, the terms described more often than not sound judgment rather than a sparkling facility with words. For example, the Chevalier de Méré, the chief exponent of the code of *honnêteté* in seventeenth-century France, wrote an entire 'Discours de l'esprit' (1677) using the term strictly in the sense of good, well-founded judgment.[5] Wit in its more modern sense of 'brilliant or sparkling conversation' was held in low esteem by the French, who tended to associate it with the laboured art of placing 'bons mots'. In England, in contrast, true wit by Congreve's time was usually associated with polished and amusing speech: according to Dryden, writing in 1677, 'the definition of wit (which has been so often attempted and ever unsuccessfully by many poets) is only this: that it is a propriety of thoughts and words; or, in other terms, thoughts and words elegantly adapted to the subject'.[6] Certainly, verbal wit was prized by English playwrights: Shakespeare had set the tone, and a whole generation of late seventeenth-century writers of comedies, especially Wycherley, Etherege and Congreve, wrote dialogue which coruscates with wit.

If Molière could not have known the term 'humour' in the English sense, he certainly knew the phenomenon it describes. We have seen that William Temple named Molière as the only non-English dramatist to make good use of humour. John Dennis coupled his name with that of England's

---

4 In J.E. Spingarn (ed.), *Critical essays of the seventeenth century*, 3 vols (Oxford 1908), vol. 3, pp 73–109 (p. 103).   **5** Chevalier de Méré, *Œuvres complètes*, ed. Charles-H. Bouhours, 3 vols (Paris 1930), vol. 2, pp 55–95.   **6** See *The critical opinions of John Dryden*, ed. John M. Alden (Nashville, Tennessee 1963), p. 279. Definitions of wit and humour do not stop with Jonson and Dryden. Gerald Wester Chapman, in *Literary criticism in England, 1660–1800* (New York 1966), gathers together eleven discourses on wit and humour (pp. 151–205), but notes that he could have easily gathered fifty or more between 1650 and 1800. Chapman notes that the discussion of wit and its meanings 'focused historic controversies of faith, ethics, tradition, class, and the value of language itself. The position one took on wit mattered' (p. 151).

leading master of the comedy of humour, Ben Jonson.[7] Indeed it has often been observed that Jonson's definition of humour fits Molière's comic vision admirably: Jonson applied the term 'by metaphor' to the 'general disposition' of the whole of humankind:

> As when some one particular quality
> Doth so possess a man, that it doth draw
> All his affects, his spirits, and his powers,
> In their confluxions, all to one way,
> This may be truly said to be a humour.
> (*Every Man out of his Humour*)[8]

In this respect, Alceste, Molière's misanthropist, described as *L'Atrabilaire amoureux* in an earlier title to the play, is a perfect example of humour, dominated as he is by the black bile of choler and melancholy which have invaded his emotions, his understanding and his very reason.

Dennis associated humorous comedy with the portrayal of the ridiculous; he praised Jonson and Molière because 'the very ground and foundation' of their comedies was the ridiculous.[9] Dennis, after Quintilian, equated the domain of humour and the ridiculous with that of *êthos*, the natural territory of the comic writer; according to Quintilian, *pathos*, the moving of the higher emotions and passions, was the domain of tragedy, while *êthos*, which included all the petty flaws and quirks of human nature, was the domain of comedy.[10] Dennis believed that Jonson and Molière were superior comic poets precisely because they preferred humour and the ridiculous to wit. He gives three reasons for the supremacy of humour. Firstly, portraying humour requires observation and judgment, while wit is the work of fancy and, if a talent for wit is rare, a true judgment is still rarer. Secondly, humour in a character necessarily gives rise to action, whereas wit, which comments on life from the outside, does not. And thirdly, humour distinguishes between characters, while wit tends to make them all sound the same. It was regarded as one of the great strengths of 'humorous' characterization that, just as no two human temperaments could ever be identical, neither could two 'humorous' characters on stage. In short, for Dennis, the humorous dramatic

---

7 See especially Dennis' parallel between Jonson and Molière, whom he presents as the two most accomplished comic poets among the ancients and the moderns in 'A defence of "Sir Fopling Flutter", a comedy written by Sir George Etheridge' (1722), collected in *The critical works of John Dennis*, ed. E.N. Hooker, 2 vols (Baltimore MD 1939, 1943), vol. 2, pp 241–50, esp. pp 249–50. **8** See *Ben Jonson*, ed. C.H. Herford and Perry Simpson, 11 vols (Oxford 1925–52), vol. 3 (1927), pp 405–604 (p. 432). **9** John Dennis, *The critical works*, vol. 2, p. 249. **10** Quintilian, *Institutio oratoria*, VI, II, 8–20.

poet shows human folly in action, while the witty poet merely comments upon it.[11]

Dennis' analysis fits *Le Misanthrope* rather well. Molière's play is composed of a set of characters with distinctive temperaments and outlooks, each of which is designed to contribute to the comic exploration of the follies of misanthropy and failed sociability. The action which results from their encounter is universal in its significance, easily measuring up to the Aristotelian ideal of turning particular experience into poetic (and timeless) truth. Characters pass through a sequence of situations and dialogues which coalesce into a piece of sustained and ordered dialectic. The process gives to Molière's comedy the unity and inevitability of tragedy. Such a process, however, involves sacrifice. Molière's characters cannot escape from their functions in the action of the play, and must obey the Aristotelian imperative of remaining consistent with themselves. Alceste's ill-judged misanthropy, like a tragic flaw, undermines his happiness and makes him unfit for friendship, for love and for the society of people in general. Worse still, it blinds him to himself and leaves him incapable of either understanding or controlling his own behaviour. The seductive Célimène, too, is trapped: she can do nothing but make fools of the men who congregate around her, deploy a quick and destructive wit, make enemies of other women, and end the play friendless and compromised. Even Acaste and Clitandre, the lavishly dressed braying *marquis*, are destined to do nothing but bray, comb their wigs, gesture extravagantly, laugh a lot in order to show their teeth, and swing violently, according to their changing company, between excessive flattery and vicious back-biting. Characters in Molière's comic world are no more likely to change their spots than the proverbial leopard. In short, Molière's composition belongs to the world of wit in the older sense of judgment and understanding. He constructs a working model of human society, and gives his characters just enough of a particular temperament to make them believable and acceptable, persuading us as spectators to accept the fiction that they are every bit as unique and real as we are, while in fact turning them into universal mechanisms, designed to demonstrate the wide range of flaws which, he believes, would tend to destroy human relationships in any epoch and context.

Given such a comic structure, one should hardly be surprised to find that Molière's play harnesses much of ancient and humanist wisdom on the topic

---

11 Dennis expounds his views on wit and humour particularly in 'A Large Account of the Taste in Poetry, and the Causes of the Degeneracy of it' (1702), in *The critical works*, ed. cit., vol. 1, pp 279–95, esp. pp 281–3.

of misanthropy. Alceste's is the age-old folly of attempting to put the world to rights, of seeking to stop the farce. As Erasmus' wise Folly says,

> If anyone tries to take the masks off the actors when they're playing a scene on the stage and show their true natural faces to the audience, he'll certainly spoil the whole play and deserve to be stoned and thrown out of the theatre for a maniac.[12]

'Nothing', Folly reminds us in the same passage, 'is so foolish as mistimed wisdom' (p. 105), and Alceste's is utterly mistimed. As Célimène points out, Alceste's excessive moralism is making him into a laughing-stock; in what I suspect is the most significant action in the portrait scene (Act II. iv), everyone laughs at Alceste while he, unable to laugh at himself, turns on them all in rage and asserts that mankind always deserves bilious hatred (ll. 681–90). At this point, Molière makes use of Éliante to demonstrate the failures in judgment of both Célimène and Alceste: she shows through her Lucretian diatribe on the behaviour of lovers that it is possible to mock the ways of humanity in general without descending to damaging gossip about individuals, and that a generous lover will normally view his mistress' faults as strengths.[13] Her smiling satire has many advantages: it is honest, it avoids malice, and it keeps the social wheels turning. In *Le Misanthrope*, Molière is taking a recognizable Democritean view of the world. In the tradition of Montaigne, Rabelais, Erasmus, Lucian, Horace and, ultimately, Socrates, he is drawing attention to a view of the world according to which to laugh at the human condition (like Democritus) is more rational than to weep at it (like Heraclitus and Timon the misanthropist). Montaigne writes in 'De Democritus et Heraclitus' (I, 50),

> J'ayme mieux la premiere humeur [that of Democritus], non par ce qu'il est plus plaisant de rire que de pleurer, mais parce qu'elle est plus desdaigneuse, et qu'elle nous condamne plus que l'autre: et il me semble que nous ne pouvons jamais estre assez mesprisez selon nostre merite.[14]

Alceste is a self-lover who displays what Montaigne describes as the two classic symptoms of the condition of philautia: he has too high an opinion of himself and too low an opinion of everyone else.[15] He is the worst kind

---

12 See *Praise of folly*, translated by Betty Radice, introduction and notes by A.H.T. Levi (London 1971), p. 104. **13** Éliante's speech occurs in lines 711–30. For a discussion of the sources and implications of this speech, see Ruth Calder, 'Molière, misanthropy and forbearance: Éliante's "Lucretian" diatribe', *French Studies*, 50, no. 2 (1996), 138–43. **14** Montaigne, *Essais*, ed. P. Villey and V.-L. Saulnier, 2 vols (Paris 1965), vol. 1, p. 303. **15** 'Il y a deux parties en cette gloire: sçavoir est, de s'estimer trop, et n'estimer pas assez autruy' (II, 17, 'De la praesumption', *Essais*, ed. cit., vol. 1, p. 633).

of satirist who chastises the whole world and excepts only himself. He has not learned that those who cannot laugh at themselves both forfeit the right to mock others and invite others to laugh at them. He is ignorant of the pragmatic truth that those who wrap themselves up in their own morose cogitations are an easy prey to this world's rogues. So it is that Alceste loses 20,000 pounds because he refuses to put up a proper defence against a well-known villain who has taken him to court (ll. 1547–50). *Le Misanthrope* is, among other things, a profound study of that almost universal phenomenon – anger at the cruel and unjust ways of the world. The fool of the play is the kind of impulsive, annoying and yet endearing lover of sincerity in whom most clear-sighted spectators will recognise something of themselves.

However, if *Le Misanthrope* is one of the most 'humorous' of Molière's comedies, it is also one of the rare plays in which he makes systematic use of verbal wit. In general, and certainly in all the comedies of Congreve, wit has a gloriously anarchic power. It can work together with physical beauty – another force for anarchy – to make immoral people irresistibly attractive and dangerously powerful. Wit generally makes innocence, goodness and virtue sound like the ornaments of dullards. It is not surprising that the literature of moral reflection had always distrusted spontaneous wit. Cicero had divided the uses of humour in oratory roughly into two kinds: 'one running with even flow all through a speech, while the other, though incisive, is intermittent; the ancients called the former "irony" and the latter "raillery"'.[16] Cicero believed that the second kind, composed of the *bons mots* of quick-witted speakers, should be used sparingly.[17] Certainly, both French and English writers in the seventeenth century dismissed punning wit as beneath contempt.[18] But Molière and his French contemporaries also distrusted other forms of verbal wit. La Fontaine loathed what he called 'mauvais rieurs':

> On cherche les rieurs; et moi je les évite.
> Cet art veut sur tout autre un suprême mérite.
> Dieu ne créa que pour les sots
> Les méchants diseurs de bons mots.
>
> (*Fables*, VIII, 8)

'Diseur de bons mots' means 'wit' and Pascal condemned wits in the *Pensées* with the celebrated aphorism 'Diseur de bons mots, mauvais caractère'.[19] La

---

16 *De Oratore*, II, 54, 218. 17 Ibid., II, 60, 243–7. 18 Molière's foppish and dim-witted *marquis* in *La Critique de l'École des femmes* is much given to worn-out *turlupinades* or laboured puns. Boileau, in *L'Art poétique*, calls such *turlupins* 'Insipides plaisans, bouffons infortunés / D'un jeu de mots grossiers partisans surannés' (ll. 131–2). Dryden, deriding the taste for puns in the poetry of Horace and in the court of King Charles II, concludes, 'but certain it is, he has no fine palate who can feed so heartily on garbage' (*Critical opinions*, ed. cit., pp 171–2). 19 Pascal, *Les Pensées*, ed.

Bruyère later repeated Pascal's phrase, adding 'je le dirais s'il n'avait été dit'.[20] For La Bruyère, those who sacrificed the reputation of others for a *bon mot* deserved nothing less than exile or imprisonment. It was a commonplace in seventeenth-century France that the *honnête homme* aimed for grace rather than wit; the end of *honnêteté* was to blend with the company of others, never to outshine them. Good laughter for the French moralists was not dependent upon sudden inspiration or quickness of wit, but upon lucidity, propriety and reason. According to La Bruyère, laughter should be reserved strictly for those things which are of themselves ridiculous; it is a mark of a fool to laugh equally at silly and well-judged remarks.[21] Taking pride in one's wit in Molière's plays is a sign of vanity; the feeble wit of such figures as Mascarille and Jodelet (*Les Précieuses ridicules*) and Trissotin (*Les Femmes savantes*) is a symptom of their self-conscious and self-admiring preciosity. Even Célimène's genuine wit, as she ridicules the whisperer, the silent woman and other absurd figures in the portrait scene, is intended to reveal flaws in her character at the same time as it entertains: her wit exposes her as another 'diseuse de bons mots, mauvais caractère' and, even as we laugh at her damning portraits, we feel that the pleasure her wit gives us — like the laughter she inspires in the *marquis* — is not quite innocent. Molière makes Célimène so enamoured of her own beauty and brilliance that she loses her judgment; the central action and dénouement of *Le Misanthrope* demonstrate that her abuse of her great gifts has sown such misery and discord in her salon that, by the end of the play, its habitués have fled in high dudgeon, and she is left alone, stripped of friends and lovers.

It would be hard to overstate the contrast between Molière's world and Congreve's. The two plays breathe a different air. For all the allusions to corruption and hypocrisy in *Le Misanthrope*, the moral climate of the play is surprisingly staid: the appearances, at least, of social etiquette are largely kept up; people fall out, but no one is threatened with degradation or poverty; Alceste, we feel, will easily survive his loss of 20,000 pounds. All four of Congreve's comedies, in contrast, are never far removed from depravity: they take place in a world of *contes galants*; his women, by and large, are citadels waiting — and usually wanting — to be taken, while his men are sexual adventurers. In *The Old Bachelor*, for example, Vainlove enjoys the preliminaries of seduction while Bellmour prefers consummation, so the one lines up assignations while the other keeps them, and audiences are invited to applaud the neatness of the arrangement. Congreve's theatre combines with its gallant

Louis Lafuma (Paris 1962), 670, p. 294.   **20** La Bruyère, 'De la cour' in *Les Caractères*, ed. R. Pignarre (Paris 1965), 80, pp 220–1.   **21** La Bruyère, 'Des ouvrages de l'esprit', in *Les Caractères*, ed. cit., 68, p. 100.

adventures frequent reminders of harsh reality, of money and marriage set-
tlements, of London's wild ways, with its pimps, prostitutes, footpads, play-
houses, courts and jails, all offering telling glimpses of the dangers of
contemporary life.

But the most striking contrast between *Le Misanthrope* and *The Way of
the World* is that all of Congreve's characters are wits; the interest of spectators is held by an almost unbroken stream of witty dialogue. Such was the
craze for wit in Congreve's time that, even had he wished, he could not have
written a play without it. The general addiction to wit can be gauged from
'A satyr against wit', written by Sir Richard Blackmore in 1700, the year in
which *The Way of the World* was first performed.[22] Blackmore's splenetic out-
burst, worthy of Alceste himself, and running on for 400 lines or so, begins:

> Who can forbear, and tamely silent sit,
> And see his Native Land undone by Wit?

The burden of his message is that wit, like some foul plague, is consuming
everything of value in England:

> O'er all the Land the hungry Locusts spread,
> Gnaw every plant, taint every flowry Bed,
> And crop each budding Virtue's tender Head.

Blackmore, though an admirer of Congreve's rich 'Funds of Standard-Sense',
suggests that even he, a man of wide culture and understanding, is guilty at
times of a surfeit of wit.

Congreve himself was acutely aware of the dangers of wit. Indeed, his
stated aim in *The Way of the World* was to make a study of good and bad wit:
he was moved, he wrote in his dedicatory epistle,

> to design some characters which should appear ridiculous not so much
> through a natural folly (which is incorrigible, and therefore not proper
> for the stage) as through an affected wit; a wit which, at the same time
> that it is affected, is also false. (p. 319)

However, the humour of the play can scarcely be said to derive from a
pathology of bad wit. Even ill-judged wit requires some small spark of
genius, and, though the quality of wit varies considerably from character to
character, everyone in *The Way of the World*, even the fools, villains and servants, has just enough self-knowing wit to make us feel their intelligence and
humanity. This feature makes Congreve's created world radically different
from Molière's, where characters displaying defective humour and judgment

22 Reproduced in *Critical essays of the seventeenth century*, ed. cit., vol. 3, pp 325–33.

are objects of ridicule, un-self-knowing mechanisms, blindly acting out their parts in the universal farce. Oliver Goldsmith wrote that 'Wit raises human nature above its level, [while] humour acts a contrary part, and equally depresses it.'[23] This echoes Aristotle's observation in his *Poetics* (1448 a) that tragedy magnifies the human condition while comedy diminishes it, and indeed it is a feature of *The Way of the World* that we are constantly surprised to find ourselves responding with tragic rather than comic emotions to the characters. At times, we are moved to the point of real admiration and pathos.[24] We become quite attached even to the fools: Lady Wishfort, a 55-year-old widow, is a blend of fool and villain; she wishes to be taken for a young beauty, longs for a new husband, and, jealous of her beautiful young niece, Millamant, and her stylish lover, Mirabell, plots to ruin both of them. However, audiences cannot wholly dislike her because her wit and her love for Mirabell, however absurd, make her so human. We warm to her in her dialogue with Foible, for example:

> LADY WISHFORT: I shall never recompose my features to receive Sir Rowland with any economy of face. This wretch has fretted me that I am absolutely decayed. Look, Foible.
> FOIBLE: Your ladyship has frowned a little too rashly, indeed, madam. There are some cracks discernible in the white varnish.
> LADY WISHFORT: Let me see the glass. – Cracks, say'st thou? Why I am arrantly flayed; I look like an old peeled wall.

Witwoud, an affected fop and conscientious wit, pours out his often strained similitudes and conceits *ad nauseam,* but never without arousing some degree of surprise and amusement. Petulant's inveterate lying and quarrelsomeness carry us along by their sheer exuberance. Even Sir Wilful, the ill-bred country squire who resembles Molière's Monsieur de Pourceaugnac, has learned a little wit by the end of the play, reassuring Mirabell that his

---

23 In Ch. XI of *An enquiry into the present state of polite learning* (1759). See *Collected works of Oliver Goldsmith,* ed. Arthur Friedman, 5 vols (Oxford 1966), vol. 1, pp 320–1.   24 There are parallels between my point here and Dr Johnson's judgment on Congreve's comedies. Johnson saw them as contests of wit, more likely to inspire tragic admiration than laughter: 'His scenes exhibit not much of humour, imagery, or passion: his personages are a kind of intellectual gladiators; every sentence is to ward or strike; the contest of smartness is never intermitted; his wit is a meteor playing to and fro with alternate coruscations. His comedies have therefore, in some degree, the operation of tragedies; they surprise rather than divert, and raise admiration oftener than merriment.' The passage, from Johnson's *Prefaces, biographical and critical, to the works of the English poets,* 10 vols (London 1779–81), vol. 6, pp 1–38, is reproduced in *William Congreve: the critical heritage,* ed. Alexander Lindsay and Howard Erskine-Hill (London and New York 1989), pp 260–71 (p. 267). I am grateful to Michael Moriarty who, in the discussion following my paper, drew my attention to this passage from Johnson.

cruel aunt, Lady Wishfort, cannot frown upon him too harshly for 'her fore-head would wrinkle like the coat of a cream-cheese' (p. 401). The villains are still more impressive than the fools. Fainall and Mrs Marwood, originally played by tragic actors, are both elegant, articulate, cruel and vengeful fig-ures, yet both, especially Mrs Marwood, are deeply unhappy. When she says in her quarrel with Fainall that 'It is not yet too late [. . .] to loathe, detest, abhor mankind, myself and the whole treacherous world,' we feel the kind of pity we have for Lady Macbeth. As for generous-hearted Mrs Fainall, who, having forgiven Mirabell for marrying her off and then abandoning her, becomes his whole-hearted supporter and tender ally, she is, quite sim-ply, a tragic figure.

Not only do we have empathy for Congreve's characters, but, even while distrusting their intentions, we find ourselves obliged most of the time to trust the shrewdness of their judgments. The opening scene, for example, pairing the chief villain Fainall with the hero Mirabell, does not, as one might expect, present two contrasting patterns of behaviour. Rather, we appear to be meeting two of a kind, two amusing men–about–town sketch-ing out equally penetrating and persuasive pictures of the way of the world; moreover, we readily see the human condition through their eyes. As the action unfolds, characters on stage present those whom we have not yet met: we first meet Witwoud through Mirabell's delightful portrait of him; as soon as Witwoud appears, he in turn paints an equally well-judged comic portrait of Petulant. Much of the moral content of the play, its substance and worldly wisdom, is expressed not through action but through raillery, through the unbroken witty commentary which the various characters keep up on events, on one another, and on the way of the world in general. It is a fea-ture of all four of Congreve's comedies that the characters on stage laugh a lot – and audiences, caught up in the stream of their sparkling dialogue, are more inclined to laugh with them than at them.

At the pinnacle of this stylish world, where everyone down to the ser-vants inspires some small degree of amusement, awe or affection, stand Mirabell and Millamant, a wondrous (*mirabilis*) hero and a beauty to inspire a thousand lovers (*mille amants*). These figures, gracious, irresistibly charming, the truest wits in the play, are both, behind their stylish affectations, deeply in love. It is through Mirabell that we first meet Millamant. He is typical of those lovers evoked in Éliante's diatribe who turn their mistress' faults into strengths. His speech is a masterpiece of eloquence, a delightful entertain-ment, and a proof of the depth of his love:

I'll tell thee Fainall, she once used me with that insolence that, in revenge I took her to pieces; sifted her, and separated her failings; I studied 'em, and got 'em by rote. The catalogue was so large that I was not without hopes one day or other to hate her heartily: to which end I so used myself to think of 'em at length, contrary to my design and expectation, they gave me every hour less and less disturbance; till in a few days it became habitual to me to remember 'em without being displeased. They are now grown as familiar to me as my own frailties; and in all probability, in a little time longer I shall like 'em as well. (p. 328)

In essence, Mirabell and Millamant are not, in the Aristotelian sense, comic characters at all. The play is a romance with echoes of Shakespeare's romantic comedies, and the tone of romances is more akin to tragedy than to comedy. The lovers' defects do not make them ridiculous. Mirabell's earlier action of marrying off a mistress to the villainous Mr Fainall in order to provide cover for her should their affair have accidentally resulted in pregnancy does not inspire mirth at the spectacle of human weakness. We are apparently to forgive this distasteful action because, as Mirabell says, 'errors which love produces have ever been accounted venial' (p. 402). In fact, we perceive the error as venial only if we have first learned, like all the women in the play, to admire and love the witty and stylish Mirabell; we must love him even for his flaws – just as he loves Millamant for hers. The climax of *The Way of the World* is the provisos scene, where the two lovers list the conditions on which they agree to be married (pp 378–82). When the apparently flighty but actually devoted Millamant ends her list with the words, 'These articles subscribed, if I continue to endure you a little longer, I may by degrees dwindle into a wife' (p. 380), audiences are moved not to laughter but to love, admiration and good humour. The true dramatic climax of the play is her short remark to Mrs Fainall following this scene: 'Well, if Mirabell should not make a good husband, I am a lost thing – for I find I love him violently' (p. 382).

Wit in *The Way of the World*, as in Congreve's earlier comedies, may perform some of the satirist's work of stripping away the glittering surface of things and exposing hidden folly, but its principal function is to make the speaker glitter more brightly than his rivals. It acts the lowly part of the mating ritual: the wittiest male will win the most beautiful woman. It is said that Congreve was in love with Mrs Bracegirdle who played the female lead in his plays, and that he watched each performance alone from a private box. This is the ideal perspective for a spectator at a Congreve comedy, a quiet retreat in which, set apart from the world, imagination can have free play. A Molière play should be seen from the body of the theatre, where we are surrounded by the laughter of other people who also find the malfunctioning human condition absurd; there, among friends whose judgments we share, we laugh freely at the spectacle of others and ourselves caricatured on stage. In *The Way of the World*, we are no less aware of our human flaws – which are more serious by and large than those of Molière's fools – but, bruised and buffeted by a harsh and unforgiving world, we are pleased to allow the power of theatrical illusion to persuade us that, whatever our past may contain, we can find forgiveness, redemption and a rare degree of happiness through the miracle of love.

The stage controversy in France and England – a confessional convergence?

HENRY PHILLIPS

The sixteenth and seventeenth centuries in Europe witness the rise and con-solidation, at somewhat different rates of evolution, of a public theatre of largely secular inspiration, endowed with fixed places of performance and professional troupes of performers. Noble and royal patronage played a role in the establishment of theatre as a significant social and political institution which attracted large audiences of varying social composition. This highly visible and crowd-pulling phenomenon of permanent and seemingly immovable disposition immediately presented problems of order, both social and moral. In England, France and Spain, the need for regulatory injunctions became apparent, and, more importantly from our point of view, the neces-sity of a moral response appeared urgent. The Churches were no strangers to dealing with theatrical performances, particularly of a religious nature. This secular and worldly theatre was, however, different. It threatened to consti-tute a rival, not only in the timing of performances, but in its claim to offer moral instruction or an explanation of the ways of the world and the human condition.

It can reasonably be asserted that hostility to theatre among the Churches was universal in Europe. Even Italy, where popes wrote plays and which we therefore might think of as tolerant, had its hardliners. In the last quarter of the sixteenth century, St Charles Borromeo was tireless in his opposition to theatre and actors in the province of Spanish-governed Milan of which he was cardinal-archbishop, and his reforming pastoral agenda reg-ularly attracted the ire of the secular authorities. His actions were supported, however, by other senior clerics in various Italian cities, including Bologna, Cremona and Asti.[1] On the other hand, within the Churches, no unanimity existed on the exact nature of the response I have alluded to. Borromeo received little encouragement from Rome, although ecclesiastical politics on

---

1 See in particular J. Dubu, *Les Églises chrétiennes et le théâtre (1550–1850)* (Grenoble 1997), and 'L'Église catholique et la condamnation du théâtre en France au XVIIe siècle', *Quaderni francesi*, 1 (1970), 319–49, but also H. Phillips, 'Italy and France in the seventeenth-century stage controversy', *The Seventeenth Century*, 11 (1996), 187–207, and 'Les acteurs et la loi au XVIIe siècle', *Littératures classiques*, 40 (2000) 87–101.

the jurisdictional role of bishops here constituted an important factor. Nor did all of Cromwell's acolytes follow his unconditional stance.[2] Similarly, in France, the Catholic Church was also divided between its moderates and hardliners, the latter taking issue with conciliatory papal approaches to a sacramental practice which had traditionally discriminated against the acting profession.[3] Undoubtedly, the situation of each state in respect of theatre was in some ways determined by internal specificities. While a close analysis of the complexities of the situation in England is beyond the scope of this article, my aim in what follows is to keep these in view and to outline points of convergence in ecclesiastical opposition to theatre in England and France.

How then could the Churches respond to the rise of a predominantly secular-inspired theatre? What arguments could and did they have recourse to in their opposition to the stage? A good deal of agreement existed among French and English writers about the corrupting influence of theatre at the level of the immediate impact of plays on the spectator. This aspect of convergence operates first at the level of subject-matter which was, in their view, intended to arouse a whole range of harmful passions in the audience. A central feature of almost all plays in the corruption of the human soul was carnal love which, for William Prynne in the *Histrio-mastix* (1633), was accompanied by 'complements, kisses and embracements'.[4] Jeremy Collier complains in 1698 that the stage is 'the best place to recover a languishing Amour, to rouse it from sleep, and retrieve it from Indifference'. Quite simply, he believes, poets can neither write nor live without it.[5] Moralists frequently included ambition and revenge as regular ingredients of plays, revenge particularly attracting the attention of Collier as worthy of reproach in the French drama he otherwise admired.[6] Revenge is further denounced by Prynne along with 'Furie, Anger, Murther, Crueltie, Tyrannie, Treacherie, [and] Treason'. Equally, Prynne puts the success of plays down to the depraved nature of the audience, who are, nonetheless, imperceptibly affected by the theatrical experience, a theme found commonly in French religious moralists, and by the deliberately deceptive nature of theatrical language which covers its evil intent.[7]

---

2 See M. Heinemann, *Puritanism and theatre. Thomas Middleton and opposition drama under the early Stuarts* (Cambridge 1980). Other aspects of the stage controversy in England are dealt with by J. Barish, *The anti-theatrical prejudice* (London 1981), and R. Fraser, *The war against poetry* (Princeton 1970).   3 See in particular Dubu, 'L'Église catholique' and Phillips, 'Les acteurs et la loi'.   4 W. Prynne, *Histrio-mastix: The player's scourge or Actors tragaedie, divided into two parts* (London 1633), p. 387.   5 J. Collier, *A short view of the immorality and profaneness of the English stage*, ed. A. Freeman (New York and London 1972), pp 280–2. The Jeremy Collier controversy has been well documented by Sister Rose Anthony, *The Jeremy Collier stage controversy, 1698–1726* (New York 1937).   6 Collier, *A short view*, ed. cit., p. 283.   7 Prynne, *Histrio-mastix*, pp 72–3, p. 958, and p. 797. See also Philippe Vincent, *Traitté des theatres* (La Rochelle 1647), p. 15.

More crucially, perhaps, theatre, as a result of the influence of subject-matter, has a deleterious effect on the Christian conduct of spectators. French moralists, from Pierre Nicole to those contributing to the bitter debate of 1694, constantly refer to the disruption of the mood required for prayer and to increasing indifference to religious teaching.[8] The moral corruption of the stage has inevitable consequences for the performance of religious and social duties which become sorely neglected.[9] Richard Wills, bishop of Winchester, and Collier insist that the stage undermines parental teaching, particularly when parents themselves allow their offspring, especially their daughters, to accompany them to this den of iniquity.[10] Prynne even puts illegitimate offspring down to the stage's encouragement of adultery.[11] Just as Prynne complains that theatre promotes worldly pomp and vanity, Pierre Coustel regards it as an enjoinder to idleness and indulgence in the 'vanitez et folies du siecle', English Protestants and French Catholics alike pointing to the baptismal vow of renunciation of worldly pleasures.[12] John Evelyn's daughter died believing the stage to be an unaccountable vanity,[13] and Richard Baxter, in his *Christian directory* of 1673, denounces 'fleshly persons' wasting the time more appropriately devoted to God.[14] In short, experience of the theatre changes us to a point where we are no longer God's creatures. Nicole refers to play-going as leading to 'fainéantise' and 'oisiveté' which, as we all know, are the seed-beds of sin.[15] Moreover, the idle rich did not give to the poor what they were prepared to spend on frequenting theatres, another example of failure to acquit oneself of religious duties.[16]

One aspect of the situation on the ground which elicited universal condemnation across the confessional spectrum from those expressing a total dislike of theatre was the timing of performances on the Sabbath or during Lent. Prynne wistfully remembers a time when a law forbade performances on Sundays: 'then those who had served God at Prayers [. . .] in the daytime, would not so seriously serve the world, the flesh, the Devill [. . .] in the night'.[17] While Pepys records that in 1662 the playhouses closed during

---

8 See H. Phillips, *The theatre and its critics in seventeenth-century France* (Oxford 1980), chapter 6. **9** Prynne, *Histrio-mastix*, pp 521–2 and p. 527. **10** R. Wills, *The Occasional Paper Number IX containing some considerations about the danger of going to plays*, ed. A. Freeman (New York and London 1974), p. 7. Collier, *A short view*, ed. cit., p. 287. **11** Prynne, *Histrio-mastix*, p. 383. **12** Prynne, ibid., p. 47 and p. 56ff, and P. Coustel, *Sentiments de L'Église et des saints pères pour servir de décision sur la comédie et les comédiens* (Paris 1694), p. 48. **13** J. Evelyn, *The diary of John Evelyn*, ed. E. S. de Beer, 6 vols (Oxford 1955), vol. 4, p. 422. **14** R. Baxter, *A Christian directory, or A summ of practical theologie* (London 1673), p. 291. **15** P. Nicole, *Traité de la comédie*, ed. G. Couton (Lyon 1961), p. 60. L. Thirouin has re-edited this text in *Traité de la comédie et autres pièces d'un procès du théâtre* (Paris 1998). See also his *Aveuglement salutaire: le réquisitoire contre le théâtre dans la France classique* (Paris 1997). **16** Coustel, *Sentiments*, p. 87. **17** Prynne, *Histrio-mastix*, p. 470. See also H. Burton, *For*

Easter, and that in 1667 no plays were performed on the Fridays of Lent, young players were allowed to set aside this prohibition.[18] No such concessions were ever needed in France, much to the chagrin of all religious moralists opposed to theatre, a chagrin greatly increased in 1694 when Thomas Caffaro, a Theatine monk consulted by the playwright Edme Boursault on the legitimacy of theatre, argued that performances during Lent constituted no infringement of the Christian life.[19] In contrast George Ridpath rails in 1698 against the very idea of a mask devoted to Merlin performed on the day set aside 'for the praise of our Redeemer'.[20] He also argues that the allowing of lawful recreations after evening prayers on Sundays, a practice endorsed by James I in 1618 and continued by Charles I in a declaration of 1634 (and, moreover, defended in the *Stage acquitted* on the grounds that a moral message from a play was better than dissolution in the tavern),[21] represented a measure destined to convert Catholics otherwise deterred by Puritan austerity.[22] The scoring of points of this sort will be discussed further below.

Another source of confessional convergence in France and England is found in the reference to Christian tradition, although its status clearly differed between the Churches. Protestants and Catholics alike shared the same sources in the Fathers' works, many of which were specifically devoted to moral and religious issues deriving from the spectacles of their own time. In France and England, sharp divisions of opinion occurred over the exact relevance of the patristic authorities in the case of contemporary drama. On one side, neither Baxter nor Prynne have any such doubts, referring to the councils of the early Church, St Jerome and St Augustine, for substantiation of their own views.[23] A *Short treatise against stage-playes* contained in the *Commonwealth tracts* mentions that the decrees of Gratian, an attempt to collate and rationalize canon law, ratified anti-theatrical pronouncements made by early councils of the Church.[24]

The strictures of the Fathers retain all their original force especially

---

God and the king (no place, 1636), p. 157.   **18** S. Pepys, *The diary of Samuel Pepys,* ed. R.C. Latham and W. Matthews, 11 vols (London 1970–83), vol. 5, p. 74; vol. 8, p. 90; vol. 3, p. 51.   **19** See Coustel, *Sentiments,* pp 50–1. See also Caffaro's work, *Lettre d'un théologien illustre par sa qualité et par son mérite consulté par l'auteur pour savoir si la comédie peut être permise, ou doit être absolument défendue* in Ch. Urbain and E. Levesque (ed.), *L'Église et le théâtre* (Paris 1930). Bossuet responds to this matter in his *Maximes et réflexions sur la comédie,* also in Urbain and Levesque, p. 240 and p. 249.   **20** G. Ridpath *The stage condem'd,* ed. A. Freeman (New York and London 1972), p.14.   **21** *The stage acquitted,* ed. A. Freeman (New York and London 1972), p. 94.   **22** Ridpath, *The stage condem'd,* ed. cit., p. 33.   **23** Baxter, *A Christian directory,* p. 462 and Prynne, *Histrio-mastix,* p. 6, p. 340, p. 475. **24** Collier, *A short treatise against stage-playes* in *Commonwealth tracts, 1625–1650,* ed. A. Freeman (New York and London 1974), p. 24. See Phillips, *The theatre and its critics,* chapter 4 and Thirouin, *Aveuglement,* chap. 1.

because the modern theatre reinstated in contemporary circumstances a genre born in idolatry, and therefore inherited vestiges of a pagan world and world-view.[25] This is particularly true of the passion of love which, for Collier and Gerbais, the latter writing in 1694, reflects the origins of the theatre in idolatry where the lover's mistress (or love itself) replaces the ancient goddess.[26] A theatre invented for un-Christian ends and which revives heathenism, Prynne argues, remains unlawful for all Christians at all times.[27] Ridpath, aware of the dangers of a Protestant leaning so heavily on Catholic tradition for the legitimization of his views, agrees that no men or councils are infallible, yet the Fathers' arguments, 'being founded upon general Scriptural rules' (themselves, we might add, not without controversy), 'ought to direct us in our Faith and Practice, as to this matter'.[28]

On the other side, a challenge was mounted to the continuing use of works relating to ancient theatre and spectacle. As in France with Pierre Corneille's *Epître* to *Théodore* in 1646, l'abbé d'Aubignac's *Dissertation sur la condamnation des théâtres* (Paris 1666) and the unfortunate Caffaro in 1694, English pro-theatre writers question the authoritative status of patristic works by arguing on the grounds of historical context.[29] The *Vindication of the stage* categorically rejects the condemnation coming down from the early centuries of the Church as having any relevance for judging the contemporary repertoire.[30] As Samuel Chappuzeau puts it in 1674, the Fathers, whom we should never contradict, had good intentions for their own time but they do not stand for ours,[31] a view advanced by Sir Richard Baker in his own defence of the stage.[32] In a typically English assertion – no French writer would dare write such a thing – the author of one of the *Collier tracts* argues that 'no man ought to pay such a respect either to Councils or Fathers, as to submit his Judgment contrary to his Reason'.[33]

One obstacle to what many regarded as the unimpeachable theological and moral authority of tradition was St Thomas Aquinas who, in his *Summa theologiae*, defends, in the context of recreation or *divertissement,* playful or humorous 'words or deeds wherein nothing further is sought than the soul's delight'.[34] Many, including among others probably Richelieu and certainly

---

25 See J. de Voisin, *La Défense du traitté de Monseigneur le prince de Conti touchant la comédie et les spectacles* (Paris 1671), p. 475, and also Vincent, *Traitté,* p. 61, and Prynne, *Histrio-mastix,* p. 16. **26** Collier, *A short view,* ed. cit., pp 282–3 and J. Gerbais, *Lettre d'un docteur de Sorbonne à une personne de qualité, sur le sujet de la comédie* (Paris 1694), pp 186–7. **27** Prynne, *Histrio-mastix,* p. 37. **28** Ridpath, *The stage condemn'd,* ed. cit., p. 73. **29** The *Epître* is included in H. T. Barnwell's *Corneille's writings on the theatre* (Oxford 1965). **30** *A vindication of the stage,* ed. A. Freeman (New York and London 1974), p. 21ff. **31** S. Chappuzeau, *Le Théâtre françois* (Lyon 1674), pp 16–17. **32** R. Baker, *Theatrum redivivum, or The theatre vindicated* (London 1662), pp 76ff. **33** 'A letter to A.H. Esq. concerning the Stage', in *Collier tracts,* ed. A. Freeman (New York and London 1974), p. 3. **34** Quoted in Phillips, *The theatre and its critics,* p. 80.

D'Aubignac, saw in this discussion a vindication of theatre, especially in the light of St Thomas' discussion of play-actors to whom he ascribes a legitimate role in human intercourse.[35] In England, the author of *The stage acquitted* shares this view along with Thomas Leke, a Catholic secular priest who was stung into replying to a prohibition from attending theatres issued by his archpriest.[36] We shall say more of this incident later.

Those whose hostility to theatre was unconditional found the example of St Thomas embarrassing and uncomfortable, and proceeded unceremoniously to cast doubt on a view which threatened their presentation of an unbroken tradition of authoritative opposition to theatre. One tactic employed by religious moralists writing in 1694 was to turn the anti-patristic argument round and to claim that the theatre as it might be envisaged by St Thomas was most certainly not reflected in modern practice, especially — and they were unanimous on this point — since the Angelic Doctor laid down a whole host of conditions concerning the legitimacy of this form of recreational activity.[37] Among English moralists, Ridpath casts doubt on the validity of St Thomas' position,[38] while Gerbais dismissed the views of the Saint on the grounds that not all points of his doctrine were 'canonisables.'[39] La Grange claimed that in any case St Thomas had never seen any plays.[40] What is at stake here is the level at which St Thomas' discussion was conducted. French critics argued that St Thomas conceived of theatre in the abstract, that is to say as an idea. This point was not lost on English critics. Collier follows this line, although not explicitly with reference to Aquinas, affirming that 'the use lies chiefly in the application,'[41] and finding an ally in Richard Wills who, also writing in 1698, warns supporters of plays to take no comfort from 'Plays at the best, pure from all those defiling Ingredients, and free from the blemish of a Vicious Resort, a condition so perfect as we never yet saw the Theater in'.[42]

The degree of convergence we have thus far highlighted should not obscure unduly the ways in which the issue of theatres and theatre-going became involved in inter-confessional rivalry not only in England, but to a certain extent in France. While this rivalry shows itself in obvious ways within the two countries that concern us, it is also evident in attitudes held by members of the English Churches to the Catholic Church in France and Rome. In contrast, French moralists rarely refer to England. Much will

---

35 Ibid., pp 179–80. **36** See I.J. Semper, 'The Jacobean theatre through the eyes of Catholic clerics', *Shakespeare Quarterly*, 3 (1952), 44–51 (p. 47). **37** Ibid., p. 49. See also Phillips, *The theatre and its critics*, especially chapter 8, and Ridpath, *The stage condemn'd*, ed. cit., pp 49–53. **38** Ridpath, *The stage condemn'd*, ed. cit., pp 52–3. **39** Gerbais, *Lettre*, p. 21. **40** C. de La Grange, *Réfutation d'un écrit favorisant la comédie* (Paris 1694), p. 42. **41** Collier, *A short view*, ed. cit., pp 1–2. **42** Wills, *Occasional paper*, ed. cit., p. 5.

therefore depend on how one religious grouping identifies itself as against another. If, as the Ordinance ordering the closure of theatres in 1647 points out, heathens condemned stage plays, how much more vehement must be this condemnation by 'Professors of the Christian Religion'?[43] Prynne evokes the 'seventh squadron of authorities', that is to say 'sundry Pagan and Christian States, Nations, Magistrates, Emperors, Princes, who have excluded, censured, banished, suppressed Plays and Actors as the greatest mischiefes'.[44] Quite simply, no Christian can be seen to tolerate what is not tolerated by another sort of Christian, especially if this 'other' turns out to be the confessional enemy. Prynne quite clearly states that the conscience of the English Churches should be moved by the fact that the whole Catholic Church, along with all the primitive Christian Fathers, has professed hostility to theatre, and he constantly calls on 'popish' authors in support of his own position. The appeal to tradition and to 'divers Moderne Christians, both Protestant and Papists' must lead Protestants to conclude that they cannot allow what 'the very Papists' condemn,[45] a view shared by Baxter.[46]

This line of argument is all the more convincing in that Catholics are also avid theatre-goers. The author of the anti-theatrical *Short treatise* notes that: 'the Papists, though they be favourers of Stage-Playes, and actors sometime upon the stage [. . .] yet they cannot for very shame justifie them, but contrariewise condemn them in their writings'.[47] That France is a point of reference in this context is made clear by Wills:

> if in a country disposed to *a lighter Temper and Air*, where the *Church* has greater Corruption, and the *Theatre* fewer, there can yet be whole Bodies of *Casuists* found, disallowing the sight of their *Modester Plays*; Methinks it shou'd not be thought an absurdity here, to go about to dissuade so *thoughtful* a *People* as we reckon ourselves, from going to ours which show so little of that Reformation to which we pretend.[48]

In a similar vein, Collier, quoting the Rotterdam *Gazette*, makes telling mention of the reported attempts of the archbishop of Paris, at this time cardinal de Noailles, to close the public theatres by degrees, 'or at least to clear them of profaneness,' referring in addition to the 1695 anti-theatrical 'mandement' of Rochechouart, bishop of Arras, and to the expulsion of Italian actors in 1697.[49]

---

43 Anonymous, 'Ordinance for suppression of all stage-playes and interludes', in *Commonwealth tracts*, ed. cit. p. 1.   **44** Prynne, *Histrio-mastix*, p. 713.   **45** Ibid., p. 569, 699, 802, p. 6, and p. 866.   **46** Baxter, *A Christian directory*, p. 462.   **47** Collier, *A short treatise*, ed. cit., p. 24.   **48** Wills, *Occasional paper*, ed. cit. p. 20.   **49** Collier, *A short view*, ed. cit., pp 243–5. For a direct response to these points of reference, see *The stage acquitted*, ed. cit., pp 93–4.

The attraction for English moralists of anti-theatrical Catholic authorities condemning theatre-loving Catholics is present most evidently in
Ridpath. Certainly, we find synods ancient and modern, and some of them
during the very darkness of popery, expressly condemning the stage. Even
Jesuits ban the reading of Terence in schools.[50] Not all Catholic writers,
however, as Ridpath knows, follow exactly the same line. Those keenest to
clutch at the straw of St Cyprian speaking out only against the plays of his
day and not ours, he asserts, turn out to be popish and Protestant doctors.
Using Caffaro in defence of theatre is to no avail either since, he asks, why
should we expect a popish divine to be hostile to theatre, especially when
Catholic worship resembles theatre?[51] The key to this seeming contradiction
lies with the word 'Protestant', Ridpath's target at home, since for him, as
with Prynne and others, the term 'Protestants' refers to Anglicans who, as we
shall see later, are considered to have renounced their pastoral duty in moral
matters, especially by supporting the king in the maintenance of theatres.
Anglicans therefore behave like Catholics, where even Catholics can condemn theatre. At the same time, Catholics are condemned as hypocrites.
Ridpath manages to have the best of three worlds at least.

Closer to his own confessional home, Ridpath quotes Chapter 14, article 28 of the *Discipline of the Reformed Church of France* which prohibited
attendance at theatre of the Huguenot faithful.[52] It is interesting therefore
that Le Brun, one of the Catholic controversialists of the *affaire Caffaro* of
1694, quotes, along with Thiers in his *Traité des jeux*, exactly the same text.[53]
This, especially for Le Brun after the revocation of the edict of Nantes in
1685, cannot be meant to elicit sympathy for the Calvinists in a kingdom
desirous of forcibly converting or expelling them. It simply means that
Catholics should not lag behind heretics in proper moral conduct. Indeed,
hostile attitudes towards theatre in France have their place in intra-Catholic
rivalries. Coustel, a former teacher at the Petites Écoles of Port-Royal,
quotes the anti-theatrical works of the Spanish Jesuit, Mariana, and records
having found other theologians and doctors not normally considered rigorist who condemn theatre.[54] Thus, moral austerity cannot be confined to
Jansenism, the suggestion being that attempts to separate Jansenism from the
body of the Church were unjust. Le Brun too, an Oratorian whose order
found itself constantly harassed by the Jesuits, identifies Escobar from among
casuists, generally not renowned for their severity, as disapproving of the
State's tolerance of plays.[55]

---

50 Ridpath, *The stage condemn'd*, ed. cit., p. 71 and p. 39. 51 Ibid., p. 64 and p. 44. 52 Ibid., p.
73. 53 See Le Père P. Le Brun, *Discours sur la comédie* (Paris 1694), p. 123, and J.-B. Thiers, *Traité
des jeux et des divertissements* (Paris 1686), p. 301 and p. 312. 54 Coustel, *Sentiments*, pp 56–7.
55 Le Brun, *Discours*, p. 133.

The importance of theatre in this game of confessional positioning emerges strongly with the French Protestant pastor Philippe Vincent. One of his central arguments focuses on the identity of Protestants as a distinctive group. The Huguenots who attend theatrical performances are guilty of what he calls 'perjure', that is to say, failing to adhere to the baptismal vow of renouncing pomp and the devil, a failure common to all confessions according to the appropriate religious moralists. In this case, the charge is accompanied by failure to 'vivre selon la Reformation Saincte qui nous distingue d'avec ceux que l'erreur tient encores dans ses liens'. Protestants at the theatre lead to the faith being mocked.[56] They are collectively responsible for the reputation of their number, especially in La Rochelle – Vincent's spiritual charge – where Huguenots, after the capitulation in 1628, found themselves in a minority among an immigrant Catholic majority.

Affirming the distinctiveness of group identity through the display of moral superiority lies behind much English commentary on the evils of the stage, evils against which the Church of England was expected to take an exemplary stand. What happened instead, according to Henry Burton, was that the king was turned against the 'true servants of Jesus Christ' by Anglican clergy not only from the pulpit but also by the actions of prelates who entertained (supposedly) religious kings and princes with an Interlude.[57] The Anglican clergy, for Ridpath, stands charged with cowardice for failing to respond to their pastoral duty, and for failing to live up to the best of their predecessors, in not speaking out for fear of the king and Laud, the latter having imposed a *Book of sports and pastimes* upon all the clergy to be read to the people on Sundays. Ridpath was simply unable to stomach the idea of a so-called saint and martyr who could sanction masks and plays on Sundays with no subsequent show of repentance.[58]

In England, the profound disaffection which arose from Anglican tolerance of the stage, and which was felt by diverse religious groupings, was compounded by the perception of theatre as the arena for the public settling of confessional scores, especially when actors were seen as the natural allies of the crown and its Church, many of them enlisting on the king's side during the war.[59] Plays, according to Ridpath, served to ridicule Puritans (the word is his), and to 'run down the Patrons of Liberty and Property'. Even under Charles II, the stage lashed 'Dissenters and Whiggs that oppos'd Tyranny'.[60] Collier complains that the Church of England is the only communion to

---

56 Vincent, *Traitté*, pp 17–18.   **57** Burton, *For God and the king*, p. 49.   **58** Ridpath, *The stage condemn'd*, ed. cit., p. 2 and pp 9–10.   **59** For this aspect of the controversy in England, consult Fraser, *The war against poetry*, and also L. Hotson, *The Commonwealth and Restoration stage* (Harvard 1928), pp 5–6.   **60** Ridpath, *The stage condemn'd*, ed. cit., p. 4.

suffer satire of the clergy on the stage.[61] The general complaint was that audiences would dismiss the teaching of religious fundamentals when the religion of those that proffered it was identified solely with (legitimate) anti-theatrical prejudice. The author of the anti-theatrical *Short treatise* remarks that theatre-goers grow weary of those who speak to them of religion, dismissing them as Puritans,[62] for Prynne a term perceived as dear to 'our Prophane Play-haunters'.[63] Prynne does not miss the opportunity to imply a direct comparison between his own religious colleagues and the early Christians, 'Christian' thus constituting the easy term of dismissal in order to avoid discussion of substance. Our Play-house censurers, Prynne argues, might as well dismiss the Fathers and modern Christian authors as Puritans or Precisians.[64] His conclusion is:

> the grand Objection of our present dissolute times for the justification of these Playes is this; That none but a company of Puritans and Precisians speake against them; all else applaud and else frequent them; therefore, certainly they are very good recreations, since none but Puritans disaffect them.[65]

Prynne's argument is accompanied, however, by the charge that 'our Roman Catholics' were much devoted to theatrical spectacle, implying yet again that Anglicanism aligns itself with Rome in these matters.[66] It is logical, therefore, especially in the light of theatre representing an officially encouraged opposition to religious rigorism, that he should comment that actors are mostly Catholics,[67] to which Sir Richard Baker replies: 'We do not question his credible *Information*, yet we justly question his incredible *Consequence*.'[68]

The demonic influence of Rome resurfaced in the question as to whether it was appropriate for priests to attend or encourage the theatre. Ridpath reproaches the Church of England for failing to follow the example of the Council of Trent which forbade theatre-going to its clergy.[69] For Prynne, this naturally extends to acting, from which activity priests are excluded, as are their children and all those intending to attend holy orders.[70]

The juxtaposition of Rome and idolatry is reaffirmed by the charge made by the author of the anti-theatrical *Short treatise* that popes seconded the urges of heathens, instructed by the devil, in solemnizing 'their Festivals and Jubilees with all sortes of Playes and Sportes for recreation'.[71] The

61 Collier, *A short view*, ed. cit., p. 108.   **62** Collier, *A short treatise*, ed. cit., pp 11–12.   **63** Prynne, *Histrio-mastix*, p. 454.   **64** Ibid., p. 702.   **65** Ibid., p. 797.   **66** Ibid., p. 12.   **67** Ibid., p. 142. **68** Baker, *Theatrum redivivum*, pp 49–50. **69** Ridpath, *The stage condemn'd*, ed. cit., p. 71. **70** Prynne, *Histrio-mastix*, p. 862.   **71** Collier, *A short treatise*, ed. cit., p. 10.

Catholic Church bears the responsibility, no less, for introducing plays into an era of Christianity:

> when that great scarlet coloured whore of Babylon with her golden cup of abominations in her hand, which hath a name written in her forehead, a misterie, great Babilon the mother of whoredomes, and which reineth over the kingdoms of the earth, was set in Peter's Chaire at Rome as the Papists say; then did the king of the Locusts, called *Abbadon* and *Apollyon*, having the key of the bottomless pitt, with full power for such a purpose, sette the Church door wide open for sundrie sports and playes to enter freely into the house of God.[72]

The opposite argument carried as much weight with Chappuzeau (a Protestant, incidentally), who, in his response to hostility from French clerics, fails to see why France should be more scrupulous than Rome, where highly placed clergymen grace the opera with their presence, and where priests appear on the public stage to sing.[73] Gerbais, on the other hand, is indignant at the mere possibility that a pope could attend a theatrical performance.[74] Henri Lelevel, echoing English writers, criticizes his own senior clergy for such an act of impiety, although he excuses their presence at plays performed at Court on the grounds that they are responding to obligation rather than exercising their personal choice.[75]

That the appearance of a priest at the theatre constitutes a dangerous argument to the extent that it seems to make plays lawful, was the position of a certain Fr John Colleton in one of the most revealing incidents to occur in England surrounding priestly countenance of theatre-going. In a controversy of 1617–18 recorded by I.J. Semper, William Harrison, the last Catholic archpriest of England, forbade secular priests from going to plays 'acted by common players upon common stages, under penalty of losing the use of their sacerdotal faculties'. The ban did not, however, affect plays performed at the Inns of Court, the royal court, the universities or private houses. One secular priest, Thomas Leke, protested, pointing out that the majority of the principal Catholics of London attended plays. Not only this but, apparently, Catholic clerics had been regular spectators at the playhouses since the turn of the seventeenth century. Colleton, in support of his superior, turns into the Catholic mirror image of Prynne and others in asserting that plays are made to sport and delight an audience consisting of young gallants and Protestants, 'for no true Puritans will endure to bee present at Playes'. It is not Anglicanism which turns out to be the moral friend of Catholicism here

---

72 Ibid., pp 8–9. **73** Chappuzeau, *Le Théâtre françois*, p. 38. **74** Gerbais, *Lettre*, p. 73. **75** H. Lelevel, *Réponse à la lettre du théologien défenseur de la comédie* (Paris 1694), p. 25 and p. 90.

but puritanism, that otherwise scourge of the scarlet-clad harlot. The prohibition was eventually revoked because Harrison preferred compromise on the question of the theatre to a situation of being 'handicapped in the troublous time of persecution by a dissension among his clerics'. Theatre was simply a distraction in the face of a more serious threat. Such was not, as we have seen, the view of French Huguenot pastors.[76]

Underpinning these arguments over priests is unquestionably the issue of scandal, thus providing another instance of common ground among English and French religious moralists alike, who certainly look back to the example of a primitive Church hostile to the idea of Christians turning up at pagan spectacles. We would expect to hear Prynne upbraid 'scandalous hystrionical Divines' who ought to have received heavy censure but for the fact that ecclesiastical discipline was found to be severely wanting.[77] Wills, however, extends the charge to all theatre-goers who 'live to the Scandal of that Religion they still make somehow to profess'.[78]

French Catholic opponents of theatre were no less rigorous in their approach to the matter of theatre-going Christians offering examples of scandalous behaviour which perniciously encouraged their weaker brethren to sin. While Suffren admits that spectators can watch some plays without necessarily being soiled by them, in other cases account had to be taken of 'le mauvais exemple que vous donneriez à ceux qui vous verroient, qui n'eussent jamais cru cela d'une personne qui fait profession d'une vertu & devotion particuliere'.[79] Nicolas Chardonnet is especially scandalized by the support actors receive from princes and noblemen:

> Cette action des Grands, ny leur qualité ne les rend pas impeccables, au contraire la parole de Dieu enseigne, que les Grands et les Puissants seront le plus puisamment chastiez, & ce, tant pour leurs propres pechez, que pour ceux où ils auront induit les autres par l'éclat de leurs mauvais exemples.[80]

The actor's remonstrance, on the other hand, identifies the presence of 'the best of the Nobility and Gentry' as the sign of a 'Civill and well-governed Theatre'.[81] The author of this anonymus letter to a certain A. H. asserts that, without the interest of the nobility, theatre can never be at its best or free

---

76 Semper, 'The Jacobean theatre', pp 44–51.   77 Prynne, *Histrio-mastix*, pp 149–50.   78 Wills, *Occasional paper*, ed. cit., p. 11. In France, the bishop of Metz extended refusal of the sacraments in his diocesan ritual of 1713 to all who had anything to do with spectacle, from actors to those who swept the floor (see Dubu, 'L'Église catholique', p. 337).   79 Le R.P.J. Suffren, *L'Année chrestienne ou le sainct et profitable emploi pour gaigner l'éternité*, 2 vols (Paris 1640–1), vol. 2, p. 863.   80 N. Chardonnet, *Le Pédagogue* (Paris 1662), p. 451.   81 *The actor's remonstrance or complaint for the silencing of their profession, and banishment from their several play-houses* (London 1643), p. 10.

from contempt and censure, since nobles possess 'all those virtues which adorn the Stage'.[82] The classic counterpoint to this recruitment of the aristocracy in the cause of theatre is the prince de Conti, former protector of Molière turned Jansenist moralizer. Wills would like his example to be followed in England:

> that the shameful *Indignities* put upon Persons of the *Highest Descent* by those of the *Meanest,* wou'd Stir up some excellent Spirit of that Eminent Rank, to shew them how much beneath them it was, to stoop so low to be thus coarsly entertained.[83]

Religious moralists were not the only ones conscious of the notion of scandal. Pepys wore his cloak over his head at the thought of being seen at a play so soon after the Plague, something bishops would not even have countenanced. He makes reference to the duchess of York organizing theatrical performances 'after the late great fast', and to her admitting to plays at Court 'the very nights before the fast for the death of the late king'.[84] But scandal for Pepys, it is true, extended to being seen in the cheap seats by four of his office-clerks who sat in the half-crown box.[85] John Evelyn, too, suffers from the agony of ambiguous feelings at attending a new opera in 1659, 'a time of such a public Consternation', it being 'prodigious that such a Vanity should be kept up or permitted'. But he had to go, being engaged with company, 'though my heart smote me for it'.[86]

Evelyn seems therefore to have shared the conviction of Burton, namely that Court encouragement of spectacle 'in the very heat and height of God's Tragedy' might move God to visit a greater plague on God's people.[87] The 1642 'Order of the Lords and Commons' banned public spectacles during the distressed Estate of Ireland, steeped in her own blood, and the distracted Estate of England 'threatened with a cloud of blood', calling for all possible means to 'appease and avert the wrath of God appearing in these Judgments'.[88] Indeed, John Rowe attributes to divine intervention the collapse of the upstairs floor of an inn at Witney, which broke under the weight of three to four hundred people watching a play which had been denied houseroom at the town hall. Other calamities of this sort had already occurred.[89] France does not escape, and for the reasons we might guess. The author of the anti-theatrical *Short treatise* reminds his readers of an incident

---

82 *Collier tracts*, ed. cit., p. 2.   **83** Wills, *Occasional paper*, ed. cit., p. 21.   **84** Pepys, *Diary*, ed. cit., vol. 7, p. 399, pp 376–7, and p. 325.   **85** Ibid., vol. 2, p. 18.   **86** Evelyn, *Diary*, ed. cit., vol. 3, p. 229. **87** Burton, *For God and king*, pp 49–50.   **88** 'An order of the Lords and Commons concerning stage-playes', dated 2 September 1642, in *Commonwealth tracts*, ed. cit., unpaginated.   **89** See J. Rowe, *Tragi-Comoedia* (Oxford 1653), p. 44.

in Lyon, at a performance by pupils of Jesuits 'to the disgrace of true religion', at which twelve people were killed by thunder and lightning sent by the 'lord from heaven'.[90]

In all that has preceded, one figure stands out as the agent of the alleged corruption associated with plays and the stage, and that is the player. As I have indicated, actors in England became associated with a particular religious grouping, understandably so since, if religious opponents to the stage managed to have their way, players stood to lose their livelihoods. In France, the acting profession certainly became a target for religious moralists, but in a rather different confessional climate. In any case, in both countries the profession had to face up to the challenge of defending itself against religious persecution. Space simply does not permit a close analysis of the laws, secular or religious, governing actors, except to say that in France, according to a severe interpretation of tradition, they could be – and sometimes were – denied the sacraments without first renouncing their profession.[91] In England, such sacramental practice did not apply, players seeming to have enjoyed a certain level of social acceptance, along with strong royal patronage, to the extent of being exempted from sumptuary laws, a statute of Henry VIII in 1510 specifically associating them in this regard with ecclesiastics and functionaries at court.[92]

On the other hand, once the theatres had been closed in the parliamentary era, it was stipulated that actors caught playing would be punished as rogues.[93] Prynne claims that two Acts of Parliament under Elizabeth I did in fact describe actors as rogues, but he concentrates in particular on their person, calling them 'the very dregs of men', and 'excessively vitious, unchaste, prophane, and dissolute in their lives'.[94] French religious moralists were no less charitable, especially towards actresses. It is Chappuzeau in France who mounts a defence of the private life of actors, noting their concern for family and especially their attendance at holy office.[95] *The actor's remonstrance* gives some hostage to fortune in claiming that actors had given up their mistresses for their wives.[96]

One of the gravest charges against players concerned the making of 'filthy lucre' from the corruption of others.[97] John Evelyn regarded the public theatre as mercenary,[98] and, as far as Collier is concerned, the argument that actors must live is 'the plea of pickpockets and highwaymen'.[99] That

90 Collier, *A short treatise*, ed. cit., p. 28. **91** For details, see in particular J. Dubu, 'L'Église' and Phillips, 'L'Acteur et la loi'. On the actor in general, see Phillips, *Theatre*, Chapter 9. **92** Fraser, *The war against poetry*, p. 137. **93** 'Ordinance of the Lords and Commons [. . .] to suppresse Stage-Playes', in *Commonwealth tracts*, ed. cit., p. 6. **94** Prynne, *Histrio-mastix*, p. 138, p. 100, and p. 32. **95** Chappuzeau, *Le Théâtre françois*, pp 128–35. **96** *Actor's Remonstrance*, p. 4. **97** Prynne, *Histrio-mastix*, p. 873. **98** Evelyn, *Diary*, ed. cit., vol. 3, p. 369. **99** Collier, *A short treatise*, ed. cit., p. 285.

actors are motivated by gain is an argument crossing the religious divide in France, with Rivet and Coustel arguing that that is their principal motivation.[100] For Pégurier, this becomes 'intérêt sordide',[101] Lelevel complaining that the only consequence of note emerging from the public stage was the actor's acquisition of immense riches,[102] and Coustel dramatically contrasting the sight of people dying of famine with fat-cat actors.[103]

In Prynne's eyes, actors, in the wearing of disguise or costume, marked the separation of Man from God's image,[104] cross-dressing, in the case of men, being in defiance of Deuteronomic law. For Prynne and Coustel, the separation already mentioned lies in the luxury of pleasure and rich apparel leading to effeminacy, a particular feature of the acting profession according to Pégurier.[105] Prynne also cannot abide the notion that actors wear the apparel of kings. This is precisely evinced by Alcandre as an argument in favour of theatre to Pridamant in Corneille's *L'Illusion comique* (1636 – ll. 134–6). Chappuzeau, almost alone in making extensive mention of England in his work, points to the need for actors to pay their court and to the importance of gifts to troupes of rich costumes by aristocrats in order to provide the appropriate visual quality of entertainment.[106] Indeed, he informs us that actors as a group could not be more devoted to monarchy,[107] a quality that becomes a fault in the eyes of some English moralists of the first half of the century.

As in the argument advanced in the letter to A.H., one defence of the actor was that the stage taught the clergy to speak English and to mend the style and form of their sermons,[108] a view echoed by Chappuzeau for whom actors have been a help to sacred orators.[109] Such a view is anathema to Ridpath who argues that, if the language of the playhouse was thought fit to offer ornaments to sermons, 'the Hearers will be apt to conclude that the Stage is not so criminal a Thing as some Men would have it accounted'.[110] How could actors possibly influence the orator if, as Collier would have it, instead of their pretension to correct, 'They laugh at Pedantry and teach Atheism, cure a Pimple and give the Plague'?[111]

Attitudes to the actor are further confirmation that a considerable degree of consensus existed across the confessional divide among those of a rigorist disposition in their belief that society could well do without theatre

---

100 For this discussion, see Phillips, *Theatre*, pp 183–4, and A. Rivet, *L'instruction chrestienne* (La Haye 1639), p. 12.   **101** L. Pégurier, *Décision faite en Sorbonne touchant la comédie* (Paris 1694), pp 62–3.   **102** Lelevel, *Réponse*, pp 43–4.   **103** Coustel, *Sentiments*, p. 63.   **104** Prynne, *Histrio-mastix*, p. 893.   **105** Coustel, *Sentiments*, p. 26, Prynne, *Histrio-mastix*, p. 47, Pégurier, *Réfutation*, p. 31 and pp 146–7.   **106** Chappuzeau, *Le Théâtre françois*, pp 169–71.   **107** Ibid., pp 151–2.   **108** *Collier tracts*, ed. cit., p. 7.   **109** Chappuzeau, *Le Théâtre françois*, pp 141–2.   **110** Ridpath, *The stage condemn'd*, ed. cit., p. 8.   **111** Collier, *A short view*, ed. cit., p. 287.

and public spectacle. It is, on the other hand, a commonplace among the defenders of the stage that the theatre contributed to the well-being of a country not only in terms of its prestige but also in terms of the policing of its populace. If people were pre-occupied with plays, they were thereby distracted from the temptation of disorder or rebellion. In England this position was hotly contested by the writers of anti-theatrical treatises. Responding to Dennis' *The usefulness of the stage* (1698), Ridpath is unconditionally opposed to the idea that the stage prevents rebellion, first on the grounds that few have the time or the money to spend on going to plays, thus greatly reducing the universal validity of the claim. Secondly, the facts are far from supportive of the case in an England which has witnessed the parliamentary revolt against Charles I, the popish plots against Charles II (a telling argument in view of Catholic associations with the stage), and the revolt against James II. Nor could theatre prevent the Fronde.[112]

The idea of the stage as the great instigator of disorder derived for Ridpath from that fact that the friends of the stage and the fomenters of civil war, here meaning those who set the king above the law, were as one. At the same time, if the supporters of the stage continued to oppose the maxims 'which contributed to the Happy Revolution', they were actually situating themselves in opposition to a regime which had ousted James II. Either way, they were the ones who found themselves in a state of illegitimacy. We see, then, that support or opposition to theatre cannot escape fundamental political consequences. Ridpath's argument was that by 'usurping upon the Sabbath, and ridiculing the Pretensions of the People to their Liberty and Property', the Brethren of the Stage carry the burden of having contributed to the calamities of the state.[113] This is categorically rejected in the letter to A.H. where it is rather the pulpit which has been more dangerous than the stage: 'Whoever learnt to cut a king's throat by seeing of Plays?'[114]

Ridpath follows criticism of such official encouragement of the stage by Charles I and the 'highest dignity in the Church' by implicitly comparing the behaviour of the crown in 1660 with the situation in France. Clearly, Ridpath has no time for the views of men such as Dennis that promoted the productive alliance of theatre and crown. Dennis had argued that Richelieu, with the very hand that wrote several plays, is credited with laying at the same time the 'Plan of the French Universal Monarchy'. Ridpath rejects this notion as heretical and wrong. In the first place, Richelieu's example is to no avail since he was 'so far over-match'd by his own Contemporary, *Oliver* the Stage-hater, that for all the courage of his tragical Pen, he could not save

---

112 Ridpath, *The stage condemn'd*, ed. cit., p. 201.   **113** Ibid., p. 204 and p. 156.   **114** *Collier tracts*, ed. cit., p. 11.

himself or his Country from trembling when the Usurper Roar'd'. Indeed, theatre is equated with tyranny.[115] In the second place, Charles II's restoration of play-houses showed a resolve 'to put cardinal Mazarin's Advice in Execution, which was to debauch the nation, in order to the better Introducing of Popery and Slavery'.[116] Not only does Ridpath allude to Mazarin as Italian, but he shows some awareness of the cardinal's reputation for unbridled spending on theatre after the miseries of the Fronde.[117] Another implication is that the restoration of theatre was responsible for ushering in the period of James II. In any case, Ridpath argues that the reintroduction of plays compared most unfavourably with Parliament times when 'the Theatre being then overturned, there was so great a Reform of Manners that [. . .] one might have walked through the city and suburbs without hearing an Oath'. For all these reasons, Ridpath is unable to understand how French Protestants, who declared against the stage, could remain the firmest friends of Louis XIV.[118]

That theatre and spectacle constituted a positive support for the cause of King and state was strongly held in France. Corneille could claim in *L'Illusion comique* that plays constituted the diversion of monarchs (ll. 1650–60), and l'abbé d'Aubignac expressed the view that theatre enhanced the prestige of the kingdom and also contributed to its policing.[119] Chappuzeau sought to advance the cause of actors in praising the service they rendered the king, also offering the view that, in monarchic regimes, plays prevent worry during times of war, whereas republics which close their theatres reduce their populations to a state of anxiety.[120]

The response of French religious moralists to such affirmations turns out to be somewhat more nuanced than that of many of their English counterparts who, as we have seen, do not hesitate to criticize their king. For them, if theatre was bad, the monarch should deprive it of his support, although no doubt some would say that he had been ill-advised by a Church less mindful than it should have been of its moral duty. On the other hand, a pious queen is held up by Baker as legitimizing a form of diversion which, had she been advised of its corruption by her confessors, she could never have allowed.[121]

115 Ridpath, *The stage condemn'd*, ed. cit., pp 199–200. **116** Ibid., p. 3. **117** On Mazarin and theatre, see J. Dubu, 'Cardinal contre Cardinal: Saint Charles Borromée en France au temps de Mazarin', in *La France et l'Italie*, ed. Jean Serroy (Grenoble 1986), pp 117–23 (pp.118–20). **118** Ridpath, *The stage condemn'd*, ed. cit., p. 36 and p. 201. **119** D'Aubignac's position is outlined most forcefully in the *Projet pour le rétablissement du théâtre* contained in P. Martino's edition of the *Pratique du théâtre* (Paris, Alger 1927). **120** Chappuzeau, *Le Théâtre françois*, pp 15–16 and pp 153–4. **121** Baker, *Theatrum Redivivum*, pp 113–14. See also Pepys, *Diary*, ed. cit., vol. 8, pp 55–6. We know that actresses were introduced to England in 1629 by Henrietta Maria, not altogether successfully,

The problem lay in the support for theatre of a king who claimed to defend and believe in his religion. How are the two to be conjugated in the same person if it is argued convincingly that theatre is corrupt? Is it possible to distinguish between private conscience and political expediency? Prynne gets as near as he can to a compromise in his suggestion that, if spectacle is to be worthy of a king and his foreign guests, it cannot be the common stage of cobblers, tinkers, whores and 'base mechanicks'. Performances must be conceived for, and confined to, the court. His dismissal of any king or high-placed individual who should stoop so low as to allow the ordinary play-house into the palace led to his ears and the end of his nose being removed as punishment for an act of *lèse-majesté*.[122]

The reaction of French Protestants in this regard ranges from the simple to the more complex. André Rivet rejects the argument that plays prevent sedition, using the same argument as Ridpath, notably that spectacles are organized for the rich rather than for the 'peuple'.[123] The more circumspect Vincent is inclined to believe that kings intend only the promotion of virtue and are beyond the prying eye of such as himself. If the confessors of kings allow such diversion, it is not for us to interfere in what does not concern us. Indeed, if actors perform before the king, they are careful to remove all offending material. On the other hand, Protestants themselves should not use the example of the king to legitimize their own behaviour in respect of theatre, since they do not share the same preoccupations. Christians live by rule, not example, however illustrious that example may be. The criterion according to which we live is not provided by the vogue of a prince's court, but whether it is in conformity with God's teaching. Vincent avoids open subversion by the suggestion that the state will not be harmed by Huguenot abstinence from spectacle.[124] However, his homily bears all the tension of the conception of a community which wishes to remain loyal in its difference, something Ridpath, as we have read, was unable to comprehend.[125]

But French Catholic moralists too have to live with the complexity of an ostensibly pious king who tolerates what they regard as morally unacceptable. How can this be explained in a situation which excludes all criticism of the king? The most detailed debate on this issue arose in 1694 during the *affaire Caffaro*. Lelevel's position is based on the different policies required in the spiritual and temporal domains. The king must provide for both. This he does by enforcing religious laws in so far as it is in his power, and by pass-

when she invited a French troupe to perform at the Blackfriar playhouse. A number of references to Henrietta Maria's participation in court spectacle are contained in M.-C. Canova-Green, *La Politique-spectacle au grand siècle: les rapports franco-anglais* (Paris, Seattle, Tübingen 1993). **122** Prynne, *Histrio-mastix*, pp 734–3. **123** Rivet, *Instruction chrestienne*, pp 76–7. **124** Vincent, *Traitté*, pp 59–60. **125** Ibid., p. 201.

ing no secular laws contrary to religious principles. However, not all his subjects have sufficient education to live according to the latter, with the consequence that some provision, like allowing the existence of theatres, must
be made to prevent any excess which would overturn civil society. It is the
role of the Church alone to enforce moral order: 'Si on ne ferme pas le
théâtre, c'est par pure politique; & si on le condamne, c'est par principe de
religion.' He adds that by refraining from going to plays, we do not harm the
state, but by going, we break our union with God.[126] Pégurier echoes
Vincent in refusing to penetrate the intentions of the king which can only
be for the good of a state where a lesser evil serves to prevent a greater
one.[127] Even Coustel, a former teacher of Port-Royal, can enunciate exactly
the same opinions in his own anti-theatrical work of 1694.[128] It might well
be held that providing this sort of justification of royal deeds was easier in
1694, that is, after the king's conversion, than, say, in 1664. Indeed, this conversion allows Gerbais to project political intentions retrospectively when he
seeks to excuse the king's own presence at theatrical performances. He wants
it all ways though. Certainly, 'raisons de politique' were, even in a previous
period, paramount. But had the king then been advised of the corrupt
nature of theatre, he would have acted in the same way as St Louis in ban-
ning plays from the kingdom.[129] Memories were surely not short enough for
this argument to have been at all convincing.

The preceding discussion has attempted to set out the various ways in
which England and France confronted the challenge of responding to the
very different sort of presence represented by the growth of a theatre of
largely secular inspiration. Areas of confessional convergence derived from
shared sources of authority, similar views regarding the impact of plays on
spectators inside the theatre, and the consequences of the theatrical experience on social and religious behaviour. At the level of this community of
Christians, the concept of scandal is common to divines on both sides of the
water through the example of Christians of the primitive Church keen to
differentiate themselves from their pagan fellow citizens. However, in that
process of attempting to establish what might be thought of as a true
Christian identity, factors relating attitudes towards the stage to politico-reli-
gious positionings emerged more strongly in England than in France during
the confrontation of two very different concepts of governance. At no time
in France did hostility to theatre threaten the position of the crown. While
to deny any political significance to the stage controversy in the kingdom
would fly in the face of historical common sense, the debate leant more to

126 Lelevel, *Réponse*, pp 26–7.   **127** Pégurier, *Réfutation*, p. 167.   **128** Coustel, *Sentiments*, p. 107.
129 Gerbais, *Lettre*, p. 95.

arguments over ways in which theatre could be situated in respect of the boundaries between religious and lay cultures, especially in the context of the Catholic Reform. Confessional rivalry of the sort manifest in England did not carry the same weight or baggage. Perhaps we might then conclude that, in the context of theatre, England and France were indeed divided by a common culture.

Conflicting cultures as reflected in some seventeenth-century English translations of French plays

J.-P. SHORT

In his *De la Comédie angloise*, which forms part of his *Sur les comédies* (written, according to René Ternois, between 1666 and 1667), Saint-Evremond, referring to Ben Jonson's methods of presenting characters, writes:

> A la vérité, ces fourberies, ces simplicitez, cette politique et le reste de ces caractères ingénieusement formez se poussent trop loin à notre avis, comme ceux qu'on voit sur notre Théâtre demeurent un peu languissants au goût des Anglais, et cela vient peut-être de ce que les Anglais pensent trop et de ce que pour l'ordinaire, nous ne pensons pas assez.[1]

On the face of it this seems an extraordinary statement. The proposition that the French do not think enough and that the English think too much is not one which, for those who like to think in general terms, would gain widespread acceptance. Nevertheless, it may prove a useful starting point for a consideration of seventeenth-century English translations of French plays for these can, on a superficial reading, provide similarly surprising and unexpected evidence supporting general statements which clash with some widely-held perceptions of the characteristics of the respective nations. To complement what Saint-Evremond says, here is a quotation from Dryden. In his *Essay of dramatick poesie*, first written in 1668 and revised in 1684, he writes, referring to the difference in approach to drama of the two nations:

> For as we who are a more sullen people come to be diverted at our plays: so they who are of an aiery and gay temper come thither to make themselves more serious; and this I conceive to be one reason why Comedies are more pleasing to us and tragedies to them.[2]

It may well be thought that this over-simplified view of the differences between the two peoples invites all sorts of questions, but the fact that a Frenchman – albeit living in England – and an Englishman both perceived

1 C. Saint-Evremond, *Œuvres en prose*, ed. René Ternois, 4 vols. (Paris 1966), vol. 3, pp 56–7.
2 John Dryden, *Of dramatick poesie, an essay*, ed. J.T. Boulton (Oxford 1964), pp 79–80.

attitudes or characteristics in their respective countrymen which affected the way they wrote plays and the way they appreciated them invites us to consider what these attitudes and characteristics are, and whether translations may enlighten us on the matter.

Let us start by reversing the order in which arguments are usually presented by producing some conclusions which may or may not be justified for these are conclusions *à la Saint-Evremond* or *à la Dryden*, that is to say over-simplified statements which suggest perceptions of English and French characteristics which are not normally associated with either nationality. These so-called conclusions are not, however, real ones. The real ones will come in their proper place. So here are some generalities which a perusal of some contemporary English translations of French plays might tempt one to make. English translations always try to make clear what in the French original could be thought to be ambiguous, uncertain or imprecise. English translations are more direct and more specific in their description either of events or of ideas. In its more extreme manifestations this takes the form of showing on the stage what in the French original is told in a *récit*. English translations are frequently imbued with political overtones, sometimes explicitly stated, which have no real parallels in the French original. English translations show emotion in open and direct ways, sometimes even in physical ways which, of course, because of *bienséance*, the French originals do not. Thus the following wonderful way of looking at things is reached: the English think more clearly, approach subjects more logically, are more interested in ideas, and display emotion more freely than do the French. Whether or not these are sensible conclusions can be decided after looking at some of the evidence.

The links between England and France in the seventeenth century were of an odd kind. There was the direct connection between the royal families of the two countries through the marriage in 1625 of Charles I to Henriette de France, the daughter of Henri IV, and then later, in 1661, through the marriage of their daughter, Henriette d'Angleterre, to the brother of Louis XIV. Thus links at the highest level are established, but how far down the social scale these links stretched is much more difficult to determine, and it is not possible to discuss this in detail here. Nor is it easy to determine how far the evolution of drama in each country was affected by the other, although after the Restoration it is possible to point to a French influence on English drama but the reverse cannot be said to be true. There is some evidence that English audiences could see French plays in London at different periods though their reception seems to have been hostile. In 1629, for instance, a performance by French actors was, according to a contemporary account, 'hissed, hooted and pippinpelted from the stage', but who they were and what they were acting is not recorded.[3] Much later in the century, Pepys mentions going to see a French play on 30 August 1661 'which was so ill done and the Scenes and company and everything else so nasty and out of order and poor, that I was sick all the while in my mind to be there'.[4] These hostile reactions to French plays in London may help to explain why so many translators claim, in their advertisements or epistles to the reader, to have greatly improved the play they have translated.

The number of translations of French plays, tragedies, tragi-comedies and comedies is not very great, and the majority of them date from the period of the Restoration.[5] The translators are, on the whole, minor playwrights or poets/poetesses who have an output of drama of their own. Pierre Corneille is the most translated author, while there are two, possibly three, translations of tragedies by Racine, and some tragi-comedies of Thomas Corneille and Quinault also found translators or adaptors. As far as comedy is concerned, Molière is, of course, very popular, but more as a source of plots and situations than as a target for direct translation. Adaptations of parts of the comedies are frequent but there are very few direct translations. *Tartuffe* is the most notable play to be directly translated,[6] and there are various versions of *Les Fourberies de Scapin*, the best of which is by Thomas Otway, the translator of *Bérénice*.[7]

The earliest tragedy to be translated in the seventeenth century is *Le Cid* in 1637–8.[8] The title page informs us that this was 'acted before their Majesties at Court and on the Cock-pit stage in Drury Lane, by the servants of both their Majesties.' The translator is one Joseph Rutter, of whom not much is known except that he was in the circle of Ben Jonson and was tutor to the children of Edward Sackville, fourth earl of Dorset and lord chamberlain to Queen Henrietta-Maria in 1628. It is also significant that Dorset had been ambassador to the court of Louis XIII in 1623 and so, presumably,

---

3 Quoted by G.E. Bentley, *The Jacobean and Caroline stage*, 7 vols (Oxford 1942–56), vol. 1, p. 25. **4** Samuel Pepys, *The diary of Samuel Pepys*, ed. R. Latham and W. Matthews, 11 vols (London 1970–1983), vol. 2, pp 165–6. **5** On seventeenth-century English translations of French plays, see the following in particular Dorothea F. Canfield, *Corneille and Racine in England* (New York 1904); André Lefevre, 'Racine en Angleterre au XVIIᵉ siècle', *Revue de Littérature Comparée*, 34 (1960), 251–7; Elizabeth Woodrough, 'Corneille et la Grande-Bretagne' in Alain Niderst (ed.), *Pierre Corneille*, Actes du Colloque de Rouen, 1984 (Paris 1985), pp 73–82; Dudley H. Miles, *The influence of Molière on Restoration comedy* (New York 1971); Peter France, 'Racine britannicus', *Œuvres et critique*, 24 (1999), 248–63. There are also references to translations in Allardyce Nicoll, *A history of Restoration Drama, 1660–1700,* 3rd edn, (Cambridge 1940) and in Derek Hughes, *English drama, 1660–1700* (Oxford 1996). **6** On this, see Matthew Medbourne, *Tartuffe or The French Puritan* (London, 1970). **7** Thomas Otway, *The cheats of Scapin* (1677) in *The works of Thomas Otway*, ed. J.C. Ghosh, 2 vols (Oxford 1932), vol. 1, pp 293–330. **8** *The Cid*, translated by J. Rutter (London 1637). The date is Old Style.

kept in touch with what was going on in France and must have known
about the success of *Le Cid*. According to Rutter, it was Dorset who 'commanded' him to translate *Le Cid*. The translation is not particularly good but
already has some of the characteristics which have been mentioned. Rutter
is not really interested in developing the expression of the conflicting
demands made on Rodrigue and Chimène. Most of the soliloquies are
omitted, and the very important one, the *stances* at the end of Act 1 where
Rodrigue tries to come to terms with what he has to do, is drastically
reduced so that his dilemma is hardly explored at all. The clue to the emphasis put on the play in England can be found in the title used which is *The
valiant Cid* and not just *The Cid*, and further light is thrown on this aspect
by the dedication by Rutter to Dorset in which he says: 'like Roderigo you
have ever preferred your honour to your affection and your King and country to anything besides'. Now in 1638 Charles I was already facing opposition in the country and Dorset was to support him staunchly throughout the
Civil War period. Thus the interest of *Le Cid* for the English audience would
seem to be as a display of valour and patriotism rather than as an exploration
of complicated relationships involving power, authority, passion, concepts of
honour and duty. Already we see the translator skewing the play in a different direction from that which the author originally intended. This alerts us
to the effect that the quite different political situations in England and
France at this time has on drama. Loyalty to the king is worthy of mention
although it is very doubtful that such a consideration would even be thought
of being mentioned in a French context. A footnote can be added which
points to another difference. *The valiant Cid* apparently remained reasonably
popular for, on 1 December 1662, Pepys saw it and describes it as 'a play I
have read with great delight but it is a most dull thing acted [. . .] there being
no pleasure in it. Nor did the King and Queene once smile all the whole
play'.[9] This may be an ambiguous appraisal but on the whole one would not
expect to 'smile' at *Le Cid*, and the fact that this should be remarked on suggests that audiences in England went to the play in a different frame of mind
from that of their French counterparts. It was not long after this that the
political situation in England worsened with the outbreak of civil war, the
defeat of the king, the flight to France of his queen and his heir, and the
installation of the Commonwealth during which time the theatres were
closed. This break in the continuity of political life had its effect on drama
because after the Restoration in 1660 and the re-opening of the theatres,
there was a great upsurge in dramatic activity and, with the return of Charles
II from France, much interest in things French, including French plays.

9 *The diary of Samuel Pepys*, ed. cit., vol. 3, pp 272–3.

Consequently, more translations were made and put on the stage in the 1660s and 1670s than at any other period in the century.

It is necessary, however, to mention that there had been some translations done in the 1650s. Sir William Lower, a minor playwright and a royalist, went into exile during the period of the Commonwealth and occupied some of this time by translating Corneille's *Polyeucte* and *Horace*. These translations were published but there is no record of their having been performed.[10] In the 1660s there were two translations of *Pompée*, one of *Horace* and two of *Héraclius*, one of which has not survived.[11] In the 1670s, another *Horace*, a *Nicomède*, a *Psyché*, an *Andromaque*, a *Tartuffe* (already mentioned), a *Bérénice* and a possible second version of *Bérénice* appeared.[12] All of these translations display the characteristics which have been identified as typical, but before considering some of these – it is not possible to look in detail at them all – it is worth drawing attention to a play which puts a comic Frenchman on the stage. This is *The playhouse to be let* by Sir William Davenant (although there is some debate as to whether it is really by him) which was acted in 1662 or 1663 and published in 1673.[13] In this we see the comic Frenchman who wants to rent the playhouse during the long vacation for his troupe of French actors. He offers to put on a farce and makes this distinction between English and French taste: 'de Engelis be more/Fantastique de de Fransh. De farce/bi also very fantastique and vil passe' and goes on: 'De vise nation bi for tings heroique/And de fantastique, vor de farce.'[14] He is able to rent the playhouse and puts on a one-act play which is, in fact, a translation of Molière's *Sganarelle ou Le Cocu imaginaire*, given in the same heavily accented frenchified English that the director speaks. It is clear from what he says that, in French eyes, English taste is

10 Sir William Lower, *Polyeuctes or The Martyr* (London 1671); *Horatius, a Roman tragedy* (London 1656).   11 These are the following: *Pompey. A translation of Corneille's La Mort de Pompée, with the addition of songs by Katherine Philips* (London 1663); *Pompey the Great, a tragedy translated out of French by certain persons of honour*, Edmund Waller, C. Sackville, Sir C. Sedley and S. Godolphin (London 1664); *Horace, translated by Katherine Philips* (London 1669); *Héraclius, emperour of the East, a tragedy Englished by Lodowick Carlell* (London 1664).   12 These are the following: *Horace, a French tragedy, Englished by Charles Cotton* (London 1671); *Nicomède, a tragi-comedy translated out of the French by John Dancer* (London 1671); Thomas Shadwell, *Psyche* (1675), *The complete works of Thomas Shadwell*, ed. Montague Summers, 5 vols (London 1927), vol. 2, pp 271–340; *Andromache, translated by a young gentleman who has a great esteem of all French playes* (London 1675); Thomas Otway, *Titus and Berenice* in *The works of Thomas Otway*, ed. cit., vol. 1, pp 251–92; John crowne, *The destruction of Jerusalem* (London 1677) in *The dramatic works of John Crowne*, ed. J. Maidment and W.H. Logan, 4 vols (New York 1874), vol. 2, pp 217–395. Although the author denies it, there are very strong resemblances to *Bérénice* in this play which suggest that Crowne did in fact use Racine's tragedy.   13 Sir William Davenant, *The playhouse to be let* (1673) in *The dramatic works of Sir William Davenant*, ed. J. Maidment and W.H. Logan, 5 vols (New York 1964) (reprinted in 5 volumes from the edition of 1872–4), vol. 4, pp 1–103.   14 *The playhouse to be let*, p. 18.

'fantastique' and that, therefore, the English go for farce while the French are 'vise' and go for 'tings heroique'. This is as blinkered a view as that held by the other side as articulated in Dryden's reference to the 'aiery and gay temper' of the French. It is Davenant, of course, who is portraying a comic Frenchman mocking English taste so it cannot be said that this is a French view of the English but, nevertheless, the existence of stereotypes is interesting.

Let us pass on from this to the *Pompey* of the 'Matchless Orinda,' Katherine Philips. This is the first real translation of the Restoration and it was put on for the first time in 1663 in the newly-opened theatre in Smock-Alley in Dublin.[15] Derek Hughes calls this play 'dull' and, although we might not agree with his opinion, he does provide a clue to the interest of the play for English and Irish audiences when he goes on to point out that it is 'one which concerns the murder of a just ruler defeated in civil war'.[16] It would be unwise to push the parallel too far but the arrival of Pompey in Egypt where he is seeking refuge may have put people in mind of Charles II seeking refuge in France after the defeats of the Civil War. It is unlikely that in France Louis XIV would be equated with the pusillanimous Ptolomée, but such a comparison would probably be quite acceptable on the English side of the Channel. *Pompey* is also remarkable for the presence in the entr'actes of scenes involving singing and dancing, the implied significance of which is that the great of the world must take time off to relax, and also that it is almost too much to ask the audience to give its attention exclusively to the unfolding of a serious dramatic plot, and that it too needs to be given time off from such stern stuff. The intervals provide these moments of relaxation but also do something else. They provide a glimpse of the future. After the third Act, Pompey's ghost appears to his wife Cornelia, who is asleep on a couch, and foretells the death of Caesar: 'His days shall troubled be and few/And he shall fall by treason too.'[17] This is an example of the English translation spelling out clearly something that is not mentioned in the French original, but it also demonstrates that, far from enhancing the original, this rewriting reduces the serious tone of the original tragedy to unacceptable levels of levity. Even where no happy ending would seem to be possible, a patched-up happy ending is partly envisaged.

The other translation of *Pompée* by 'certain persons of honour', one of whom was Charles Sackville, grandson of the earl of Dorset mentioned above, was acted in London in 1664. It does not have the interludes which

---

15 On this, see W.S. Clark, *The early Irish stage* (Oxford 1955), pp 52–6 and 62–4. On Katherine Philips, see also the article in this volume by Deana Rankin.   16 Derek Hughes, *English drama, 1660–1700*, p. 37.   17 *Pompey. A translation of Corneille's La Mort de Pompée, with the addition of songs by Katherine Philips*, op. cit., entr'acte between Acts 3 and 4.

Mrs Philips' translation has, but in some ways it has a more direct political message. In Corneille's text, Cléopâtre, talking about a possible marriage to César, says:

> Achevons cet hymen, s'il se peut achever;
> Ne durât-il qu'un jour, ma gloire est sans seconde
> D'être du moins un jour la maîtresse du monde
>
> (II. i. 428–30)

In the English version, just before the translation of these lines, Cleopatra states:

> And if propitious Heaven but bless my Bed
> With any branch of his illustrious seed
> That happy union of our Blood will Joyn
> Our Interest so, he'll be for ever mine.
>
> (II. i. 425–8)

This reference to the role of a child in securing a succession was particularly relevant at this time when the childlessness of Charles II was becoming, and was to become more so later on, an issue in the politics of the time. And in the epilogue to this play we find the following lines addressed to the King:

> This great example of false Egypt's fate
> Instructed Kings to set a higher Rate
> Upon their faith and hold their fame too dear
> To treat him ill for whom we languished here.

This is a direct reference to the asylum given to Charles II and makes a point which the author of *Pompée* would have found extraordinary.

As well as the two *Pompeys* mentioned above, there were two translations of *Héraclius* published in 1664, of which only one has survived. The author of the surviving translation was the oddly named minor playwright Lodowick Carlell. Two points are made in the author's advertisement, one is that this play is about 'the restoration of a Gallant Prince to his just inheritance', and the other is 'that the continuance of a just and Royal line [is] not one of the least blessings to the nation'. Pepys saw this play on 8 March 1664 and enjoyed it. He says, among other things, that:

> The play hath one very good passage well managed in it; about two persons pretending and yet denying themselves to be son to the Tyrant Phocas and yet heire of Mauricius to the crowne [. . .] At the beginning, at the drawing up of the curtain, there was the finest Scene of the Emperor and his people about him, standing in their fixed and different

postures in their Roman habits, above all that ever I yet saw at any of the Theatres.[18]

Spectacle is once again what attracts, and indeed it is spectacle that is sought in many translations. But in this translation of *Héraclius*, as well as spectacle and the extraordinary complication of the plot, there runs through a thread of political commentary on the nature of rule and the nature of power. The love interest (if it can be called that), which in Corneille's play is of prime importance, is played down. Much of the dialogue between Héraclius and the woman he loves, Eudoxe, is cut down or omitted altogether, and where in the French there is no explicit reference to Civil War, in the English translation there is at least one specific reference showing that in the English consciousness the Civil War had left its mark. Once more we note the presence of contemporary political overtones completely absent from the French original.

Finally in this group of translations of plays by Corneille is the *Horace* of Sir Charles Cotton (1671), not that of Mrs Philips which appeared in 1669 and which does not offer the same interest as the later one. Like her *Pompey*, however, Cotton's *Horace* has songs and choruses between the Acts which perform various functions. One is to foretell what will happen, thus removing any doubt that the audience might have about the outcome. For instance, at the end of Act I the following song is sung:

> Oh poor Camilla! How art thou
> Exalted in thy fortune now!
> Whom fate so soon will headlong throw
> Into a precipice of woe!
> Betray'd by Riddles and Loves Charms
> Thou dreamst thy self in Curiace arms
> Wrapt in chast pleasures, when alas!
> Thou only must could death embrace.

The fluctuation of fortunes in Corneille's play which pushes the action on, now in this direction, now in that, is not to the taste of the English translator who wants it made clear from the beginning that, however possible it may *seem* that a happy outcome may happen, it is *not* going to happen. What is even more significant in this translation is what seems to be the deliberate undermining of the Cornelian values of heroism and patriotism. For instance, this song is sung at the end of Act II:

---

18 *The diary of Samuel Pepys*, ed. cit., vol. 5, pp 78–9.

> Deluded Heroes! How they fly
> To meet a cruel destiny
> And sacrifice themselves to Fame
> A nothing, a meer airy name
> When in th'unnatural contest
> Who conquer'd falls is happiest

And this comment is made on war:

> Tis emulation animates
> The fury and the spleen of states
> And till that emulation cease
> The world will never be at peace.

This raises all sorts of questions about the meaning of Corneille's tragedies. Hughes makes the point that the French *Horace* portrays 'families divided by what is essentially a civil war',[19] and was therefore of interest to an English audience despite the fact that, by 1671, the Civil War was some years in the past. Nevertheless, the slant that the English translator puts on the play does show a marked difference in his aims from those of Corneille.

The same difference can be seen, in another way, in the translations of Racine's plays that were acted in this period. These were *Andromaque*, translated by an 'unknown young gentleman' and then tidied up by the dramatist John Crowne, and *Bérénice*, translated by the rather better-known dramatist Thomas Otway. The translation of *Andromaque* is based on the first edition which was published in 1668 and which contains the scene where Andromaque appears on the stage after the death of Pyrrhus, a scene which Racine suppressed in subsequent editions. It is tempting to say that the success of *Andromaque* in France prompted the 'unknown young gentleman' to want to make it known in England. However, doubt is cast over this theory by what we are told about him. He had, according to Crowne, 'a great esteem of all French plays', but he had a greater esteem of himself for he says that 'this of French plays is far from being the worst', and criticizes the absence of action on the stage which, he says, he has corrected as 'may be seen in the last act, where what is only dully recited in the French play, is there represented, which is no small advantage'.[20] In keeping with this claim, the translator puts on the stage the wedding of Andromache and Pyrrhus complete with music, songs and processions, and shows the assassination of Pyrrhus by Greek soldiers. There is no doubt that he has used ingeniously extracts from

---

19 Derek Hughes, *English drama, 1660–1700*, p. 37.   **20** *Andromache* (London 1675), Epistle to the Reader.

the *récits* in the original, describing what happens in the temple to build his reconstruction, including the dragging round the stage of the corpse of Pyrrhus and the appearance of Hermione with a 'naked poniard' in her hand. Thus violence, stark and vivid, is unleashed in this last act, but far from compensating for the 'dullness' of the *récits,* the tragedy is diminished by this display. The translator, used to seeing violent emotions portrayed in physical terms, does not appreciate that it is possible for such emotions to be portrayed equally effectively in the more subtle form of *récits*.

The same cannot be said of *Titus and Berenice*, Thomas Otway's translation of *Bérénice,* performed in 1676 and published in 1677. The play is much condensed in passing from Racine to Otway, for instead of five acts there are three, and this is achieved by cutting the length of many speeches and by running scenes together. In an interesting article discussing this translation, Jessica Munns suggests that the main difference between the tragedy of Racine and the tragedy of Otway is that in the latter Titus, instead of being portrayed as a man coming to terms with an impossible position, becomes a man who accepts his position but changes as he does so. She says that the play could just as well be called *Titus* as *Titus and Berenice*: 'Berenice's role is that of a catalyst; she helps to set processes in motion which turn Titus from a man to a monster.'[21] This interpretation is open to question, but certainly a comparison between the last words of both plays is illuminating. Everybody remembers the haunting lines spoken by Bérénice at the end of Racine's tragedy:

> Adieu. Servons tous trois d'exemples à l'univers
> De l'amour la plus tendre et la plus malheureuse
> Dont il puisse garder l'histoire douloureuse.
>
> (V. vii. 1502–4)

In Otway's play the valediction is pronounced by Titus:

> Henceforth all thoughts of pitty I'll disowne
> And with my arms the Universe ore-run
> Rob'd of my love, through Ruins purchase fame
> And make the world as wretched as I am.
>
> (III. i. 476–9)

We see very clearly here the very different emphasis in the English play compared to the French original. The emphasis shifts in other ways as well. The relationships between Titus, Berenice and Antiochus are much cruder

---

21 Jessica Munns, 'Thomas Otway's *Titus and Berenice* and Racine's *Bérénice'*, *Restoration,* 7 (1983), 58–67 (p. 63).

and more violent. Much of the subtlety of Racine's play is lost. There is, as we know, some, but not very much, physical expression of mental distress in *Bérénice*. Titus weeps, Bérénice becomes dishevelled, but this in no way detracts from the high emotional level that is maintained throughout the tragedy. The difference in this respect between the original and the translation is well illustrated by the final scene of *Titus and Berenice*. We see here how a display of emotion on the stage can lead to what seems a ludicrous scene. Titus hands Berenice over to Antiochus for protection, saying 'Never forsake her in sad distress' (460), and the stage direction says 'falling on his neck', a physical expression presumably of his own distress, but this is followed by Antiochus turning to Arsaces and saying to him 'Arsaces! On thy bosom let me lye/Whilst I but take one last dear look and dye' (463–4). It may be frivolous to wonder whether Antiochus had disentangled himself from Titus before falling on the bosom of Arsaces or whether the two collapse together on the wretched Arsaces, but this kind of action does show up the hazards of trying to represent mental distress in a physical manner. Words may be more powerful after all.

At the beginning of this article some real conclusions were promised instead of the spurious ones offered then. The aim has been to show how superficial those preliminary statements were. What separates the English translations from their French originals is the desire for spectacle, the taste for cruder representation of violence and violent emotion, and the wish to discern a political message in a given situation. The first two aims are responsible for the way English translators distort the originals, and spring from the wish to fit the plays into an English framework. The main lines of the differences in the development of the drama in the two countries are well known: the taste for spectacle and violence on the one hand, and the movement away from these on the other. This is clearly illustrated in these translations but it would appear that the defining difference is to be found in the political aspect. The challenging of authority, while it did exist in France as the wars of Fronde demonstrate, never reached the same intensity as it did in England. The frame of mind which brought about this challenge in England can be discerned in these translations, even in their more extreme and absurd aspects, and they therefore display, even if they do not explain, the conflict of two cultures in dramatic form.

'If Egypt now enslav'd or free A Kingdom or a Province be': translating Corneille in Restoration Dublin

DEANA RANKIN

The quotation in the title of this article is taken from Corneille's *La Mort de Pompée* as it was staged in Dublin in late January 1663. The lines are not to be found in Corneille's original but in a song to which the Dublin Cleopatra listens in the *entr'acte* between Acts IV and V, that is to say, just after Caesar leaves her to deal with her brother Ptolemy's rebellion, and just before Pompey's widow, Cornelia, enters carrying an urn containing her murdered husband's ashes. At the end of the play Cleopatra will, with Caesar's blessing, be crowned queen of Egypt. For the moment, however, uncertain of her realm, she stands poised between the opposing possibilities of Rome's protection and Rome's revenge. At precisely this point in Corneille's play, then, Dublin's Cleopatra pauses to listen to a song addressed to her ancestral gods:

> Alas! In vain our Dangers call;
> They care not for our Destiny;
> Nor will they be concern'd at all
> If Egypt now enslav'd, or free,
> A Kingdom or a Province be.[1]

The song was one of five written both for performance and for incorporation in the published text by the poet Katherine Philips, 'the Matchless Orinda,' also the translator of *Pompey. A tragoedy* (Dublin and London, 1663).[2] Her *Pompey* was one of two translations of Corneille produced and per-

---

1 *The collected works of Katherine Philips: the matchless Orinda*, ed. G. Greer, R. Little and P. Thomas, 3 vols (Stump Cross 1991–3), vol. 3, p. 72, ll. 34–8. Unless otherwise stated, all references are to this edition. References to Corneille's originals are to *Corneille: Œuvres complètes,* ed. André Stegman (Paris 1963). My reading of Corneille has been informed by G. Couton, *Corneille et la Fronde* (Paris 1955), S. Dubrovsky, *Corneille ou la dialectique du héros* (Paris 1963), R.J. Nelson, *Corneille, his heroes and their worlds* (Philadelphia 1963) and on *Nicomède* in particular, M. Greenberg, *Corneille, Classicism and the ruses of symmetry* (Cambridge 1986), pp 146–65. I am also grateful to Wes Williams for his comments on this essay.   2 Philips' poems are addressed to a 'circle of friendship', where the correspondents go by names taken from French and English romances and plays. Philips also translated Corneille's *Horace* (see below) and 'Mr Corneille upon ye Imitation of Jesus Christ [. . .] Englished'. The following fragments were first published in *Poems* (1667): 'Tendres desirs out of a French prose', 'La solitude de St Amant', 'A pastoral of Mons: de Scudery's in the first volume

formed in Dublin in the decade after the Restoration of Charles II. The second, *Nicomède. A tragi-comedy* (London, 1671), was by John Dancer, an officer in the service of the duke of Ormond, the king's lord lieutenant of Ireland during most of the period in question. While Philips had been in Wales with her husband throughout the Civil Wars and Republic, both Ormond and Dancer had spent a good deal of time in royalist exile in France.

This essay, with its tales of translations, *entr'acte* insertions and liminary materials, addresses the aftermath of conflicts beyond the borders of the French nation, in particular the English Civil Wars and the Wars of the Three Kingdoms, which made their peculiar mark on the literary culture of seventeenth-century France. I shall seek to locate both Katherine Philips' *Pompey* and John Dancer's *Nicomède* within a political web of translation and representation in a city where the label of 'Kingdom or Province' was as fraught for the emerging Anglo-Irish elite as it was for Philips' version of Corneille's story of Cleopatra. For both plays are, I shall argue, part of the broader project to rehabilitate the monarchy in the Three Kingdoms – England, Scotland and Ireland – which had been radically reshaped by republic and regicide. Furthermore, as both of these writer-translators turn to Corneille to articulate their anxieties in a time and a place of political instability, they draw our attention anew to the original texts and to the explorations of the tensions between the metropolitan centre and the colonial margins which fuel Corneille's soldier-heroes.

In 1662, John Ogilby, together with Thomas Stanley, was appointed master of the revels for Ireland by the lately-restored king. Together they built the Smock Alley Theatre which remained the central focus of Dublin drama until its closure in 1786. For Ogilby, this was a return to familiar territory. His short-lived Werburgh Street Theatre, the first purpose-built theatre outside London in the Three Kingdoms, flourished in Dublin between 1636 and 1640. It attracted the patronage of numerous members of the Irish nobility, including the young Ormond, before escalating political unrest in the build-up to the 1641 Irish Rebellion forced its closure. In contrast to his earlier, financially disastrous, escapade, Ogilby's Dublin theatre had official sanction. In the words of the king's patent, the masters of the revels were to produce plays that were 'decent and becoming and not prophane and obnoxious'.[3] In this quest for 'decent and becoming' theatre, they turned to

of Almahide, Englished', and from the Italian, 'Amanti ch'in pianti & c'. All are included in *Collected works,* ed. cit., vol. 3.   **3** Quoted in W.S. Clark, *The early Irish stage* (Oxford 1955), p. 182. See also M. Schuchard, *John Ogilby, 1600–76: Lebensbild eines Gentleman mit vielen Karrieren* (Hamburg 1973), and K. van Erde, *John Ogilby and the taste of his times* (Folkestone 1976).

translations from the French, to drama from Paris. For it was there, in the city of royalist exile, that the English court and its hangers-on had been exposed to French theatre.[4] More specifically, they had witnessed at first hand the importance assigned to theatre in the building of the nation-state. So it was that, as they sought to reconstitute themselves in the new Restoration world order, to extricate themselves from a recent history of rebellion and republic, Dublin looked towards Paris, and returned exiles returned to Corneille.

The few critics who have written on theatre in Restoration Dublin have tended to figure it as a court in exile from the metropolitan centre that was London. P. Kavanagh argued that members of Dublin society considered themselves 'more as English exiles than as citizens of Ireland', and D. Canfield, although more effusive, resorted to a similar argument:

> Dublin was at this time a brilliant edition of London [. . .] The brilliant cultured people who ruled it regarded themselves as exiles, and felt that keen desire to keep in touch with the movements of the great world centres which characterises exiles.[5]

I suggest that more was at stake than these characterizations of the Dublin cultural scene allow. The story of French translation in Dublin is not simply a story of exile from, or jealous competition with, London. In choosing to translate Corneille's *La Mort de Pompée* and *Nicomède*, both Philips and Dancer chose to translate plays which do more than thematize the distance from the metropolitan seat of colonial power. For both plays address the question of autonomy on the margins of empire, and they also explore the possibilities of language as a force for mediation, as a system of terms to be adopted and adapted in the transition from military to civic order. Restoration Dublin turned, then, to Paris and to Corneille to explore the language of a regal but civil society.

Corneille's *La Mort de Pompée* was probably written in late 1641, the year of the outbreak of the Irish Rebellion and of the English Civil War. It was finally published, with a dedication to Mazarin, in 1644. In the prefatory 'Au lecteur', Corneille acknowledges his debt to a text which also served as a sub-text for English writers, politicians, and soldiers on all sides throughout the English Civil War, namely Lucan's *Pharsalia*. Gesturing towards his

---

4 *Le Cid* was immediately popular in England. The British Library copy of Rutler's translation, *The Cid, a tragi-comedy*, is dated 26 January 1637; in France *Le Cid* was entered for publication on 21 January 1637. Rutler also published a sequel in 1640, described as 'A Tragi-comedy', in which Chimène's father, presumed dead, returns. 5 P. Kavanagh, *The Irish theatre* (Tralee 1946), p. 66; D. Canfield, *Corneille and Racine in England* (New York 1904), pp 32–3. See also A. Mulert, *Pierre Corneille auf der Englischen Bühne und in der Englischen Übersetzungs-Literatur des siebzehnten Jahrhunderts* (Erlangen and Leipzig 1900).

own act of translation for the stage, Corneille celebrates the Roman
Republican poet,

> dont la lecture m'a rendu si amoureux de la force de ses pensées et de
> la majesté de son raisonnement, qu'afin d'en enrichir notre langue, j'ai
> fait cet effort pour réduire en poème dramatique ce qu'il a traité en
> épique.[6]

La Mort de Pompée presents the aftermath of Lucan's civil wars. It appeals
for the recognition and reward of true loyalty and for recuperation and
accommodation of the disruptions of civil war to a new order, the better to
ensure the future security of the state. In the 1660 'Examen', Corneille revis-
ited his play remarking that:

> Il y a quelque chose d'extraordinaire dans le titre de ce poème, qui porte
> le nom d'un héros qui n'y parle point; mais il ne laisse pas d'en être en
> quelque sorte le principal acteur, puisque sa mort est la cause unique de
> tout ce qui s'y passe.[7]

If the dead Pompey is the main actor who broods over Corneille's play,
then the executed Charles I is the unspoken and unspeaking presence in
Katherine Philips' translation. In an early poem, Philips linked the death of
Charles I with that of Pompey:

> Unhappy Kings, who cannot keep a Throne,
> Nor be so fortunate to fall alone!
> Their weight sinks others: Pompey could not fly,
> But half the world must bear him company;[8]

It was such poetry which, under the Republic and Commonwealth of the
1650s, brought her family close to disaster. In spite of her puritan upbring-
ing and strong republican family connections – Philips' husband, Captain
James Philips, was a staunch Cromwellian and her mother had married the
parliamentary commander Skippon – she developed a reputation as a lyric
poet with royalist tendencies. Another of her poems, 'Upon the double

---

6 Corneille, *Œuvres complètes*, ed. cit., p. 315. On the use and influence of Lucan's *Pharsalia* in
England, see D. Norbrook, *Writing the English Republic: poetry, rhetoric and politics, 1627–1660*
(Cambridge 1999), pp 1–23. Abraham Cowley also (unsuccessfully) models his unfinished royalist
epic, *The Civil War*, begun in 1643, on Lucan.　　**7** Corneille, *Œuvres complètes*, ed. cit., p. 316.　　**8** 'On
the 3d September, 1651', *Collected works*, ed. cit., vol. 1, pp 82–3, ll. 21–4. For further details of
Katherine Philips' biography and works, see P. Souers, *The matchless Orinda* (Cambridge, Mass.
1931), P. Thomas, *Katherine Philips ("Orinda")* (Aberystwyth 1988), and E. Hageman 'Katherine
Philips: the matchless Orinda', in K.M. Wilson (ed.), *Women writers of the Renaissance and Reformation*
(Athens and London 1987), pp 566–608.

murther of K. Charles, in answer to a libellous rime made by V.[avasor] P.[owell]', fell into the hands of one J. Jones, a rival of her husband's. His political downfall, as a result of his wife's writing, was only narrowly averted.

By 1662, however, the year in which Katherine Philips arrived in Dublin, the tables had turned. Under the newly restored monarchy, Philips' husband was now the culprit, threatened with execution on account of his past maltreatment of a royalist captain. He kept his life but lost his seat in parliament. Once more faced with ruin, this time in a very different political climate, Philips' was far from being a threat to her husband's position. Rather, both her writing and her royalist reputation became an important tool in the quest to rehabilitate her family and, as we shall see, her friends.

Philips journeyed to Ireland to accompany her friend, Anne Owen (*Lucasia*), to her new marital home. She also had pressing business of her own. For Philips' much-vaunted royalism did not prevent her from seeking to capitalize on her father's early investments in the Company of Adventurers, established by Cromwell in 1642 to fund the relief and conquest of Ireland. She aimed to pursue her father's land claims through the Irish courts and restore some family income. Throughout her stay in Ireland, she continued a correspondence with *Poliarchus*, more commonly known as Charles Cotterell, the king's master of ceremonies in London and himself a translator of La Calprenède's *Cassandra*. It was Cotterell who would ensure that manuscript and printed copies of both *Pompey* and occasional poems were presented to the queen as Philips requested. Cottrell's preservation of Philips' letters further ensured that the business of the translation, performance and publication of the Dublin *Pompey* is well documented.[9] It is from these letters that we learn how Philips travelled to Dublin within a few days of Ormond's arrival to take up his post as lord lieutenant. Though less ceremonious, the arrival of the poetess attracted the attention of others in the same Restoration boat. The letters make it clear that her translation of *Pompey*, begun for private amusement, was destined to become a corporate event. It was Roger Boyle, earl of Orrery, who first came upon a fragment of Philips' work, a scene from the third act. He quickly despatched the latest edition of Corneille's original, that of 1660, for her use, together with a characteristically fulsome poem of encouragement:

> You English Corneil's Pompey with such flame,
> That you both raise our wonder and his fame.
> If he could read it, hee like us would call,

---

9 See Sir Charles Cotterell, *Cassandra: the fam'd romance* (London 1652), also republished in 1661, 1664, 1667, 1676. Cotterell also translated Davila with W. Aylesbury as *The historie of the civill warres of France* (London 1647[48]). *Letters from Orinda to Poliarchus* was first published in 1705.

The copy greater than th'Originall.

. . .

Who your translation sees cannot but say,
That tis Orinda's work and but his play.
The French to learn our language now will seek,
To hear their greatest wit more nobly speak.[10]

Orrery's own interest in French literature had begun on his 'grand tour' on the continent in 1639–41. He took only cursory note of the *Querelle du Cid* raging in Paris at the time. Later, in a letter to his draconian father from Saumur, he apologized for reading French romances 'to pass a lazy houre', despite strict instructions to the contrary.[11] His halting engagement with literature was suspended when he returned to Ireland on the eve of the Irish Rebellion, and he found himself thrust into a military career. Orrery's youthful transgressive reading was, however, later recuperated to more gentlemanly pursuits when he composed *Parthenissa*, a long and fairly tortuous romance and the first written in English to announce Madame de Scudéry's work as its model. In 1662, he made his own theatrical debut in Dublin with *Altamira*, later renamed *The generall* for its London production. With the personal encouragement of Charles II, Orrery went on to become one of the Restoration's most successful and prolific writers of heroic verse drama.[12]

Orrery's interest in Philips' translation project was, however, more than aesthetic, for he too had a political past which needed recuperation, if not translation, into new and better terms. After the execution of Charles I, Orrery did not join the royalist exile in France, rather – under severe duress, he and his loyal biographer maintained – he served as Cromwell's chief commander in Ireland, becoming a close friend and confidant. Although Orrery later became one of the chief instruments of the Restoration in Ireland, he remained anxious to prove and re-prove his loyalty to the crown. Whatever his reasons, Orrery provided strong moral support for Philips' enterprise and, when the translation was complete, suggested that it should also be performed. He donated, moreover, the substantial sum of £100 for costumes.[13]

10 Katherine Philips, *Poems by the most deservedly admired Mrs Katherine Philips* (London 1667), f. b1v; *Collected works*, ed. cit., vol. 2, pp 46–9. **11** K. M. Lynch, *Roger Boyle, first earl of Orrery* (Knoxville 1965), p. 20. See also E. Budgell, *Memoirs of the life and character of the late earl of Orrery* (London 1732). **12** Roger Boyle, *Parthenissa: a romance in four parts* ([Waterford 1651] London 1655); *Dramatic works of Roger Boyle, earl of Orrery*, ed. W. Smith Clark II, 2 vols (Cambridge, Mass. 1937). See also N. Klein Maguire, *Regicide and Restoration: English tragi-comedy, 1600–1671* (Cambridge 1992). **13** Orrery was only one of a number of prominent Dublin figures involved in the production. The earl of Roscommon composed a prologue, Edward Dering an epilogue, and John Ogilby was choreographer. Others contributed the settings for the songs. See Philips, *Collected works*, ed. cit., vol. 2, pp 74–6; vol. 3, pp 3–4, 90–1.

The whole was performed before Ormond, a well-known francophile. Not only had he recently returned from French exile, but he had also traced his aristocratic ancestry with some pride to the Anglo-Norman invasion of Ireland in the twelfth century.[14]

The printer's prefatory remarks to the published version of Philips' play state that 'the hand that did it is responsible for nothing but the English and the Songs between the Acts, which were added only to lengthen the Play, and make it fitter for the Stage'.[15] It is, however, these very interventions – the act of translation and the 'minor' additions – which substantially alter the tone of Corneille's original. Philips' translation is both fluent and fluid, probably the best and certainly the most performed of the seventeenth-century English versions of Corneille. She transposes the Cornelian alexandrines into what was fast becoming the poetic vehicle for the Restoration drama, the decasyllabic heroic couplet. Her correspondence with Cotterell reveals the care with which she approached her task.[16] The letters also reveal acute anxiety when it appears that a rival translation by 'Certain persons of Honour' working in London might be published first. With the encouragement of Orrery and company, the Philips' version beat the metropolitan competition. While she remained modestly deferential in public, in private Philips was fiercely critical of the London version, taking some glee in the fact that 'this way of garbling Authors is fitter for a Paraphrase than a Translation'.[17]

Above all, the mechanics and metaphors of translation are used to articulate and explore the complicated relationships between Rome and Egypt, empire and colony. This is perhaps best illustrated through the comparison of Corneille's original and Philips' translation in the second act, as Cleopatra and Ptolemy separately receive news of Rome's arrival in Egypt and consider their future. In Corneille's play, in the account given to Cleopatra of Septimus' role in the killing of Pompey, the treachery and violence done to the Roman ruler by his compatriots in a foreign land is linguistic as well as physical:

---

14 According to his library catalogue, Ormond owned many sadly unidentified volumes of French drama in addition to all of the texts published in the *Querelle du Cid*. See *Calendar of the manuscripts of the marquis of Ormonde*, 8 vols (London, 1902–20), vol. 7, p. 515.   15 Philips, *Collected works,* ed. cit., vol. 3, p. 2.   16 See for example her exchanges with Cotterell over the best translation for the French word 'effort', *Collected works,* ed. cit., vol. 2, pp 64, 69–70, 78, 79.   17 Philips, *Collected works*, ed. cit., vol. 2, p. 103. *Pompey the Great. A tragedy* (London 1664) was translated by Edmund Waller, Edward Filmore, Charles Sedley, Lord Buckhurst and Sidney Godolphin (see Mulert, *Pierre Corneille*, p. 38). On Philips' criticism of the anachronistic monarchism of this translation, see A. Shifflett,' "How many virtues must I hate?": Katherine Philips and the politics of clemency', *Studies in Philology*, 94 (1997), 103ff.

> Septime se présente et lui tendant la main
> Le salue Empereur en langage romain
> (*La Mort de Pompée*, ed. cit., II. ii. 479–80)

Philips' translation both thematizes and enacts the function of language in the pursuit of power:

> *Septimius* then, to get him in his Pow'r,
> I'th Roman Language call'd him Emperour;
> (*Pompey*, ed. cit., II. ii. 33–4)

Cleopatra responds to Achoreus' report with an appeal to the Gods for future justice. In the French this reads as follows:

> Vous qui livrez la terre aux discordes civiles
> Si vous vengez sa mort, Dieux, épargnez nos villes!
> N'imputez rien aux lieux, reconnaissez les mains:
> Le crime de l'Egypte est fait par des Romains.
> (*La Mort de Pompée*, ed. cit., II. ii. 509–13)

In Philips' translation there are certain alterations, due in part to the exigencies of rhyme, which beg further attention:

> You Gods, who Nations do chastise with War,
> When you Revenge this Death, our Cities spare;
> And not the place, but Actors look upon,
> The crime of *Egypt* was by Romans done.
> (*Pompey*, ed. cit., II. ii. 63–7)

How are we to read this shift from 'discordes civiles' to 'War'? Simply as a matter of scansion, or as a reluctance to stir the memories of recent conflict? Certainly, for such as Orrery, keen to exorcize his Cromwellian ghosts, it was more valuable to define his service in Ireland as a just war against Irish rebels, than as part and parcel of the civil strife between parliament and king.

In this passage, the future queen demonstrates her nascent Roman citizenship; the good of the empire, particularly her part of the empire, depends on the health of its centre. Rome must lead by example. Cleopatra's brother, on the other hand, is more than ready to follow the bad example of Rome, as personified in Septimus. At the end of Act II, Ptolemy listens to bad advisors, as Photin instructs him on how to receive Caesar. Corneille's original styles this imagined first encounter as a linguistic performance; the young king is advised both to play the good colonial agent and to play for time:

> Quoi qu'il en fasse enfin, feignez d'y consentir,
> Louez son jugement, et laissez-le partir.
> Après, quand nous verrons le temps propre aux vengeances,
> Nous aurons et la force et les intelligences.
>
> (*La Mort de Pompée*, ed. cit., II. iv. 707–10)

Philips' translation presses even further the theatricality of the event:

> Entire submission to his Orders shew
> Applaud his Judgment but then let him go.
> That time forever for our Revenge will be most fit,
> When we can Act as well as think of it.
>
> (*Pompey*, ed. cit., II. iv. 63–6)

When Caesar, surrounded by soldiers, does eventually make his first appearance on stage, Ptolemy greets him with a single deferential line: 'Seigneur, montez au trône, et commandez ici' (*La Mort de Pompée*, III. ii. 807). Philips repeats the grand gesture but, with one crucial alteration, she steers the emphasis of her translation away from the historically charged threat of military command to the more joyful prospect of civil rule: 'Great Sir, ascend the Throne and *govern* Us' (*Pompey* , III. ii. 89, italics mine).

At the level of words and sentences, then, Philips' translation gives Corneille's version of Lucan's tale of the 'mopping-up' operation after the Civil War particular resonance in Dublin. But what of the 'minor additions' claimed with such reticence? The final tone of Philips' translation is substantially different from Corneille's original, notably because her decasyllabic couplets seem to shift Corneille's formal alexandrines into more buoyant optimism. This mood is further strengthened by the original insertions with which this essay began, namely the songs at the end of each act. In some cases, the songs are only loosely linked to the action of Corneille's original. The song which Ptolemy and Photin listen to at the end of Act 1, for example, which begins 'Since affairs of the State are already decreed, /Make room for Affairs of the Court', stands alone. Indeed, it was a popular hit throughout the 1660s, reproduced in various collections of airs.[18] The songs at the close of the third and fifth act, however, both attempt to shape the main action by pre-empting and guiding the audience's reaction. In doing so, moreover, they seek to strengthen the potential for tragi-comic vision in the play. Both songs focus on the problem of the Roman citizen Cornelia and her desire for revenge. The third act closes with her vow to avenge the death

---

18 *Pompey*, ed. cit., I. iii. 124–43. See also 'To my Lady Elizabeth Boyle, singing "Since Affairs of the State &c."', *Collected works*, ed. cit., vol. 1, pp 177–8 and commentary.

of her husband, Pompey. But Philips' *entr'acte* song, which follows immediately on, has Pompey's ghost sing over the sleeping Cornelia. The song effectively delivers in prophetic mode the vengeance she desires, as Pompey reveals of Caesar that 'His dayes shall troubled be, and few, / And he shall fall by Treason too' (*Pompey*, ed. cit., III, iv. 113–14). Yet the presence of her temporarily resurrected husband, and indeed the fact that he reveals the future in what amounts to a lullaby, both serve to soften the stark force and dramatic tension of the widow's vow. His song concludes with a vision of future peace:

> Thy stormie Life regret no more,
> For Fate shall waft thee soon a shoar,
> And to thy *Pompey* thee restore.
>
> Where past the fears of sad removes,
> We'l entertain our spotless loves,
> In beauteous and Immortal Groves.
>
> There none a Guilty crown shall wear,
> Nor *Caesar* be Dictator there.
> Nor shall *Cornelia* shed a Tear.
> (*Pompey*, ed. cit., III. iv. 118–26)

This song is then followed by a 'Military Dance', still part of Cornelia's dream, after which she wakens to deliver a short speech, the only invented speech of Philips' version:

> What have I seen? And whether is it gone
> How great the vision! and how quickly done!
> Yet if in Dreams we future things can see,
> There's still some Joy, laid up in Fate for me.
> (*Pompey*, ed. cit., III. iv. 128–31)

This is a move of reconciliation when the bereaved speak with the dead, when present uncertainties become future resolutions, when even Cornelia can imagine a return to 'Joy'. It is further reinforced in the closing scenes when a grand masque performed before Cleopatra and Caesar resolves, for the moment, the problematic elements of the play. The final song summarizes the happy fates of the main characters. Even as Cornelia resists the play's move to restoration and closure by departing to Africa to stir her sons to revenge, she is recuperated to the play's final image – a tragi-comic ending with a vision of her beauty in grief:

> *Cornelia* yet, would challenge Tears
> But that the sorrow which she wears,
> So charming is, and brave.
> (*Pompey*, ed. cit., V. v. 77–9)

In spite of the revenge and disruption to come, there the play pauses at a moment of resolution, moving from the 'Tragoedy' of Philips' title to the borderlands of tragi-comedy. Within this structure, the women are held up as examples of model citizenship. Even as Pompey's vengeful widow Cornelia calls for vengeance, her duty as a Roman citizen drives her to save Caesar from Ptolemy's treacherous rebellion. In spite of her familial ties to Egypt, Cleopatra displays an acute sense of duty to Rome and to Caesar. Yet alongside such moments of transcendent devotion to Rome, the play continually gestures towards the uneasy balance of power between Rome and its colonies. Indeed, in the end, Cornelia leaves for Africa, for the lands of that great and primal threat to the Roman state, Queen Dido, to stir up Rome's colonial sons to revenge. Cleopatra remains, for the present, Caesar's loyal servant, but this increasingly personal loyalty will come to destabilize Rome and contribute to Caesar's ruin. The closing scene, the day of celebration, is merely a temporary respite.

Some seven years later, in 1669–70, John Dancer's version of Corneille's *Nicomède* was also produced in the Smock Alley Theatre. His translation is no masterpiece. Like *Pompey*, it is, for the most part, in decasyllables, but it is much less accomplished than Philips' work. The rhythm, for example, is uneven and the lines do not always rhyme. Dancer does not leave behind an equivalent to Philips' 'Letters to Poliarchus', but the final text does not suggest that he debated the finer points of translation with his friends. He is, all in all, a minor figure in the history of the Dublin stage, described by Canfield as 'a moderate versifier and a literary man of taste and intelligence'.[19]

Turning to Corneille's *Nicomède* (1651), Stegman proclaims it to be the playwright's first great political tragedy since *La Mort de Pompée*, describing it as 'sa pièce politique la plus complète'.[20] Contemporary critics were quick to identify the eponymous hero with Condé and his role in the Fronde, and whilst audiences flocked to the play, critics condemned the playwright. Indeed, Corneille did not return to writing for the stage until *Œdipe* in 1659.[21] In the light of this, John Dancer's choice to translate this particular play in Dublin in the late 1660s, and to do so in distinctly military terms, is

---

19 Canfield, *Corneille and Racine in England*, p. 85. **20** Corneille, *Œuvres complètes*, ed. cit., p. 519. **21** Ibid. See also Gouton, *Corneille et la Fronde*.

particularly interesting and merits further attention. The translator was an officer in the army, possibly born in Ireland, and certainly resident there after the Restoration in the service of Ormond, whom he had also served during his French exile. Dancer is one of many soldier-writers in Ireland who give literary form to military ambition, his voice speaking forth at the nexus of courtly patronage and military service.[22]

Like Katherine Philips, Dancer is the author of a number of translations, including Tasso's *Aminta: the famous pastoral* (London, 1660), and Renaud Rapin's *The comparison of Plato and Aristotle* (London, 1673). Nor was *Nicomède* his only translation from the French for the Dublin stage. The titlepage of Dancer's version of Quinault's play, *Agrippa king of Alba or The false Tiberinus* (London, 1675), announces that it was 'several times Acted with great Applause before his Grace the Duke of *Ormond* then Lord Lieutenant of *Ireland* at the Theatre Royal in Dublin'.[23] Quinault's verse tragi-comedy – more suited to opera libretto than to the French classical stage – might seem far removed from Dancer's later preoccupation with *Nicomède*, yet there are also points of contact. The tension between the soldier and the politician, more forcefully articulated in Corneille's play, resonates in the character of Agrippa's father. This consummate politician, having faked Agrippa's death and arranged for him to return to court disguised as the hated tyrant Tiberinus, fails to adjust to changing circumstances. When tempers mount against 'Tiberinus', the father risks losing his own son rather than revealing his deception. The possibility of a straightforwardly tragi-comic plot of mistaken identities and *doppelgängers* is complicated by the father's insistence on *not* revealing the truth, on playing the political rather than the military card. In counterpoint to this, Quinault's play is full of commanders putting their military training and the respect of their men to good use. The play presumably appealed to Dancer's military interests as well as to the growing Restoration passion for honour and courage.

It is in *Nicomède* that Dancer brings his profession fully to bear on his translation. Like *La Mort de Pompée*, the play deals with life in the outreaches of Empire. Indeed, Corneille expressly states this in both the 'Au lecteur' (1651) and the revised 'Examen' of 1660:

> Mon principal but a été de peindre la politique des Romains au dehors, et comme ils agissaient impérieusement avec les rois leurs alliés, leurs maximes pour les empêcher de s'accroître, et les soins qu'ils prenaient de

---

22 See my 'The art of war: military writing in Ireland in the seventeenth century' (D.Phil., Oxford, 2000). **23** It was, therefore, acted between 1666 and 1669. See Philippe Quinault, *Agrippa roi d'Albe, ou Le faux Tiberinus* (Paris 1660).

traverser leur grandeur, quand elle commençait à leur devenir suspecte à force de s'augmenter et de se rendre considérable par de nouvelles conquêtes.[24]

If, as Corneille suggests in the 'Au lecteur', this is a soldier's play, then Dancer's translation stresses the idea of the military and soldier's language far beyond that of the French original. In Act I Scene v, for example, Arsinoé divulges to Cléone her plan to ensure that the throne should remain in her hands, describing how she will cause a rift between the king and his oldest son. In the French this reads:

> Sans prendre aucun souci de m'en justifier
> Je saurai m'en servir à me fortifier.
> > (*Nicomède*, ed. cit., I. v. 337–38)

The English translation engages more fully the metaphors of military siege:

> His Accusations as my Engines move
> Will fortifie me in his father's Love.
> > (*Nicomède*, ed. cit., I. v. 337–38)[25]

At the opposite end of the spectrum, the soldierly integrity and honour of Nicomède is also more forcibly expressed in English. In Act IV Scene II, for example, he appears before King Prusias to ask for the punishment of those who have endangered Queen Laodia and to implore him to put royal duty before family interests. In the French this reads:

> C'est gloire et non pas crime à qui ne voit le jour
> Qu'au milieu d'une armée et loin de votre cour,
> Qui n'a que la vertu de son intelligence,
> Et vivant sans remords, marche sans défiance.
> > (*Nicomède*, ed. cit., IV. ii. 1165–8)

Dancer's translation gives to Nicomède's speech the language and the force of the military handbook:

> 'Tis Glory this, and not a crime for one
> Who lives in Camps, where no Court Tricks are known;
> Who scorning baseness, does not Thunder fear,
> And knows no Strategems, but those of War.
> > (*Nicomède*, ed. cit., IV. ii. 1165–68)

---

24 Corneille, *Œuvres Complètes*, ed. cit., p. 520. For a reading of the internal politics, see J. Scherer, 'Les intentions politiques dans *Nicomède*' in Alain Niderst (ed.), *Pierre Corneille, Actes du Colloque tenu à Rouen, octobre 1984* (Paris 1985), pp 493–9. **25** John Dancer, *Nicomède, a tragi-comedy* (London, 1671).

As with Philips' *Pompey,* however, there is more to Dancer's translation than
the interpretation of individual words. *Nicomède* was originally produced and
published as a 'Tragédie' whereas Dancer's translation was entitled *Nicomède,
a tragi-comedy* (London, 1671). The sub-title might suggest that, as with
Katherine Philips' earlier translation, pressure had been brought to bear on
dramatic genre, that alterations – those 'songs and minor additions' once
again – had been made to the original. This is not the case. Dancer's translation remains entirely faithful to the spirit of Corneille, and his choice of
the label 'tragi-comedy' does not indicate any textual intervention. Rather
it signals the long shadow cast by the execution of Charles I on the English
Restoration stage. The representation of tragedy remained problematic, and
play descriptions were often changed accordingly.[26] Yet this sub-title also
invites a re-consideration of Corneille's own uneasiness with the ending of
Nicomède, as he articulates it in the 'Examen'. Had he followed his sources to
the letter, Corneille would have replicated Justinian's tale of Nicomède's parricide. Rather than risk accusations of moral corruption, this time seeking
to avoid the fraught moral and aesthetic issues of the *Querelle du Cid,*
Corneille bows to audience opinion. Nicomède is rescued from Roman
captivity by Attalus, his step-brother. The male hereditary line is reunited in
the final scene, and the curtain falls as the hero, still uncorrupted, prepares to
rule and to marry. As Corneille summarizes in the 'Examen' (1660):

> D'abord j'avais fini la pièce sans les [Nicomède and Attalus] faire revenir
> [. . .] Cela ne démentait point l'effet historique, puisqu'il laissait sa mort
> en incertitude, mais le goût des spectateurs, que nous avons accoutumés
> à voir rassembler tous nos personnages à la conclusion de cette sorte de
> poèmes fut cause de ce changement, où je me résolus pour leur donner
> plus de satisfaction, bien qu'avec moins de régularité.[27]

Still smarting perhaps from the *Querelle du Cid,* Corneille effectively adopts
– and thereby lulls his audience into accepting – the structures of tragi-comedy without the title. Dancer is not so coy. Indeed, the very values which
cause Corneille concern are the root of the play's appeal to Dancer. For his
translation celebrates the uncompromising and uncompromised ideals of the
soldier-hero. To prove the point, he dedicates the play to Thomas, earl of
Ossory and son of Ormond, who had earned a national reputation for his
part in the Four Days' War with the Dutch in 1666. Ossory had also proved

---

26 See, for example, N. Klein Maguire, *Regicide and Restoration: English tragi-comedy, 1600–1671.*
Perhaps the most notorious example of alteration to suit Restoration taste was Nahum Tate's
History of King Lear (London 1681) which gave Shakespeare's original a happy ending.
27 Corneille, *Œuvres complètes,* ed. cit., p. 521.

heroic (if ultimately unsuccessful) in his defence of his father's reputation under the attacks of the consummate politician Buckingham. Dancer allies himself with an Anglo–Norman Irish dynasty, whose past loyalty to the king was constantly called into question as enemies stirred up unwelcome memories of Ormond's proximity to the Irish Catholic Confederation during the Wars of the Three Kingdoms. The Ormonds are identified with soldierly honour, their enemies with political treachery.[28] Corneille's dramatic exploration of the complexities of national and imperial allegiance, with its variation on the theme of love versus war, centres on an examination of just such opposing types. On the one hand, the soldier, Nicomède, conquers territory, annexes kingdoms and, when necessary, raises rebellion. On the other, the politician-ambassador, the Roman envoy Flaminius, attempts to educate new Roman citizens, build family alliances with the Empire, and disrupt autonomous power bases. In Corneille's play, the soldier firmly defeats the ambassador. The reunited royal family overthrows the false family proposed by the stepmother, Arsinoé, a family which depends quite literally on being held hostage to Rome. Moreover, Nicomède, through his projected marriage to the queen of Armenia, is poised to create a powerful and threatening royal alliance on the verges of the Roman empire. The play celebrates the soldier at the height of his powers, stopping short of his descent into tyranny.

I conclude with one final scene from Restoration Dublin, or rather, not a scene at all. For Katherine Philips' translation of Corneille's *Horace* was never performed there. When she died of small pox, aged 32, just over a year after the curtain went down on *Pompey*, her *Horace* was left unfinished.[29] It breaks off towards the end of Act IV Scene VI, just after the Roman hero Horace has killed his sister Camilla for her ambivalent reaction to his victory over the Albans and her lover. The last words she translated are:

> Proclus   What have you done?
> Horace   An honourable act
>   Such an offence does such revenge exact.
>   (*Horace*, ed. cit., IV. vi. 72–4)

<hr />

28 See J.C. Beckett, *The cavalier duke: a life of James Butler, first duke of Ormond* (Belfast 1990), pp 96–7, 105–6. Dancer translates Corneille's 'Trois sceptres' as 'Three Kingdoms,' emphasizing the relevance to the Stuart monarchy, Corneille, *Œuvres complètes*, ed. cit., p. 522; Dancer, *Nicomède*, p. 4.   **29** Philips' translation was partially completed by Sir John Denham, often performed, and first published in *Poems* (London 1669). Sir Charles Cotton's translation, *Horace, a French tragedy of Monsieur Corneille* (London 1671) was used to complete Philips' translation in the 1705 edition.

> [Procule   Que venez-vous de faire?
> Horace   Un acte de justice,
>   Un semblable forfait veut un pareil supplice.]
>   (*Horace*, ed. cit., IV. vi. 1323–4)

By chance, then, Philips' translation breaks off at the very point which her earlier version of *Pompey* continually sought to defer, namely the threat posed to the state by personal vengeance. How can Horace, warrior champion of Rome, be reconciled with the brother who has murdered his sister? The legacy of fratricide, parricide and the problematic aftermath of civil war is left hanging in mid air.

The recuperation of vengeance into the foundations of the civil state is a problem which haunts Corneille's work. It is amplified by both Philips and Dancer as they produce translations and performances in a new theatre, in a would-be vice regal city on the edges of a fledgling empire. As the Dublin settler elite of which they were a part pondered the aftermath of the English Civil Wars, as they wondered whether Ireland would henceforth be a sister- or subject-kingdom, these translations of Corneille, a French-Norman-Jesuit writer, came to play a formative role in the emergence of a distinct Protestant Anglo-Irish cultural voice. In terms mediated by women and ex-soldiers, these texts explore how and whether the soldier should turn statesman. At the heart of such cultural readjustment stood the Cornelian figure of the soldier-hero, faced with the conflicting claims of past and future, charged with the task of reconciling past military action with the demands of fostering peace and stability in the new nation-state.

Rebel hearts: La Calprenède's transformation of political conflict into drama

GUY SNAITH

Gautier de Costes, sieur de La Calprenède (1610–63), wrote nine plays during the late 1630s and early 1640s, six tragedies and three tragi-comedies.[1] As recommended by Aristotle and as practised by dramatists since the revival of tragedy in the sixteenth century, La Calprenède, like his contemporary Pierre Corneille, dramatizes 'quelque grand intérêt d'état'.[2] Sedition, conspiracies, usurpation and rumours of regicide characterize five of his six tragedies in which La Calprenède plays variations on the theme of rebellion and political upheaval holds the fate of states in the balance. In this article, I shall look at five of La Calprenède's tragedies in the light of their exploitation of political conflict.[3]

In his first play, *La Mort de Mithridate* (season of 1635–6), La Calprenède dramatizes the last day in the life of the king of Pontus as the Romans finally incorporate his kingdom into their empire under Mithridate's son, Pharnace, who has betrayed his father and sold himself to Rome. In his second tragedy, *Jeanne, reine d'Angleterre* (1636–7),[4] La Calprenède depicts the collapse of the nine-day reign of Jane Grey as queen of England. Jeanne and her supporters are besieged in London. Her father-in-law Northbelant (Northumberland) and her husband Gilfort (Guildford) claim to uphold the last will and testament of Edward VI against the supporters of Mary Tudor's legitimacy. The rebellion lost, the usurpation overturned, Northbelant and Gilfort are tried and executed. Haunted by the memory of her father's reign, Marie does not want to execute Jeanne who she feels has sinned only by

---

1 Represented in the Aspin collection conserved at Trinity College Dublin are six individual plays of La Calprenède as well as a bound volume of six plays. 2 See Pierre Corneille, 'Discours de l'utilité et des parties du poème dramatique', in H.T. Barnwell (ed.), *Writings on the theatre* (Oxford 1965), p. 8. 3 There are modern editions of three of La Calprenède's plays. *La Mort de Mithridate* (Paris 1637) and *Le Comte d'Essex* (Paris 1639) are included in the second volume of *Théâtre du XVIIe siècle*, ed. Jacques Scherer and Jacques Truchet (Bibliothèque de la Pléiade, Paris 1986). My edition of *La Mort des enfants d'Hérodes* (Paris 1639) is in the University of Exeter's 'Textes Littéraires' series (LXIX, 1988). For the other plays, references will be to the original edition. La Calprenède's tragedy *Phalante* (Paris 1642) will not be included in this discussion; it deals with a love triangle between three friends, one of whom is the queen of Corinth, but there is no rebellion nor even any 'grand intérêt d'état'. 4 La Calprenède, *Jeanne, reine d'Angleterre* (Paris 1638).

obeying her father-in-law. She nevertheless inevitably gives in to the *raison d'état* and begins her reign with the spilling of what she considers to be innocent blood. In *Le Comte d'Essex* (1637–8), the rebellion of the earl of Essex in 1601 is the subject matter. Essex, the headstrong favourite of Elizabeth I, has returned from Ireland, abandoning his campaign against Tyrone, and has marched through London to see the queen, it being rumoured by his enemies that he wants to seize power. The crown and the queen's life are thus threatened. Essex is arrested, tried and condemned to death while the queen waits for him to ask for mercy. He does so by sending a ring which, however, only reaches its destination after his death. In La Calprenède's next tragedy, *La Mort des enfants d'Hérode* (1637–8), there is only a rumour of sedition. Hérode's two sons by Mariane, Alexandre and Aristobule, are slandered and tried on trumped-up charges of plotting against their father, charges backed up by forged letters. 'Ceste funeste Cour' (I. i. 85) is how one of the sons describes the Herodian court, and Hérode's two sons end up sacrificed to its fetid atmosphere, as was their mother. In La Calprenède's last extant play, *Herménigilde* (1641–2),[5] there is civil war in Visigothic Spain. The national religion is Arianism, and Herménigilde, who has converted to Roman Catholicism, has rebelled against his father by withdrawing to Seville where he has been besieged for the last two years. Factions at court centring on the queen, Herménigilde's stepmother, spread rumours that Herménigilde is plotting to seize power and even has designs on the king's life. Appeals are made to him to recant, and also to his father Lévigilde to give way, but, for the good of Spain, Herménigilde is sent to his death.

Such are the situations of transgression for which, it might seem, there are two causes: self-promotion or self-protection. Certainly Mithridate is under no illusions as to his son's motivation: 'Il veut porter un Sceptre en me privant de vie' (I. ii. 157). Northbelant is certainly accused of dynastic ambition in pushing his daughter-in-law's claim to the throne, and even Jeanne admits to having been dazzled momentarily by the crown. 'Quel espoir de grandeurs te pouvait éblouir?', Elisabeth asks Essex (I. i. 43), and although he proclaims that the welfare of the state was his aim, that 'welfare' is conceived personally – to rid Elisabeth of such ministers and counsellors as Cécile (Robert Cecil) whom Essex feels are poisoning the queen's mind against him. In the darker atmosphere of the later plays, characters simply try to protect themselves. Persecution at court forces Hérode's children by Mariane to consider fleeing, but, before they are able to, charges of conspiracy against

---

5 La Calprenède, *Herménigilde* (Paris 1643).

their father are brought against them. Persecution at court forced Herménigilde and his supporters to withdraw to Seville where they have remained solely on the defensive against the king. Tricked into leaving the city, Herménigilde is arrested but bears no ill-will: 'En posant les armes, j'ai obéi à mon père, j'ai obéi à mon Roy, quelques prétextes que j'eusse dans ma rébellion, j'étais toujours criminel' (*Herménigilde*, ed. cit., III. 1). *Criminel*, *crime*, accompanied by adjectives such as *lâche* and *noir*, suggest that rebellion is never considered an appropriate course of action in La Calprenède's drama. Indeed, it is the most heinous of crimes as it cuts across all that a subject owes his monarch, namely *devoir, obéissance, services*, and even threatens that which is the most sacred: the very life of the monarch. So it is that *Jeanne* opens with the loyal Clocestre (Gloucester) chiding the English over their support of the usurper Jeanne and the rebels:

> Oui peuple je rougis de honte et de colère,
> Et cette lâcheté si visible et si claire,
> Qui vous laisse survivre à vos Princes trahis,
> Me défend aujourd'hui d'avouer mon pays.
> [. . .]
> O piété bannie! O foi que nous devons
> Aux Princes souverains de qui nous relevons.
> O Majesté jadis si sainte et si sacrée,
> Faut-il que ta grandeur soit si peu révérée?
>   (*Jeanne*, ed. cit., 1. i)

Civil war tears countries apart, the horror of which Herménigilde's brother, Recarède, points out:

> Lévigilde est armé contre son fils, Herménigilde est armé contre son père, l'Espagne est armée contre l'Espagne, et dans cette horrible confusion, quelque but qu'on se propose et quelque succès qu'aient vos armes, aucun des partis ne peut espérer que la destruction de soi-mesme.
>   (*Herménigilde*, ed. cit., 1. iii)

Rebellion gives rise to a host of political questions. What should be done when great noblemen rebel? Given the different qualities of great military figures and sedentary court advisers, what is the respective value to the state and the monarch of such different servants? When the great do wrong, indeed great wrong, how much weight should be attached to past services? How can innocence survive at a Machiavellian court? How can one know the truth when factionalism is so pernicious? How can one live with a tyrannical monarch? What are the duties of subjects and monarchs to each other? Is such a thing as 'liberté de conscience' outside the sovereign's purview? Can a monarch ever break his word? And, of course, is clemency such a dangerous policy, or must the *raison d'état* always be invoked?[6]

In La Calprenède's drama, rebellion is set as a political problem which is to be worked out over the course of five acts. The crisis must be averted, order must be restored, and justice is expected. With the exception of *Mithridate*, in all four tragedies monarchs have to steer a path through conflicting evidence and conflicting advice to some approximation of the truth. Trials of the rebels are convened. Clemency and severity make their conflicting claims. But the resolution of the political problem is always pursued on a personal level. Sometimes one feels that all La Calprenède wants is the premise of a rebellion to give himself the opportunity to explore the human repercussions of such an event. He therefore makes life even more difficult for his rulers. Mithridate has been betrayed by his own son; Elisabeth loves Essex; it is Hérode's own children who are accused of plotting against him; Lévigilde must proceed against his son and heir. Political problems, indeed topical problems, are aired in the plays, but encounters between protagonist and antagonist, confrontations between one court faction and another, cross-examinations at trials, are all marked more by the personal than the political. So it is that La Calprenède chronicles the conflict between political abstractions and the call of humanity.

La Calprenède's archetypal tragedy deals with a rebellion or intrigue, real or supposed, followed by a trial, a condemnation, and vain appeals from secondary characters, before ending with the execution of the rebel. Such a schema works with variations for four of the tragedies mentioned above. *La Mort de Mithridate* deals with rebellion but does not contain a trial. In *Herménigilde* a trial is promised but never takes place. The pattern is established of two poles, the protagonist and the antagonist, between which the tragedy develops. Behind each is generally a group of people, the one hoping to save the hero and/or heroine and the other hoping to be rid of them. The aim of the hero's supporters is to bring the two poles together in the hope that, through discussion, the problems will be resolved. Communication represents an attempt to close the gap, to reach the truth which will save the hero from execution, reunite father and son, and bring lovers together. And as an indispensable cog in the machinery of suspense, the antagonist must be persuaded to see the hero again or to grant another reprieve. Therefore, the appeals are made, the interviews are arranged, and

6 Some of these problems facing the monarch are explored in my article "'Le Poids d'une couronne": The Dilemma of Monarchy in La Calprenède's Tragedies', in Keith Cameron and Elizabeth Woodrough (ed.), *Ethics and politics in seventeenth-century France: essays in honour of Derek A. Watts* (Exeter 1996), pp 185–99.

the trials are set up. The aim is communication, the one thing which is rarely achieved. Ranged against the protagonist and his supporters is a band of enemies equally intent on keeping the poles apart. If communication is going to mean an improvement in the lot of their victim, then the central characters must not be allowed to talk, or at least must be kept under close surveillance. In these tragedies we are interested in the fates of two characters: in that of Pharnace as well as that of Mithridate, in Marie's as well as in Jeanne's, in Elisabeth's as well as in that of Essex. The interdependence of the two poles is an essential part of La Calprenède's tragic vision. The alienation of father and son, of husband and wife, the estrangement of lovers, the increasing isolation of two people related by bonds of family or affection, all underscored by the failure of dialogue, constitute the basis of La Calprenède's dark vision.

La Calprenède chronicles battles for power, but such battles seem murkier from *Hérode* onward. In *Mithridate* and *Jeanne* the crown is at stake and the life of the monarch endangered; in *Essex* we are on the threshold of the later plays and are never sure whether the safety of the crown really is in jeopardy or whether the conflict is rather between Essex and Cécile. What we can be sure of in all three cases, however, is that acts which could be considered rebellious have indeed been committed and the security of the state has thereby been threatened. *Hérode* and *Herménigilde*, on the other hand, present devastating pictures of the power of slander. The crown is at stake, as in the earlier plays, but the danger to it does not stem from the ostensible rebels but rather from malign counsellors to the king. The villainous elements build upon the precariousness of the position of the monarch to convince him that his power is coveted, that conspiracy is rampant, that his life is in danger, and that it is the hero who is to blame. In this respect we see that, although La Calprenède seems to prefer his protagonists to be tragic victims of external pressures, schemed against, going to their death head held high, admired and pitied, it is the sovereigns whom we find more interesting, their dilemmas and psychological struggles providing the plays with their dynamism. The obscurity of motivation of the royal counsellors who hate, conspire, slander and finally win, contributes to the pervasive atmosphere of malevolence which is such a part of court life in the later plays. With communication almost impossible and with trials so ineffective, the good are rendered impotent in the face of near-motiveless evil. Stays of execution, interviews, appeals are merely placebos which cannot halt the spread of the cancer. The rather traditional rebellions of *Jeanne* and *Essex* look clear-cut and healthy beside the domestic machinations and the atmosphere of corruption of the later plays where calumny paves the road to power.

Beginning in political strife and ending with the rebel disposed of, these tragedies do move in a traditional way from chaos to order. But this order is not one accompanied by the winds that bring refreshment or by the rain that cleanses and washes away the sin. Instead, the antagonist and the audience are left contemplating a near void. Throughout five acts, monarchs have battled with themselves over their interests versus those of the state. They have opted for the latter, sometimes compromising their principles, always going against their nature, and yet, for the monarchs concerned, they, and in several instance the state itself, are definitely worse off for this victory of *raison d'état*. The rebel is no more, the rebellion, real or supposed, has been suppressed, but is the future any brighter? Is the country really safer? In the earlier plays, the bleak future of the monarch is balanced by a relatively good fate for the state. Although Jeanne and Essex may die and Marie and Elisabeth suffer, England is more secure. Although in despair, the monarch could well recover in spite of herself. Because of the needless deaths of his sons, however, Hérode faces the future without a legitimate heir to the throne, a thought even more disturbing in that, by the end of the play, he has abdicated all responsibility so that the reins of government would seem to be falling even more firmly into the hands of his counsellors. Is Judaea really better off? With Herménigilde executed and Recarède, next in line to the throne, having withdrawn from court into a self-imposed exile, what is to be Lévigilde's future? And that of Spain? A progression from chaos to order may be chronicled by La Calprenède, but if that order is represented by a new order on the lines of the counsellors of Hérode and Lévigilde, the view of the future for Judaeans and Spaniards is indeed bleak.

After the destruction, confronted as we are by a void, we are left pondering the events of the play and contemplating the future. La Calprenède refuses to grant his audience the luxury of an 'incomprehensible repose'.[7] Absurdity is instead the keynote. The predominant feeling as the canon develops is that conspiracies will continue to flourish, innocence will still be victimized, the wrong people will continue to be condemned, states will remain insecure, and no matter how hard good men may try to harness the absurdity, the world will grind inexorably onward in the same way. The overall impression we are left with is one of waste – the waste of good rulers, the waste of young lives, the cruellest waste of all being that of the innocent young couples like Jeanne and Gilfort, Glaphira and Alexandre, Indégonde and Herménigilde, who ask nothing but to love each other, are pushed into situations not of their own making, and are sacrificed to higher priorities,

7 The phrase is George Steiner's. See *The death of tragedy* (London 1961; reprinted 1974), p. 9.

whether those priorities are genuine or alleged. So it is that, as one progresses through La Calprenède's dramatic career and one continues to search for that reassurance that the destruction of the hero's life and the blighting of the antagonist's must at least have served some worthwhile purpose, one realizes increasingly that it all seems to have been for nothing.

La Calprenède has a tragic sense of life which taps the cruel absurdity of existence, exposes the evil in the world while offering little explanation, appreciates the tragic gap between aspiration and achievement, and which, most achingly of all, explores the all-too-human difficulties of communication and isolation. We watch powerless as characters, bound by the closest of ties and yet cut off from each other, reach out but fail to communicate and, in not doing so, slide helplessly to disaster. But amidst their own suffering, whether in a prison cell or on their march to the scaffold, La Calprenède's heroes are still capable of a dignity, a nobility, and above all of a consideration of others which raises them above the absurdity of the inevitable. A positive value is discovered by the victim amidst the wasteful destruction, whereas for the antagonist the political issue has been a burden which, when resolved, has only negative results. Having renounced family and honour, Pharnace survives to live alone with his conscience, chafing beneath the yoke of a Rome which no longer needs him, while his family has preserved its dignity and unity in death. A prisoner of her role as queen, Marie flees the stage in horror while Jeanne glides majestically to the scaffold. Unjustly cursed by her lover, betrayed by her counsellor and lady-in-waiting, Elisabeth survives to suffer in solitude Essex's posthumous revenge. Having sacrificed his family, Hérode vows to lock himself away with his remorse while his sons can look on Heaven as a release from their hell on earth. Knowing he is going to die, Herménigilde can proclaim: 'Oui la victoire est à moi' (*Herménigilde*, ed. cit., v. i), a cry which his father cannot raise. In La Calprenède's works, then, tragic voracity is never satisfied with just the death of the protagonist: the antagonist who is left is also its victim.

Just before the collapse of her nine-day reign, Jeanne apostrophizes the crown: 'Charmeresse des sens, dangereuse Méduse,/Vaine & folle grandeur dont l'éclat nous abuse.' Her string of metaphors then runs to: 'Mer . . . Polipe . . . Miroir . . . Jouet de la Fortune, ombre, chimère, vent' (*Jeanne*, ed. cit., I. v). In its lushness Jeanne's lament stands out from the disenchantment voiced by other monarchs of La Calprenède as a kind of *morceau de bravoure* whose sentiment is common throughout the plays, but whose expression is not. Highlighting the traditional problems of theatrical kingship, such a lament also evokes the disillusionment, uncertainty, instability and impermanence of the world in general, themes which bear witness to the consciousness of La Calprenède's age, a spirit which Ehrmann discreetly referred to as 'cette sensibilité qu'il est convenu d'appeler baroque'.[8]

The tale of France during the last years of Louis XIII's reign, when La Calprenède's plays were written, is told just by looking at the titles of chapters in Tapié: 'La Grande Epreuve (1636–1638)', 'La Lutte jusqu'au dernier souffle . . . (1639–1643)', or at those in Briggs under the section 'The Ministry of Richelieu': 'Noble conspiracy and rebellion'; 'Resistance to war finance; the popular revolts'.[9] Descimon and Jouhaud begin their chapter 'Ordre et désordre' thus: 'La première moitié du XVIIe siècle est le théâtre d'une longue suite de guerres civiles, prises d'armes, complots, révoltes. Le désordre paraît ainsi installé au centre de la vie politique de l'époque.'[10] Richelieu begins his *Testament politique*, published in 1638, with a short history of the reign of Louis XIII. The names of Chalais, Bouteville, Marillac, Montmorency and others are all testimony to the intrigues, to the rebellions of noblemen, and to the conspiracies against the state characteristic of the period. Chalais had dared to plot against Louis XIII in favour of Gaston d'Orléans and was executed in 1626; Bouteville had dared to fight a duel after the ban on duelling and was executed in 1627; in 1630, Marillac was arrested ostensibly for embezzlement, tried, condemned, and executed in 1632; the duc de Montmorency later the same year led a revolt in Languedoc, was captured, tried, condemned, and executed. To quote Descimon and Jouhaud again: 'Pendant le règne de Louis XIII (1610–1643), il ne se passe guère d'année sans expédition contre des sujets révoltés ou sans la découverte d'un complot, suivie de poursuites judiciaires et parfois aussi de prise d'armes.'[11] La Calprenède did not, therefore, have to look far for inspiration. The pattern of the archetypal Calprenedian tragedy echoes the fate of each of the rebel noblemen mentioned above. To take just Montmorency as an example, the history of his rebellion provides some remarkable parallels with that of Essex in La Calprenède's tragedy, *Le Comte d'Essex*. There is the curious mixture of political and personal ambitions behind the rebellion, and above all the aim of ridding Louis XIII of his principal minister, as Essex hoped to deliver Elisabeth from Cécile. There are the dashing antics on the battlefield at Castelnaudary, like those of Essex at

---

8 See also Jacques Ehrmann, *Un paradis désespéré: l'amour et l'illusion dans 'L'Astrée'* (New Haven and Paris 1963), p. 115. Madeleine Bertaud calls *Le Comte d'Essex* 'l'une des dernières grandes compositions baroques', in 'D'un *Comte d'Essex* à l'autre, La Calprenède et Thomas Corneille', in M. Bertaud and A. Laberit (ed.), *Amour tragique, amour comique, de Bandello à Molière*, Centre de philologie et de littératures romanes de l'Université de Strasbourg 2 (Paris 1989), pp 99–133 (p. 100).   **9** Victor L. Tapié, *La France de Louis XIII et de Richelieu* (Paris 1952); Robin Briggs, *Early modern France, 1560–1715* (Oxford 1977).   **10** Robert Descimon and Christian Jouhaud, *La France du premier XVIIᵉ siècle, 1594–1661* (Paris 1996), p. 71.   **11** Ibid., p. 71.

Cadiz, and, indeed, even more reminiscent of battles in one of La Calprenède's romances. There is even the anecdote of the wounded Montmorency asking for a ring to be delivered to his wife.[12] The duke's trial was swift and, for once, unaccompanied by criticism of Richelieu as to its fairness. The appeals made on Montmorency's behalf emphasized his great name, his connections, his personal qualities and the promise of his future services to the crown. But the intercessions of his wife, of the princesse de Condé, of the duc d'Angoulême, of the queen, of Monsieur, combined with the foreign appeals of the queen mother, of the duc de Savoie and even of the pope could do nothing to save him. Richelieu is severe in his chapter 'Peines et récompenses': 'En matière de crime d'Etat, il faut fermer la porte à la pitié, mépriser les plaintes des personnes intéressées et les discours d'une populace ignorante, qui blâme quelquefois ce qui lui est le plus utile et souvent tout à fait nécessaire.'[13] 'Compensant un mal présent par le bien passé' is dismissed as a dangerous indulgence (p. 345). Sent to the scaffold, as Church comments, 'like so many others in this period, [Montmorency] met death with great fortitude'.[14] Indeed, Bertaud comments:

> Essex a la fierté proche de l'insolence des grands féodaux que dut combattre Richelieu pour renforcer le pouvoir monarchique. Il était certainement moins, pour les spectateurs du temps, une figure élisabéthaine qu'un des leurs – et qu'il fût soupçonné de conspiration ne pouvait que renforcer cette certitude.[15]

Similarly, the *récits* of the executions of Jeanne (*Jeanne*, v. v) or Herménigilde (*Herménigilde*, v. vi) show La Calprenède's protagonists behaving in a fashion not only worthy of tragedy, but also of the real rebels of Louis XIII's reign.

Montmorency was executed five months after Marillac, and the nobility was shocked by this series of trials and executions which they blamed on Richelieu and on his avowed policy to 'rabaisser l'orgueil des Grands' (*Testament politique*, ed. cit., p. 95). The theme of the evil counsellor was, then, as strong in the real political world as in La Calprenède's plays. Chalais, Montmorency, and later Cinq-Mars all felt it was for the good of the country, as well as for their own, to rid France of the tyranny of Richelieu. Ironically, Richelieu himself in the *Testament* warned against the dangers often posed by those close to the King. In his chapter entitled 'Flatteurs et intrigants', he writes: 'Il n'y a point de peste si capable de ruiner un État que

---

12 Henri Griffet, *Histoire du règne de Louis XIII, roi de France et de Navarre*, 3 vols (Paris 1758), vol. 2, p. 304.   13 Armand-Jean Duplessis, Cardinal de Richelieu, *Testament politique*, ed. Louis André, 7th edn (Paris 1947), p. 342.   14 William F. Church, *Richelieu and reason of state* (Princeton 1972), p. 236.   15 Bertaud, *Amour tragique*, p. 104.

les flatteurs, les médisants et certains esprits, qui n'ont autre dessein que de former des cabales et des intrigues dans les Cours' (*Testament politique*, ed. cit., p. 365). In his attempts to open Hérode's eyes to the machinations of Salome and Antipatre, La Calprenède's Melas might well have voiced the following comment made by Richelieu to his king: 'A peine pourrais-je rapporter tous les maux dont ces mauvais esprits ont été auteurs pendant le règne de V.M.' (*Testament politique*, ed. cit., p. 367). Moreover, La Calprenède dedicates *La Mort des enfants d'Hérode* to the Cardinal and offers Herod's strong rule as a source of admiration:

> Acceptez, MONSEIGNEUR, ce Politique que je vous offre. S'il eut des vices que vous detestez, il eut des vertus que vous estimez sans doute, & son courage & sa bonne conduite ont effacé une partie des taches de sa vie.[16]

In the later plays of La Calprenède, women are often the ringleaders of the conspiracies, and certainly the reign of Louis XIII offered examples of female machinations as well. Particularly notable is the conspiracy in which Chalais was involved, which is often called the 'conspiration des dames'. It was Montmorency's wife who ultimately persuaded her husband to throw in his lot with Gaston d'Orléans, the king's brother, and women like the duchesse de Chevreuse and Marie de Medici, the queen mother, keep reappearing behind intrigues as indefatigably as Salome in *Hérode* and Goisinte in *Herménigilde*. A dramatist, therefore, had before him pictures of rebellion within the royal family, for factions centring on the king's mother or brother plunged the country into turmoil with Chalais in 1626, with Montmorency in 1632, and with Cinq-Mars in 1642. Such was the political atmosphere in which La Calprenède was turning rebellion into drama.[17]

As reflections of contemporary events, La Calprenède's tragedies must have struck chords of recognition in the mind of his audience without necessarily being perceived as direct allusions. Certainly, given the seventeenth-century public's passion for *clés*, topicality could well have constituted part of the appeal of these plays, even if no allusion was meant. Jane Conroy points out that at the time when La Calprenède was writing *Jeanne*, for example, problems of succession similar to those in the play were preoccupying the French and would persist until the birth of Louis le Dieudonné in 1638.[18] Similarly, a number of allusions to contemporary events could be

---

16 La Calprenède, *La Mort des enfants d'Hérode*, ed. cit., p. 4.   **17** In the same period, other playwrights were dramatizing conspiracy as well. One thinks, among others, of Georges de Scudéry's *La Mort de César* (1635), Pierre Corneille's *Cinna* (1640–41), and Tristan L'Hermite's *La Mort de Sénèque* (1644).   **18** Jane Conroy, *Terres tragiques: l'Angleterre et l'Ecosse dans la tragédie française du XVIIe siècle* (Tübingen 1999), p. 207.

perceived in a tragedy like *Herménigilde*, although they are possibly unintended. It is hard to imagine, however, that Recarède's three-page set-piece on the horrors of civil war (*Herménigilde*, 1. iii) would not have produced a ripple of acknowledgement as to its appropriateness during the season of 1641–2, when the treasonous disturbances of Soissons and Cinq-Mars were in people's minds. The problem of the division of a nation for religious reasons would still be topical in a country which had known civil war provoked by similar divisions less that fifteen years earlier. Herménigilde is besieged in Seville; so the Huguenots had holed up in La Rochelle. And is it not possible that, if the play was performed after the rebellion of Cinq-Mars, the last to centre on Monsieur, the King's brother, at least one patron in the audience might have nudged his neighbour on hearing Recarède cry out in this plea for reconciliation: 'Ah! Monsieur; ah! mon frère' (*Herménigilde*, ed. cit., 1. iii)? It is clear that to reflect the political atmosphere of the time, the plays do not need to be committed to a specific cause, nor do they require a sustained allegorical treatment of a contemporary event.

Although one does not know why or how La Calprenède chose his subject matter, the sheer power and dramatic possibilities of the subject must have constituted the major attraction. For example, in *Jeanne* there is no reference to Mary Tudor having been Roman Catholic and Jane and Elizabeth Protestant. Religion is even almost completely absent from *Herménigilde*, his martyr tragedy. It would seem, then, that the clash between characters on the stage before an audience is more important than the dynastic or religious controversies which constitute the major historical issues. The basic attraction of all of the subjects dramatized by La Calprenède is that they provide good stories of conflict which are exceedingly dramatic.

As Georges Forestier writes: 'Dramatiser l'histoire, c'est toujours peu ou prou *récrire* l'histoire'.[19] La Calprenède's historical sources tended to provide detailed treatment of the events but often only rudimentary comments on the characters or conflicts of the participants. For example, in Appian and Plutarch there are no confrontations between Mithridate and his treacherous son, Pharnace, who is only briefly introduced near the end of the tale. In Pollini, one of the Italian historians with an account of Jane Grey, Mary Tudor, characterized by her 'rarissima bontà', has a horror of bloodshed and would like to follow the principle of 'vincere co' benefici', but the punishment of the rebels is not turned into a dilemma for her.[20] In Camden, Elizabeth is uncertain as to what course to take after Essex's trial, and it is

19 Georges Forestier, 'Corneille poète d'histoire', *Littératures Classiques*, 11, supplement (1989), 37–47 (p. 38). 20 Girolamo Pollini, *Historia ecclesiastica della Rivoluzion d'Inghilterra* (Rome 1594), pp 321, 349, 403.

rumoured that regret for her lover's death haunts her on her own deathbed two years later. De Thou even goes so far as to talk of 'une affection secrète' for Essex.[21] However, it is the oral tradition which must already have gone one step further, elevating the two into that star-crossed pair 'Elizabeth and Essex'. In chronicling the facts, then, the historian provides the skeleton to be fleshed out by the dramatist through the personalities of his characters. In this respect, La Calprenède works within the established conventions of historical tragedy inherited from Aristotle. The essential facts of his subject matter are respected, but the gaps are filled in, psychological explanations for actions are provided, emotional bonds are enhanced, personal animosities are heightened or, indeed, created. In this way, La Calprenède's drama personalizes the historical. His embellishments do, of course, always remain compatible with historical fact, that is, La Calprenède writes in the tradition of the ideal tragedy of his time, a tradition recommended by the likes of D'Aubignac and called 'une tragédie historique anhistorique' by Forestier.[22]

Certain inventions obviously have the public in mind; La Calprenède must not forget *le roman d'amour*. In answer to a question about how he had contrived to introduce love into his play, the playwright Puff, in Sheridan's *The critic*, replies thus: 'Love! Oh nothing so easy; [. . .] where history gives you a good heroic out-line for a play, you may fill up with a little love at your own discretion' (II. i).[23] La Calprenède too fills up his good heroic outline with a little love: Pharnace has Bérénice; Mithridate, Hypsicratée; Jeanne, Gilfort; Elisabeth, Essex; Alexandre, Glaphira; Herménigilde, Indégonde. These, then, are love tragedies as well. La Calprenède also knows that his audience is eagerly awaiting the *scène à faire*. Both Bérénice and Mithridate must have their chance to confront Pharnace. Queen Mary and usurper Jane Grey must meet, although they never did in reality. The ecstatic farewells of husband and wife before Herménigilde's execution cannot be sacrificed to the historical truth of Indégonde being in Africa at the time. The scenes just mentioned are not in his sources. In fact, the roles of Bérénice and Hypsicratée have virtually been invented by La Calprenède.

21 William Camden, *Histoire d'Elizabeth royne d'Angleterre*, translated by Paul de Bellegent (Paris 1627), pp 346, 412; Jacques-Auguste de Thou, *Histoire universelle depuis 1543 jusqu'en 1607*, 16 vols (London 1734), vol. 13, p. 587. La Calprenède would have had access only to the Latin original of the latter text. **22** Georges Forestier, 'Théorie et pratique de l'histoire dans la tragédie classique', *Littératures Classiques*, 11 (1989), 95–107 (p. 98). He explains: 'La substance de l'argumentation est, en effet, la suivante: la poésie, quoique supérieure à l'histoire, doit en même temps être historique, tout en étant autorisée à s'écarter de l'histoire' (p. 98). The distinction that Forestier makes between Corneille's approach to historical tragedy and that of his fellow dramatists is that, for the former, history is 'le *sujet* de l'action' whereas for the others it is just 'le "lieu" de l'action' (p. 100). **23** Richard Brinsley Sheridan, *The critic*, in Cecil Price (ed.), *Sheridan's plays* (Oxford 1975), pp 331–85 (p. 358).

And yet he has been criticized for 'le souci de faire oeuvre d'historien', an alleged aim which Pierre Médan sees as having marred Mithridate.[24] Because, in the 'Au Lecteur', La Calprenède mentions having consulted Appian, Plutarch and Florus, the dramatist is criticized for too slavishly demonstrating 'le plus grand respect pour la vérité historique' (p. 48). However, as Forestier has warned:

> On n'invoque la vérité historique que pour expliquer que l'on avait les meilleures raisons de prendre des libertés avec elle. Mais ces raisons aboutissent à faire considérer que, globalement, on a été supérieurement fidèle à l'histoire, puisqu'on n'y a ajouté des 'ornements' que pour mieux la servir auprès du public.[25]

So, in the *Au Lecteur* to *Mithridate*, La Calprenède justifies his invention of Bérénice: 'cet incident est assez beau pour mériter qu'on luy pardonne' (p. 146). Audience reaction constitutes vindication, he continues in his defence:

> Et je ne mentirai point, quand je dirai que les actions de cette femme ont donné à ma Tragédie une grande partie du peu de réputation qu'elle a, et que celle qui les a représentées dans les meilleures compagnies de l'Europe a tiré assez de larmes des plus beaux yeux de la terre pour laver cette faute.[26]

Just like Puff who boasted: 'Now I rather think I have done this with some success'(*The critic*, II. i),[27] La Calprenède's attitude to his sources seems to have been dictated both by dramatic necessity and by a quest for dramatic effect. Since he depicts the last stages of a crisis, incidents before these final critical events are either discarded or streamlined to fit into the dialogue. For example, the succession of Mithridatic wars carefully chronicled by Appian is relegated to an atmospheric blur of forty years of non–stop war as first Pompée and later Mithridate recall the past (*Mithridate*, I. i; IV. iii). The death of Edward VI, his will, and the plight of the disinherited sisters, Mary and Elizabeth Tudor, are served up as food for heated debate between the sisters or the usurper and the queen (*Jeanne*, II. i; II. ii). The endless vicissitudes of Herod the Great's children, involving several previous trials, are reduced to expository laments or recriminations between half-brothers (*Hérode*, I. i; II. i).

The unities, which La Calprenède in his enthusiasm to be modern is conscious of obeying, impose changes. An event like the Wyatt rebellion,

---

24 Pierre Médan, 'Un Gascon précurseur de Racine: *La Mort de Mithridate* de La Calprenède et le *Mithridate* de Racine', *Revue des Pyrénées*, 19 (1907), 44–63 (p. 58). **25** Forestier, 'Théorie et pratique', 101. **26** La Calprenède, 'Au lecteur', *Mithridate*, p. 146. **27** Sheridan, ed. cit., p. 359.

instrumental in the death of the historical Jane Grey, cannot be fitted in, just as Essex's rebellion cannot involve two trials as it historically did. Time demands the greatest compression. Seven months cannot be allowed to pass between Jane Grey's reign (9–19 July 1553) and her death (12 February 1554), just as the seventeen days between Essex's arrest and execution (8 February and 25 February 1601) are telescoped into a busy twenty-four hours. The headlong rush to disaster in *Hérode* gives no impression of some twenty-two years having elapsed between the execution of Mariane (29 BC) and that of her sons (7 BC). Interestingly, such temporal foreshortening actually contributes to the tragic pleasure.

Pilfered historical detail can be put to use to enrich the plays stylistically. In *Mithridate*, for example, the anecdotes of Mithridate's past military exploits, especially those about Pompey (I. ii), not only establish the events of the tragedy as the last stage of the hunt, but also evoke a contrast between the vastness of vistas preceding the play and the claustrophobia of the besieged palace before us. The ignominious and untenable state to which Mithridate has been reduced is thus underlined. In the past, Romans have fallen to Mithridate, and their names ring in our ears as the father hurls them at his son, Pharnace: 'Flacce, Cotta, Fimbrie, et Triaire, vaincus' (IV.iii.1203). Kings have fallen to Rome as well, and Mithridate does not let Pharnace forget:

> Tu peux encore mieux confirmer ta pensée,
> En m'alléguant Syphax, ou Jugurte, ou Persée.
> (*La Mort de Mithridate*, ed. cit., IV. iii. 1213)

All of these names are found in Appian, Plutarch and Florus, and are used here as indicative, on the one hand, of Mithridate's warrior past, and, on the other, of what awaits Mithridate at Rome's hands. At the same time they impart a temporal depth to the play. Stripped of the individual histories attached to them – naturally enough since Pharnace would be fully conversant with such – and forged into enumerations, they also offer the public the pleasures of euphony.

La Calprenède falls, then, into the respectable contemporary tradition of choosing an historical subject of which he honours the essential facts while inventing and embellishing for the greatest dramatic effect. 'C'est toute la difficulté, mais c'est aussi ce qui fait l'essence de la création dramatique,' comments Forestier.[28]

There are rebellions, usurpations and conspiracies in La Calprenède's plays. Political conflict is the source material he sought out, material which

---

28 Forestier, 'Corneille poète d'histoire', 38.

often mirrored the reality of the times he lived in. Transforming the rebellions that he witnessed into drama, La Calprenède served up political conflict as a prime source of entertainment. But just what effect did La Calprenède hope that his plays would have upon his audiences?[29] He will certainly have fallen in with the general seventeenth-century consensus on tragic pleasure as described by Jean-Claude Vuillemin:

> Au XVIIe siècle en effet, tout le monde s'accordait à concevoir la tragédie comme une forme théâtrale qui devait d'abord agir directement sur les nerfs des spectateurs, exciter leurs 'passions' selon la terminologie du temps, ce qui le plus souvent revenait à leur faire verser de 'douces larmes'.[. . .]
>
> Le spectacle tragique doit provoquer chez ceux qui le regardent des émotions de nature quasi-physiologique. On ne vient pas chercher au théâtre un plaisir d'esthète ou des satisfactions intellectuelles, mais on demande à la représentation de déclencher un 'transport', c'est-à-dire une émotion spontanée et incoercible qui procède du plus profond du corps.[30]

Passions, larmes, transport, élévation, frisson, frémissement are all words used in the seventeenth century to describe the pleasure to be had from tragedy. La Calprenède seems to have succeeded in awakening such emotions in *Mithridate*; Grenaille confirms that the success of the play arose from the fact that it caused 'de si grandes émotions dans les âmes des spectateurs.'[31]

What was La Calprenède wanting to do or make happen with words and actions? He wanted to excite audiences, to make them gasp at the scenes of arrest where physical violence is threatened, or thrill to the clash of enemies locked into life and death struggles, or side with those supporters of the hero vying with those in the rival camp for the ear of the monarch, their friend's or lover's life being at stake. He wanted to create suspenseful drama which would have people coming back after the interval. Acts thus end on notes of curiosity, dependent on the appeal with its alternations between hope that the protagonist will be saved and despair that yet another appeal has failed. He wanted to move his audience. As just mentioned, in the *Au Lecteur* to

---

29 For a more detailed answer to this question, see my articles 'Plaisir à La Calprenède', *Seventeenth-Century French Studies*, 9 (1987), 55–73, and 'Suspense as a source of theatrical pleasure in the plays of La Calprenède', in Alan Howe and Richard Waller (ed.), *En marge du classicisme: essays on the French theatre from the Renaissance to the Enlightenment* (Liverpool 1987), pp 95–121. 30 Jean-Claude Vuillemin, 'Nature et réception du spectacle tragique sur la scène française du XVIIe siècle', *Revue d'Histoire du Théâtre*, 159 (1988), 217–26 (p. 219). 31 François Chatounières de Grenaille, 'Ouverture générale à toute la pièce, avec un discours sur les Poëmes Dramatiques de ce temps', prefacing his *Innocent malheureux; ou, La Mort de Crispe* (Paris 1639), sig. ẽ2r.

Mithridate, La Calprenède defends his invention of Bérénice on the grounds that she had the audience in tears. Scherer tells us too that audiences were moved by the pathos of prison scenes.[32] Indeed, in four of the plays under discussion, La Calprenède's heroes find themselves in prison. Particularly effective scenes are the *adieux* of Jeanne and Gilfort half heard through the prison walls (*Jeanne*, VI. iii and iv), and the touching exaltations of Herménigilde and Indégonde who are allowed to share the same cell (*Herménigilde*, v. i).

La Calprenède wanted to impress aurally, ergo the length of the monologues, the appeals, the trial accusations and defences. There is no denying the power that an actress could inject into the kind of grandiloquence required from Elisabeth as she discovers, too late, that Essex has sent the ring as an appeal to her mercy (*Le Comte d'Essex*, V.vii). Likewise, Glaphira's four-page threnody over the dead bodies of her husband and brother-in-law which ends *Hérode* is a *tour de force* which D'Aubignac criticizes as falling into the category of 'des Discours inutiles,' but which any actress would have fought tooth and nail to keep in the play.[33]

La Calprenède wanted to impress with spectacle. From his first play one sees that he has a flair for the great dramatic moment and a baroque eye for effect. In the last act of *Mithridate* the poison is poured, the cup passed around, the *adieux* and last embraces are made, Mithridate stabs himself and is put on the throne, so that the tableau which greets Pharnace, the rebel son, in the last scene of the play, is of his whole family arranged around the throne, dead. Such scenes have about them a pictorial quality which one will find again in La Calprenède's romances. Drama is fluid, the tableau forms and dissolves, but one feels that if it were possible to freeze the moment of Pharnace collapsing in front of Mithridate and Hypsicratée dead on their thrones, their family dead at their feet, or Glaphira fainting, or Recarède and Mathilde on their knees before Lévigilde, the images would recall those great historical machines produced for the Salon by academic painters of the nineteenth century such as Paul Delaroche, Victor-Julien Giraud, or Paul-Joseph Jamin.[34]

The trial, of course, constitutes La Calprenède's most consistently spectacular *scène à effet*. Rebellion has led to this. Massed judges or peers crowd the stage. The accused defends himself or refuses to, preferring instead to hurl insults. Personal enmity drags the proceedings into name-calling; tables are

---

32 Jacques Scherer, *La Dramaturgie classique en France* (Paris 1950), p. 167.   **33** François Hédelin, abbé d'Aubignac, *La Pratique du théâtre*, ed. Pierre Martino (Paris 1927), p. 140.   **34** In fact, a powerful, although historically inaccurate, equivalent in paint of Derby's *récit* of Jane's execution can be seen in London at the National Gallery in Paul Delaroche's painting of 1834 entitled 'Execution of Lady Jane Grey'.

turned as the accused accuses; fervent protestations necessitate order being restored to the court. The trial in *Le Comte d'Essex* may lack discipline in detail, but the picture of Essex and Cécile at each other's throats is never unsatisfying as drama. In this respect, La Calprenède's approach to the set-piece of the trial might well constitute the strongest proof that his interest is in the dramatic, the rhetorical, the personal rather than the political.

Rebellions, sedition, conspiracies, trials, executions – La Calprenède is fully of his time. He reflects the world around him, echoing the political preoc-cupations of the age, working within an established literary tradition at the same time as responding to the theatrical developments of the 1630s, and all with the aim of entertaining an audience. In that formative decade, along with Corneille, Du Ryer, Mairet, Rotrou, Scudéry, Tristan L'Hermite and others, La Calprenède, in his dramatizing of political conflict and thus in his rewriting of history, contributes to the flourishing of 'ce phénomène politico-littéraire que constitue la tragédie française'.[35]

---

35 Jacques Truchet, *La Tragédie classique en France* (Paris 1975), p. 92.

Conflicting signals: images of Louis XIV in Benserade's ballets

JULIA PREST

Louis XIV danced regularly in court ballets between 1651 and 1670.[1] The concept of a dancing king, particularly one to whom the label 'absolute' is so closely attached, immediately raises a number of pressing issues which need to be addressed. Which roles did he play? Why did he dance and to what effect? Was it a politicized act or was it merely for pleasure? How did the act of dancing enhance, or, indeed, detract from, Louis' carefully controlled kingly image?

While the majority of Louis XIV's activities have attracted sustained and extensive interest among scholars for the past three centuries, his dancing exploits have tended to be overlooked or, at best, given short shrift. The appearance in 1984 of Philippe Hourcade's article bearing the mildly equivocal title 'Louis XIV travesti' and dedicated entirely to the dancing Louis was, therefore, a most welcome innovation.[2] Hourcade's article provides a useful introduction to the subject, including a list of the known ballet roles taken by Louis XIV, and its strength lies above all in its assessment of what he aptly calls the 'extrême diversité' (p. 262) of roles performed by the king.[3] For Louis did not, as some critics have rashly claimed, dance only majestic, exalted roles:[4] his repertoire is highly heterogeneous, as the appendix to this article demonstrates.

A second article devoted to the dancing king and written by dance historian and performer Régine Astier was published in 1992.[5] Astier also provides a list of Louis XIV's dancing roles in court ballets in an article which

1 Whether the last ballet roles taken by Louis XIV were in Benserade's *Ballet de Flore* (1669) or Molière's *Les Amants magnifiques* (1670) is a matter for some debate. While it is clear that the roles of Neptune and Apollo in *Les Amants magnifiques* were written for Louis, there is some evidence to suggest that he did not, in the end, perform them. On this, see my article 'Dancing king: Louis XIV's roles in Molière's *Comédies-ballets*, from court to town', *The Seventeenth Century*, 16, no. 2 (Autumn 2001), 283–98. 2 Philippe Hourcade, 'Louis XIV travesti', *Cahiers de Littérature du XVIIe siècle*, 6 (1984), 257–71. 3 His list includes a number of minor inaccuracies which I hope to have corrected in the appendix to the present article. 4 See for example, Fiona Garlick in her otherwise stimulating article, 'Dances to evoke the king: the majestic genre chez Louis XIV', *Dance Research*, 15, no. 2 (Winter 1997), 10–34 (p. 27). 5 Régine Astier, 'Louis XIV, "Premier Danseur"' in David Lee Rubin (ed.), *Sun King: the ascendancy of French culture during the reign of Louis XIV* (Washington, London and Toronto 1992), pp 73–102.

focuses on the significance of dance at Louis XIV's court and the impact of the foundation of the Académie Royale de Danse in 1661.[6] A more theorized approach to the subject is advocated by Mark Franko in an article examining Louis XIV's female roles in court ballets.[7] Franko's theoretical stance is often illuminating, particularly in his examination of the relationship between kingly power and kingly performance as a dancer, although he has a tendency to arrive at seemingly radical conclusions sometimes based on rather flimsy evidence or argument. One of my own articles on Louis' dancing roles in Molière's *comédies-ballets* aims to examine the significance of the king's occasional participation in this genre, his presence as a dancer at court and his absence from town productions of the same works.[8] This small flurry of articles reflects a modest but significant increase of interest in the question of the dancing Louis, a trend also reflected in sections of larger publications, such as the chapters concerned with dance in Philippe Beaussant's *Louis XIV, artiste* (Paris 1999) and in Sarah R. Cohen's *Art, dance, and the body in French culture of the Ancien Régime* (Cambridge 2000).

The aim of the present article is to explore the images of the dancing Louis XIV produced by Benserade's ballet verses. Louis' dancing career coincided almost exactly with Benserade's career as author of ballets, as both began with the *Ballet de Cassandre* in 1651 and both effectively ended with the *Ballet de Flore* in 1669.[9] Ideally, an examination of French court ballet would include among its principal components the music, choreography, sets and costumes as well as the *livrets* (or programmes). Unfortunately, no choreography for these ballets is extant and much of the music is lost, but some set and costume designs do survive, the majority of which are conserved in the Cabinet des Estampes, the Bibliothèque de l'Institut and the Musée Carnavalet in Paris. The most complete sources of information nonetheless remain the *livrets*, which provide the structure of the ballets, brief summaries of the action of each scene, the names of the dancers and singers and, what interests us most here, lines of verse, most of them written by Benserade, commenting on the courtly dancers as well as on the professional dancers, and their adopted roles.[10]

6 Astier's list also contains some minor inaccuracies. **7** Mark Franko, 'The king cross-dressed: power and force in royal ballet' in Sara E. Melzer and Kathryn Norberg (ed.), *From the royal to the republican body: incorporating the political in seventeenth- and eighteenth-century France* (Berkeley, Los Angeles and London 1998), pp 64–84. Previously published as 'Double bodies: androgyny and power in the performances of Louis XIV', *Drama Review*, 38, no. 4 (Winter 1994), 71–82. **8** Julia Prest, 'Dancing King'. **9** As indicated above, Louis XIV may have performed in *Les Amants magnifiques* in 1670. The *Ballet de Flore* marked Benserade's retirement from ballet composition, although he was brought out of retirement to write the verses for the *Ballet du triomphe de l'amour*, performed in 1681 (and which really belongs to the era in which ballet had effectively been subsumed into the new popular entertainment, *tragédie-lyrique*). **10** Access to Benserade's ballet

Before embarking upon an investigation of the ballet verses written specifically to accompany Louis XIV as he performed his various roles, it is important to discuss the nature of these verses and how they functioned. The verses were not pronounced on stage, but were written to be read silently by the spectator during the performance. They nevertheless served a dramatic function, providing subtle nuances of character and interpretation which could not be conveyed simply through dance. The curious way in which references to the performer and to the adopted role are combined is summarized by Charles Perrault, who wrote with reference to Benserade's verses for Louis XIV:

> Le coup portoit sur le Personnage, & le contre-coup sur la Personne; ce qui donnoit un double plaisir en donnant à entendre deux choses à la fois, qui belles séparément, devenoient encore plus belles estant jointes ensemble.[11]

As will be seen in the course of this study, ballet verses are often more concerned with the noble performer than with the character he or she portrays. In the case of Louis' courtiers, they included frequent references – some more opaque than others and many of them openly mocking – to aspects of the performer's personal life, often couched in the vocabulary of the assumed character. In the case of the king, this was a delicate operation, as open mockery would not have been politic. But Louis XIV was not simply a human being whose personal life had to be treated with delicacy; his official image as invincible king also had to be upheld, a concept we shall return to below. Certainly, the tension inherent in ballet verses, particularly in the case of Louis XIV, is clear as different levels of reality and fiction co-exist.

The tension between person and adopted role was further complicated when the dancer performed as a member of the opposite sex. At the end of the reign of Louis XIII, the majority of ballets were performed by all-male casts, with the exception of the ballets 'De la reine' in which the queen and female members of her entourage danced in the 'grand ballet' at the close of the entertainment. Under the reign of Louis XIV, female courtiers were to dance more and more frequently and female professional dancers were

livrets has been greatly facilitated by Marie-Claude Canova-Green's edition of them entitled *Benserade: ballets pour Louis XIV*, 2 vols (Toulouse 1997). This edition will form the principal source for this article, and all page references to quotations from the ballets will be to it. The attribution of certain ballets to Benserade is occasionally problematic, owing to the fact that ballet texts were sometimes multi-authored (one author might write the *vers* while another wrote the musical *récits*, for example); under the classification of 'Benserade's ballets', I include all those which feature in Canova-Green's edition.   11 Charles Perrault, *Les Hommes illustres qui ont paru en France*, 2 vols (Paris 1696 and 1700), vol. 2, p. 80.

introduced, but many female roles continued to be performed by cross-dressed men. As indicated above, the king was not exempt from this practice.

The theatre critic and Jesuit priest, Claude-François Ménestrier, considered it to be inappropriate for a king to perform anything other than noble roles alongside noble dancers, but, in the face of Louis' varied incarnations, he was obliged to preach the merits of such behaviour.[12] His concern draws our attention not only to the question of seemly, kingly behaviour, but, by extension, to the predicament facing Benserade of how to write verses for a supposedly invincible king parading his frail, mortal body in a variety of different roles, many of them unbecoming, in court ballets. The official images of Louis XIV as a superlative king, images which were handed down to posterity, are famous for having been scrupulously crafted and manipulated, a highly complicated procedure overseen first by Mazarin, but most significantly by Colbert, and later, to a lesser extent, by his successor, Louvois. Official accounts of Louis' achievements written by carefully selected historiographers, medals struck to celebrate significant events of the reign, commemorative statues, paintings and so on were, from 1663 onwards, subject to the watchful and controlling eye of the Petite Académie. Court ballets, on the other hand, enjoyed greater freedom of expression, ideologically, artistically and, in this case, dramatically. Louis XIV's very presence, not to mention his active participation in ballets, was itself political – this was the man who was to make a political act out of getting up in the morning and going to bed at night – but it is important to remember that, unlike commemorative medals or other official chronicles of the reign, ballets were not primarily political in their purport. That they were used for political purposes is in no doubt, but they also functioned as entertainment, and the bodily presence of Louis XIV on stage was a physical reminder both of Louis the man who enjoyed ballet and of Louis the king who also used ballet to further his political ends.

The doctrine of the king's two bodies, as expounded most famously in Ernst H. Kantorowicz's study of 1957,[13] will serve to illuminate this tension.[14] The principle is neatly exposed in the following extract from Edmund Plowden's *Reports*, collected and written under Queen Elizabeth:

12 See Canova-Green, *Benserade: ballets pour Louis XIV*, vol. 1, p. 27.   13 Ernst H. Kantorowicz, *The king's two bodies: a study in mediaeval political theology* (Princeton 1995; first published 1957). 14 Franko's use in 'The king cross-dressed' of the concept of the king's two bodies to distinguish between masculine and feminine roles is contested by Sarah Cohen, who objects to the resulting unhelpful and inaccurate generalizations regarding male and female models (see her chapter on Court Ballet in *Art, dance and the body*, p. 50). While I concur that the paradigm of the king's two bodies as employed by Franko is misleading, I maintain that it may usefully be applied to illuminate

For the King has in him two Bodies, *viz.*, a Body natural, and a Body politic. His Body natural [. . .] is a Body mortal, subject to all Infirmities that come by Nature or Accident, to the Imbecility of Infancy or old Age, and to the like Defects that happen to the natural Bodies of other People. But his Body politic is a Body that cannot be seen or handled, consisting of Policy and Government, and constituted for the Direction of the People, and the Management of the public weal, and this Body is utterly void of Infancy, and old Age, and other natural Defects and Imbecilities, which the Body natural is subject to, and for this Cause, what the King does in his Body politic, cannot be invalidated or frustrated by any Disability in his natural Body.[15]

According to this definition, Louis XIV, as he performs in court ballets, may reasonably be understood to be performing his body politic by means of his body natural, as suggested, for example, by Jean-Marie Apostolidès.[16] Contrary to the understanding of the notion of the king's two bodies noted by Plowden, however, I maintain that the frailties of the natural body can indeed thwart the invincibility of the body politic, and that the image of Louis XIV was constantly struggling against this phenomenon.

In an age of eulogistic magnitude surrounding the figure of Louis XIV, it is not surprising to find that the overwhelming theme of the verses written to accompany his dancing roles is the expression of his superlative kingly qualities – his glory, majesty, virtue, nobility, grandeur, goodness and supreme greatness. In this respect, the tenor of Benserade's ballet verses is strongly reminiscent of that of the more regulated official accounts of the reign. In the early ballets, when he was still a child, Louis' latent qualities were stressed and his future glory anticipated. For example, we read in the verses accompanying his role as the wine-loving female Bacchante in the *Ballet des fêtes de Bacchus* (1651):

> De là ie quitte en peu de temps
> Tous ces petits vins, & pretens
> Aualer à longs traits du grand vin de la gloire,
> Déja la Nature & les Cieux
> En naissant m'en ont tant fait boire,
> Qu'on voit qu'il me sort par les yeux.
> <div align="right">(<i>Benserade</i>, ed. cit., vol. 1, p. 73)</div>

the indisputable tension between the official images of Louis XIV and the reality of the man behind that image. **15** Edmund Plowden, *Commentaries or reports* (London 1816), 212a. Cited in Ernst H. Kantorowicz, *The king's two bodies*, p. 7. **16** Jean-Marie Apostolidès, *Le Roi-machine: spectacle et politique au temps de Louis XIV* (Paris 1981), pp 129–30.

The imagery is consistent with Louis' adopted role, and references to the bacchanalian pursuits of wine and love are not eschewed, but his future glory which will crown his inherited, God-given glory takes pride of place.

In the verses for Louis playing the glorious role of Apollo in the first entry of the *Ballet des noces de Pélée et de Thétis* (1654), his supreme kingly qualities are expounded:

> Plus brillant & mieux fait que tous les Dieux ensemble,
> La Terre ny le Ciel n'ont rien qui me ressemble,
> De rayons immortels mon front est couronné:
> Amoureux des beautez de la seule victoire,
> Ie cours sans cesse apres la gloire
> Et ne cours point apres Daphné.
> (Benserade, ed. cit., vol. 1, p. 181)

We notice that, in addition to the conventional qualities ranging from physical attractiveness, a desire for victory and glory to brilliance and even immortality, part of Louis' greatness is perceived to be his lack of interest in pursuing the female sex or, to put it another way, his lack of interest in pursuing the desires of his body natural. Louis' attitude towards sexual love is a recurring theme throughout the ballets and one which develops and changes over the years. In the early ballets, he is seen to be immune to love, and then gradually he awakens to the inevitable call of its charms, becomes a source of love for admiring women and ultimately the epitome of the consummate lover (we shall return to the theme of love and pleasure below). These examples from the *Ballet des fêtes de Bacchus* and the *Ballet des noces de Pélée et de Thétis* demonstrate that Louis' qualities were praised in Benserade's verses both in traditionally glorious roles, such as that of Apollo, and in more morally and sexually dubious roles, such as that of a Bacchante. Different methods are used (the more dubious role requires a greater manipulation of associated imagery, for example), but both are encomiastic to a greater or lesser degree.

One of the most overt examples of encomium in Benserade's ballet verses is to be found in the opening stanza for Louis playing Renaud in *Les Amours déguisés* (1664):

> Sage & vaillant
> Rien ne peut égaler ses trauaux & ses peines,
> Le sang de Charlemagne heroïque & boüillant
> A pris vn nouueau feu dans ses Royales vaines,
> Son coeur est genereux, est noble, est fier, est grand,
> De tous les autres coeurs c'est le plus magnanime,

> Vn coeur de vray Monarque, vn coeur de Conquerant,
> Qui court apres l'honneur & qui cherche l'estime.
>> (*Benserade*, ed. cit., vol. 2, p. 671)

More significant than this expression of adulation, however, are the references to Louis' less kingly pursuits which feature in the same set of verses. The first stanza continues,

> C'est là précisément tout ce que j'en diray,
> Et quelque autre talent qui luy tombe en partage,
> Sur le fait de ce coeur je ne m'expliqueray
> Pas dauantage.
>> (*Benserade*, ed. cit., vol. 2, p. 671)

This must surely be an oblique reference to one or other of Louis' mistresses and probably to Mlle de la Vallière. While Benserade is willing to extol the virtuous qualities to be found in the king's heart, he will only allude in passing to the less virtuous qualities also contained therein. He continues in the next stanza to remind the ballet audience (as a means of justification of Louis' behaviour?) that even kings have much in common with other human beings:

> Les plus grands Rois
> Ne laissent pas pourtant d'estre ce que nous sommes,
> Au moins s'ils ne le sont, par de certains endrois
> Ils ont beaucoup de l'air de tous les autres hommes.
>> (*Benserade*, ed. cit., vol. 2, p. 671)

Having praised Louis XIV's body politic, Benserade now comments on his body natural, and specifically his fondness for the female sex. Whereas an immunity to love had been perceived as a quality desirable in the young king, here Benserade attempts to incorporate the weaknesses of the body natural into the strength and greatness of the body politic as he writes that, with regard to the formation of a hero, 'La Nature & la Gloire ont-elles commencé? / L'Amour acheue' (*Benserade*, ed. cit., vol. 2, p. 672). The problem of praising a supposedly perfect and divinely-chosen king who yet displays human weaknesses is becoming manifest.

The problem of praising a human king is related to, but distinct from, the problem of praising a king who is (supposed to be) beyond praise. As early as in the *Ballet de l'impatience* (1661), Benserade had declared that Louis XIV was superior to his ancient models, writing of him as someone 'qui passe de bien loin nos Heros fabuleux' (*Benserade*, ed. cit., vol. 2, p. 513), although he continued to use these models, somewhat awkwardly at times, as a means to praise the king. As he called into question the usefulness of allusions to ancient heroes as a topos of praise for the modern, superior king, Benserade simultaneously revealed the difficulties inherent in the encomiastic medium with a human being as its object, and hinted at a debate which was to rage a little later in Louis' reign, that is, the 'Querelle des Anciens et des Modernes'.

The cracks are beginning to show in a number of other examples of attempts at high praise, as when Benserade, having in earlier ballets likened Louis XIV to a number of Roman gods, goes one step further in the verses for Louis, evoking him as the sun in the *Ballet d'Hercule amoureux* (1662):

> Cet Astre à son Autheur ne ressemble pas mal,
> Et si l'on ne craignoit de passer pour impie,
> L'on pourroit adorer cette belle Copie
> Tant elle aproche prés de son Original.
> *(Benserade*, ed. cit., vol. 2, p. 594)

Not only has Louis surpassed his human and mythological models, but Benserade, in his quest for new methods of praise, suggests that he is on a par with the creator God himself. The poet, aware of the blasphemous implications of his words, does not press the point, but the hiatus between the image of the body politic being described and the reality of the body natural performing the role can only have increased as the level of praise reached heavenly proportions. Far from furthering the Ludovician political cause, one might argue that excess praise subverted it by drawing attention to the disparity between the king's two bodies.

With regard to court ballet, the crisis of representation (to borrow Peter Burke's phrase)[17] reached breaking point in 1669 with the *Ballet de Flore*. In the verses accompanying Louis' role as the sun in the first entry, Benserade wrote frankly of the inability of art (in his case poetry) to convey the king's unparalleled greatness:

> SOLEIL, de qui la gloire acompagne le cours,
> Et qu'on m'a veu loüer toûjours
> Auec assez d'éclat quand vostre éclat fut moindre,
> L'Art ne peut plus traiter ce sujet comme il faut,
> Et vous estes monté si haut
> Que l'Eloge, & l'Encens ne vous sçauroient plus joindre.
> *(Benserade*, ed. cit., vol. 2, p. 833)

---

17 See Peter Burke, *The fabrication of Louis XIV* (New Haven and London 1992), chapter nine.

These lines reveal not so much the ultimate and sublime greatness of the king, however, as the dead end to be found at the limits of hyperbolic praise. It is not so much the case that words cannot live up to the king, but rather that the king cannot live up to the words which are used to describe his endeavours. This is not a crisis of language but rather a crisis concerning the very nature of the monarch and the monarchy. The precarious balance between the body politic and the body natural is in jeopardy.

In addition to praise of his great qualities, one of the most frequent themes found in the verses for Louis' dancing roles is that of war, including repeated references to contemporary military conflicts and to peace, as and when appropriate. War is an intrinsically problematic phenomenon for a supposedly perfect king, and it features in Benserade's verses in relation both to peace and to love. The final lines written for Louis' role as a Titan in the *Ballet des fêtes de Bacchus* express the wish that he should be both 'aymé dans la paix' and 'craint dans la guerre' (*Benserade*, ed. cit., vol. 1, p. 82). Similarly, in the *Ballet de la raillerie*, Benserade gives the following text to Louis who is playing a 'Gentilhomme François':

> Quand vn voisin m'offence, ou m'a fait quelque iniure,
> Ie me bas contre luy s'il est de mon estoc:
> Puis ie cherche la Paix, & voudrois ie vous iure
> Que les armes fussent au croc.
> (Benserade, ed. cit., vol. 2, p. 463)

Peace is preferable, but Louis will go to war if necessary. A subtly different nuance is given in the *Ballet des saisons* (1661) where Louis played the corn goddess Cérès:

> Destin, vous le vouliez, par vostre ordre tout pur
> La Terre a dû souffrir qu'vn fer trenchant & dur
> Luy déchirast le sein dans vne rude Guerre;
> Maintenant s'en est fait, & de ma propre main
> Je séme heureusement sur cette mesme Terre
> Dequoy donner la vie à tout le genre Humain.
> (Benserade, ed. cit., vol. 2, p. 545)

The Thirty Years War, which had recently ended, is attributed to destiny and not to any king, while peace is attributed specifically to Louis. The shift in emphasis with regard to war, which is here given a wholly negative image, cannot be accounted for solely by the particular historical context of the ballet, that is, a context of recent and welcome peace. It is more in keeping with the concept of Louis as a source of all things good and of no thing bad, as expounded in the verses for Louis as Jupiter in the *Ballet de l'impatience* (1661):

> Le monde cependant m'adore & connoist bien
> Qu'à son vtilité ie dispose les Astres,
> Et suis la source de son bien,
> Sans estre autheur de ses desastres.
>
> (Benserade, ed. cit., vol. 2, p. 510)

Here again, negative events are presented as having been 'des fiers Destins l'ouurage necessaire' (*Benserade*, ed. cit., vol. 2, p. 510). The device whereby negative occurrences are acknowledged, but responsibility for them is located beyond the king's natural or political body, is a clever but ultimately unconvincing one, for if the king is as powerful and omnipotent as we have been led to believe, he must necessarily be in control of events and therefore responsible for them. Here, too, the cracks are beginning to show.

War imagery is also used in association with love, particularly to describe Louis' nascent sexual love. For example, in Benserade's verses for Louis playing a 'Curieux' in the *Ballet de la nuit* (1653), we read of his ambivalent attitude towards love in the following terms:

> Je sçauray triompher de ma personne & d'elles [les passions]
> Ainsi que d'ennemis,
> Et me conter moy–mesme entre tous mes rebelles
> Combatus & soûmis.
>
> (Benserade, ed. cit., vol. 1, p. 140)

The metaphor of love as a battle is, of course, a conventional one, and one which recurs many times in the verses for the young king. Representations of the relationship between love and (non-metaphorical) war take on a number of facets, including the notion that the king may turn his attention to love once he has successfully dealt with any current conflict (see for example the *Ballet de l'impatience*, *Benserade*, ed. cit., vol. 2, p. 509). The war-love tension culminates, however, in the image of Louis XIV as simultaneously both war hero and consummate lover, and is characteristic of the tensions underlying his portrayal in general. This is best illustrated in the following verses accompanying Louis' role as Spring in the *Ballet de Psyché* (1656):

> Que de ce doux Printems on ayme le retour,
> O la bonne saison pour les biens de la terre!
> Elle est toute propre à la Guerre,
> Et toute faite pour l'Amour.
>
> (Benserade, ed. cit., vol. 1, p. 295)

One might not expect the season of love also to be the season of war, but while the king's body politic may inspire his soldiers ('Que sa jeune vigueur anime de Guerriers', *Benserade*, ed. cit., vol. 1, p. 295), his body natural will inspire love among the court beauties, just as they, in turn, will inspire love in him.

The heavy emphasis in Benserade's ballet verses on the theme of the king's nascent love, and later on his amorous exploits, draws our attention to his human side and to the desires of his body natural even when these urges are couched in the laudatory vocabulary of the king's body politic. It is, of course, the king's duty to provide a son and heir in order to ensure the immortality of his body politic, and it is fitting that the birth of the dauphin be celebrated in the verses for the dancing king and queen in the *Ballet d'Hercule amoureux* (1662) (*Benserade*, ed. cit., vol. 2, p. 564). The theme of the king as consummate lover has, however, more to do with carnal desires and pleasure-seeking than with the commendable kingly pursuits associated with images of praise and the body politic. This was best illustrated when Louis XIV performed on stage alongside his current mistresses as, for example, when he played a shepherd to Mlle de la Vallière's shepherdess in the *Ballet des arts* (1663) (*Benserade*, ed. cit., vol. 2, p. 605). Although Benserade's verses for the king, while hinting at his susceptibility to love, stress the fact that the requirements of his body politic will always take precedence over the desires of his body natural ('Ne croyez pas que son plaisir l'emporte,' *Benserade*, ed. cit., vol. 2, p. 605), the verses written for Mlle de la Vallière include thinly veiled references to their not-so-secret love:

> Elle a dans ses beaux yeux vne douce langueur,
> Et bien qu'en apparence aucun n'en soit la cause,
> Pour peu qu'il fût permis de foüiller dans son coeur,
> On ne laisseroit pas d'y trouuer quelque chose.
>
> (*Benserade*, ed. cit., vol. 2, p. 607).

The tension between the demands of the king's two bodies are encapsulated in the opposition between business and pleasure, a recurring theme of Benserade's verses and one which is best illustrated in the opening stanza of the verses for Louis' role as a shepherd in the *Ballet des muses* (1666–67):

> Ce Berger n'est jamais sans quelque chose à faire,
> Et jamais rien de bas n'occupe son loisir,
> Soit plaisir, soit affaire,
> Mais l'affaire tousiours va deuant le plaisir.
>
> (*Benserade*, ed. cit., vol. 2, p. 782).

While it was undoubtedly the case that Louis XIV was ultimately more concerned with matters of state than with personal self-indulgence, the problem was that when he participated in court ballets, pleasure appeared to be taking precedence. Had the ballets set out to be void of political purport and purely pleasurable in aim, the discrepancy between the king's two bodies would have been less apparent. It is the co-existence and uncomfortable proximity of references to the king's body politic and body natural, exacerbated by the visible presence of the king's human body on stage, which led to a series of images of the king in conflict with his official image. While ballets could be used, and indeed were, for the promotion of the king's official image, the risk remained that this image would be undermined in performance and by the tensions inherent in Benserade's accompanying verses.

There is a lone example in which Benserade overtly challenges the suitability of the king's ballet role, and that is when he played a 'débauché' in the *Ballet des plaisirs* (1655). Given their singularity and import, I shall quote the accompanying verses in full:

> Sire, quel spectacle pour nous?
> Et d'où peut proceder en vous
> Ce changement qu'on y remarque?
> Sur quelle herbe auez vous marché,
> Quoy, faut-il qu'vn si grand Monarque
> Deuienne vn si grand Desbauché?
>
> C'est l'ordre que vos ieunes ans
> S'attachent aux suiets plaisans,
> Et qu'ils ne demandent qu'à rire;
> Mais ne soyez point emporté,
> Esuitez la Desbauche, SIRE,
> Passe pour la fragilité.
>
> Il n'est ny Censeur ny Regent
> Qui ne soit assez indulgent
> Aux voeux d'vne ieunesse extresme,
> Et pour embellir vostre Cour,
> Qui ne trouue excusable mesme
> Que vous ayez vn peu d'amour.
>
> Mais d'en vser comme cela,
> Et de courre par cy par là
> Sans vous arrester à quelqu'vne,

> Que tout vous soit bon, tout égal
> La blonde autant comme la brune,
> Ha! SIRE, c'est vn fort grand mal.
>   (*Benserade*, ed. cit., vol. 1, pp 260–1)

Benserade's words are prophetic. Written when Louis XIV was still only sixteen years old and several years before his weakness for the female sex became a reality at court, these verses already highlight the tension between duty and pleasure, between strength and weakness, between the body politic and the body natural, a tension which was to dog his reign and which was to be performed before the court again and again as Louis danced his many roles in court ballets. Rather than projecting the image of an immortal, invincible, superlative king (through the body natural), Louis' dancing roles and their accompanying verses subtly highlighted the discrepancy between his two bodies, leaving the defects of his body natural dangerously exposed. It is no wonder that Louis XIV and Benserade abandoned court ballet in 1670, leaving the forbidding and complex task of praising the king for other media to tackle.

APPENDIX: LOUIS XIV'S DANCING ROLES IN BENSERADE'S BALLETS

Date	Ballet	Roles[18]
1651	*Ballet de Cassandre*	Un Chevalier de la suite de Cassandre (3)
		Un Tricotet poitevin (11)
1651	*Ballet des fêtes de Bacchus*	Un Filou traîneur d'épée (4)
		Un Devin (8)
		Une Bacchante (18)
		Un Homme de glace (22)
		Un Titan (27)
		Une Muse (30)
		Une Coquette (Entrée supprimée)[19]
1653	*Ballet de la nuit*	Une Heure (I, 1)
		Un Jeu (II, 2)
		Un Ardent (III, 6)
		Un Curieux (III, 11)
		Un Furieux (IV, 2)
		Le Soleil levant (IV, 10)

18 Entry numbers (and parts, where appropriate) are given in parentheses. **19** This role was originally written for Louis XIV but omitted from performance.

1654	*Ballet des proverbes*	Tout ce qui reluit n'est pas or (I, 4)
		Un Maure (I, 10)
		Un Attaquant (II, 2)
		Un Espagnol (II, 11)
1654	*Ballet des noces de Pélée et de Thétis*	Apollon (1)
		Une Furie (4)
		Une Dryade (6)
		Un Académiste (8)
		Un Courtisan (9)
		La Guerre (10)
1654	*Ballet du temps*	Un Moment (I, 2)
		Le Siècle d'or (I, 12)
		Le Printemps (II, 6)
		Le Feu (II, 11)
1655	*Ballet des plaisirs*	Un Berger (I, 1)
		Un Egyptien (I, 12)
		Un Débauché (II, 1)
		Le Génie de la danse (II, 11)
1655	*Ballet des bienvenus*	[En lui-même] (II, 2)
1656	*Ballet de Psyché*	Le Printemps (I, 2)
		Un Esprit follet (I, 12)
		Pluton (II, 12)
1657	*Ballet de l'Amour malade*	Le Divertissement (1)
		Un des parents et amis des mariés (10)
1658	*Ballet d'Alcidiane*	La Haine (I, 1)
		Eole (II, 1)
		Un Démon (II, 6)
		Un Maure (III, 7)
1659	*Ballet de la raillerie*	Le Ris (1)
		Le Bonheur (5)
		Un Gentilhomme français (12)
1661	*Ballet de l'impatience*	Un Grand amoureux (I, 1)
		Jupiter (II, 4)
		Un Chevalier de l'ancienne chevalerie (III, 3)
1661	*Ballet des saisons*	Cérès (4)
		Le Printemps (8)
1662	*Ballet d'Hercule amoureux*	La Maison de France (1 & 2)
		Pluton (8)
		Mars (9)
		Le Soleil (17)
1663	*Ballet des arts*	Un Berger (1)
1663	*Les Noces de village*	Une Fille de village (8)

		Un Bohémien (13)[20]
1664	*Les Amours déguisés*	Renaud (7)
1665	*Ballet de la naissance de Vénus*	Alexandre (II, 6)
1666–1667	*Ballet des muses*	Un Berger (4)
		Un Espagnol (6)
		Cyrus (8)
		Une Nymphe (12)
		Un Maure de qualité (14)
1668	*Le Carnaval*	Un Plaisir (1)
		Un Masque sérieux (6)
1669	*Ballet de Flore*	Le Soleil (1)
		Un Européen (15)

20 The verses for Louis' role as a gypsy read 'Pour LE ROY, qui deuoit representer vn Bohesmien'. This suggests that he may not have performed the role, a hypothesis supported by the fact that he is not mentioned in the list of performers playing 'Bohémiens' in the *livret* (see *Benserade*, ed. cit., vol. 2, pp 636–7).

IV. MILITARY CONFLICT

Franco-Irish military relations in the Nine Years War, 1689–97

HARMAN MURTAGH

War is the ultimate form of conflict, when divisions between the ideals, ideologies or interests of diverse groupings degenerate into systematic organized violence. Near incessant war, coupled with widespread revolution and political and social disorder, characterized Europe in the seventeenth century, which historians regard as a time of general crisis.[1] The upheavals of that period were shaped and energized by a parallel military revolution in the size, organization, technology and tactics of armies and navies.[2]

Under Louis XIV, France had become the pre-eminent military power in Europe. Like so many other facets of his reign, Louis' militarism was on a grand scale. By the 1690s, the French army of 340,000 outshone all others in size and proficiency, and the navy of nearly 200 fighting ships was 'more numerous and better [than that] of any other European prince'.[3] Louis did not scruple to use his military strength to achieve political and diplomatic goals: for two out of three of the fifty-five years of his personal reign (1661–1715) France was at war. This brought her considerable gains, but the success of Louis' bullying diplomacy and periodic recourse to violence as a tool of state policy alarmed and antagonized other European powers. By 1688, as another war loomed, France had many enemies and only one potential ally, James II, the king of England and, therefore, of Ireland also.

Moves towards an Anglo-French alliance alarmed James' son-in-law, William prince of Orange, who was the *stadthouder* of the Dutch Republic and Louis' most inveterate enemy. James' Roman Catholicism and autocratic ways were disliked in England. William took advantage of his father-in-law's unpopularity to mount an invasion in November 1688 which overthrew

1 On this, see Geoffrey Parker and Lesley M. Smith (ed.), *The general crisis of the seventeenth century* (London 1978). 2 On this, see Clifford J. Rogers (ed.), *The military revolution debate: readings on the military transformation of Early Modern Europe* (Boulder/San Francisco/Oxford 1995); Geoffrey Parker, *The military revolution: military innovation and the rise of the West, 1500–1800* (Cambridge 1988); Jeremy Black, *A military revolution? Military change and European society, 1550–1800* (London 1991). 3 John A. Lynn, *Giant of the Grand Siècle: the French army, 1610–1715* (Cambridge 1997), p. 340; Louis-François de Bourchet, Marquis de Sourches, *Mémoires*, cited in Francois Bluche, *Louis XIV*, translated by Mark Greengrass (Oxford, 1990), p. 299.

James and established William and his wife, Mary, on the English throne in the so-called Glorious Revolution.[4] Louis' hope of securing the support of England's significant financial, military and naval powers was dashed, and instead, at a key moment, these resources went to strengthen his enemies.

In Ireland, James continued to enjoy the support of his Catholic co-religionists who formed three-quarters of the population. Their objective was to reverse the political and economic losses they had suffered in the wars and plantations of the preceding hundred years. A Catholic recovery that had started under James was now threatened, and the Irish Catholics determined to resist William.[5]

Tyrconnell, their able leader, had been placed in charge of the Irish government by James.[6] He responded to the Glorious Revolution by a huge expansion of his army, and successfully consolidated his authority over the whole island except in the western parts of pro-Williamite Protestant Ulster.[7] A Dublin parliament made the changes to land ownership that the Catholics sought.[8] Negotiations with William in early 1689 delayed British military intervention while Tyrconnell completed clandestine arrangements for French support.[9]

The idea of Ireland becoming some sort of French protectorate was not new: Tyrconnell himself had alluded to it in 1686 as a possible option in the event of a Protestant succession, and it would be surprising if the concept had not again crossed his mind at the time of the Glorious Revolution.[10] It was observed in 1689 that if Tyrconnell had been a Frenchman he could not have been more zealous for the interests of the king of France, and in 1690 Lord Clare, a leading Jacobite – as James' supporters are known to history

---

4 On this, see Thomas Babington Macaulay, *The history of England from the accession of James II* (London 1849); John Miller, *James II: a study in kingship* (London 1989); *John Childs, the army, James II and the Glorious Revolution* (Manchester 1980); J.R. Jones, *The Revolution of 1688 in England* (London 1988); Mark Kishlansky, *A monarchy transformed: Britain, 1603–1714* (London 1996), pp 263–86. **5** On this, see J.G. Simms, *Jacobite Ireland, 1685–91* (London 1969), passim. **6** See John Miller, 'The earl of Tyrconnell and James II's Irish policy, 1685–1688', *Historical Journal*, 20 (1977), 803–23. Richard Talbot (1630–91), earl and titular duke of Tyrconnell, was from a leading Hiberno-Norman family. He was a close associate of James since their shared exile in the 1650s, and subsequently became a spokesman for Irish Catholics at the English court. In 1686 he had been put in charge of the Irish army, and in 1687 became lord deputy. He used his office to improve the lot of his fellow Irish Catholics, especially those of Norman ancestry. He was in France in late 1690 to consolidate his position with James and solicit further military support from Louis. **7** On this, see Diarmuid Murtagh & Harman Murtagh, 'The Irish Jacobite army, 1689–91', *Irish Sword*, 18, no. 70 (winter 1990), 32–48; Simms, *Jacobite Ireland*, pp 48–57. **8** See Thomas Davis, *The Patriot parliament of 1689*, ed. C. Gavan Duffy (London 1893); J.G. Simms, *The Jacobite parliament of 1689* (Dundalk 1966). **9** See Simms, *Jacobite Ireland*, pp 50–2, 58–60. Tyrconnell was adaptable to circumstances, and his negotiations with William may not have been entirely insincere. **10** See Miller, 'The earl of Tyrconnell', 807–8, 821–2.

from the Latin version of his name – urged the French to take over Ireland.[11] However, although a subsidiary motive for French involvement in Ireland was to increase commercial links, a more formal political or constitutional connection does not appear to have been on the agenda of the hard-headed statesmen at Versailles.[12]

Louis and his ministers recognized that the Glorious Revolution had been a significant setback for their plans. An effective counterstroke would be an attempt to use Ireland as a springboard to restore James with the help of the Irish Catholics.[13] This would sufficiently destabilize the British Isles to divert William and many of his resources from the Continental war. Certainly, there was some recent history of military relations between Ireland and France.[14] Irish regiments, raised by military contractors, had formed part of the French army in the Thirty Years War. In the Dutch war (1672–8), a British brigade which fought with the French included an Irish Catholic regiment which was responsible for training many of the senior officers of Tyrconnell's army, including Justin MacCarthy, Patrick Sarsfield and Richard Hamilton.

The French marine minister, the marquis de Seignelay, was in favour of an overseas expedition to Ireland with the new French navy, fostered by himself and his father, the great Colbert. He had a favourable report from the baron de Pointis, a naval gunnery officer whom he had sent to Ireland to assess the situation.[15] The only comparable overseas operation of Louis' reign was the French intervention in Sicily in the 1670s, which had been a moderate success.[16] Louvois, the war minister, disapproved of diverting resources from the European mainland, as it was clear France would be hard-pressed to hold simultaneously fronts in Flanders, Germany, Catalonia and

11 See *Négociations de M. le comte d'Avaux en Irlande, 1689–90*, with an introduction by James Hogan (Dublin 1934), p. 148; *Franco-Irish correspondence, December 1688 – February 1692*, ed. Sheila Mulloy, 3 vols (Dublin 1983–4), vol. 3, pp 135–6. Daniel O'Brien (1630?–90), 3rd Viscount Clare, was a francophile. In 1675 he had been accused of spying for France and was dismissed from command of an Irish regiment in the Anglo-Dutch brigade. In 1690 his regiment was sent from Ireland to France as part of the Mountcashel brigade under the command of his eldest son who had been a page at the French court in 1679. 12 On commercial expectations, see *Franco-Irish correspondence*, ed. cit., vol. 1, p. x. 13 See J.W. Grant, 'The government of Louis XIV' in A.W. Ward, G.W. Prothero and Stanley Leathes (ed.), *The Cambridge modern history*, vol. 5 (Cambridge 1908), p. 57; John Childs, *The Nine Years War and the British army, 1688–1697: the operations in the Low Countries* (Manchester 1991), p. 24. 14 Pierre Gouhier, 'Mercenaires irlandais au service de la France (1635–64)', *Irish Sword*, 7, no. 26 (summer 1965), 58–75; C.T. Atkinson, 'Charles II's regiments in France, 1672–78', *Journal of the Society for Army Historical Research*, 24 (1946), 53–64, 128–36, 161–71; Harman Murtagh, 'Irish soldiers abroad, 1600–1800' in Thomas Bartlett & Keith Jeffery (ed.), *A military history of Ireland* (Cambridge 1996), pp 297–8. 15 See Simms, *Jacobite Ireland*, pp 59–60. 16 See John A. Lynn, *The wars of Louis XIV, 1667–1714* (London/New York 1999), pp 143–4, 148–9.

Savoy.[17] The policy differences between Louvois and Seignelay reflected the long-standing rivalry of their respective Le Tellier and Colbert families, a rivalry which ensured that Louvois was certain to oppose anything which favoured the navy. Louis' own interest was in land warfare, but Seignelay was a favourite of Madame de Maintenon, the king's wife, and his view prevailed.[18] Once the policy was decided upon, it fell to Louvois, brilliant administrator that he was, to organize the cumbersome process of marshalling men and supplies for transport to Ireland.

What followed was a sustained effort over three years during which eight convoys brought French officers and supplies, and, in 1690, French troops to ports and anchorages on the south and west coasts of Ireland. More than 40 men-of-war sailed in the two principal convoys of 1689, and 50 in the three convoys of 1690.[19] The largest of all convoys, which sailed in March of that year, comprised 36 warships, 15 smaller vessels and 25 merchantmen. Sixty warships sailed in the three convoys of 1691.

The English navy failed to disrupt French communications with Ireland. In addition to the standard intelligence, climatic and navigational difficulties of the period, it was handicapped by its disorganization at the commencement of hostilities, by the mediocrity of its admirals, and by uncertainty as to its objectives arising from policy differences between William and his naval advisers. Only one French convoy was intercepted. This was off Bantry Bay in May 1689 when the French had the best of a rather inconclusive six-hour engagement involving, between both fleets, more than 40 warships, 10,000 sailors and 2,000 cannon.[20] French naval superiority was confirmed at the larger battle off Beachy Head in 1690. However, the French failed to exploit their naval advantage. William was dependent on sea transport to prosecute both the Continental war and the war in Ireland, and Seignelay's ships made no attempt to disrupt his communications with either theatre of operations.

The first French convoy in March 1689 brought James and a number of French officers and officials to Ireland.[21] A second convoy followed in May. The thousands of new soldiers raised by Tyrconnell were little more than a

---

17 See André Corvisier, *Louvois* (Paris 1983), pp 288–9, 453–5, 464–7. 18 On this, see Sheila Mulloy, 'The French navy and the Jacobite War in Ireland, 1689–91', *Irish Sword*, 18, no. 70 (Winter 1990), 18–31. 19 *Franco-Irish correspondence*, ed. cit., vol. 1, pp xlii-xliii. 20 On this, see E.B. Powley, *The naval side of King William's war* (London 1972), passim; Peter le Fevre, 'The battle of Bantry Bay, 1 May 1690', *Irish Sword*, 18, no. 70 (winter 1990), 1–16; A.W.H. Pearsall, 'The war at sea' in W.A. Maguire (ed.), *Kings in conflict: the revolutionary war in Ireland and its aftermath, 1689–1750* (Belfast 1990), pp 92–105. 21 The full list of those who embarked is given in *A Jacobite narrative of the war in Ireland, 1688–1691*, ed. John T. Gilbert (Dublin 1892; reproduced Shannon 1971), pp 315–16.

rabble, lacking arms, clothing, training, discipline and pay.[22] The immediate task was to form them into an effective military force. Conrad von Rosen, the senior French general, took charge of the situation.[23] He consolidated the Irish army into a 35,000-strong force organized into 45 regiments of infantry, 8 of dragoons (mounted infantry), 7 of cavalry and 2 troops of life guards.[24] The higher commands were given to experienced officers, including a number of French generals. Middle-ranking and junior French officers were distributed amongst the new regiments to overcome the inexperience of the Irish, and to meet artillery, engineering and commissariat needs. By 1690 approximately 10 per cent of the Irish army's officer corps was French, a total of almost 250 commissioned personnel.[25] However, all the French were withdrawn towards the close of hostilities that year, although in 1691 a small number of senior French officers came to lead the Jacobite army for its last independent campaign.

As important as the personnel were the military supplies. In 1689 the French fleets brought 17,000 muskets, 3,000 swords, 17,000 sabres, 1,000 pairs of pistols and 100,000 lbs. of powder to arm the Irish soldiers.[26] Further munitions were sent in 1690, and 8,000 muskets and 16,000 hand-grenades were supplied in 1691. Cannon, tents, horse-harness, medical equipment, clothing, tools, carts, sacks, food, drink and money also came from France.

The French involvement generated a large correspondence between Ireland and the highly developed French administration, especially the Departments of Foreign Affairs, War and Marine.[27] For the historian, the

---

22 See *Négotiations de M. le comte d'Avaux*, ed. cit., pp 79, 82, 85, 100, 272, 376ff.   **23** Conrad von Rosen (1628–1715) was a tough professional soldier of Livonian birth whose career was in the French army. He became a marshal of France in 1703. He was popular with the Irish, but his blunt manner and advocacy of harsh treatment towards the Ulster Protestants caused his relations with James to deteriorate and he was recalled to France early in 1690.   **24** On this, see Murtagh & Murtagh, 'The Irish Jacobite army, 1689–91', 33.   **25** *Franco-Irish correspondence*, ed. cit., vol. 1, p. 399.   **26** Ibid., pp xlii–xliii.   **27** The letters of the comte d'Avaux, the experienced and perceptive French diplomat who accompanied James to Ireland, are the most important part of the foreign ministry papers at the Quai d'Orsay. They were published privately, in a work of 756 pages, in England *c.* 1845, and then republished in facsimile by the Irish Manuscripts Commission (IMC) in 1934, under the title *Négociations de M. le comte d'Avaux en Irlande, 1689–90* with an introduction by James Hogan. An index to the *Négotiations*, prepared by Lilian Tate, and an additional thirty-six documents relating to d'Avaux contributed by Hogan, followed (Dublin 1958). The War Ministry papers comprise 2442 documents, bound in thirteen volumes, now located at the Service Historique de l'Armée de Terre in Vincennes. Two volumes and a portion of a third, edited by Tate, were published by the IMC in 1958. See Lilian Tate, 'Franco-Irish correspondence, December 1688-August 1691' in *Analecta Hibernica*, 21 (1959). In 1983–4 IMC published the remaining ten and a half volumes in a three-volume set of 1313 pages, introduced, edited and indexed by Dr Sheila Mulloy, under the title *Franco-Irish correspondence, December 1688-February 1692*. Collectively, these works surely represent the largest *œuvre* in the French language ever published in Ireland. Copies of many of the Irish-related papers in the marine ministry are in the *Dépôt de la guerre* collection.

letters, reports, assessments, lists, wants and comments of the French are by far the most important source we have for the Jacobite side of the war. They tell in detail the story of the French involvement, and reflect the French view of Ireland. This was not favourable. If service in Ireland brought the officers temporary promotion, which was occasionally made permanent as a reward for merit, most of the French were unhappy with their lot. They found the hardship of campaigning in Ireland difficult to endure: the Irish, 'la nation du monde la plus brutale et qui a le moins d'humanité', were impossible allies, there was no hope of victory, and the French were all uniformly possessed of 'la rage de retourner en France'.[28] The exception was General St Ruth, the commander in 1691, who settled into campaigning in Ireland with enthusiasm and was popular with his Irish troops.[29]

The French soon realized that, even with their assistance, the Irish army lacked the military strength to restore James to the English throne.[30] Indeed, James' involvement with the Irish Catholics was in one sense counterproductive, as it only further antagonized his English Protestant subjects and made more difficult any reconciliation with them. However, sufficient military success to strengthen Tyrconnell's bargaining power with William was possibly on the cards. Unfortunately for the Irish, the French saw Ireland as a sideshow, whereas for William, once Louis became involved, total victory in Ireland was crucial to consolidate his grip on the British Isles which, in turn, was essential to the alliance against France. England's military involvement in the alliance actually arose as a direct response to the French intervention in Ireland, although William doubtless would have found some other pretext to persuade the English parliament to enter the war had Louis not conveniently provided that one.[31]

In Ireland, the war in 1689 was for Ulster. The failure of the amateurish Jacobite army to capture Derry, where two French generals, Maumont and Pusignan, were killed, or to subdue Enniskillen, gave the Williamites a bridgehead in the north from which to take the initiative the following year with an offensive against Dublin and the rich provinces of Leinster and Munster.[32] Both sides built up their forces for the critical 1690 campaign. Rosen and d'Avaux were recalled, and Louis reinforced the Jacobites with a 6,500-strong French infantry brigade.[33] It was led by the comte de Lauzun,

28 *Franco-Irish correspondence*, ed. cit., vol. 1, p. xi; vol. 2, p. 8.   29 *Franco-Irish correspondence*, ed. cit., vol. 2, pp 283–4; see also Charles O'Kelly, *Secret history of the war of the revolution in Ireland, 1688–1691, written under the title of 'Destruction of Cyprus'*, ed. John Cornelius O'Callaghan (Dublin 1850), pp 134–5.   30 *Franco-Irish correspondence*, ed. cit., vol. 1, p. xi.   31 On this, see Childs, *The Nine Years War*, p. 24.   32 For modern accounts of the course of the war, see Simms, *Jacobite Ireland*, passim; Harman Murtagh, 'The war in Ireland, 1689–91' in W.A. Maguire, *Kings in conflict*, pp 61–91, and Richard Doherty, *The Williamite war in Ireland* (Dublin 1998).   33 *Franco-Irish correspondence*,

a courtier with a chequered past who had been appointed at James' request and was quite unfit for high military command.[34] Effectively, military leadership of the French brigade largely devolved to the lieutenant general, the marquis de la Hoguette, a competent professional soldier. The impact of the French was substantially lessened by Lauzun's overriding concern for their preservation.[35] These were his orders from Louvois whom he greatly feared and whose misgivings about the Irish venture had been increased by Lauzun's appointment.

In exchange for the French troops, 5,000 Irish soldiers were sent to France under Lord Mountcashel, a senior Jacobite general who had served there in the 1670s.[36] On arrival, the Irish were formed into three regiments and posted to the fronts in Savoy and Catalonia, where they proved to be first-class soldiers and soon won distinction.

The Williamite army was also strengthened for the 1690 campaign. It was comprised of contingents of many nationalities, reflecting the multinational character of the alliance against Louis, and it included four regiments of French Huguenots.[37] William, himself a Calvinist when in Holland, regarded the Huguenots highly and also made use of their propaganda value as victims of Louis' alleged tyranny. He appointed the most celebrated of the refugees, the duke of Schomberg, a former marshal of France, as commander of his forces in Ireland in August 1689. However, the elderly marshal's autumn offensive was a costly failure, and in frustration William came to Ireland in person to conduct the campaign of 1690. With 35,000 men he routed James' army of 25,000 at the battle of the Boyne. As the Jacobites fled, they were saved from massacre by the disciplined rearguard action of the French brigade – virtually its only positive contribution to the campaign.[38] During the battle, the Huguenots were severely mauled by the Irish cavalry and Schomberg was killed.

The Irish rallied behind the line of the Shannon and repulsed William's attack on Limerick, the city's defence being capably organized by the French general, the marquis de Boisseleau.[39] In September, however, all the French

---

ed. cit., vol. 1, p. 193.   **34** Ibid., pp xxvi–xxvii; *Négociations de M. le comte d'Avaux*, pp 521, 618; Lilian Tate, 'Letter-book of Richard Talbot', *Analecta Hibernica*, 4 (1932), 101, 104–5.   **35** See Simms, *Jacobite Ireland*, p. 141.   **36** See John A. Murphy, *Justin MacCarthy, Lord Mountcashel, commander of the first Irish Brigade in France* (Cork 1959), pp 26ff; John C. O'Callaghan, *History of the Irish brigades in the service of France* (Glasgow 1869); Murtagh, 'Irish Soldiers abroad', pp 297–8. There is much information on the selection and preparation of the Irish brigade in the *Négociations de M. le comte d'Avaux*.   **37** See Harman Murtagh, 'Huguenot involvement in the Irish Jacobite war, 1689–91' in C.E.J. Caldicott, H. Gough and J.-P. Pittion (ed.), *The Huguenots and Ireland: anatomy of an emigration* (Dublin 1987), pp 225–38.   **38** On this, see Sheila Mulloy, 'French eyewitnesses of the Boyne', *Irish Sword*, 15, no. 59 (Winter 1982), 105–11.   **39** *Franco-Irish correspondence*, ed. cit., vol. 2, pp 99–101, 106–7; J.G. Simms, 'The siege of Limerick, 1690' in E.

embarked at Galway for home.[40] The fleet that evacuated them might have been better employed against the English and Dutch vessels that transported the earl of Marlborough's army to Munster that same month to besiege and capture Cork and Kinsale.

Despite conditions of great hardship, the Irish continued to hold out in the west, inspired by their most dynamic soldier, Patrick Sarsfield, who had served his military apprenticeship in France in the 1670s.[41] The Irish resistance impressed Louis sufficiently for him to support the Jacobites again in 1691. He sent supplies and money but no personnel apart from some generals.[42] To the chagrin of Sarsfield, who felt the appointment should have been his, the new army commander was the marquis de St Ruth, a courageous and experienced officer who had been favourably impressed by the Irish he commanded in Savoy in 1690.[43] Experience of war had hardened the Irish army into a more professional force, and St Ruth's vigour in preparing for the summer campaign lifted morale and won respect.[44] The Irish never fought better than in 1691, and St Ruth was close to victory at the bloody pitched battle of Aughrim in County Galway when a chance cannon-shot killed him, and the Jacobite army went down to a heavy defeat, to which the Huguenot general, Ruvigny, made an important contribution.[45] St Ruth has been justly criticized for carelessness over the earlier loss of the key Jacobite fortress of Athlone, but accusations of rashness over the decision to fight at Aughrim are probably misplaced. A seventeenth-century army needed territory to subsist, and the threat to so much of his country once the Williamites crossed the Shannon made a stand to oppose their advance into Connacht his only realistic alternative to surrender or starvation.

Without St Ruth, the remaining French generals, d'Usson, de Tesse and La Tour Montfort, were powerless to counter the defeatism that pervaded

Rynne (ed.), *North Munster studies: essays in commemoration of Monsignor Michael Moloney* (Limerick 1967), pp 308–15. Alexandre de Rainier de Droue, marquis de Boisseleau (d. 1698) came to Ireland in 1689 and was given command of a two-battalion infantry regiment. **40** *Franco-Irish correspondence*, ed. cit., vol. 2, pp 115–21. **41** See Piers Wauchope, *Patrick Sarsfield and the Williamite war* (Dublin 1992), pp 12–13; Henry Mangan, 'Sarsfield's Defence of the Shannon, 1690–1', *Irish Sword*, 1, no. 1 (1949), 24–32. **42** *Franco-Irish correspondence*, ed. cit., vol. 1, p. xii; ii, pp 145–49, 163–90. **43** Ibid., pp xxviii–xxix. **44** See O'Kelly, '*Destruction of Cyprus*', ed. cit., pp 114–17. **45** See George Story, *A continuation of the impartial history of the wars of Ireland* (London 1693), pp 121–38; K. Danaher and J.G. Simms (eds), *The Danish force in Ireland, 1690–1691* (Dublin 1962), pp 119–24; G.A Hayes McCoy, *Irish battles* (London 1969), pp 238–72. A monument to St Ruth in the form of a Celtic cross stands on the battlefield, with an inscription in English, Irish and French. Henri de Massue, marquis de Ruvigny (1648–1720), an officer in the French army and deputy general of the Protestant churches in France, had gone into exile in 1689 and joined the army in Ireland after the death of his brother, La Caillemotte, at the Boyne. He was created a viscount (and later earl of Galway) in recognition of his service at Aughrim.

the demoralized Jacobite army.[46] Tyrconnell was dead, and Sarsfield and the other senior army officers ended the war with the treaty of Limerick in October. The tardy arrival soon afterwards of the last French supply fleet did not tempt the Jacobites to renege on the Limerick agreement.[47] Louis had continued his support to the finish, but the conclusion of hostilities in Ireland caused neither surprise nor upset in France. Seignelay and Louvois were both dead, and the feeling was that any further involvement was a waste of time and resources.

A key issue for France was the fate of the Irish army, still about 20,000 strong. Facing her enemies on all fronts, France needed as much military manpower as she could get, and the recruitment of a substantial number of Irish veterans became the overriding French objective as the war neared its end.[48] The military articles of the treaty of Limerick were of particular significance for Louis because they allowed those of the Irish army who so wished to go to France.[49] This was readily acceded to by Ginkel, the Williamite commander, who was so anxious to end the war and thereby release his forces for service in Flanders, that he agreed to supply the necessary shipping to transport the Jacobite soldiers to fight for Louis. In all, between 15,000 and 16,000 Irish soldiers appear to have gone to France after the treaty in addition to the 5,000 men of the Mountcashel brigade who had preceded them in 1690.[50]

For the Wild Geese, as these migrant Irish soldiers came to be called, the war now switched to mainland Europe. Mountcashels' men had been incorporated into the French army, but the new arrivals, formed into twelve regiments, were nominally king James' army, although paid for and under the operational control of the French.[51] They were first mustered in Normandy for an invasion of England, but the defeat off Cape La Hogue in May 1692 ended French naval superiority, and with it the possibility of reopening

---

46 *Franco-Irish correspondence*, ed. cit., vol. 2, pp 385–7, 400–2, 410–13. Both d'Usson and de Tesse were promoted to lieutenant general on being sent to Ireland. Jean de Bonnac, marquis d'Usson (1652–1705), played the leading role after the death of St Ruth, with whose aggressive approach he had disagreed. His role was the defence of towns (see René de Laportalière, 'Jean d'Usson de Saint Martin, lieutenant général des armées du roi, 1652–1705', *Société Ariégeoise*, 32 (1977), 73–114). Philibert-Emmanuel de Froullay, Chevalier de Tesse (d. 1701) was St Ruth's second-in-command at Aughrim where he was wounded. He 'acted nothing but by the approbation of d'Usson' (O'Kelly, '*Destruction of Cyprus*', ed. cit., p. 147). Henri de la Tour Montfort (d. 1703) was the governor of Limerick and, like St Ruth, had more faith in the Irish army than d'Usson and de Tesse. **47** *Franco-Irish correspondence*, ed. cit., vol. 1, pp xii–xiii, xliii. **48** Ibid., p. x; vol. 2, pp 511–12, 520–2, 524–5, 529. The issue had earlier concerned d'Avaux and Louvois. **49** Story, *Continuation*, pp 239–48; J. G. Simms, *The treaty of Limerick* (Dundalk 1961), pp 8–12. **50** *Franco-Irish correspondence*, ed. cit., vol. 1, p. xliii. **51** On this, see O'Callaghan, *History of the Irish brigades*, passim; Murtagh, 'Irish Soldiers abroad', pp 297–300.

hostilities in the British Isles.[52] The Irish were then dispersed to the fronts on the Continent where they participated with distinction in the remaining campaigns and actions of the war, notably at the battles of Steenkirk (1692) and Landen (1693).

The war finally ended in 1697 with the treaty of Ryswick. James' distinctive army was abolished. Half the regiments, much reduced in size, were incorporated into the French army to join the existing Irish brigade.[53] About 10,000 Irish soldiers were demobilized and endured considerable hardship until the outbreak of the the Spanish War of Succession in 1701 provided them with fresh opportunities for military employment in the service of the Bourbons. Thereafter, Irish regiments remained part of *ancien régime* France and Spain until the Revolution. After Ryswick, William's four Huguenot regiments were brought back to Ireland for demobilization, and many of the officers settled in Ireland, notably at Portarlington, a confiscated Jacobite estate granted to Ruvigny.[54]

How, finally, should we assess the balance sheet of Franco-Irish military relations during the Nine Years War? French support enabled the Irish Jacobites to fight a three-year war of resistance to the Williamite takeover. The volume of aid sent by Louis was impressive, but with his resources already stretched by his enormous commitments on the Continent, what came to Ireland fell far short of what was required for a Jacobite military victory, and was even more inadequate for the declared aim of restoring King James.

In the end, the Jacobites went down to a decisive defeat which ended all hope of a Catholic recovery in Ireland. But at least, thanks to Louis, their civilization died honourably, not with a whimper but with a bang that engaged the attention of Europe; and, in the aftermath, France provided a refuge for the Irish army and military employment for Irish Catholic exiles for the next century. Certainly up to the time of Napoleon a possible invasion of Ireland continued to be a factor in French military planning against England.[55] Had Louis' successors managed to restore France to the pre-eminence she had known at the height of his reign, the Wild Geese might

52 See Demetrius Charles Boulger, *The battle of the Boyne together with an account based on French and other unpublished records of the war in Ireland (1688–91) and of the formation of the Irish Brigade in the service of France* (London 1911), pp 294–307.   **53** On this, see Micheline Kerney Walsh, 'The Wild Goose tradition', *Irish Sword*, 17, no. 66 (summer 1987), 12–13.   **54** See Raymond Hylton, 'The Huguenot settlement at Portarlington, 1692–1771' in Caldicott, Gough and Pittion (ed.), *The Huguenots and Ireland*, pp 297–320.   **55** See, *inter alia,* Marcus de la Poer Beresford, 'Ireland in French strategy during the American War of Independence, 1776–83', *Irish Sword*, 12, no. 49 (winter 1976), 285–97; 13, no. 50 (summer 1977), 20–9; John A. Murphy (ed.), *The French are on the sea: the expedition to Bantry Bay, 1796* (Cork 1997); Harman Murtagh, 'General Humbert's campaign in the West' in Cathal Poirteir (ed.), *The great Irish rebellion of 1798* (Cork 1980), pp 115–24.

have returned to fight again in Ireland as they always wished. The defeat of
the Irish and the failure to restore James to the throne were setbacks for
Louis' policy and damaging to his prestige. However, save possibly in the
early stages, informed French opinion had never really expected any other
outcome. The real objective of French policy was to divert William and his
resources from the war in Flanders, thus giving the French forces there the
local superiority they needed to blunt offensive operations by the allies, and
achieve military victories such as the battle of Walcourt (1690) and the capture of Mons (1691).[56] These early successes helped France endure the
extended war of attrition that ensued.[57] There was the added bonus of
20,000 battle-hardened Irish soldiers for the French army at a time when
Louis needed all the military manpower he could get. The reduction of
Ireland had been an expensive process for William, and the wartime damage
to his country's economy reduced its capacity to contribute further to the
allied war effort. For these reasons it is fair to say that Louis' intervention in
Ireland was of a limited success. On balance, France secured a good return
on a comparatively modest investment of military resources in Ireland and
the Irish during the Nine Years War.

---

56 See Childs, *The Nine Years War*, passim.   **57** See Lynn, *The Wars of Louis XIV*, pp 191–265.

Voltaire's slanted vision of the Fronde as *Commedia buffa* in *Le Siècle de Louis XIV*[1]

MARC SERGE RIVIÈRE

For his tableau of the Fronde in *Le Siècle de Louis XIV*, probably first drafted as early as 1735 and constantly revised until 1775, Voltaire had at his disposal a large number of written sources.[2] These consisted largely of memoirs left by those close to Louis XIV and by eyewitnesses – Mme de Motteville, cardinal de Retz, Guy Joli, Pierre Lenet, Mme de Nemours, Omer Talor, Mlle de Montpensier, Jean Hérault de Gourville and Pierre de La Porte, among others. On the one hand, the main corpus of historical facts was readily available at the time of composition and this made Voltaire's task easier in some respects. On the other hand, the historian was fully aware of the difficulty of reconciling these testimonies, which were often contradictory and smacking of personal bias. So it is that in *Le Siècle* (1751), he writes: 'Il est difficile de concilier tous les détails rapportés par le cardinal de Retz, Mme de Motteville, l'avocat général Talon, et tant d'autres; mais tous conviennent des principaux points' (p. 646). In this respect, the best comment on Voltaire's handling of sources as a historian is to be found in an *alinéa* on Pope in the Kehl edition of Voltaire's *Lettres philosophiques*: 'Il en est des livres comme du feu dans nos foyers: on va prendre ce feu chez son voisin, on l'allume chez soi.'[3]

The problem, then, for Voltaire was not how to seek out vital information, but rather how to sift through a considerable number of sources and collect significant yet often disparate material, before integrating the borrowings into a unified, informative and entertaining account of events. This he largely succeeded in doing. Initially, he set out to give a corpus of objective and factual information; his discussion of the economic causes of the Fronde is a good example of this and is based on the memoirs of de Retz, Mme de Motteville, Guy Joli and Omer Talon (*Le Siècle*, pp 643–4). However, Voltaire had no scruples in selecting and highlighting anecdotal

1 An earlier version of this article was published under the title 'Voltaire and the Fronde', in *Nottingham French Studies*, 26, no. 1 (June 1987), 1–18. 2 In this article, *Le Siècle de Louis XIV* will be referred to in its shortened form as *Le Siècle*. All references are to René Pomeau's edition of the *Œuvres historiques* (Paris 1957). 3 Quoted by H.T. Patterson in his introduction to Voltaire, *Traité de métaphysique* (Manchester 1937), pp xii-xiii.

details that served his main polemical purpose, namely to underline the futility and absurdity of civil wars in general, and of the Fronde in particular, and to preach the cause of strong monarchic government. In the final analysis, chapters IV and V of *Le Siècle* constitute a slanted history of what was, in Voltaire's eyes, the most ludicrous and farcical of all French civil wars. In his article 'Historiographe',Voltaire went out of his way to stress the moral purpose of history thus:

> Heureusement même un peuple entier trouve toujours bon qu'on lui remette devant les yeux les crimes de ses pères: on aime à les condamner, on croit valoir mieux qu'eux. L'*historiographe* ou l'historien les encourage dans ces sentiments, et en retraçant les guerres de la Fronde, et celles de la religion, ils empêchent qu'il n'y en ait encore.[4]

Voltaire the moralist and propagandist accordingly produced a satirical tableau which bore the stamp of his unique personality and was largely dependent for its effect on a carefully chosen pot–pourri of *petits fait* and *historiettes*, which also provide an accurate historical framework. This tableau sheds much light on Voltaire's method of work as a historian; he relied as a rule on two or three major sources, here de Retz and Motteville, and then proceeded to add to this corpus of essential data a collection of anecdotes and entertaining details which added spice to the narrative and characterized what the historian called 'l'esprit du temps'.

This article will examine what Voltaire's personal vision of the Fronde was, to what extent it was echoed or modified eighteen years later in the more serious *Histoire du parlement de Paris* of 1769, and how Voltaire transformed what was intrinsically a serious crisis into a farcical and burlesque 'guerre des pots de chambre' (*Le Siècle*, p. 651).To analyse all of Voltaire's borrowings would fall outside the scope of this brief survey; instead, I shall confine myself here to a few *échantillons* by way of illustration of the manner in which Voltaire's main thesis predetermined both the selection and adaptation of material borrowed from a range of sources.

To say that the propagandist always has the better of the historian and chronicler of events would be a gross oversimplification. For in *Le Siècle*, as in his other historical works, there is a constant tension between, on the one hand, the need for impartiality dictated to Voltaire by his high ideals of writing history and, on the other, his personal commitment to the philosophical crusade. In this respect, the main conclusions reached by J.H. Brumfitt remain essentially valid: 'especially in his major works, he is constantly

---

4 Voltaire, *Œuvres alphabétiques*, ed. J.Vercruysse, in *The complete works* (Genève and Oxford 1968–), vol. 33, I, p. 220.

restrained not only by the need for caution forced on him by an intolerant society, but by a high ideal of objectivity and impartiality and by a genuine concern for the truth for its own sake'.[5] Voltaire's frequent statements about *Le Siècle*, made during a twenty-year period of gestation and composition (1732–51), reflect this paradoxical position, although they must, of necessity, be taken with a pinch of salt. Fully aware as he was of the hostile attitude of the French authorities to the forthcoming publication, in a letter sent from Berlin and written on 25 June 1751 he argued to Michel Lambert that in *Le Siècle* 'l'auteur disparaît absolument pour ne laisser voir qu'un siècle illustre dans tous les genres'.[6] At the same time, he acknowledged on 31 August 1751 that, as a historian, he had taken it upon himself to assess the contributions and conduct of kings, generals, clerics and magistrates: 'Je me suis constitué de mon autorité privée juge des rois, des généraux, des parlements, de l'église, des sectes qui la partagent.'[7] Despite his commitment to the philosophical cause, Voltaire seems sincere enough in advocating that history ought never to stoop to the level of satire: 'On sait assez que l'histoire ne doit être ni un panégyrique, ni une satire, ni un ouvrage de parti, ni un sermon, ni un roman.'[8]

This persistent tension, characteristic of much of Voltaire's historical writing and apparent in his treatment of the Fronde in *Le Siècle*, has been resolved more happily in the *Histoire du parlement de Paris* (1769). However, despite greater self-imposed discipline in the later work, the propagandist cannot help himself at times and gives free rein to an uncontrollable urge to pass judgment on 'la bêtise humaine' in history, of which he views the Fronde a prime example. This arguably ludicrous, albeit crucial, episode in French history played clearly into the hands of the witty and effervescent satirist. Voltaire's attitude towards the Fronde remained constant from the *Lettres philosophiques* of 1733 onwards. In his catalogue of civil insurrections in France, he deemed the Fronde to be the most illogical: 'Nos guerres civiles sous Charles VI avaient été cruelles, celles de la Ligue furent abominables, celle de la Fronde fut ridicule.'[9] Taking the opposite point of view, modern historians have stressed the serious implications and the lasting impact of the Fronde as a political and social crisis. A notable example is P.J. Coveney, who, in his book, *France in crisis, 1620–1675*, astutely summed up thus the significant impact of the civil strife on internal policies in the early

5 J. H. Brumfitt, 'History and propaganda in Voltaire', *Studies on Voltaire*, 24 (1963), 271-87 (p. 287).
6 Voltaire's *Correspondence*, ed. T. Besterman, in *The complete works*, ed. cit., vol. 96, p. 11 (D 4494).
7 Ibid., Voltaire to the duc de Richelieu (D 4561), vol. 96, p. 272.   8 *Défense de Louis XIV*, in *Œuvres historiques*, ed. cit., p. 1293.   9 Voltaire, *Lettres philosophiques*, ed. F.A. Taylor (Oxford 1965), p. 24.

part of Louis XIV's personal reign: 'The confused imbroglio-like quality of certain phases of the Fronde – the Parisian Fronde of de Retz for example – should not be taken as evidence of its triviality, but rather of the complexity and depth of the crisis in the state.'[10] He goes on to argue that fears of the recurrence of civil unrest remained long uppermost in Louis XIV's mind in his dealings with the *parlements* and the *noblesse d'épée*: 'Just as the origins of the Fronde stemmed from developments over a very long period, so its consequences affected the consolidation of the monarchy and the whole future of the *ancien régime*. It is by far the most important single fact of the French seventeenth century.'[11]

In his tableau in *Le Siècle*, Voltaire purposely focused on the 'imbroglio-like quality' of the Fronde and highlighted the triviality of what he deemed to be a tragi-comic episode. His views of the Fronde may well have been partly inspired by de Retz's private evaluation of the civil strife as a 'galimatias d'actions': 'Ces remarques, trop légères par elles-mêmes, ne sont dignes de l'histoire que parce qu'elles marquent très naturellement l'extravagance de ces sortes de temps, où il n'est pas permis aux plus sensés de parler et d'agir toujours en sages.'[12] De Retz's perception of his role is underlined in J.H.M. Salmon's excellent study: 'He had been less the heroic *chef de parti* than the theatrical director of a farce in which the actors kept assuming roles for which they had not originally been cast. But up to a point, at least, he had coordinated the production and his memoirs could reflect his pride in his achievement.'[13] Early in the 1720s, Voltaire had read de Retz's memoirs where the Fronde was presented as a spectacle which had much in common with the Commedia dell'arte, of which the *coadjuteur* represented himself as the *capocomico*. No doubt the literary artist in Voltaire was quick to realize the dramatic potential of this succession of plots and counter-plots, marked by the voluntary and involuntary masking and unmasking of heroes and villains. As Paul Morand has judiciously noted in his preface to the *Mémoires du cardinal de Retz*, the Fronde, as a spectacle, frequently descended to the levels of *commedia buffa*:

> La Fronde c'est la Commedia dell'arte, un canevas très simple où l'action et les dialogues sont laissés à l'invention d'acteurs de génie [. . .] La pièce est une *recreazione comico-tragica*, sur un *libretto* élémentaire: exécutif contre législatif, féodalité contre droit divin.[14]

---

10 P.J. Coveney, 'Introduction', in P. J. Coveney ed., *France in Crisis, 1620-1675* (London 1977), pp 1–64 (p. 37). **11** Ibid. **12** P. de Gondi, Cardinal de Retz, *Mémoires*, ed. P. Morand, 2 vols (Paris 1965), vol. 1, p. 319. **13** J.H.M. Salmon, *Cardinal de Retz: the anatomy of a conspirator* (London 1969), p. 132. **14** Paul Morand, introduction to the *Mémoires* of the Cardinal de Retz, ed. cit., vol. 1, pp 8–9.

This would appear to have been precisely the view taken by Voltaire of the civil war throughout his career – it combined the ingredients of a burlesque comic opera with those of *commedia buffa* and those of the Commedia dell'arte, with its improvisations on a given theme, its parody of political intrigues, its unpredictable characters, the bragging Capitan Condé, the ridiculous *dottori* of the *parlement* and the ludicrous figure of Pantalon represented by Mazarin. Just as, in Voltaire's view, the Commedia dell'arte had degenerated into a series of stale and vulgar jokes and could no longer be considered fit as family entertainment in his day, so too the Fronde had become an occasion for tasteless vaudevilles and such improper public jokes as the reactions to the decree which put a price on Mazarin's head:

> Les Blot et les Marigny, beaux esprits, qui portaient la gaieté dans les tumultes de ces troubles, firent afficher dans Paris une répartition des cent cinquante mille livres: tant pour qui couperait le nez au cardinal, tant pour une oreille, tant pour un oeil, tant pour le faire eunuque. (*Le Siècle*, p. 658)

Even in the early historical works such as the *Essay upon the civil wars of France*, first published in England in 1727, Richard Waller has noted a similar tendency on Voltaire's part to insert sardonic comments on

> the lack of fundamental seriousness of character in the French temperament which means that the kingdom is invariably governed by what is accepted at Court and which allowed the Parisians in 1590 to sing 'Ballads in the Streets and Lampoons' against the man who was besieging their city and threatening to starve them to death.[15]

Likewise, in the *Lettres philosophiques*, Voltaire summed up the Fronde as a farce played out on the stage of history and in which the main performers had earned not the applause but the jeers of posterity: 'Pour la dernière guerre de Paris, elle ne mérite que des sifflets.'[16] One of Voltaire's favourite metaphors in his historical works was 'le théâtre de la guerre' (*Le Siècle*, p. 728); the conduct of Condé, de Retz, Mazarin or that of the *parlementaires* between 1648 and 1653, belonged to the world not of Cornelian and epic theatre, but of low comedy marked by the type of satirical drinking songs which Voltaire had deplored in the *pièces du théâtre de la foire* by Lesage and Fuzelier. Moreover, in his article 'Bouffon' in the *Dictionnaire philosophique*, he wrote of Scarron's *Mazarinades*:[17] 'Ces saletés font vomir, et le reste est si

---

15 R. Waller, 'Voltaire's civil wars: history and anecdote', in U. Kölving and C. Mervaud (eds), *Voltaire et ses combats* (Oxford 1997), vol. 2, pp 1401–12 (p. 1404).   **16** Voltaire, *Lettres philosophiques,* ed. cit., p. 23.   **17** 'The name given to the very numerous pamphlets and satires, in prose and verse,

exécrable qu'on n'ose le copier. Cet homme était digne du temps de la Fronde.'[18]

Indeed, whenever Voltaire wished to evoke the atmosphere of the Fronde in his writings, he resorted either to the world of the *cabarets,* to which the *petit peuple* thronged, or to *Mazarinades* and sordid intrigues unworthy of the great names involved. In his *Leningrad notebooks,* among entries which appear to date back to 1735 when he was composing the first draft of the chapters on the Fronde, one finds the following remark: 'La grand'salle devenue un théâtre de la guerre, la débauche et la gaieté régnant au milieu de ces horreurs.'[19] Elsewhere in his *Notebooks,* as in *Le Siècle,* the spotlight is turned on a reprehensible 'légèreté d'esprit' prevalent in the capital: 'En ce temps les horreurs les plus honteuses à l'humanité se commettoient avec un esprit de plaisanterie, et on faisoit la guerre au son des chansons et des vaudevilles.'[20] These early remarks may well contain the seed of the central idea behind Voltaire's attempt to trivialize the Fronde in *Le Siècle*: 'Les cabarets et les autres maisons de débauche étaient les tentes où l'on tenait les conseils de guerre, au milieu des plaisanteries, des chansons et de la gaieté la plus dissolue' (*Le Siècle,* p. 651). All along, the social historian saw in this levity a national trait to be compared to the natural propensity towards gravity characteristic of the English nation during its civil wars. In his article 'Français', completed for the *Encyclopédie* in 1756, Voltaire described the typical Parisian as 'impétueux dans ses plaisirs, comme il le fut autrefois dans ses fureurs', and he added: 'En général, l'impétuosité dans la guerre, et le peu de discipline, furent toujours le caractère dominant de la nation.'[21] Similar observations on the mood of levity that seized the capital in times of crises are found in the *Essai sur les guerres civiles de France,* which appeared at the Hague in 1729 and was probably a translation of the English version by Abbé Granet:

> Les misérables Parisiens, trompés d'abord par l'espérance d'un prompt secours, chantaient dans les rues des ballades et des lampons contre Henri: folie qu'on ne pourrait attribuer à quelque autre nation avec vraisemblance; mais qui est assez conforme au génie des Français, même dans un état si affreux.[22]

---

issued against cardinal Mazarin at the time of the Fronde. The name was sometimes extended to all satires published on the occasion of the conflict in question.' (*The Oxford companion to French literature,* ed. P. Harvey and J. E. Clarendon, Oxford 1959, p. 467).   **18** Voltaire, *Œuvres complètes,* 70 vols (Kehl 1784–89) vol. 34, p. 339.   **19** Voltaire, *Notebooks,* ed. T. Besterman, in *The complete works,* ed. cit., vol. 81, p. 210.   **20** Ibid., p. 250.   **21** Voltaire, *Œuvres alphabétiques,* ed. cit., in *The complete works,* ed. cit., vol. 33, p. 98.   **22** Voltaire, *The English essays of 1727,* ed. R. Waller, in *The complete works,* ed. cit., vol. 3 B, p. 105.

Although the tone becomes more serious in the four chapters of the *Histoire du parlement de Paris* where Voltaire returns to the Fronde (chapters LIV–LVII of the Kehl edition), one leitmotiv remains the burlesque portrayal of the civil war. References to *vaudevilles* and *cabarets* persist. Quoting a popular satirical song of the time, the propagandist highlights what he sees as one of the most objectionable aspects of the conflict: 'Cette chanson ridicule montre l'esprit du temps auquel les plus grandes affaires avaient été traitées au cabaret et en vaudevilles'.[23] That Voltaire, who enjoyed composing *facéties* – a genre which flourished as a powerful political and satirical weapon during the Fronde[24] – should in turn have objected so strongly to the mood of levity prevalent at the time, is another aspect of his ubiquitous personality. In *Le Siècle*, he uses the term *facétie* to describe Condé's hypocritical behaviour during the procession in honour of Sainte Geneviève in 1652: 'Mais en même temps y a-t-il rien de plus ridicule que de voir le grand Condé baiser la châsse de sainte Geneviève dans une procession, y frotter son chapelet, le montrer au peuple, et prouver par cette facétie que les héros sacrifient souvent à la canaille?' (pp 663–4). The tableau of the Fronde has, indeed, much in common with Voltaire's own *facéties* by its witty and satirical tone. Diana Guiragossian's definition of the genre could equally apply to whole sections of the tableau in *Le Siècle*, 'The term was generally applied to collections of amusing and satirical anecdotes and to racy short stories.'[25] A similar proclivity towards anecdotes and *bons mots* can be observed in Voltaire's early attempts at writing history in the *Essay upon the civil wars of France* (1727).[26]

This apparent contradiction between Voltaire the author of *facéties* and the critic of the jocular Frondeurs is more easily understood if one examines closely the underlying political themes of his tableaux of the Fronde both in *Le Siècle* and in the *Histoire du parlement de Paris*. As J.H. Brumfitt has noted, one of Voltaire's chief philosophical objectives was to establish a sharp contrast between the general anarchy which had marked the prelude to Louis XIV's personal reign and the subsequent period of lasting stability ascribed to the king's strong leadership: 'To enhance the achievement of Louis he minimizes that of Mazarin. He describes the Fronde as a sort of comic-opera rebellion.'[27] Seen in this light, Voltaire's own production of the *commedia buffa* becomes not just a source of entertainment for his readers, but also a highly effective medium for conveying a clear political message which he summarized thus in his article 'Tyrannie', first published in the *Correspondance littéraire* of 1 October 1764: 'Sous quelle tyrannie aimeriez-

23 Voltaire, *Œuvres complètes*, ed. cit., vol. 26, p. 260. 24 See D. Guiragossian, *Voltaire's facéties* (Genève 1963), p. 13. 25 Ibid. 26 On this, see R. Waller, 'Voltaire's civil wars', pp 88–9. 27 J.H. Brumfitt, *Voltaire, historian* (Oxford 1958), p. 61.

vous mieux vivre? Sous aucune; mais s'il fallait choisir, je détesterais moins la tyrannie d'un seul que celle de plusieurs.'[28]

As a partisan of the *thèse royale*, Voltaire was only too glad to seize upon this burlesque episode in order to draw attention to the real dangers posed by the constant elbowing for position of a powerful and uncontrolled *noblesse d'épée* and an irresponsible and ambitious *noblesse de robe* represented by the *parlements*. Such is the conclusion drawn by Peter Gay in *Voltaire's politics*: 'Voltaire's admiration of Louis XIV should be read as a political preference for the king over his opponents, a reasoned and reasonable judgment that with all its dangers a strong monarchy is preferable to a strong nobility.'[29] By drawing attention to the political ambitions of the *parlement de Paris* during the civil war, Voltaire makes this point forcefully: 'Sous un gouvernement vigoureux, le parlement n'était rien: il était tout sous un roi faible' (*Le Siècle*, p. 648). And in a paragraph added in 1768 as a result of further research for the *Histoire du parlement de Paris,* the propagandist applauded the young king's stern measures, taken in 1653, which aimed to outlaw future assemblies of the *chambres* and keep the *parlement de Paris* in check: 'Le parlement voulut remontrer; on mit en prison un conseiller, on en exila quelques autres; le parlement se tut: tout était déjà changé' (*Le Siècle*, p. 667). An equally distorted picture emerges from the narrative of events in the *Histoire du parlement de Paris*: 'On se tut, on obéit; et depuis ce moment l'autorité souveraine ne fut plus combattue sous ce règne.'[30] What Voltaire omitted to say was that the crisis did not come to an abrupt end in 1653. In his eagerness to see the 'naughty boys' of the insurrection chastised, in particular the magistrates whom he likened in the *Lettres philosophiques* to 'des écoliers qui se mutinent contre le préfet d'un collège, et qui finissent par être fouettés',[31] Voltaire oversimplified the issues and minimized the lasting political impact of the Fronde by presenting the royal victory as complete. So it is that the most flagrant infringements of the truth in the tableau of the Fronde in *Le Siècle* frequently reside less in the omission of important data, than in a sustained effort to put the entire episode in a satirical perspective.

However, to be fair to Voltaire, both in *Le Siècle* and in the *Histoire du parlement de Paris* he does go some way towards seriously unravelling the complex issues of the crisis, such as its economic causes – the burden of new taxes imposed on a populace which was at the time below subsistence levels, the financial deficits inherited from Richelieu's government and the venality of offices to which Emeri resorted (*Le Siècle*, pp 643–4). Voltaire's

28 Voltaire, *Dictionnaire philosophique*, ed. C. Mervaud, in *The complete works,* ed. cit., vol. 36, p. 579. **29** P. Gay, *Voltaire's politics* (Princeton 1959), pp 110–11. **30** Voltaire, *Œuvres complètes,* ed. cit, vol. 26, p. 262. **31** Voltaire, *Lettres philosophiques*, ed. cit., p. 23.

analysis of the crisis in the making comes fairly close to P.J. Coveney's informed assessment: 'The crisis of the Fronde was the product of a harsh counterpoint between the most adverse external and internal factors.'[32]

The opening pages of chapter IV of *Le Siècle* seem to augur well in terms of the balanced and objective approach chosen by Voltaire, but it is not long before the satirist upstages the detached chronicler and the social historian; neither does Voltaire convey adequately the real concern of the *noblesse de sang* with the restoration of their privileges which had been eroded under Richelieu, nor does he present the Fronde *parlementaire* as a revolt of office-holders on behalf of their legal rights. Furthermore, Voltaire's depiction of the main protagonists betrays the full extent of his own *parti pris* and pre-conceptions. As a defender of the *thèse royale,* he goes out of his way to cast Anne of Austria in the role of the frail and innocent victim of opposing factions, while he omits to point out that her obstinacy greatly fuelled the conflict. Drawing on one of his main sources, Mme de Motteville's *Mémoires pour servir à l'histoire d'Anne d'Autriche,* Voltaire seeks to arouse pity for a regent abused by the populace.[33] Thus the *raconteur* makes a meal of the unflattering nickname 'Dame Anne' given by the 'petit peuple' to Anne of Austria. 'La reine ne pouvait paraître en public sans être outragée; on ne l'appelait que *dame Anne*; et si l'on y ajoutait quelque titre, c'était un opprobre' (*Le Siècle*, p. 649). Voltaire had found the appellation in Guy Joli's *Mémoires*: 'La reine était tombée dans un mépris si général que le menu peuple ne la nommait que madame Anne.'[34] To drive the point home, Voltaire then focuses on the type of ignominious *vaudevilles* and improper songs said by Mme de Motteville to have hurt the regent deeply.[35] Furthermore, in his prosecution of the *canaille parisienne,* Voltaire draws attention to the integrity of his witness in order to add weight to his charge of victimisation: 'Mme de Motteville dit, avec sa noble et sincère naïveté, que ces "insolences faisaient horreur à la reine et que les Parisiens trompés lui faisaient pitié"' (*Le Siècle*, p. 649).

After the court's flight from Paris, we are told in fairly melodramatic terms: 'Presque toute la cour coucha sur la paille [. . .] Le roi manqua souvent du nécessaire. Les pages de sa cour furent congédiés parce qu'on n'avait pas de quoi les nourrir' (*Le Siècle*, p. 649). Likewise, the regent is said by

---

32 P. J. Coveney, *France in crisis,* ed. cit., p. 11.   **33** F. B. de Motteville, dame de Langlois, *Mémoires pour servir à l'histoire d'Anne d'Autriche,* 6 vols (Amsterdam 1739). Also reproduced in C.B. Petitot, *Mémoires relatifs à l'histoire de la France,* 78 vols (Paris 1820–8).   **34** G. Joli, *Mémoires,* in C.B. Petitot, *Mémoires relatifs à l'histoire de la France,* ed. cit., vol. 57, p. 53. As one of the Frondeurs, Joli had ascribed much of the blame for this to the regent herself. It is to be noted that Joli, in fact, uses the formula 'madame Anne' which Voltaire renders as the more pejorative 'dame Anne' to arouse his readers' indignation.   **35** *Corpus des notes marginales* (Berlin 1979–94), vol. 5, p. 789: *signet.*

Voltaire to have been deeply hurt by the battle of Saint-Antoine in 1652:'La reine en larmes était prosternée dans une chapelle des Carmélites' (*Le Siècle*, p. 662).[36] By putting his trust exclusively in Mme de Motteville's account of the fate of the queen mother, Voltaire makes no allowances for the courtier's pro-royalist feelings, undoubtedly because they matched his own.

In his treatment of the *parlements,* Voltaire's hostility towards the troublesome magistrates is much more pronounced in *Le Siècle* than it is in the *Histoire du parlement de Paris*. His bias leads him early in 1735 to sift through his sources in search of lapidary anecdotes that might assist him in his campaign. For example, according to Mme de Motteville, on the occasion of the Battle of Lens (August 1648), young Louis rejoiced at this important setback for the magistrates: 'Le Roi sçachant qu'il avoit gagné une bataille, s'écria tout haut et avec une grande exclamation *que le Parlement seroit bien fâché de cette nouvelle.*'[37] Voltaire took the trouble to underline this detail by means of a marker, a *signet*, in his own copy of the source with the express purpose of using it in *Le Siècle* (p. 645). In so doing, he fails once more to make allowances for Mme de Motteville's royalist bias, for he is only too glad to select anecdotes that give him greater ammunition in his attack on the magistrates. Moreover, he leaves the reader in no doubt as to his own position by drawing a tendentious conclusion at the end: 'Ces paroles faisaient voir assez que la cour ne regardait alors le parlement de Paris que comme une assemblée de rebelles' (*Le Siècle,* p. 645).

Almost continuously, therefore, Voltaire forgets his pledge to be a moderate and objective historian in his handling of the Fronde *parlementaire*. Instead, he portrays the magistrates as a scheming and unreasonable group of politicians dominated by radicals who take spontaneous and unconstitutional decisions aimed at safeguarding their positions, irrespective of the lasting damage done to the nation and to the monarchy. In reality, while it is true that the *parlement* acted on many occasions out of self-interest,[38] several of its decisions were the result of serious compromises reached after long deliberations between moderates and radicals.

Following a generally objective account of the Fronde *parlementaire,* Voltaire seems to have decided, early in the process of the composition of *Le Siècle*, that by offering a purely chronological survey of the civil war, he

36 See Motteville, F.B.L., dame Langlois de, *Mémoires pour servir à l'histoire d'Anne d'Autriche* [. . .], in C.B. Petitot, *Mémoires relatifs à l'histoire de la France,* ed. cit., vol. 39, p. 338.   **37** Motteville, *Mémoires pour servir à l'histoire d'Anne d'Autriche,* ed. cit., vol. 2, p. 332. This reference is to the 1739 edition used by Voltaire. His copy of this source is to be found in the public library of Leningrad. See *Corpus des notes marginales,* ed. O. Golubiéva (Berlin 1994), vol. 5, p. 789 The italics in the quotation are Motteville's.   **38** See R. Mousnier, 'Some reasons for the Fronde', in *France in crisis,* pp 169–200 (p. 182).

would be on well-trodden ground. There is, accordingly, a noticeable change of direction, even in the first edition of 1751:

> On ne veut point répéter ici tout ce qui a été écrit sur ces troubles et copier des livres pour remettre sous les yeux tant de détails alors si chers et si importants et aujourd'hui presque oubliés; mais on doit dire ce qui caractérise l'esprit de la nation, et moins ce qui appartient à toutes les guerres civiles que ce qui distingue celle de la Fronde. (*Le Siècle*, pp 648–9)

From this point onwards, the social historian, intent on defining 'l'esprit du temps,' resorts to a substantial collection of *historiettes* and *petits faits* which present the double advantage of entertaining the reader and heaping ridicule on the Frondeurs and the populace. The tone quickly degenerates to the level of the *commedia buffa* as Voltaire plays to the *parterre*, for whom, as a practising dramatist, he had little regard. Thus, in his writing, historical facts generally make way for an increasing number of anecdotal minutiae collected over several years.

As the text of chapters IV and V of *Le Siècle* was revised and expanded over the years, the tone became increasingly satirical and more in keeping with Voltaire's growing preoccupation with his main thesis of depicting the Fronde *noble* as irresponsible, unjustifiable and even degenerate. To prove his case, Voltaire relies on an endless catalogue of carefully chosen *petits faits*, tantamount to circumstantial evidence, such as the defeat of the *Régiment de Corinthe*, so called because de Retz, as titular archbishop of Corinth, had set it up. The satirist gleefully reports this reversal for the cardinal: 'Tout se tournait en raillerie; le régiment de Corinthe ayant été battu par un petit parti, on appela cet échec *la première aux Corinthiens*' (*Le Siècle*, p. 651, Voltaire's italics). Voltaire resorts to techniques of caricature later employed in *Candide* and, to this end, Joli's expression, 'un parti des ennemis',[39] is transformed into 'un petit parti'. Mazarin's poor French accent likewise adds to his caricature, as Voltaire incorporates into his text a detail borrowed from the memoirs of Mme de Nemours, namely the cardinal's mispronunciation of 'l'arrêt d'union' as 'l'arrêt d'ognon' (*Le Siècle*, p. 644).[40] In Voltaire's production of this *commedia buffa*, a motley crew of colourful characters occupy the stage in turn, among them the 'roi des Halles,' a nickname for the duc de Beaufort (*Le Siècle*, p. 651).[41] Moreover, mock-heroic scenes become ideal raw material in

---

39 Joli, in Petitot, *Mémoires relatifs à l'histoire de la France,* ed. cit., vol. 47, p. 52.   **40** *Mémoires de Mme de Nemours* (Amsterdam 1730), p. 6.   **41** The source is Mme de Motteville, *Mémoires pour servir à l'histoire d'Anne d'Autriche* in Petitot, *Mémoires relatifs à l'histoire de la France,* ed. cit., vol. 38, p. 164.

Voltaire's plan to convey the 'esprit de vertige' of the time; such is the sketch of Retz's grand entrance into the *parlement* armed with a dagger (*Le Siècle*, p. 652). The amusing paradox was not lost on the satirist whose portrait of the *coadjuteur* is reminiscent of that of the Jesuit commandant in *Candide*, with 'la robe retroussée, l'épée au côté, l'esponton à la main'.[42] To round off the scene, Voltaire inserted into his text, by way of suitable *bons mots*, an irreligious *boutade*, stooping thereby to the level of the *parterre*. For these details, the satirist had delved into the *coadjuteur's* own memoirs: '*Voilà le bréviaire de notre archevêque.*'[43] The end result is that, because the readers are caught up in a fast-moving sequence of farcical *intermèdes,* they regrettably lose sight of serious political issues, such as the complex reasons for the growing rivalry between the Prince de Condé's faction and the old Frondeurs gathered around de Retz.

Another example of this oft-employed technique of *reductio ad absurdum* is the 'affaire du tabouret', which is presented by Voltaire as 'une preuve [. . .] sensible de la légèreté d'esprit qu'on reprochait aux Français' (*Le Siècle*, p. 652). Mme de Motteville had discussed the question of *préséance* with her customary degree of seriousness by describing the political manoeuvres of the various factions in the *coulisses*.[44] For his part, Voltaire ignores the keen sense of injustice felt by the nobility which perceived Anne of Austria's action as yet another slight against their depleted privileges. Instead, in a manner once again reminiscent of the *conteur's* approach, the satirist turns the spotlight on the disproportion between the small cause – a *tabouret* offered to Mme de Pons – and the serious effect and exaggerated response, namely the convening of the *états généraux*, thereby placing the incident firmly within an ironic framework (*Le Siècle*, p. 652). In a similar vein, the satirist patronizingly labels the Fronde 'noble', 'une affaire de femmes' (*Le Siècle*, p. 652), despite giving the leading roles to Condé, Conti, de Retz, Mazarin and many other male protagonists in the previous scenes. As evidence of this female take-over of what he considers to be men's business, Voltaire quotes, out of context, a mere *boutade* in a letter from Gaston d'Orléans to his daughters: 'A mesdames les comtesses, maréchales de camp dans l'armée de ma fille contre le Mazarin,' a detail borrowed from the *Mémoires de mademoiselle de Montpensier*[45] which is then blown up out of all proportion (*Le*

42 Voltaire, *Candide*, ed. M. Béguin and J. Golzink (Paris 1998), p. 95.   **43** De Retz, *Mémoires*, 4 vols (Amsterdam 1731), vol. 3, p. 372. The italics are Voltaire's.   **44** Petitot, *Mémoires relatifs à l'histoire de la France*, ed. cit., vol. 38, p. 372.   **45** Mademoiselle de Montpensier, Louise d'Orléans, duchesse de, *Mémoires de mademoiselle de Montpensier* [. . .] (Amsterdam 1730), 6 vols. Voltaire possessed this edition in his library (BV 2507) and a *signet* is to be found at the point where the anecdote is told (vol. 2, pp 42–3). See *Corpus des notes marginales*, vol. 5, p. 774.

Siècle, p. 653). To add to the general tone of the *commedia buffa*, the satirist also finds room for a number of grandiloquent, albeit insignificant, speeches by the bragging *Capitan*, Condé, at the expense of *Pantalon*, Mazarin. Consider, for example, the inclusion of Condé's defiant words to the cardinal, 'Adieu Mars!'(*Le Siècle*, p. 653),[46] and the prince's contemptuous remarks in broken Italian about the cardinal, 'All'illustrissimo signor Faquino,' episodes which are borrowed from Joli's *Mémoires*, but which fit in well with the burlesque tone of the Commedia dell'arte.[47]

Comedy would not be complete, in the seventeenth-century tradition of the Molière-Lulli partnership, without the inclusion of ballet. The endless changing of partners among the Frondeurs is seized upon by Voltaire to turn the civil war into a cheap version of *comédie-ballet*. The volatile nature of the protagonists is brought home by scenes in which they are engaged in a series of clumsy quadrilles: 'La guerre finit et recommença à plusieurs reprises; il n'y eut personne qui ne changeât souvent de parti' (*Le Siècle*, p. 653). Similarly, the masking and unmasking of the chief villains, as Voltaire saw them, namely de Retz, Conti, Longueville, the *parlement* and *Capitan*-Condé, become an integral part of burlesque comedy, as it was in the Commedia dell'arte or in Molière's *Le Bourgeois Gentilhomme* or *Les Fourberies de Scapin*. Voltaire also draws attention to unusual costumes in the spectacle of the Fronde: 'Les Parisiens sortaient en campagne, ornés de plumes et de rubans; leurs évolutions étaient le sujet de plaisanterie des gens du métier' (*Le Siècle*, p. 651). In this extravaganza, each faction is characterized by its own colours: 'Chaque parti avait alors son écharpe' (*Le Siècle*, p. 658). Not wanting to be left out of the military parade, cardinal-general Mazarin designed a distinctive uniform for his own troops out of sheer vanity. To add to the mood of public levity, Condé, turned supporter of the court, presented to the queen mother 'un petit nain bossu, armé de pied en cap: "Voilà, dit-il, le généralissime de l'armée parisienne." Il voulait par-là désigner son frère, le prince de Conti, qui était en effet bossu, et que les Parisiens avaient choisi pour leur général' (*Le Siècle*, p. 651).[48] The burlesque spectacle is thus complete thanks to the presence of a court jester. As for the *petit peuple* of Paris, they play the role of the vulgar *parterre*, booing and cheering the protagonists and thereby contributing an indispensable ingredient to Voltaire's version of the *commedia buffa*: 'Les troupes parisiennes, qui sortaient de Paris et revenaient toujours battues, étaient reçues avec des huées et des éclats de rire' (*Le Siècle*, p. 651).

To conclude, then, it would appear that, in his treatment of the Fronde,

---

46 The source is the *Mémoires de Mme de Nemours*, ed. cit., p. 47.   **47** Joli, *Mémoires*, ed. cit., p. 73.
48 The source is the *Mémoires de Mme de Nemours,* ed. cit., p. 34.

Voltaire strives after objectivity, but not earnestly enough to achieve it. In other words, Voltaire emerges, paradoxically at times, as an 'homme de passion', to use René Pomeau's phrase,[49] and at other times as the 'premier historien scientifique', in Charles Rihs' words.[50] As a lover of rational history and a critic of 'la bêtise humaine', he saw in the Fronde an example of mass hysteria, an irrational and inexcusable attempt to undermine the monarchy, as well as a deplorable lapse in behaviour on the part of several volatile sections of the nation. In his handling of sources for the tableau of the civil war, the unresolved tension between the high degree of objectivity expected of the historian and his personal commitment to preconceived philosophical aims is very much in evidence. The suppression of important data and the blurring of serious issues contribute to the general caricature. Voltaire responds chiefly as a royalist, a staunch defender of the *thèse royale,* a lover of stability and a vocal opponent of divided government. He also frequently fails to heed his own warning about the dangers of bias in the memoirs of Louis XIV's contemporaries: 'Il n'y a que trop de traits, dans ces mémoires, ou falsifiés par la passion, ou rapportés sur des bruits populaires' (*Le Siècle,* p. 642). While he is on his guard against the prejudices of some eyewitnesses, notably de Retz, La Porte and Gourville, he is at the same time guilty of inconsistency; he makes no allowances for Mme de Motteville's royalist *parti pris* because it suits him to convey her strong views. On the one hand, just as in his theoretical writings on tragedy the classicist in Voltaire deplored the mixture of genres,[51] so too he could not accept that, with the future of the monarchy in jeopardy, the scenes of the Fronde could have been played out in an atmosphere of jocularity and mirth. On the other hand, the philosopher was capable of reflecting on the strange paradox that this general levity in fact constituted the Fronde's saving grace, since it prevented the kind of bloodshed that had marked the Ligue: 'Au milieu de ces désordres il régna toujours une gaieté qui les rendit moins funestes' (*Le Siècle,* p. 664). One ought to be grateful for small mercies: 'Les chefs de parti furent moins cruels et les peuples moins furieux que du temps de la Ligue; car ce n'était pas une guerre de religion' (*Le Siècle,* p. 659).

Finally, if one were to try and determine Voltaire's originality in *Le Siècle* and the extent to which he has furthered our understanding of the civil war, one would have to say that, strictly in terms of historical information, he uncovered little that was relatively new, for there was already a substantial corpus of sources on this eventful episode in French history. What is novel

---

49 R. Pomeau, *La Religion de Voltaire* (Paris 1956), p. 384.   **50** C. Rihs, *Recherches sur les origines du matérialisme historique* (Genève 1962), p. 119.   **51** For example in his comments on the 'Alas! Poor Yorick' scene of *Hamlet* in Letter 18 of the *Lettres philosophiques.*

is Voltaire's own subjective, often unfair, yet generally sound interpretation of events. That is to say, any originality consists chiefly in his contribution as propagandist, philosopher and social historian, rather than as chronicler of events. For in the end, Voltaire's greatest merit consisted of having sifted through a large number of contradictory eyewitness reports and of having transformed his borrowings into a unified, lively, informative and reasonably comprehensive narrative. As E.H. Carr has rightly pointed out in his thought-provoking book, *What is history?*, 'the historian and the facts of history are necessary to one another. The historian without his facts is rootless and futile; the facts without the historian are dead and meaningless.'[52] Voltaire's creative mind established the right balance between analysis and narrative; his art of exposition, his mastery of story-telling techniques and his natural talent as a *raconteur* ensured that the tableau of the Fronde met with the approval of his public. So it is that, in a letter to Devaux on 9 December 1738, Mme de Graffigny expressed her rapture at Cirey during her first reading of the unfinished manuscript of *Le Siècle de Louis XIV*, and in particular waxed lyrical about the merits of the chapters on the Fronde: 'Il y a un abrégé de la Fronde qui est divin.'[53] The lasting success of Voltaire's tableau has been due primarily to his highly individualistic manner of presentation. As always in such matters, Voltaire would have wished to have the final say; in his article 'Style', he concluded: 'Presque toujours les choses qu'on dit frappent moins que la manière dont on les dit; car les hommes ont tous à peu près les mêmes idées de ce qui est à la portée de tout le monde. L'expression, le style fait toute la différence.'[54]

52 *What is history?* (London 1964), p. 30.   **53** Mme de Graffigny, *Correspondance*, ed. E. Showalter (Oxford 1985), vol. 1, p. 206.   **54** Voltaire, *Œuvres complètes*, ed. cit., vol. 43, p. 227.

Bibliography

I. PRINTED SOURCES

Abbott, C., 'The portrait as text: two depictions of Madame de Saint-Balmon 1607–1660,' *Atlantis: Revue d'Études sur les femmes, numéro special sur la femme sous l'Ancien Régime*, (1993), 122–33.

Adam, A., *Histoire de la littérature française au XVII⁰ siècle*. 5 vols, Paris 1954–62.

—— *Du Mysticisme à la révolte: les Jansénistes du XVII⁰ siècle*. Paris 1968.

Agrippa, H.C., *De nobilitate et praecellentia foeminei sexus*. Antwerp 1529.

Alden, J. M. (ed.), *The critical opinions of John Dryden*. Nashville, Tennessee 1963.

Alter, J., 'Vers des re-lectures du *Roman bourgeois*: du lisible, du scriptible, de l'illisible et du relisible' in Michel Bareau, Jacques Barchilon, Donna Stanton and Jean Alter (ed.), *North American Society for Seventeenth-Century French Literature, Actes de Banff* (Paris, Seattle, and Tübingen 1987), pp 237–48.

Anon., *The actor's remonstrance or complaint for the silencing of their profession, and banishment from their several play-houses*. London 1643.

—— *Scarron's city romance, made English*. London 1671.

—— *Andromache, translated by a young gentleman who has a great esteem of all French playes*. London 1675.

—— *Factum pour Élie Seignette apoticaire et exerçant l'art de la pharmacie à La Rochelle, intimé. Contre la communauté des maistres apoticaires de la mesme ville appellans*. [La Rochelle] [1676].

—— *Factum pour Élie Richard, Élie Bouhéreau et Jean Seignette contre Jacques du Mont....* [La Rochelle] [1683].

—— *The stage acquitted*, ed. A. Freeman. New York and London 1972.

—— *A vindication of the stage*, ed. A. Freeman. New York and London 1974.

—— *Collier tracts*, ed. A. Freeman. New York and London 1974.

—— *Commonwealth tracts 1625–1650*, ed. A. Freeman. New York and London 1974.

Anthony, R., *The Jeremy Collier stage controversy 1698–1726*. New York 1937.

Apostolidès, J.-M., *Le Roi-machine: spectacle et politique au temps de Louis XIV*. Paris 1981.

Aquinas, St Thomas, *Summa theologiae*, ed. T. Gilby and others. 61 vols, London 1964–81.

Arnauld, A., *Œuvres*, ed. Gabriel Du Pac de Bellegarde and Jean Hautefage. 42 vols, Paris 1775–81.

—— and Nicole, Pierre, *La Logique ou l'art de penser*, ed. Pierre Clair and François Girbal, Bibliothèque des Textes Philosophiques, 2nd edn. Paris 1993.

Asslineau, C., *Le Roman bourgeois*. Paris 1854.

Astier, R., 'Louis XIV, "Premier Danseur"', in David Lee Rubin (ed.), *Sun King: the ascendancy of French culture during the reign of Louis XIV*. Washington, London and Toronto 1992.

Atkinson, C.T., 'Charles II's regiments in France, 1672–78', *Journal of the Society for Army Historical Research*, 24 (1946), 53–64, 128–36, 161–71.

Aubignac, F. H., Abbé d', *Projet pour le rétablissement du théâtre* in P. Martino (ed.) *Pratique du théâtre*. Paris and Alger 1927.

Aubigné, A. d'., *Les Tragiques*, ed. A. Garnier and J. Plattard. Paris 1990.

Audibert, R., and Bouvier, R., *Saint-Amant: capitaine du Parnasse*. Paris 1946.

Augustine, St, *De civitate Dei*, ed. J.E.C. Welldon. 2 vols, London, 1924.

—— *De spiritu et littera/On the spirit and the letter*, translated by W.J. Sparrow Simpson. London 1925.

—— *Confessions*, edited and translated by H. Chadwick. Oxford 1998.

Avaux, J.-A. d', *Negociations de M. le comte d'Avaux en Irlande 1689–90 with an introduction by James Hogan*. Dublin 1934.

—— *Negociations de M. le comte d'Avaux en Irlande (1689–90)* supplementary volume, ed. Hogan J., with indexes by L. Tate. Dublin 1958.

Baker, R., *Theatrum redivivum, or The theatre vindicated*. London 1662.

Barish, J., *The anti-theatrical prejudice*. London 1981.

Barles, L., *Les Nouvelles Decouvertes sur les organes des femmes, servans à la generation*. Lyon 1674.

Barnwell, H. T., *Corneille's writings on the theatre*. Oxford 1965.

Baulot, I., *Mutus liber*. La Rochelle 1677.

Baxter, R., *A Christian directory, or A summ of practical theologie*. London 1673.

Bayle, P., -*Nouvelles de la république des lettres*, (juillet 1684), I: 536.

—— *Nouvelles de la république des lettres*, (mai 1685), III: 553.

—— *Nouvelles de la république des lettres*, (octobre 1685), IV: 1130–1.

—— *L'Histoire du fœtus humain, recoeüillie des extraits de Monsieur Bayle; & publiée par Monsieur du Rondel*. Leyden 1688.

—— *Dictionnaire historique et critique*. 1697.

Beccaria, C., marchese di, *Dei delitti e delle pene. Traité des délits et des peines* / Traduit de l'italien. Neuchatel 1797.

Beckett, J. C., *The cavalier duke: a life of James Butler, first duke of Ormond*. Belfast 1990.

Bellegarde, J.B. Morvan de, *Réflexions sur ce qui peut plaire ou déplaire dans le commerce du monde*. Paris 1689.

—— *Réflexions sur le ridicule et sur les moyens de l'éviter*. La Haye 1729.

Benserade, I., *Benserade: ballets pour Louis XIV*, ed. Marie-Claude Canova-Green, 2 vols. Toulouse 1997.

Bentley, G.E., *The Jacobean and Caroline stage*, 7 vols. Oxford 1942–56.

Bertaud, M. 'D'un *Comte d'Essex* à l'autre, La Calprenède et Thomas Corneille', in M. Bertaud and A. Laberit (ed.), *Amour tragique, amour comique, de Bandello à Molière* (Paris 1989), pp 99–133.

Beugnot, B., 'La figure de Mecenas', in Roland Mousnier and Jean Mesnard (ed.), *L'Âge d'or du mécénat (1598–1661)* (Paris 1985), pp 285–93.

Black, J., *A military revolution? Military change and European society, 1550–1800*. London 1991.

Bluche, F., *Louis XIV* [trans. Mark Greengrass]. Oxford 1990.

Boileau, N., *Œuvres complètes* , ed. A. Adam. Paris 1966.

Bordaille, M. de, *Éclaircissement de la doctrine de l'Église touchant le culte des saints, pour servir de réponse à un sermon* . . . La Rochelle 1675.

—— *Défense de la foi de l'Église touchant l'Eucharistie, contre le livre de Mr de Lortie de la sainte cène*. La Rochelle 1676.

—— *Défense de la doctrine de l'Église touchant le culte des saints, contre le livre de Mr de Lortie*. La Rochelle 1677.

Boucher de Beauval, J., *Traité de la populaire colique bilieuse du Poitou*. La Rochelle 1673.

Boulanger, M., 'Justice et absolutisme: la grande ordonnance de 1670', *Revue d'Histoire Moderne et Contemporaine*, 47, no. 1 (2000), 8–11.

Boulger, D.C., *The battle of the Boyne together with an account based on French and other unpublished records of the war in Ireland (1688–91) and of the formation of the Irish Brigade in the service of France*. London 1911.

Boyle, R., *Parthenissa: A romance in four parts*. [Waterford 1651] London 1655.

—— *Dramatic works of Roger Boyle, earl of Orrery*, ed. W. Smith Clark II, 2 vols. Cambridge Mass. 1937.

Brenner, A. A., *The Israelite woman: social role and literary type in biblical narrative*. Sheffield, 1985.

Briggs, R., *Early modern France, 1560–1715*. Oxford 1977.

Brockliss, L., and C. Jones, *The medical world of modern France*. Oxford 1997.

Broomhall, S. M., 'Connaissances et pratiques de santé chez les femmes françaises de la Renaissance'. Unpublished *mémoire de DEA* supervised by J.-P. Pittion and submitted to the Centre d' Études Supérieures de la Renaissance, Tours 2000.

Brumfitt, J. H., *Voltaire historian*. Oxford 1958.

—— 'History and propaganda in Voltaire', *Studies on Voltaire*, 24 (1963), 271–87.

Bruneau, M.-F., *Racine, le Jansénisme et la modernité*. Paris 1986.

Budgell, E., *Memoirs of the life and character of the late earl of Orrery*. London 1732.

Burke, P., *The fabrication of Louis XIV*. New Haven and London 1992.

Burton, H., *For God and the King*. No place, 1636.

Bury, E., *Littérature et politesse: l'invention de l'honnête homme 1580–1750*. Paris 1996.

Caffaro, T., *Lettre d'un théologien illustre par sa qualité et par son mérite consulté par l'auteur pour savoir si la comédie peut être permise, ou doit être absolument défendue*, Ch. Urbain and E. Levesque (ed.), *L'Église et le théâtre*. Paris 1930.

Calder, R., 'Molière, misanthropy and forbearance: Éliante's "Lucretian" diatribe', *French Studies*, 50, no. 2 (1996), 138–43.

Callières, F. de, *Des bons mots et des bons contes, de leur usage, de la raillerie des Anciens, de la raillerie et des railleurs de notre temps*. Amsterdam 1692.

Camden, W., *Histoire d'Elizabeth royne d'Angleterre*, translated by Paul de Bellegent. Paris 1627.

Calvin, J., *Institition de la religion chrétienne*, ed. Jean-Daniel Benoît. 5 vols, Paris 1957–63.

Camus, J.-P., *Les Diuersitez*. Paris 1613.

—— *La Pieuse Jullie*. Paris 1623.

—— *Petronille*. Lyon 1626.

—— *Les Euenemens singuliers*. Lyon 1628.

—— *Les Spectacles d'horreur*. Paris 1630; Genève 1973.

—— *L'Amphitheatre sanglant*. Paris 1630.

—— *Les Rencontres funestes*. Paris 1644.

Canfield, D. F., *Corneille and Racine in England*. New York 1904.

Canova-Green, M.-C., *La Politique-spectacle au grand siècle: les rapports franco-anglais*. Paris, Seattle, Tübingen 1993.

Carlell, L., *Héraclius, emperour of the East, a tragedy Englished by Lodowick Carlell*. London 1664.

Carr, E.H., *What is history?* London 1964.

Casamayor, *nom de plume* of Serges Fuster. See Fuster, S.

Castle, T., 'Lab'ring Bards: Birth topoi and English Poetics, 1660–1820', *Journal of English and Germanic Philology*, 78 (1979), 193–208. .

Caussinat-Nogaret, G. (ed.), *Histoire des élites en France*. Paris 1991.

Chapman, G. W., *Literary criticism in England, 1660–1800*. New York 1966.

Chappuzeau, S., *Le Théâtre françois*. Lyon 1674.

Chardonnet, N., *Le Pédagogue*. Paris 1662.

Chatelain, U.-V., *Le Surintendant Nicolas Foucquet, protecteur des lettres, des arts et des sciences*. 1905; Genève 1971.

Chatounières de Grenaille, F., 'Ouverture générale à toute la pièce, avec un discours sur les Poëmes Dramatiques de ce temps', prefacing his *Innocent malheureux; ou, La Mort de Crispe*. Paris 1639.

Chedozeau, B., 'Le Tragique d'Athalie', *Revue d'Histoire Littéraire de la France*, (juillet-septembre 1967), 494–501.

Childs, J., *The army, James II and the Glorious Revolution*. Manchester 1980.

—— *The Nine Years War and the British army, 1688–1697: the operations in the Low Counties*. Manchester 1991.

Cholières, N. de, *La guerre des males et des femelles*. Paris 1588.

Church, W. F., *Richelieu and reason of state*. Princeton 1972.

Cicero, *De Oratore*, ed. A.S. Wilkins. Oxford 1879–92.

Clark, J.C., *La Rochelle and the Atlantic economy during the eighteenth century*. Baltimore and London 1981.

Clark, W.S., *The early Irish stage*. Oxford 1955.

Cognet, L., *Le Jansénisme*, Que sais-je?, 6th edn. Paris 1991.

Cohen, S., *Art, dance and the body in French culture of the Ancient Regime*. Cambridge 2000.

Collier, J., *A short treatise against stage-playes* in *Commonwealth tracts 1625–1650*, ed. A. Freeman. New York and London 1974.

—— *A short view of the immorality and profaneness of the English stage*, ed. A. Freeman. New York and London 1972.

Congreve, W., *The comedies of William Congreve*, ed. Eric S. Rump. London 1985.

Conroy, J., *Terres tragiques: l'Angleterre et l'Ecosse dans la tragédie française du XVIIe siècle*. Tübingen 1999.

Corneille, P., *Œuvres complètes*, ed. André Stegman. Paris 1963.

—— 'Discours de l'utilité et des parties du poème dramatique', in H.T. Barnwell (ed.), *Writings on the Theatre*. Oxford 1965.

Corvisier, A., *Louvois*. Paris 1983.

Cotterell, C., *Cassandra: the fam'd romance*. London 1652.

—— and Aylesbury W., *The historie of the civill warres of France*. London 1647 [1648].

Cotton, C., *Horace, a French tragedy of Monsieur Corneille*. London 1671.

Coulet, H., *Le Roman jusqu'à la Révolution*. Paris 1967.

Coustel, P., *Sentiments de l'église et des saints pères pour servir de décision sur la comédie et les comédiens*. Paris 1694.

Couton, G., *Corneille et la Fronde*. Paris 1955.

Coveney, P.J. (ed.), *France in crisis, 1620-1675*. London 1977.

Crowne, J., *The dramatic works of John Crowne*, ed. W. Patterson, 4 vols. New York 1874.

Cuénin, M., *La Dernière des Amazones: Madame de Saint-Baslemont*. Nancy 1992.

Cullière, A., 'La vie culturelle en Lorraine dans la seconde moitié du XVIe siècle', Université de Nancy II, Ph.D. thesis. Nancy 1978.

Cunningham, A., 'Fabricius and the "Aristotle Project" at Padua', in A. Wear, R.K. French and I.M. Lonie (ed.), *The medical renaissance of the sixteenth century* (Cambridge 1985), pp 195–222.

Danaher, K. and Simms, J.G. (ed.), *The Danish force in Ireland, 1690–1691*. Dublin 1962.

Dancer, J., *Nicomède, a tragi-comedy*. London, 1671.

Davenant, W., *The dramatic works of Sir William Davenant*, ed. W. Patterson, 5 vols. New York 1964 (reprint of the edition of 1872–4)

Davies, B., *The thought of Thomas Aquinas*. Oxford 1992.

Davis, T., *The patriot parliament of 1689*, ed. C. Gavan Duffy. London 1893.

Delaizement, D.H., *Histoire des réformés de La Rochelle depuis l'année 1660 jusqu'à l'année 1685*. Amsterdam 1689.

De la Tour du Pin de La Charce, P., *Histoire de Madameoiselle de la Charce de la maison de la Tour du Pin, ou mémoires de ce qui s'est passé sous le règne de Louis Quatorze*. Paris 1731.

Delmas-Marty, M. (ed.), *Procès pénal et droits de l'homme*. Paris 1992.

Dennis, J., *The critical works of John Dennis*, ed. E. N. Hooker, 2 vols. Baltimore MD 1939, 1943.

Dens, J.-P., *L'Honnête homme et la critique du goût: esthétique et société au XVIIe siècle*, French Forum Monographs, 28. Lexington, Kentucky *c.*1981.

Denzinger, H. (ed.), *Enchiridion symbolorum, definitionum et declarationum de rebus fidei et morum*, revised by Adolf Schönmetzer, 35th edn. Barcelona, Freiburg im Breisgau, Rome, New York 1973.

De Retz, P., *Mémoires*, 4 vols. Amsterdam 1731.

Derrida, J., *Les Marges de la philosophie*. Paris 1972.

Des Billons, Le Père, *Histoire de la vie chrétienne et des exploits militaires d'Alberte-Barbe d'Ernecourt connue sous le nom de madame de Saint-Balmon*. Liège 1773.

Descartes, R., *Les Passions de l'âme*, ed. Geneviève Rodis-Lewis. Paris 1970.

Descimon, R., and Jouhaud, C., *La France du premier XVIIe siècle, 1594–1661*. Paris 1996.

Dessert, D., *Fouquet*. Paris 1987.

—— 'Finances et société au XVIIe siècle : à propos de la Chambre de Justice de 1661', *Annales E.S.C.*, 29, no. 4 (juillet-août 1974), pp 847–81.

Dionis, P., *L'Anatomie de l'homme suivant la circulation du sang, & les dernières découvertes, démontrées au Jardin Royal*. Paris 1690.

Doherty, R., *The Williamite war in Ireland*. Dublin 1998.

Döring, U., *Antoine Furetière: Rezeption und Werk*. Frankfurt am Main 1995.

—— 'La réception critique du *Roman bourgeois* au dix-neuvièm^e siècle', *Œuvres & Critiques*, 2, no. 2 (hiver 1977–8), 99–115.

Driver, S.R., *The Hebrew scriptures*. New York 1963.

Dryden, J., *Of dramatick poesie, an essay*, ed. J.T. Boulton. Oxford 1964.

Dubrovsky, S., *Corneille ou la dialectique du héros*. Paris 1963.

Dubu, J., *Les Églises chrétiennes et le théâtre (1550–1850)*. Grenoble 1997.

—— 'L'Église catholique et la condamnation du théâtre en France au XVIIᵉ siècle', *Quaderni francesi*, 1 (1970), 319–49.

—— 'Cardinal contre Cardinal: Saint Charles Borromée en France au temps de Mazarin', in *La France et l'Italie*, ed. Jean Serroy (Grenoble 1986), pp 117–23.

Dumaître, P., 'Autour d'Ambroise Paré: ses adversaires, ses ennemis', *Histoire des Sciences médicales*, 32 (1998), 203–10.

Duplessis, A.-J., cardinal de Richelieu, *Testament politique*, ed. Louis André, 7th edition. Paris 1947.

Dupuis, G, and Guédon, M.-J., *Institutions administratives*. Paris 1988.

Durand-Lapie, P., *Un académicien du XVIIᵉ siècle: Saint-Amant, son temps, sa vie, ses poésies*. Paris 1898.

Ehrmann, J., *Un paradis désespéré: l'amour et l'illusion dans 'L'Astrée'*. New Haven and Paris 1963.

Erasmus, D., *Praise of folly*, translated by Betty Radice, introduction and notes by A.H.T. Levi. London 1971.

Erde, K. van, *John Ogilby and the taste of his times*. Folkestone 1976.

Esmein, A., *Histoire de la procédure criminelle*. Amsterdam 1882.

Evelyn, J., *The diary of John Evelyn*, ed. E. S. de Beer, 6 vols. Oxford 1955.

Fabricius, H., *De formatio foetu*. Venice 1604.

—— *De formatione ovi et pulli*. Padua 1621.

Falkiner, C. L., and Ball, F. E., *The manuscripts of the marquis of Ormonde*, 8 vols. London 1902–20.

Feuillée-Kendall, P., 'La Réforme de la justice: velléité, ou réalité?', *French Politics and Society*, 16, no. 3 (1998), 30–7.

Ficino, M., *De amore*, translated by Sears Reynolds Jayne. Columbia 1944.

Forestier, G., 'Corneille poète d'histoire', *Littératures Classiques*, 11, supplement (1989), 37–47.

—— 'Théorie et pratique de l'histoire dans la tragédie classique', *Littératures Classiques*, 11 (1989), 95–107.

Foucault, M., *Histoire de la folie*. Paris 1961.

—— 'Qu'est-ce qu'un auteur', *Bulletin de la Société française de Philosophie*, 44 (1969), 73–104.

—— *Surveiller et punir*. Paris 1975.

—— *Dits et écrits*. Paris 1994.

France, P., 'Racine britannicus', *Œuvres et Critiques,* 24 (1999), 248–63.

Franko, M., 'The king cross-dressed: power and force in royal ballet', in Sara E. Melzer and Kathryn Norberg (ed.), *From the royal to the republican body: incorporating the political in seventeenth- and eighteenth-century France* (Berkeley, Los Angeles and London 1998), pp 64–84. Previously published as 'Double bodies: androgyny and power in the performances of Louis XIV', *Drama Review*, 38, no 4 (winter 1994), 71–82.

Fraser, R., *The war against poetry*. Princeton 1970.

Fronton du Duc, Le Père, *L'Histoire tragique de la pucelle de Dom-Remy, aultrement d'Orléans*. Nancy, 1581.

Furetière, A., *Le Dictionnaire universel d'Antoine Furetière*, ed. A. Rey. 3 vols, Paris 1978.

—— *Roman bourgeois*, ed. Jacques Prévot. Paris 1981.

Fuster, S., *Les Juges*. Paris 1957.

Gaber, S., *La Lorraine meurtrie*. Nancy, 1979.

Garapon, A., *Le Gardien des promesses*. Paris 1996.

Garasse, F., *La Doctrine curieuse des beaux esprits de ce temps, ou pretendus tels*. Paris 1623.

Garlick, F., 'Dances to evoke the king: the majestic genre chez Louis XIV', *Dance Research*, 15, no 2 (winter 1997), 10–34.

Gaxotte, P., *Histoire des Français*. Paris 1951.

Gay, P., *Voltaire's politics*. Princeton 1959.

Gerbais, J., *Lettre d'un docteur de Sorbonne à une personne de qualité, sur le sujet de la comédie*. Paris 1694.

Gével, C., 'Une héroine du dix-septième siècle: Madame de Saint-Balmont', *Revue de Paris,* (octobre 1930), 168–80.

Gilbert, J. T. (ed.), *A Jacobite narrative of the war in Ireland 1688–1691.* Dublin 1892; reprinted Shannon 1971.

Gilson, E., *La Liberté chez Descartes et la théologie.* Paris 1913.

—— *Introduction à l'étude de saint Augustin.* Paris 1929.

Goldsmith, O., *Collected works of Oliver Goldsmith,* ed. Arthur Friedman, 5 vols. Oxford 1966.

Gombaud, A. de, chevalier de Méré, *Œuvres complètes,* ed. Charles-H. Boudhors, 3 vols. Paris 1930.

Gondi, P. de, Cardinal de Retz, *Mémoires,* ed. P. Morand, 2 vols. Paris 1965.

Gouhier, P., 'Mercenaires irlandais au service de la France (1635–1664)', *Irish Sword,* 7, no. 26 (summer 1965), 58–75.

Gracián, B., *L'Art de la prudence,* translated by Amelot de la Houssaie. Paris 1994.

Graffigny, F. de, *Correspondance,* ed. E. Showalter. Oxford 1985.

Grant, J. W., 'The government of Louis XIV', in A.W. Ward, G.W. Prothero & S. Leathes (ed.), *The Cambridge modern history,* 13 vols. Cambridge 1902–11.

Greenberg, M., *Corneille, classicism and the ruses of symmetry.* Cambridge 1986.

Griffet, H., *Histoire du règne de Louis XIII, roi de France et de Navarre,* 3 vols. Paris 1758.

Grmek, M. D., 'Le Concept de maladie', in M. M. Grmek & B. Fantini (ed.), *Histoire de la pensée médicale en Occident* (Paris 1997), pp 163–7.

Guez de Balzac, J.-L., *Les Entretiens* [1657], ed. B. Beugnot, 2 vols. Paris 1972.

Guibelet, J., *Traité de la génération de l'homme.* Evreux 1603.

Guiragossian, D., *Voltaire's Facéties* (Genève 1963).

Hageman, E. 'Katherine Philips: The Matchless Orinda', in K.M. Wilson (ed.), *Women writers of the Renaissance and Reformation* (Athens and London Press 1987), pp 566–608.

Harvey, P. and Clarendon, J. E. (ed.), *The Oxford companion to French literature.* Oxford 1959.

Harvey, W., *Anatomical exercitations, concerning the generation of living creatures.* London 1653.

Hayes McCoy, G. A., *Irish battles.* London 1969.

Hédelin, F., abbé d'Aubignac, *La Pratique du théâtre,* ed. Pierre Martino. Paris 1927.

Heinemann, M., *Puritanism and theatre. Thomas Middleton and opposition drama under the early Stuarts.* Cambridge 1980.

Hespérien, P., *Sermon sur St Jean iv 22.* La Rochelle 1674.

Hotson, L., *The Commonwealth and Restoration stage.* Harvard 1928.

Houppeville, G. de, *La Génération de l'homme par le moyen des œufs.* Rouen 1676.

Hourcade, P., 'Louis XIV travesti', *Cahiers de littérature du XVIIe siècle,* 6 (1984), 257–71.

Huarte, J., *Anacrise, ou Parfait jugement et examen des esprits propres & naiz aux sciences,* translated by Gabriel Chappuis. Lyon 1580.

Hughes, D., *English drama 1660–1700.* Oxford 1996.

Humbert, H., *Combat à la barrière.* Nancy, 1627.

Hylton, R., 'The Huguenot settlement at Portarlington, 1692–1771', in C.H.G. Caldicott, H. Gough and J.-P. Pittion (ed.), *The Huguenots and Ireland* (Dublin 1987), pp 297–320.

James, E.D., *Pierre Nicole, Jansenist and humanist: a study of his thought.* The Hague 1972.

Jansenius, C., *Augustinus.* 3 vols, Rouen 1643.

Johnson, S., *Prefaces, biographical and critical, to the works of the English poets,* 10 vols. London 1779–81.

Joli, G., *Mémoires,* in C.B. Petitot (ed.), *Mémoires relatifs à l'histoire de la France,* 78 vols. Paris 1820–8. Vol. 57.

Jones, J.R., *The Revolution of 1688 in England.* London 1988.

Jonson, B., *Ben Jonson,* ed. C. H. Herford and Perry Simpson, 11 vols. Oxford 1925–52.

Jouhaud, C., and Merlin, H., 'Mécènes, patrons et clients. Les médiations textuelles comme pratiques clientélaires au XVIIe siècle', *Terrain,* 21 (octobre 1993), 47–62.

Kant, E., *Critique of pure reason,* translated by J.M.D. Meiklejohn, with an introduction by A.D. Lindsay, Everyman's Library. London and New York 1934.

Kantorowicz, E. H., *The king's two bodies: a study in mediaeval political theology.* Princeton 1995; first published 1957.

Kavanagh, P., *The Irish theatre.* Tralee 1946.

Kerney Walsh, M., 'The Wild Goose tradition', *Irish Sword,* 17, no. 66 (summer 1987), 12–13.

Kishlansky, M., *A monarchy transformed: Britain 1603–1714.* London 1996.

Klein Maguire, N., *Regicide and Restoration: English tragi-comedy 1600–1671.* Cambridge 1992.

Koyré, A., *Du monde clos à l'univers infini.* Paris 1957.

Kremer, E. J., 'Grace and free will in Arnauld', in E. J. Kremer (ed.), *The great Arnauld and some of his philosophical correspondents* (Toronto 1994), pp 219–39.

—— 'L'Accord de la grâce avec la liberté selon Arnauld', *Antoine Arnauld (1612–1694): philosophe, écrivain, théologien,* Chroniques de Port-Royal, 44 (1995), 145–61.

Kriegel, B., *Les Chemins de l'état.* Paris 1986.

Kuhn, T., *The structure of scientific revolutions.* Chicago 1962.

Labrousse, E., '*Une foi, une loi, un roi?' La révocation de l'édit de Nantes.* Genève 1985.

La Bruyère, J. de, *Les Caractères.* Paris 1688; ed. R. Pignarre. Paris 1965.

La Calprenède, G., *La Mort des enfants d'Hérodes.* Exeter 1988.

Lagny, J., *Le Poète Saint-Amant (1594–1661): essai sur sa vie et ses œuvres.* Paris 1964.

La Grange, C. de (Le Père), *Réfutation d'un écrit favorisant la comédie.* Paris 1694.

Lair, J., *Nicolas Foucquet, procureur général, surintendant des finances, ministre d'état de Louis XIV.* 2 vols, Paris 1890.

Laportalière, R. de, 'Jean d'Usson de Saint Martin, lieutenant général des armées du roi, 1652–1705', *Société Ariégeoise,* 32 (1977), 73–114.

La Rochefoucauld, duc de, *Maximes et réflexions diverses,* ed. Jean Lafond. Paris 1976.

Le Bret, C., *De la souveraineté du roy.* Paris 1632.

Le Brun, P. (Le Père), *Discours sur la comédie* Paris 1694.

Lefevre, A., 'Racine en Angleterre au XVIIᵉ siècle', *Revue de Littérature Comparée,* 34 (1960), 251–7.

Le Fevre, P., 'The battle of Bantry Bay, 1 May 1690', *Irish Sword,* 18, no. 70 (winter 1990), 1–16.

Leibniz, G.W., *Essais de théodicée,* ed. J. Brunschwig. Paris 1969.

Lelevel, H., *Réponse à la lettre du théologien défenseur de la comédie.* Paris 1694.

Le Moyne, Le Père, *La Gallerie des femmes fortes.* Paris 1647.

Lépage, H., 'Étude sur le théâtre en Lorraine', *Mémoires de l'Académie de Stanislas',* 14 (1886), 265–303.

Lespinasse, R., (ed.), *Les Métiers et corporations de la ville de Paris XIVᵉ-XVIIIᵉ,* 3 vols (Paris 1886–97), vols 1 and 3.

Lessius, L., *De praedestinatione et reprobatione angelorum et hominum disputatio.* Antwerp 1610.

—— *De providentia numinis et animi immortalitate libri duo adversus atheos et politicos.* Antwerp 1613.

Lewis, G., *Le Problème de l'inconscient et le cartésianisme.* Paris 1950.

Lindsay, A., and Erskine-Hill, H. (ed.), *William Congreve: the critical heritage.* London and New York 1989.

Lortie, A., *Traité de la sainte cène.* La Rochelle 1674.

—— *Défense du sermon de Mr Hespérien sur S. Jean ch.iv v.22.* Saumur 1675.

Lower, W., *Horatius a Roman tragedy.* London 1656.

—— *Polyeuctes or The Martyr.* London 1671.

Luther, M., *De servo arbitrio* in *Luthers Werke in Auswahl,* ed. Otto Clemen. 4 vols, Berlin 1966–7.

Lynch, K. M., *Roger Boyle, first earl of Orrery.* Knoxville 1965.

Lynn, J. A., *Giant of the Grand Siècle: the French army, 1610–1715.* Cambridge 1997.

—— *The wars of Louis XIV 1667–1714.* London and New York 1999.

Macaulay, T. B., *The history of England from the Accession of James II.* London 1849.

Magendie, M., *La Politesse mondaine et les théories de l'honnêteté en France au XVIIᵉ siècle.* Genève 1970.

Malachy, Th., '*Esther:* une tragédie de Racine et de l'Ancien Testament', *Lettres Romanes* (août 1989), 143–5.

Mangan, H., 'Sarsfield's defence of the Shannon, 1690–1', *Irish Sword,* 1, no. 1 (1949), 24–32.

Marchant, J., *Candelabrum mysticum septem lucernis adornatum, sacramentorum ecclesiae doctrinam pastoribus, concionatoribus, sacerdotibus pernecessariam illustrans.* Mons 1630.

—— *Hortus pastorum et concionatorum sacrae doctrinae floribus Polymitus.* Paris 1638.

Marin, L., *Le Portrait du roi.* Paris 1981.

Martin, E., *L'Université de Pont-à-Mousson et les problèmes de son temps.* Nancy 1972.

McCallum, R, I., *Antimony in medical history: an account of the medical uses of antimony and its compounds since early times to the present day.* Edinburgh 1999.

Médan, P., 'Un Gascon précurseur de Racine: *La Mort de Mithridate* de La Calprenède et le *Mithridate* de Racine', *Revue des Pyrénées*, 19 (1907), 44–63.

Medbourne, M., *Tartuffe or The French Puritan.* London 1670.

Mellor, A., *La Torture.* Paris 1949.

Ménage, G., *Menagiana, ou bons mots, rencontres agréables, pensées judicieuses, et observations curieuses.* Amsterdam 1693.

Méré, Chevalier de, *Œuvres complètes*, ed. C.-H. Bouhours, 3 vols. Paris 1930.

Mersenne, M., *Quaestiones celeberrimae in Genesim.* Paris 1623.

Mervault, P., *Journal des choses plus mémorables que ce sont passées au dernier siège de La Rochelle.* No place, no date [1641].

Metivier, H., *L'Ancien Régime en France.* Paris 1981.

Miles, D. H., *The influence of Molière on Restoration comedy.* New York 1971.

Miller, J., *James II: a study in kingship.* London 1989.

—— 'The Earl of Tyrconnell and James II's Irish policy, 1685–1688', *Historical Journal*, 20 (1977), 803–23.

Molina, L. de, *Liberi arbitrii concordia cum gratiae donis, divina praescientia, providentia, praedestinatione et reprobatione.* Antwerp 1609.

Montaigne, M. de, *Essais*, ed. P. Villey and V.-L. Saulnier, 2 vols. Paris 1965; ed. Alexandre Micha. 3 vols, Paris 1979.

Montpensier, A.M.L.H. d'Orléans, duchesse de, *Mémoires de mademoiselle de Montpensier* [. . .], 6 vols. Amsterdam 1730.

Motteville, F.B.L., dame Langlois de, *Mémoires pour servir à l'histoire d'Anne d'Autriche.* Amsterdam 1739.

Mousnier, R., 'Some reasons for the Fronde', in P.J. Coveney (ed.), *France in crisis, 1620-1675* (London 1977), pp 169–200.

Mouy, P., *Le Développement de la physique cartésienne 1646–1712.* Paris 1934.

Mulert, A., *Pierre Corneille auf der Englischen Bühne und in der Englischen Übersetzungs-Literatur des siebzehnten Jahrhunderts.* Erlangen and Leipzig 1900.

Mulloy, S., 'French eye-witnesses of the Boyne', *Irish Sword*, 15, no. 59 (winter 1982), 105–11.

—— 'The French navy and the Jacobite war in Ireland, 1689–91', *Irish Sword*, 18, no. 70 (winter 1990), 18–31.

Mulloy, S. (ed.), *Franco-Irish correspondence December 1688-February 1692.* 3 vols. Dublin 1983–4.

Munns, J., 'Thomas Otway's *Titus and Berenice* and Racine's *Bérénice*', *Restoration*, 7 (1983), 58–67

Murphy, J. A. (ed.), *The French are on the sea: the expedition to Bantry Bay, 1796.* Cork 1997.

Murphy, J. A., *Justin MacCarthy, Lord Mountcashel, commander of the first Irish brigade in France.* Cork 1959.

Murtagh, H., 'General Humbert's Campaign in the West', in Cathal Poirteir (ed.), *The great Irish rebellion of 1798* (Cork 1980), pp 115–24.

—— 'Huguenot involvement in the Irish Jacobite war, 1689–91', in C.E.J. Caldicott, H. Gough and J.-P. Pittion (ed.), *The Huguenots and Ireland: Anatomy of an Emigration* (Dublin 1987), pp 225–38.

—— 'The war in Ireland, 1689–91', in W.A. Maguire (ed.) *Kings in conflict: the revolutionary war in Ireland and its aftermath, 1689–1750* (Belfast 1990), pp 61–91.

—— 'Irish soldiers abroad, 1600–1800', in Thomas Bartlett & Keith Jeffery (ed.), *A military history of Ireland* (Cambridge 1996), pp 297–8.

—— with Murtagh, D., 'The Irish Jacobite army, 1689–91', *Irish Sword*, 18, no. 70 (winter 1990), 32–48.

Nicolas, A., *La Torture.* Amsterdam 1681.

O'Callaghan J. C., *History of the Irish brigades in the service of France.* Glasgow 1869.

O'Kelly C., *Secret history of the war of the revolution in Ireland, 1688–1691, written under the title of 'Destruction of Cyprus'*, ed. John Cornelius O'Callaghan. Dublin 1850.

Ormesson, O. Lefevre d', *Journal d'Olivier Lefèvre d'Ormesson*, ed. M. Chéruel. Paris 1860.

Otway T., *The works of Thomas Otway*, ed. J.C. Ghosh, 2 vols. Oxford 1932.

Paré, A., *Œuvres complètes.* Paris 1598.

Pariset, F. G., 'Claude Deruet', *Gazette des Beaux Arts*, 1 (1952), 153 –72;

—— 'Les Amazones de Claude Deruet', *Le Pays Lorrain*, (1956), 97–114.

Parker, D., *La Rochelle and the French monarchy: conflict and order in seventeenth-century France.* London 1980.

Parker G., *The military revolution: military innovation and the rise of the West, 1500–1800.* Cambridge 1988.

—— and Smith L.M. (ed.), *The general crisis of the seventeenth century.* London 1978.

Pascal, *Les Pensées*, ed. Louis Lafuma. Paris 1962.

Pearsall A.W.H., 'The war at sea', in W.A. Maguire (ed.), *Kings in conflict: the revolutionary war in Ireland and its aftermath 1689–1750* (Belfast 1990), pp 92–105.

Pégurier L., *Décision faite en Sorbonne touchant la comédie.* Paris 1694.

Pellisson, P., *Œuvres diverses de Monsieur Pellisson de l'Académie françoise.* 3 vols, Paris 1735.

Pepys S., *The diary of Samuel Pepys,* ed. R. C. Latham and W. Matthews, 11 vols. London 1970–83.

Pérouas, L., *Le Diocèse de La Rochelle: sociologie et pastorale.* Paris 1964.

Perrault, C., *Les Hommes illustres qui ont paru en France pendant ce siècle.* 2 vols. Paris 1696–1700.

—— *Mémoires de ma vie*, ed. Paul Bonnefon. Paris 1909; reprinted with an essay by Antoine Picon, Paris 1993.

Petitot, C. B., *Mémoires relatifs à l'histoire de la France*, 78 vols. Paris 1820–8.

Philips, K., *The collected works of Katherine Philips: the matchless Orinda*, ed. G. Greer, R. Little and P.Thomas, 3 vols. Stump Cross 1991–3.

—— *Pompey. A translation of Corneille's La Mort de Pompée, with the addition of songs by Katherine Philips.* London 1663.

—— *Poems by the most deservedly admired Mrs Katherine Philips.* London 1667.

—— *Horace,* translated by Katherine Philips. London 1669

Phillips, H., *The theatre and its critics in seventeenth-century France.* Oxford 1980.

—— 'Italy and France in the seventeenth-century stage controversy', *The Seventeenth Century*, 11 (1996), 187–207.

—— 'Les acteurs et la loi au XVIIe siècle', *Littératures classiques*, 40 (2000) 87–101.

Pinto-Correia, C., *The ovary of Eve: egg and sperm and preformation.* Chicago 1997.

Plato, 'The symposium' in *Dialogues on Love and Friendship*, translated by Benjamin Jowett. New York 1968.

Plowden, E., *Commentaries or reports.* London 1816.

Poer Beresford, M. de la, 'Ireland in French strategy during the American War of Independence, 1776–83', *Irish Sword*, 12, no. 49 (winter 1976), 285–97.

Poissenot, B., *Nouvelles Histoires tragiques*, ed. J.-C. Arnould and R. A. Carr. Genève 1996.

Poli, S., *Storia di storie: considerazioni sull'evoluzione della storia tragica in Francia dalla fine delle guerre civili alla morte di Luigi XIII.* Abano Terme 1985.

—— *Histoire(s) tragique(s): anthologie/typologie d'un genre littéraire.* Fasano and Paris 1991.

—— 'Autour de Rosset et de Camus', *Romanciers du XVIIe siècle*, *Littératures Classiques*, 15 (octobre 1991), 29–39.

Pollini, G., *Historia ecclesiastica della Rivoluzion d'Inghilterra.* Rome 1594.

Pomeau, R., *La Religion de Voltaire.* Paris 1956.

Porchnev, B., *Les Soulèvements populaires en France de 1623 à 1648.* Paris 1963.

Porter, R., 'Introduction', in Roy Porter (ed.), *The popularization of medicine, 1650–1850.* London and New York 1992.

Poullain de la Barre, F., *De l'Égalité des deux sexes.* Paris 1673; reprinted 1984.

Powley, E.B., *The naval side of king William's war*. London 1972.

Prest, J., 'Dancing king: Louis XIV's roles in Molière's *Comédies-ballets*, from court to town', *The Seventeenth Century*, 16, no. 2 (autumn 2001), 283–98.

Prynne, W., *Histrio-mastix: the player's scourge or actors tragaedie, divided into two parts*. London 1633.

Quinault, P., *Agrippa roi d'Albe, ou le faux Tiberinus*. Paris 1660.

Quintilian, *Institutio oratoria*, 4 vols. London 1921–2.

Racine, J., *Théâtre complet*, ed. J. Morel and A. Viala. Paris 1980.

Ramsey, M., 'The Popularization of Medicine in France, 1650–1900', in Roy Porter (ed.), *The popularization of medicine, 1650–1850* (London and New York 1992), pp 97–133.

Ridpath, G., *The stage condem'd*, ed. A. Freeman. New York and London 1972.

Rieger, D., '"Histoire de loi" – "Histoire tragique": authenticité et structure de genre chez F. de Rosset', *XVIIe Siècle*, 184 (juillet-septembre 1994), 461–77.

Rihs, A., *Recherches sur les origines du matérialisme historique*. Genève 1962.

Rivet, A., *L'instruction chrestienne*. La Haye 1639.

Riviere, M. S., 'Voltaire and the Fronde', *Nottingham French Studies*, 26, no. 1 (June 1987), 1–18.

Roger, J., *Les Sciences de la vie dans la pensée française du 18e siècle*. Paris 1971.

Rogers, C. J. (ed.), *The military revolution debate: readings on the military transformation of early modern Europe*. Boulder, San Francisco, Oxford 1995.

Rohault, J., *Entretiens sur la philosophie*. Paris 1671.

Romain, N., *Maurice. Tragoedie*. Pont-à-Mousson 1606.

Ronzeaud, P., 'La femme au pouvoir ou le monde à l'envers', *Dix-septième siècle*, 108 (1975), 9–33.

Roth, O., 'L'Honnête-Homme chez La Rochefoucauld', in Alain Montandon (ed.), *L'Honnête-homme et le dandy* (Tübingen 1993), pp 59–76.

Rowe, J., *Tragi-Comoedia*. Oxford 1653.

Roy, H., 'La vie à la cour de Lorraine sous le Duc Henri II', *Mémoires de la Société d'Archéologie Lorraine et de Musée Historique Lorrain*, 63 (1913), 53–206.

Royer, J.-P., *Histoire de la justice en France*. Paris 1995.

Rublack, U., 'Wench and maiden: women, war and the pictorial function of the feminine in German cities of the early modern period', *History Workshop Journal*, (autumn 1997), 1–21.

Rutler, J., *The Cid a Tragi-comedy*. London 1637.

Saint-Amant, Marc-Antoine Girard, sieur de, *Œuvres*, ed. J. Lagny and J. Bailbé, 5 vols. Paris 1967–79.

Saint Balmont, Mme de, *Les Jumeaux martyrs*, ed. C. Abbott and H. Fournier. Genève 1995.

Saint-Evremond, C., *Œuvres en prose*, ed. René Ternois, 4 vols. Paris 1966.

Sales, F. de, *Traicté de l'amour de Dieu*. Rouen 1626.

Salmon, J.H.M., *Cardinal de Retz: the anatomy of a conspirator*. London 1969.

Scherer, J., *La Dramaturgie classique en France*. Paris 1950.

—— 'Les intentions politiques dans *Nicomède*', in *Pierre Corneille: Actes du Colloque tenu à Rouen, octobre 1984*, ed. Alain Niderst (Paris 1985), pp 493–9.

Schuchard, M., *John Ogilby 1600–76: Lebensbild eines Gentleman mit vielen Karrieren*. Hamburg 1973.

—— and Truchet, J. (ed.), *Théâtre du XVIIe siècle*. Paris 1986.

Scudéry, G. de, *La Mort de César*. Paris 1635.

Seignette, J., *Apologie pour le sel polychreste de Monsieur Seignette, maistre apoticaire de la Rochelle*. [La Rochelle] [1674].

Semper, I. J., 'The Jacobean theatre through the eyes of Catholic clerics', *Shakespeare Quarterly*, 3 (1952), 44–51.

Serroy, J., *Roman et réalité. Les Histoires comiques au XVIIe siècle*. Paris 1981.

Sévigné, Madame de, *Lettres*, ed. B. Raffalli. Paris 1976.

Shadwell, T., *The complete works of Thomas Shadwell*, ed. M. Summers, 5 vols. London 1927.

Sheridan, R. B., *Sheridan's plays*, ed. Cecil Price. Oxford 1975.

Shifflett, A., ' " How many virtues must I hate?": Katherine Philips and the Politics of Clemency', *Studies in Philology*, 94 (1997), 103–35.

Simms, J.G., *The treaty of Limerick*. Dundalk 1961.

—— *The Jacobite parliament of 1689*. Dundalk 1966.

—— *Jacobite Ireland, 1685–91*. London 1969.

—— 'The siege of Limerick, 1690', in E. Rynne (ed.), *North Munster studies: essays in commemoration of Monsignor Michael Moloney* (Limerick 1967), pp 308–15.

Snaith, G., 'Plaisir à La Calprenède', *Seventeenth-Century French Studies*, 9 (1987), 55–73

—— 'Suspense as a source of theatrical pleasure in the plays of La Calprenède', in A. Howe and R. Waller (ed.), *En marge du classicisme: essays on the French theatre from the Renaissance to the Enlightenment* (Liverpool 1987), pp 95–121.

—— '"Le Poids d'une couronne": the dilemma of monarchy in La Calprenède's tragedies', in K. Cameron and E. Woodrough (ed.), *Ethics and politics in seventeenth-century France: essays in honour of Derek A. Watts* (Exeter 1996), pp 185–99.

Soergel, P., *Wondrous in his saints: counter-Reformation propaganda in Bavaria*. Berkeley and Los Angeles 1993.

Somaize, A.B. de, *Grand dictionnaire historique des prétieuses*. Paris 1661.

Souers, P., *The matchless Orinda*. Cambridge Mass. 1931.

Soulez Larivière, D., *Les Juges dans la balance*. Paris 1987.

Spingarn, J. E. (ed.), *Critical essays of the seventeenth century*, 3 vols. Oxford 1908.

Stanton, D. C., *The aristocrat as art: a study of the 'honnête homme' and the dandy in seventeenth- and nineteenth-century French literature*. New York and Guildford 1980.

Steiner, G., *The death of tragedy*. London 1961; reprinted 1974.

Story, G., *A continuation of the impartial history of the wars of Ireland*. London 1693.

Suárez, F., *Disputaciones metafísicas*, edited and translated by Sergio Rábade Romeo, Salvador Caballero Sánchez and Antonio Puigcerver Zanón, 7 vols. Madrid 1960.

Suchon, G., *Traité de la morale et de la politique*. Lyon 1693; Paris 1999.

Suffren, Le R. P. J., *L'Année chrestienne ou le sainct et profitable emploi pour gaigner l'éternité'* , 2 vols. Paris 1640–1.

Swammerdam, J., *Biblia mundi* (published posthumously in 1680).

Tapié, V. L., *La France de Louis XIII et de Richelieu*. Paris 1952.

Tate, L. (ed.), 'Franco-Irish correspondence December 1688-August 1691', *Analecta Hibernica*, 21 (Dublin 1959). Whole volume.

Tate, N., *History of King Lear*. London 1681.

Thiers, J.-B., *Traité des jeux et des divertissements*. Paris 1686.

Thirouin, L., *Aveuglement salutaire: le réquisitoire contre le théâtre dans la France classique*. Paris 1997.

—— *Traité de la comédie et autres pièces d'un procès du théâtre*. Paris 1998.

Thomas, P., *Katherine Philips ("Orinda")*. Aberystwyth 1988.

Thou, J.-A. de, *Histoire universelle depuis 1543 jusqu'en 1607*, 16 vols. London 1734.

Tristan L'Hermite, F., *La Mort de Sénèque*. Paris 1644.

Truchet, J., *La Tragédie classique en France*. Paris 1975.

Van Delft, L., *Le Moraliste classique: essai de définition et de typologie*. Genève 1982.

Van Deursen, A. Th., *Professions et métiers interdits; un aspect de l'histoire de la révocation de l'édit de Nantes*. Groningen 1960.

Vanini, G.-C., *Amphitheatrum aeternae providentiae divino-magicum, christiano-physicum, nec non astrologo-catholicum*. Lyon 1615.

Vaucher Gravili, A. de, *Loi et transgression: les histoires tragiques au XVIIᵉ siècle*. Lecce 1982.

Venette, N., *Traité du scorbut*. La Rochelle 1673.

—— *De la génération de l'homme, ou tableau de l'amour conjugale. Septième edition, reueuë, corrigée, augmentée & enrichie de figures*. Cologne [i.e. Paris] 1696.

Vernon, J.-M., *L'Amazone chrestienne ou les avantures de Madame de Saint Balmon, qui a joint une admirable dévotion et la pratique de toutes les vertus avec l'exercice des armes et de la guerre*. Paris 1678; reedited by R. Muffat, Paris 1873.

Vialet, M., 'L'écriture de l'incohérence', in Michel Bareau, Jacques Barchilon, Donna Stanton and Jean Alter (ed.), *North American Society for Seventeenth-Century French Literature, Actes de Banff* (Paris, Seattle, and Tübingen 1987), pp 373–88.

Vincent de Paul, Saint, *Correspondance*, ed. Pierre Costa, 7 vols. Paris 1920–2.

Vincent, P., *Traitté des theatres*. La Rochelle 1647.

Voisin, J. de, *La Défense du traitté de Monseigneur le prince de Conti touchant la comédie et les spectacles*. Paris 1671.

Voltaire, F. M. Arouet de, *Œuvres complètes*, 70 vols. Kehl 1784–9.

—— *Traité de métaphysique*, ed. H. T. Patterson. Manchester 1937.

—— *Œuvres historiques*, ed. R. Pomeau. Paris 1957.

—— *Lettres philosophiques,* ed. F.A. Taylor. Oxford 1965.

—— *The complete works*. Genève/Oxford 1968–.

—— *Candide*, ed. M. Béguin and J. Golzink. Paris 1998.

Vuillemin, J.-C., 'Nature et réception du spectacle tragique sur la scène française du XVIIe siècle', *Revue d'Histoire du Théâtre*, 159 (1988), 217–26.

Waller, E., Sackville, C., Sedley, C. and Godolphin, S., *Pompey the Great, a tragedy translated out of French by certain persons of honour*. London 1664.

Waller, R., 'Voltaire's civil wars: history and anecdote', in U. Kölving and C. Mervaud (ed.), *Voltaire et ses combats*. 2 vols. Oxford 1997.

Warner, M., *Joan of Arc: the image of female heroism*. London 1981.

Wauchope, P., *Patrick Sarsfield and the Williamite war*. Dublin 1992.

Wear, A., 'The popularization of medicine in early-modern England', in Roy Porter (ed.), *The Popularization of Medicine 1650–1850* (London and New York 1992), pp. 17–41.

White, S.A., 'Esther' in C.A. Newsom and S.H. Ringe (ed.), *The women's Bible commentary*. London 1992.

Wills, R., *The occasional paper Number IX containing some considerations about the danger of going to plays*, ed. A. Freeman. New York and London 1974.

Woodrough, E., 'Corneille et la Grande-Bretagne', in A. Niderst (ed.), *Pierre Corneille*, Actes du Colloque de Rouen, 1984 (Paris 1985), pp 73–82.

Wright, C., *The French painters of the seventeenth century*. London 1985.

Zimmermann, E., *La Liberté et le destin dans le théâtre de Jean Racine*. Saratoga 1982.

II. MSS

Bodleian Library, Oxford
Locke, J., *Journal*, MS Locke.

Marsh's Library, Dublin
"Memoires et pieces pour servir a l'histoire generale de la persecution faitte en France contre ceux de la religion Reformée depuis l'année, 1656, jusqu'a la Revocation de l'Edit de Nantes, faitte par celuy donné a Fontainebleau au Moys d'Octobre, 1685', a collection of legal documents gathered by a contemporary, Abraham Tessereau, conserved under the classification 'Bouhéreau MS'.

Index

Académie Française, 72, 80 n. 19
Académie Royale de Danse, 228
Adam, Antoine, 72, 73, 81
Agrippa, Heinrich Cornelius, 48 n. 19
Amelot de la Houssaie, Abraham-Nicolas, 133
Angoulême (*see* Valois, Charles de).
Anne, queen of Austria, 264, 267
Anthony, Sister Rose, 164 n. 5
Antoine, Louis, cardinal de Noailles, 169
Apostolidès, Jean-Marie, 231
Appian, 220, 222, 223
Aquapendente, Hieronymus Fabricius d', 43
Aquinas, Thomas, St, 104, 105, 107, 108, 110,
    111, 112, 114, 115, 116, 167, 168
Arc, Jeanne d', 30, 35, 37, 40
Aristotle, 41, 48 and n. 19, 112, 114, 159, 210,
    221
Arnauld, Antoine, 12, 37, 45 n. 10, 59, 103–16
Aspin, Geoffrey, 9
Asslineau, Charles, 72
Astier, Régine, 227, 228 n. 6
Aubignac (*see* Hédelin, François)
Aubigné, Agrippa d', 46, 47
Aubigné, Françoise d', marquise de
    Maintenon, 248
Augustine of Hippo, St, 22, 104, 105, 108, 110,
    111, 113, 114, 116, 166
Augustus, Caius Julius Caesar Octavianus, 74,
    76, 80, 81, 144
Avaux (*see* Mesmes, Jean-Antoine de)
Ayrault, Pierre, 142, 144

Baker, Sir Richard, 167, 172, 179
Bandello, Matteo, 117
Bar-le-Duc, 31, 33, 34
Barles, Louis, 45, 49, 50–1
Baulot, Isaac, 54 and n. 9, 55, 61 and n. 32
Baxter, Richard, 165, 166, 169
Bayle, Pierre, 41–2, 43, 44, 51, 133
Beaussant, Philippe, 228
Beccaria, Cesare, 145
Belleforest, François de, 117
Belle-Ile, 90
Benserade, Isaac de, 15, 227–41
Blackmore, Sir Richard, 158
Blondel, David, 133
Boaistuau, Pierre, 117

Boethius, 122
Boileau-Despréaux, Nicolas, 45 n. 10, 72, 76,
    77, 128
Boisseleau (*see* Rainier de Droue, Alexandre
    de)
Bomier, Pierre, 57
Bonaparte, Napoléon, 139
Bonaventure, St, 107
Bonnac, Jean de, marquis d'Usson, 252, 253 n.
    46
Bordaille, Michel de, 58, 59
Borromeo, Charles, St, 163
Bossuet, Jacques-Bénigne, 45 n. 10, 115, 116
Boucher de Beauval, Jacques, 54 n. 5, 55
Bouhéreau, Élie, 52, 53, 54 n. 9, 55, 60, 61, 62
Bourbon, Anne-Geneviève de, duchesse de
    Longueville, 268
Bourbon, Louis de, comte de Soissons, 220
Boursault, Edme, 166
Bouteville (*see* Montmorency, François de)
Boyle, Roger, earl of Orrery, 198–201
Bracegirdle, Mrs, 161
Brant, Sebastian, 151
Briggs, Robin, 217
Brumfitt, John H., 257, 262
Bruneau, Marie-Florine, 27
Buckhurst, Lord (*see* Sackville, Charles)
Burke, Peter, 234
Burton, Henry, 171, 175
Butler, James, duke of Ormond, 195, 198, 200,
    205, 207–8

Caffaro, Thomas, 166, 167, 170, 180
Callières, François de, 129, 130, 131, 132
Callot, Jacques, 30 n. 1
Calvin, Jean, 104, 107
Camus, Jean-Pierre, 12, 117–27
Canaries, 91
Canfield, Dorothea, 196, 204
Carlell, Lodowick, 189
Carr, E. H., 270
Casamayor (Serges Fuster), 141
Cecil, Robert, 1st Earl of Salisbury, 211, 214,
    217, 226
Chalais (*see* Talleyrand-Périgord, Henri de)
Chalmont, Charles, marquis de Saint Ruth,
    250, 252, 253 n. 46

Champfleury (Jules Husson), 73
Chapelain, Jean, 76
Chappuzeau, Samuel, 167, 173, 176, 177, 179
Chardonnet, Nicolas, 174
Charles I, king of England, 166, 178, 184, 186, 197, 198, 199, 107
Charles II, king of England, 43, 171, 178–9, 186, 188–9, 195, 199
Charles III, duc de Lorraine, 32 n. 10, 35
Charles IV, duc de Lorraine, 10, 31 n. 7, 32, 33, 39
Charpentier, François, 80 n. 18
Chatounières de Grenaille, François de, 224
Chedozeau, Bernard, 28
Chevreuse (*see* Rohan-Montbazon, Marie de)
Cholières, Nicolas de, 48 n. 19
Churchill, John, 1st duke of Marlborough, 252
Cicero, Marcus Tullius, 13, 144, 156
Cinq-Mars, Henri de, 218, 219, 220
Clare, Lord (*see* O'Brien, Daniel)
Claude, Jean, 59
Clement VIII, pope, 121
Cohen, Sarah, 228, 230 n. 14
Colbert, Jean-Baptiste, 12, 53, 55, 58, 74, 75, 76, 77, 135, 137, 138, 139, 230, 247–8, 253
Colleton, Father John, 173
Collier, Jeremy, 164, 165, 167, 169, 171, 176–7
Colomiés, P., 52
Compagnie du Saint-Sacrement, 56–7
Condé, Louis, prince de, 204, 260, 262, 267–8 (*see also* Montmorency, Charlotte de)
Congreve, William, 13, 151–62
Conroy, Jane, 219
Constantin, Jean, 142
Conti, Armand, prince de, 175, 267–8
Corneille, Pierre, 14, 75, 167, 179, 185, 187, 189–1, 194–8, 200–9, 210, 219 n. 17, 226
Corneille, Thomas, 185, 217 n. 8
Cornet, Nicolas, 106, 111
Costes, gautier de, sieur de la Calprenède, 15, 198, 210–26
Cotterell, Charles, 198, 200
Cotton, Sir Charles, 14, 190, 208 n. 29
Coulet, Henri, 73
Coustel, Pierre, 165, 170, 177, 181
Coveney, P. J., 258, 264
Cowley, Abraham, 197 n. 6
Cromwell, Oliver, 164, 178, 198, 199
Crowne, John, 191
Cyprian, St, 170

Dancer, John, 14, 195, 196, 204–9
Davenant, Sir William, 187–8
De la Baume Le Blanc, Louise, duchesse de La Vallière, 233, 237
Delaroche, Paul, 225

Delaizement, Daniel Henri, 57 n. 14
De la Tour du Pin de La Charce, Philis, 30 and n. 2
Democritus, 155
Denham, Sir John, 208 n. 29
Dennis, John, 152, 153, 154, 178
Dering, Edward, 199 n. 13
Derrida, Jacques, 45
Deruet, Claude, 31
Des Billons, le Père, 10, 30, 31, 34, 36–8
Descartes, René, 60 and n. 29, 61 n. 30, 130
Descimon, Robert, 217
Desjeans, Jean-Bernard-Louis, baron de Pointis, 247
Des-Yveteaux, Monsieur, 93
Devaux, François Antoine, 270
Devereux, Robert, 2nd earl of Essex, 211, 213–8, 220–1, 223, 225, 226
Diderot, Denis, 73
Dillon, Wentworth, 4th earl of Roscommon, 199 n. 13
Dionis, Pierre, 49
Domrémy, 31
Dorset (*see* Sackville).
Drelincourt, Charles, 42 n. 3, 44, 48 n. 20
Dryden, John, 152, 183, 184, 188
Dublin, 14, 15, 188, 194–209, 210 n. 1, 246, 250
Dudley, John, duke of Northumberland, 210, 215, 225
Dudley, Lord Guilford, 210
Dumont, J., 52, 55
Dumoulin, Charles, 142
Du Plessis, Armand-Jean, cardinal/duc de Richelieu, 83, 90, 136, 167, 178, 217–9, 263, 264
Du Ryer, Pierre, 226

Edward VI, king of England, 210, 222
Ehrmann, Jacques, 217
Elizabeth I, Queen of England, 176, 211, 213, 214–7, 220–2, 225, 230
England, 152 ff, 163 ff, 183 ff, 195, 196 n. 4, 197 n. 6, 210, 215, 245–6, 249 n. 27, 250, 253, 254, 260
Ent, George, 49, 50
Erasmus (Desiderius Erasmus Roterodamus), 13, 151, 155
Ernecourt, Barbe d', Madame de Saint Balmont, 9–10, 30–40
Ernecourt, Marie Claude d', 32
Ernecourt, Simon d', 31
Escobar, Antonio, 170
Estrepis, Madame d', 32
Essex (*see* Devereux, Robert)
Etherege, Sir George, 152
Evelyn, John, 165, 175, 176

Faret, Nicolas, 98
Fernel, Jean, 60
Ficino, Marsilio, 46
Filmore, Edward, 200 n. 17
Florus, Publius Annius, 222, 223
Fontainebleau, 98
Fontanges, Jacques de, marquis de Maumont, 250
Forestier, George, 220, 221, 222, 223
Foucault, Michel, 10, 41–2, 43, 51, 145, 146
Fouquet, Nicolas, 11, 74, 75, 77 and n. 15, 79
Franko, Mark, 228, 230 n. 14
Frederik Herman, duke of Schomberg, 251
Fronde, 16, 17, 135, 136, 141, 178, 179, 193, 204, 256–70
Froullay, Phillibert-Emmanuel de, chevalier de Tesse, 252, 253 n. 46
Furetière, Antoine, 11, 72–81
Fuzelier, Louis, 260

Galen, 41, 48, 60
Gallois, Monsieur, 132
Garasse, François, 123
Gaxotte, Pierre, 138
Gay, Peter, 263
George, P., 52
Gerbais, Jean, 167, 168, 173, 181
Gibieuf, Guillaume, 104
Gille, I., 52
Ginkel, Godart van, 253
Girard, Marc-Antoine, sieur de Saint-Amant, 11, 82–100
Giraud, Victor-Julien, 225
Goibaud du Bois, Philippe, 45 n. 10
Goldophin, Sidney, 200 n. 17
Goldsmith, Oliver, 159
Gombaud, Antoine, chevalier de Méré, 129, 130, 131, 152
Gondi, Paul de, cardinal de Retz, 256–7, 259, 260, 266–9
Gonzague, Marie de, 82–87, 99 n. 13
Gourville, Jean Hérault de, 256, 269
Goyer, Mathias, 54
Graaf, Reinier de, 44, 45, 49, 50 and n. 25, 51
Gracián, Baltasar, 133
Graffigny (*see* Issembourg, Françoise d').
Gramont, Antoine, maréchal de, 131
Granet, Abbé, 261
Gregory IX, pope, 144
Grey, Jane, queen of England, 210–2, 214–6, 218, 221–3, 225
Grignan, Madame de, 145
Groningen, 60, 61
Guerre, Martin, 124
Guez de Balzac, Jean-Louis, 74, 75, 76, 79, 81
Guibelet, Jourdain, 48 n. 19

Guigou, Elisabeth, 142
Guildford (*see* Dudley, Lord Guildford)
Guiragossian, Diana, 262

Habert, Isaac, 103–4, 106, 107, 115
Hales, Alexander of, 107
Hamelot, P., 52, 54
Hamilton, Richard, 247
Haraucourt, Jacques d', seigneur de Saint Balmont, 32, 33
Harrison, William, 173, 174
Harvey, William, 43 and n. 4, 44, 45 n. 10, 49, 60 n. 29, 61 n. 30
Hédelin, François, Abbé d'Aubignac, 167, 168, 179, 221, 225
Henri II, duc de Lorraine, 32
Henri II, duc de Montmorency, 217–9
Henri IV, king of France, 47, 184
Henrietta-Maria, queen of England, 179 n. 121, 184
Henry VIII, king of England, 176
Heraclitus, 155
Herod Antipas, king of Judaea, 222
Hespérien, Pierre, 57, 58
Horace (Quintus Horatius Flaccus), 77, 79, 155
Hourcade, Philippe, 227
Houppeville, Guillaume de, 45 n. 10
Huarte, Juan, 46
Hughes, Derek, 188, 191

Inquisition, 144
Ireland, 9, 16, 245–55 (*see also* Dublin)
Issembourg, Françoise d', madame de Graffigny, 270

James I, king of England, 166
James II, king of England, 16, 178, 179, 245–8, 250–1, 253–5
Jansenius, Cornelius, 12, 103–16
Jouhaud, Christian, 217
Jerome, St, 22, 166
Joli, Guy, 256, 264, 266, 268
Johnson, Samuel, Dr, 159 n. 24
Jonson, Ben, 151, 152 n. 6, 153, 183, 185
Justinian I, emperor, 207

Kant, Emmanuel, 114 n. 44
Kantorowicz, Ernst, 230
Kavanagh, Peter, 196
Koyré, Alexandre, 41
Kriegel, Blandine, 139
Kristeva, Julia, 27–8
Kuhn, Thomas, 41

La Bruyère, Jean de, 128, 133, 157
La Calprenède (*see* Costes, Gautier de)

La Fontaine, Jean de, 75, 79, 156
La Grange, Charles de, 168
La Hoguette, Charles Fortin, marquis, 251
Lambert, Michel, 258
Lamoignon, Chrétien de, 138, 139, 143, 145
La Mothe le Vayer, François, 111
Lamy, François, 45 n. 10
La Porte, Pierre de, 256, 269
La Rochefoucauld, François, duc de, 128, 130, 132
La Rochelle, 52–71
La Tour Monfort, Henri de, 252, 253 n. 46
Lauzun (*see* Nompar de Caumont, Antonin)
Laval, Henri de, bishop of La Rochelle, 57
La Vallière (*see* De la Baume Le Blanc, Louise de)
La Voisin, Catherine Deshayes, 145
Le Brun, Charles, 75
Le Brun, Pierre, le Père, 170
Le Camus, Jean, marquis de Pusignan, 250
Le Fèvre, Monsieur, 132
Leibniz, Gottfried Wilhelm, 113 n. 44
Leke, Thomas, 168, 173
Lelevel, Henri, 173, 177, 180
Lenet, Pierre, 256
Lenoir, Rémi, 142
Le Nôtre, André, 75
Leroy-Ladurie, Emmanuel, 138
Lesage, Alain-René, 260
Lessius, Leonardus, 121, 122, 124
Le Tellier, Michel, marquis de Louvois, 230, 247–8, 251, 253
Leyden, 42 n. 3, 60, 61
Licetus, Fortunius, 45 n. 10
Ligue, 90
Locke, John, 53, 54 n. 9
Lombard, Peter, 107
Longueville, Marie de, duchesse de Nemours, (*see also* Bourbon, Anne-Geneviève de)
Lorraine, 16, 30 ff
Lortie, André, 57, 59
Louis XIII, king of France, 10, 15, 35, 185, 217, 218, 219, 229
Louis XIV, king of France, 12, 15, 30, 56, 57 n. 14, 73, 75, 76, 90, 128, 133, 135, 136, 137, 138, 140, 143, 144, 179, 184, 188, 219, 227–41, 245, 247, 250–5, 256, 259, 262–3, 265, 269
Louis, St, king of France, 181
Louvois (*see* Le Tellier, Michel)
Lower, Sir William, 14, 187
Loyseau, Charles, 135
Lucian, 155
Lucan (Marcus Annaeus Lucanus), 196, 197, 202
Lulli, Jean-Baptiste, 268

Luther, Martin, 104, 107, 108
Lynn, John, 30

Maignart de Bernières, Charles II, 97
Maintenon (*see* Aubigné, Françoise d')
Mairet, Jean, 226
Malachy, Th., 23, 24
Malebranche, Nicolas, 44, 45 n. 10
Malingre, Claude, 117
Marchant, Jacques, 122 n. 11 and 12
Mariana, Juan, 170
Marillac, Louis de, 217, 218
Marlborough (*see* Churchill, John)
Mary I, queen of England, 210, 214–6, 220–2, 246
Massue, Henri de, marquis de Ruvigny, 252, 254
Maumont (*see* Fontanges, Jacques de)
Mazarin, Jules, cardinal, 75, 136, 138, 179, 196, 230, 260, 261 n. 17, 262, 266–8
McCarthy, Justin, Viscount Mountcashel, 247, 253
Mecenas, Caius Cilnius, 74, 76, 77, 79, 80, 81
Médan, Pierre, 222
Medici, Marie de, 219
Ménage, Gilles, 132 n. 22
Ménestrier, Claude-François, 230
Méré (*see* Gombaud, Antoine)
Mersenne, Marin, 124
Mesmes, Jean-Antoine de, comte d'Avaux, 249 n. 27, 250, 253 n. 48
Molière, François de, 95
Molière (Jean-Baptiste Poquelin), 13, 50 n. 25, 75, 128, 151–62, 175, 185, 187, 268
Molina, Luis de, 105, 115, 121
Montaigne, Michel Eyquem de, 13, 47, 155
Montmorency, Charlotte de, princesse de Condé, 218
Montmorency, François de, comte de Bouteville, 217
Montpensier (*see* Orléans, Louise d')
Morand, Paul, 259
Morvan de Bellegarde, Jean-Baptiste, 129, 130, 132
Motteville, Françoise Bertaut, dame de Langlois de, 16, 256, 257, 264, 265, 266 n. 41, 267, 269
Mountcashel (*see* McCarthy, Justin)
Munns, Jessica, 192

Nancy, 31 and n. 7, 32, 38
Nemours, madame de (*see* Bourbon, Anne-Geneviève de).
Neuville-en-Verdunois, 10, 31, 32
Nicolas, Augustin, 144

Nicole, Pierre, 45 n. 10, 59, 112 n. 36, 165
Noailles (*see* Antoine, Louis)
Nompar de Caumont, Antonin, comte de
  Lauzun, 250, 251
Northbelant (*see* Northumberland)
Northumberland (*see* Dudley, John)

O'Brien, Daniel, 3rd viscount Clare, 246, 247
  n. 11
Ogilby, John, 195, 199 n. 13
Orange, William, prince of, 245–8, 250–1,
  253–5
Orinda (*see* Philips, Katherine)
Orléans, Gaston, duc d', 217, 219, 267
Orléans, Louise d', duchesse de Montpensier,
  256, 267
Ormesson, Olivier Lefebvre d', 75
Ormond (*see* Butler, James)
Orrery (*see* Boyle, Roger)
Ossory, Thomas, earl of, 207
Otway, Thomas, 185, 191, 192
Ovid (Publius Ovidius Naso), 99
Owen, Anne, 198

Paré, Ambroise, 45 n. 10, 47, 48
Paris, 98, 151 n. 1, 169, 196, 199, 228, 257 ff
Parival, Jean-Nicolas de, 117
Pascal, Blaise, 103, 104 n. 3, 128, 129, 156, 157
Paul, St, 104
Pégurier, Laurent, 177, 181
Pellisson, Paul, 75, 76
Pepys, Samuel, 165, 175, 185, 186, 189
Perrault, Charles, 131, 133, 229
Philips, James, 197
Philips, Katherine, 14, 188–90, 194–209
Plato, 46
Plowden, Edmund, 230, 231
Plutarch, 220, 222, 223
Pointis (*see* Desjeans, Jean-Bernard-Louis)
Poissenot, Bénigne, 118
Poli, Sergio, 117
Pollini, Girolamo, 220
Pomeau, René, 269
Pomponazzi, Pietro, 120
Pons, Madame de, 267
Pont-à-Mousson, 35, 38
Pope, Alexander, 256
Porchnev, B., 136
Port-Royal, 22, 170, 181
Prynne, William, 164–7, 169–70, 172–4, 176–7,
  180
Pusignan (*see* Le Camus, Jean)
Pussort, Henri, 139, 140, 143, 145

Quinault, Philippe, 185, 205, 206 n. 23
Quintilian, Marcus Fabius, 153

Rabelais, François, 151, 155
Rabutin-Chantal, Marie de, marquise de
  Sévigné, 145
Racine, Jean, 9, 21–9, 72, 128, 138, 185, 191,
  192, 193
Rainier de Droue, Alexandre de, marquis de
  Boisseleau, 251, 252 n. 39
Rangeard, Jean, 55 n. 11
Rapin, Renaud, 205
Régnier, Mathurin, 128
Restif de la Bretonne, Nicolas Edmé, 73
Retz (*see* Gondi, Paul de)
Retz, duc de, 90
Richard, Élie, 52, 53, 55, 56, 59–64, 65
Richelieu (*see* Du Plessis, Armand-Jean)
Ridpath, George, 13, 166–8, 170–2, 177–80
Rihs, Charles, 269
Riolan, Jean, the Younger, 61
Rivet, André, 177, 180
Rochechouart, Guy Seve de, évêque d'Arras,
  169
Rohan-Montbazon, Marie de, duchesse de
  Chevreuse, 31 n. 7, 219
Rohault, Jacques, 60
Romain, Nicolas, 38
Ronsard, Pierre de, 85, 86
Ronzeaud, Pierre, 27
Rose, Monsieur, 133
Rosen, Conrad von, 249, 250
Rosset, François de, 117, 118, 127 n. 18
Rotrou, Jean de, 226
Rouvroy, Louis de, duc de Saint-Simon, 138
Rowe, John, 175
Royer, Jean-Pierre, 137, 138, 139, 140
Rueil, 136
Rutter, Joseph, 14, 185, 186
Ruvigny (*see* Massue, Henri de)

Sackville, Charles, 6th earl of Dorset, 188, 200
  n. 17
Sackville, Edward, 4th earl of Dorset, 185,
  186
Saint-Amant (*see* Girard, Marc-Antoine)
Saint-Balmont (*see* Haraucourt, Jacques d', and
  Ernecourt)
Saint-Cyr, 21
Saint-Denis, Charles de, sieur de Saint-
  Evremond, 183, 184.
Saint-Evremond (*see* Saint-Denis, Charles de)
Saint Ruth (*see* Chalmont, Charles)
Saint-Simon (*see* Rouvroy, Louis de), 138
Saint Victor, Hugh of, 107
Saint Victor, Richard of, 107
Sales, François de, 118, 120 n. 7, 122
Salisbury, lord (*see* Cecil, Robert)
Salmon, J.H.M., 259

Sarfield, Patrick, 247, 252–3
Sarrasin, Jean-François, 129
Savoie (*see* Victor Amadeus)
Scarron, Paul, 75, 78 n. 17
Scherer, Jacques, 206 n. 24, 225
Schomberg (*see* Frederik Herman)
Scudéry, George de, 219 n. 17, 226
Scudéry, Madeleine de, 75, 199
Sedley, Charles, 200 n. 17
Seguier, Pierre, 36
Seignelay (*see* Colbert, Jean-Baptiste)
Seignette, Élie, 52, 54 n. 9, 58–9
Seignette, Jean, 52, 53
Semper, Isidore Joseph, 173
Sévigné (*see* Rabutin-Chantal)
Shakespeare, William, 152, 161, 207 n. 26
Sheridan, Richard Brinsley, 221
Skippon, Philip, 197
Socrates, 155
Soissons (*see* Bourbon, Louis de)
Somaize, Antoine Baudeau de, 75 n. 10
Sorel, Charles, 72, 79
Soulez-Larivière, Daniel, 143
Stanley, Thomas, 195
Stegman, André, 204
Suárez, Francisco, 105
Suffren, Jean, le Père, 174
Swammerdam, Jan, 44, 50 n. 25

Talbot, Richard, earl and titular duke of
    Tyrconnell, 246–8, 250, 253
Talor, Omer, 256
Talleyrand-Périgord, Henri de, comte de
    Chalais, 217–9
Tapié, Victor, 217
Tasso, Torquato, 205
Tate Nahum, 207 n. 26
Taylor, F.A., 258 n. 9
Temple, Sir William, 151, 152
Tesse (*see* Froullay, Philibert-Emmanuel de)
Tessereau, Abraham, 55

Thiers, Jean-Baptiste, 170
Thou, Jacques-Auguste de, 221
Timon, 155
Toul, 32
Trent, Council of, 106, 109, 110, 121, 172
Tristan L'Hermite, François, 219 n. 17, 226
Tudor, Edward (*see* Edward VI)
Tudor, Elizabeth (*see* Elizabeth I)
Tudor, Mary (*see* Mary I)
Tyrconnell, (*see* Talbot, Richard)

Usson, (*see* Bonnac, Jean de)

Valles, Francisco, 60
Valois, Charles de, duc d'Angoulême, 218
Vanini, Giulio-Cesare, 123
Vaucher Gravili, Anne de, 117
Venette, Nicolas, 52, 53, 55, 56, 60–4
Verdun, 31
Vernon, Jean-Marie, 10, 30, 31, 34, 36–8
Viau, Théophile de, 95
Victor Amadeus, duc de Savoie, 218
Vincent de Paul, St, 146
Vincent, Philippe, 171, 180, 181
Virgil, 76, 77, 79
Vitry-le-François, 32
Voiture, Vincent, 131
Voltaire (François Marie Arouet), 16–17, 145,
    256–70
Vuillemin, Jean-Claude, 224

Waller, Edmund, 200 n. 17
Waller, Richard, 260
William III, prince of Orange, 16, 245–8,
    250–1, 253–5
Wills, Richard, bishop of Winchester, 165, 168,
    169, 174
Wyatt, Sir Thomas, the Younger, 222
Wycherley, William, 152

Zola, Émile, 73